The
Territories of the
Russian Federation
2024

The
Territories of the
Russian Federation
2024

25th Edition

LONDON AND NEW YORK

25th edition published 2024
by Routledge
4 Park Square, Milton Park, Abingdon, Oxon, OX14 4RN

and by Routledge
605 Third Ave, New York, NY 10158

Routledge is an imprint of the Taylor & Francis Group, an informa business

© 2024 Routledge

All rights reserved. No part of this publication may be reprinted or reproduced or utilised in any form or by any electronic, mechanical, or other means, now known or hereafter invented, including photocopying and recording, or in any information storage or retrieval system, without permission in writing from the publishers.

Trademark notice: Product or corporate names may be trademarks or registered trademarks, and are used only for identification and explanation without intent to infringe.

First published 1999

ISBN: 978-1-032-49282-7 (hbk)
ISBN: 978-1-003-46686-4 (ebk)
ISSN: 1465-461X

DOI: 10.4324/9781003466864

Typeset in Times New Roman
by Data Standards Limited, Frome, Somerset

Editor: Dominic Heaney

Senior Editor, Statistics: Philip McIntyre

Editorial Assistant: Avi Sharma

Statistics Researchers: Mohd Khalid Ansari (Senior Team Leader), Ankita Nigam, Niti Rawat, Koustubh Saxena, Ambica Sharma

Contributor: Catriona Marcham

The Publishers make no representation, express or implied, with regard to the accuracy of the information contained in this book and cannot accept any legal responsibility for any errors or omissions that may take place.

Foreword

The 25th edition of THE TERRITORIES OF THE RUSSIAN FEDERATION aims to furnish a clear and comprehensive introduction to Russia's regions, without which an understanding of the world's largest country must remain opaque.

This book is divided into four parts. Part One is an introduction, with an authoritative article covering federal-regional relations in Russia since Vladimir Putin returned to the presidency in 2012. There is also a chronology of Russian history and politics, together with fully revised economic and demographic statistics, and information on the federal administration, including the executive and legislative organs and the principal political parties. Outline information is given of the Russian administrations installed in four disputed territories internationally recognized as constituting Ukrainian territory which remained active zones of military conflict, and of which Russia announced the annexation in September 2022. Part Two comprises the territorial surveys, the principal section of the book, with individual chapters on each of the 85 federal units (including Sevastopol City and the Republic of Crimea, annexed from Ukraine in 2014, and not internationally recognized as Russian territories). The geographical and historical background, the current political situation and an economic outline are accompanied by the names and contact details of the main officials in every territory, and names of the territorial representatives in both chambers of the federal parliament. Each chapter includes a map of the federal unit, and there are, in addition, two maps covering wider geographical areas. A select bibliography appears in Part Three. Finally, Part Four provides an alphabetical listing of the territories, and an additional index groups them according to their geographical location within the Federal Okrugs into which Russia is divided. A gazetteer detailing the territories renamed or abolished after 1991 is provided. There is also an index of the principal cities of the Russian Federation, with details of the territories in which they are located.

Much of the content of THE TERRITORIES OF THE RUSSIAN FEDERATION is available online at www.europaworld.com. This prestigious resource incorporates sophisticated search and browse functions as well as specially commissioned visual and statistical content. An ongoing programme of updates of key areas of information ensures currency of content.

Since the 24th edition of this book was published, public and political life in the Russian Federation has been dominated by the consequences of the continuing full-scale conflict in Ukraine. Increasingly, regions of Russia bordering that country (and on occasion those further away, including Moscow City) were subject to drone and other attacks launched from across the border. In this wartime context, the federal authorities sought further to consolidate their already extensive powers, especially after they briefly appeared threatened, in June 2023, by a rebellion led by Yevgenii Prigozhin and his paramilitary Wagner Group. After that rebellion was peacefully subdued, in August Prigozhin and other senior members of Wagner (which was to be disbanded) were killed in a plane crash. Meanwhile, further charges were brought against the prominent imprisoned opposition activist, Aleksei Navalnyi. Having been found guilty of extremist activity and 'rehabilitating Nazi ideology', he was sentenced to a further 19 years' incarceration and in December he was transferred to a 'special regime' camp in the Arctic. In regional legislative and gubernatorial elections held in September 2023 the de facto ruling party, Yedinaya Rossiya (United Russia), had, in almost all cases, increased its share of support, although this was generally accompanied, particularly in the legislative polling, by untypically low rates of electoral participation. Meanwhile, preparations for a presidential election, due to be held in March 2024, commenced, although it appeared improbable that any substantive challenge to the re-election of Putin, 24 years after he first became President, would emerge.

January 2024

Acknowledgements

The editors gratefully acknowledge the co-operation, interest and advice of all who have contributed to this volume. We are indebted to many organizations within the Russian Federation, particularly the Federal Service of State Statistics, Rosstat. We are also grateful to Eugene Fleury, who originally prepared the maps included in this book.

Contents

Abbreviations ix

PART ONE
Introduction

Developments in Russian Federal–Regional Relations since 2012
  RASMUS NILSSON 3
Chronology of Russia 19
Statistics 36
The Government of the Russian Federation 43
Disputed and Annexed Territories 50

PART TWO
Territorial Surveys

Map of European Russia 54
Map of Asian Russia 55
Notes, Acronyms of Political Parties used in the Territorial Surveys 56

Central Federal Okrug
Moscow City	57	Oryol Oblast	83
Belgorod Oblast	63	Ryazan Oblast	85
Bryansk Oblast	66	Smolensk Oblast	87
Ivanovo Oblast	69	Tambov Oblast	89
Kaluga Oblast	71	Tula Oblast	91
Kostroma Oblast	73	Tver Oblast	93
Kursk Oblast	75	Vladimir Oblast	95
Lipetsk Oblast	78	Voronezh Oblast	97
Moscow Oblast	80	Yaroslavl Oblast	100

North-Western Federal Okrug
St Petersburg City	102	Murmansk Oblast	121
Republic of Kareliya	106	Novgorod Oblast	123
Republic of Komi	109	Pskov Oblast	125
Archangel Oblast	112	Vologda Oblast	128
Kaliningrad Oblast	115	Nenets Autonomous Okrug	130
Leningrad Oblast	119		

Southern Federal Okrug
Sevastopol City	133	Krasnodar Krai	152
Republic of Adygeya	137	Astrakhan Oblast	156
Republic of Crimea	141	Rostov Oblast	159
Republic of Kalmykiya	149	Volgograd Oblast	162

North Caucasus Federal Okrug
   Chechen Republic   165
   Republic of Dagestan   172
   Republic of Ingushetiya   178
   Kabardino-Balkar Republic   183
   Karachai-Cherkess Republic   188
   Republic of North Osetiya—Alaniya   192
   Stavropol Krai   197

Volga Federal Okrug
   Republic of Bashkortostan   200
   Chuvash Republic   204
   Republic of Marii-El   207
   Republic of Mordoviya   210
   Republic of Tatarstan   213
   Udmurt Republic   217
   Perm Krai   220
   Kirov Oblast   223
   Nizhnii Novgorod Oblast   226
   Orenburg Oblast   229
   Penza Oblast   231
   Samara Oblast   233
   Saratov Oblast   236
   Ulyanovsk Oblast   239

Urals Federal Okrug
   Chelyabinsk Oblast   241
   Kurgan Oblast   244
   Sverdlovsk Oblast   246
   Tyumen Oblast   249
   Khanty-Mansii Autonomous Okrug—Yugra   252
   Yamalo-Nenets Autonomous Okrug   255

Siberian Federal Okrug
   Republic of Altai   258
   Republic of Khakasiya   261
   Republic of Tyva   264
   Altai Krai   267
   Krasnoyarsk Krai   270
   Irkutsk Oblast   273
   Kemerovo Oblast—Kuzbass   276
   Novosibirsk Oblast   279
   Omsk Oblast   282
   Tomsk Oblast   285

Far Eastern Federal Okrug
   Republic of Buryatiya   287
   Republic of Sakha (Yakutiya)   290
   Kamchatka Krai   294
   Khabarovsk Krai   297
   Maritime (Primorskii) Krai   300
   Transbaikal Krai   303
   Amur Oblast   306
   Magadan Oblast   309
   Sakhalin Oblast   311
   Jewish Autonomous Oblast   315
   Chukot Autonomous Okrug   317

PART THREE
Select Bibliography
Select Bibliography (Books)   323

PART FOUR
Indexes
Index of Principal Cities   329
Territories Renamed or Abolished after 1991   331
Alphabetical List of Territories   332
Federal Okrugs   333

Abbreviations

Adm.	Admiral	m	metre(s)
AO	Avtonomnyi Okrug (Autonomous Okrug)	m.	million
ASSR	Autonomous Soviet Socialist Republic	nab.	naberezhnaya (embankment, quai)
		NL	Partiya Novyye Lyudi (New People Party)
BCE	before the common era		
		per.	pereulok (lane, alley)
c.	circa	pl.	ploshchad (square)
CE	common era	PR	Patrioty Rossii (Patriots of Russia)
CIS	Commonwealth of Independent States	pr.	prospekt (avenue)
		PRe	Partiya Rehioniv (Party of the Regions)
Co	Company		
Col	Colonel		
cu	cubic	Rep.	Republic
		retd	retired
EU	European Union	RPPS	Rossiiskaya Partiya Pensionerov za Spravedlivosti—Partiya Pensionerov (Russian Party of Pensioners for Social Justice—Party of Pensioners)
f.	founded		
FSB	Federalnaya Sluzhba Bezopasnosti (Federal Security Service)		
		RSFSR	Russian Soviet Federative Socialist Republic
Gen.	General		
GP	Grazhdanskaya Platforma (Civic Platform)	SPS	Soyuz Pravykh Sil (Union of Rightist Forces)
GRP	gross regional product	sq	square (in measurements)
ha	hectares	SR	Spravedlivaya Rossiya (A Just Russia), Spravedlivaya Rossiya—Patrioty—Za Pravdu (A Just Russia—Patriots—For Truth)
km	kilometre(s)		
KPRF	Kommunisticheskaya Partiya Rossisskoi Federatsii (Communist Party of the Russian Federation)		
		SSR	Sovetskaya Sotsialisticheskaya Respublika (Soviet Socialist Republic)
KPSS	Kommunisticheskaya Partiya Sovetskogo Soyuza (Communist Party of the Soviet Union)	St	Saint
		tel.	telephone
KR	Kommunisty Rossii (Communists of Russia)	UK	United Kingdom of Great Britain and Northern Ireland
		ul.	ulitsa (street)
		UN	United Nations
kWh	kilowatt hour(s)	USSR	Union of Soviet Socialist Republics
		UTC	Coordinated Universal Time
LDPR	Liberalno-demokraticheskaya Partiya Rossii (Liberal Democratic Party of Russia)	Yeo-YeR	Yedinstvo i Otechestvo-Yedinaya Rossiya (Unity and Fatherland-United Russia)
Lt	Lieutenant	YeR	Yedinaya Rossiya (United Russia)

PART ONE
Introduction

Developments in Russian Federal-Regional Relations since 2012

RASMUS NILSSON

INTRODUCTION

Many features of the federal structure within the Russian Federation originated in the Union of Soviet Socialist Republics (USSR). The Soviet system was highly centralized from its creation in 1922. The Moscow-based ruling party, which subsequently became the Kommunisticheskaya Partiya Sovetskogo Soyuza (KPSS—Communist Party of the Soviet Union), retained practical and symbolic supremacy across the land. Nevertheless, the communist leadership could not ignore regional affairs. In order to accommodate national aspirations and limit nationalist protests, the USSR allowed territorial units to exist within the Union Republics. Such territorial units were often dedicated to specific ethnic groups in what was a multinational state. Furthermore, Soviet elites depended on regional strongholds to secure power or recognition within Union-wide institutions. Thus, Leonid Brezhnev attained high office, including 18 years (1964–82) as General Secretary of the KPSS, not least due to his experience and connections in the east of the Ukrainian Soviet Socialist Republic. Moreover, regional elites could build power bases with autonomous features. This power could be built on the charismatic authority of individuals, or on the importance that a given region held for the Union as a whole, such as in the case of the West Siberian regions, which contained extensive hydrocarbon reserves.

Following the disintegration of the USSR in 1991, the President of the Russian Federation, Boris Yeltsin, enjoyed public prominence and became closely linked to the rapid political and economic transformations that enveloped Russia during the 1990s. Although Yeltsin sought to retain a substantial role for Russia and for himself on the world stage, he could not ignore the plight of Russia's regions, which regularly appealed to his Government for economic support in the face of a crumbling economy and decaying infrastructure. Yet the Yeltsin administration often lacked the capability to assist and was also forced to enter into specific agreements with those regions from which his Government could gain economic benefits, such as the energy-rich Republic of Tatarstan. Despite Yeltsin's success in holding the Russian Federation together during these troubled years, the resulting state—as formalized in the 1993 Constitution—was an unwieldy amalgam of ill-defined rights held by central and regional authorities, which repeatedly led to disputes, prolonged regional dissatisfaction or simply regional non-compliance with federal demands.

Nowhere was this more obvious than in the bloody conflict which erupted in Chechnya in 1994. In part, the conflict demonstrated the willingness of the central state to oppose and destroy serious regional challenges to its political supremacy. It was telling that the Yeltsin administration would go to such lengths to keep control over what otherwise seemed an inconsequential region. However, although the military attack stymied Chechen statehood, consequences for the centre were dire. Intensive fighting for more than 18 months resulted in the deaths of thousands of civilians and soldiers and presented a chaotic image far from the federal stability and harmony sought by Yeltsin.

When Vladimir Putin became premier and subsequently President in 1999–2000, his growing popular support built on perceptions that he would turn such chaos into order. Taking advantage of the disputed circumstances surrounding terrorist bombings in Moscow and other Russian cities during August and September 1999, Putin restarted the war in Chechnya. Yet while his early approach to the North Caucasus region was aggressive, Putin otherwise presented himself as a modern, rational leader of a state with huge economic potential, offering deals to political and economic elites across the country. The rise of Putin was accompanied by regional power shifts as allies from his home city of St Petersburg began to replace Muscovite elites remaining from Yeltsin's tenure. At the same time, the retreat from the 2000 presidential election by former premier and Minister of Foreign Affairs Yevgenii Primakov, who had been supported by the Mayor of Moscow, Yurii Luzhkov, represented Putin's triumph over a significant, regional-backed challenger.

In place of such political veterans, ambitious oligarch Mikhail Khodorkovskii gained in economic and political influence, notably through his energy company, Yukos. It was therefore a significant boost to Putin's centralization of power when Khodorkovskii was arrested in 2003 and subsequently imprisoned for alleged economic crimes. Having removed the most significant remaining oligarch from the Yeltsin era, Putin then sought to institutionalize political control by spreading the dominance of Yedinaya Rossiya (YeR—United Russia). By 2003 this party (initially formed in 2001) controlled almost one-half of the seats in the lower legislative chamber, the Gosudarstvennaya Duma (State Duma). Across Russia, YeR increasingly dominated regional affairs. However, it was debatable whether YeR constituted a unified group of politicians loyal to Putin. While open dissent against presidential or governmental directives rarely included members of YeR, many of its members had joined not due to ideological affinity but for reasons of political expediency. Such politicians might challenge the regime if it ever ceased to provide for them. This would periodically happen after Putin's return to the presidency in 2012. Few went to the lengths of former leader of the Chuvash Republic, Mikhail Ignatyev, who brought a case against Putin in the federal Supreme Court following his dismissal in 2020. Ignatyev never had much chance of success and he died of pneumonia later that year. Yet the willingness of a former ally to challenge Putin openly was a brief demonstration that, even after two decades, the centre remained unable fully to control regional elites. In specific parts of the country extra-judicial challenges had remained pronounced, too. The North Caucasus had continued to host regional insurgents, even after the nadir of insurgent attacks in September 2004, when hundreds of children and adult hostages were killed at a school in Beslan, North Osetiya—Alaniya.

POLITICAL DEVELOPMENTS

One reason for the many deaths in Beslan had been the heavy-handed intervention by federal security institutions. Putin, however, used the atrocity to place blame on the local administration, and on power devolution more generally. In 2004, shortly after the crisis, Putin announced that regional leaders would be directly responsible to, and appointed by, the President. With this announcement, the centralization of Russian federal politics increased. During Putin's second presidential term (2004–08) this included new rules on the size of political parties and the installation of regional 'strongmen', such as Ramzan Kadyrov, who became premier of Chechnya in 2006 and its President in 2007 (later Head of the Republic, and in the Chechen form of his title, Father of the People). From 2008 the new Russian President, Dmitrii Medvedev, presented himself as a defender of transparency and the rule of law, yet in terms of federal relations little changed. Due to such executive inertia public dissatisfaction with the regime grew—markedly so around 2011–12, when Medvedev and Putin effectively decreed the return of the latter as President (Putin having served as premier for the duration of Medvedev's presidency) and the electoral fortunes of YeR fell. Subsequent public protests were violently suppressed by the authorities. Medvedev and Putin realized that political reform, however symbolic, was needed to reduce public dissatisfaction. In early 2012 legislation enacted by Medvedev consequently reintroduced direct gubernatorial elections, as well as changes to regulations on political parties, reducing the minimum number of members for a party to obtain registration from 40,000 to 500.

Clearly, the returning President Putin believed that such minor political concessions to the regions would do little to challenge his overall control. The following years would mostly prove him right. Between Putin's presidential inauguration in May 2012 and the end of 2023 a total of 75 of the 83 heads of federal subjects (as the territories are known) were replaced (in addition to the heads of Crimea and Sevastopol, which were annexed in 2014, and those of four Ukrainian regions annexed de jure, if not de facto, in 2022). While these changes mostly occurred following gubernatorial resignations, there was little doubt that the President had initiated the changes, inserting regional leaders loyal to himself. Some regional leaders moved on to other, arguably more important, state positions. Conversely, a few regional leaders lost more than their jobs in the reorganizations. Before and after the 2018 presidential election, regional leaders were rapidly being supplanted. In regions such as the Republic of Marii-El, the Udmurt Republic, Sakhalin Oblast, the Komi Republic and Khabarovsk Krai (where former Governor Viktor Ishayev had even been a federal minister in the past), criminal charges, sometimes resulting in convictions of corruption, against former leaders followed, or—as in the case of Chelyabinsk Oblast Governor Boris Dubrovskii—emerged during their tenure. Those convictions could vary; sometimes lower-profile local officials were punished less severely. For instance, in October 2020, following an ecological catastrophe caused by the spill of thousands of tons of diesel oil, the Mayor of Norilsk, in Krasnoyarsk Krai, Rinat Akhmetchin, received only six months' correctional work and a minor financial penalty for negligence. Yet in the same month the much more high-profile Aleksandr Solovyov, former Head of the Udmurt Republic, was sentenced to 10 years in prison for taking bribes. Since criminality was widespread in the political system it was not always clear why individuals were singled out. When a federal Minister of Economic Development could be removed from office—as happened to Aleksei Ulyukayev in November 2016—and be charged with corruption and subsequently convicted, nobody was safe. Regional leaders who had openly challenged the President were particularly vulnerable. Notably, Kirov Oblast Governor Nikita Belykh—formerly allied with murdered opposition leader Boris Nemtsov—was in 2016 deposed and charged with corruption, and in February 2018 was sentenced to eight years' imprisonment.

Conversely, those who had earned Putin's trust could be protected by the state. Having been Governor of Kemerovo Oblast (now Kemerovo Oblast—Kuzbass) since 1997, Aman-Geldy Tuleyev had stood against Putin in the 2000 election. Nevertheless, the new President understood the value of retaining an experienced leader in a resource-rich region and Tuleyev had regained such trust during the first years of Putin's rule. So, when Tuleyev was forced to resign in April 2018, following a deadly fire at an ill-maintained shopping centre, he was elected Chairman of the regional parliament shortly afterwards (remaining in the post until the next elections in

INTRODUCTION

September, when he became the rector of a regional institute; he eventually died in November 2023). Almost two years after the fire a co-owner of the shopping centre in question was extradited from Poland to stand trial over the incident, and in late 2021 two senior officials of the company that owned the shopping centre received lengthy custodial sentences for the violation of fire safety regulations. Tuleyev, as head of the local administration, might also have been held accountable for the blaze. Nevertheless, with federal goodwill Tuleyev avoided this. Other regional administrations required more wide-ranging assistance. After Crimea and Sevastopol were annexed from Ukraine in 2014, the federal centre repeatedly emphasized internal and external threats to their stability. Particularly around the time of Putin's March 2018 re-election as President, both territories were lavished with attention. If Russia were ever to achieve similar control over the four territories purportedly annexed from Ukraine in 2022, such focus on their security, too, would be required.

In addition to keeping a close watch over individual federal subjects, the Putin regime also strengthened its oversight through the post of Presidential Representative, which was created in 2000. This post was a conduit through which federal requests could be conveyed formally and informally to regional administrations. The envoys were carefully selected from experienced personnel, such as the former Minister of Justice and Prosecutor-General, Vladimir Ustinov, for the highly sensitive Southern Federal Okrug, which until 2010 included the North Caucasus, and which from 2016 incorporated the Crimean peninsula. Even after Putin returned the right of elections to regional leaders, the supervision of Presidential Representatives meant that the Kremlin's control was never seriously relaxed. Between 2007 and 2017, an exception to this 'power vertical' had been Tatarstan, which had retained a political and economic power-sharing agreement with the federal centre. Eventually, however, Putin let this arrangement expire. Now, promoters of Tatar culture and language were challenged or even persecuted by the state. Some local resistance appeared, including from Tatarstan's parliament in late 2021, against federal plans to change the region's Constitution, abolishing the title of 'President' (which had already disappeared from all other federal subjects) and removing references to Tatarstan's state sovereignty. By the end of 2022, however, Tatarstan's parliamentarians had ceded to pressure; the presidential title was eventually abolished in February 2023. In the context of Russia's continuing invasion of Ukraine, Tatarstan had to submit to the Kremlin's need for domestic control. During 2023 sporadic public protest and opposition in Tatarstan would receive little support from regional elites. Moreover, the taming of Tatarstan had ramifications far beyond the republic. The existence of an (at least officially) ethnically distinct republic, with a leader presented as autonomous, had been one of the last vestiges of federalism in Russia. Going forward, the Russian polity would appear centralized in form, as well as in normal practice.

At times of potential political risk, however, the centre would still need the support of the regions. In presidential or State Duma elections, regional executives were expected to ensure broad support in their territory for the federal administration. For the latter, this was not just a matter of winning elections, but also of producing a legitimacy-endowing turnout. That became particularly important in the 2020 consultative constitutional referendum. The Kremlin was certain of victory, yet still used all means to secure a high turnout. That aim was only partly fulfilled, with an official turnout of 67.3%. Noticeable, however, was the familiar pattern of substantial victories and turnout rates in regions dependent on federal funds. Similarly, in the 2018 presidential election, Putin received over 90% of the vote across the North Caucasus republics. In return for such loyalty, the federal centre could allow these republics unusual freedoms, including the negotiated transfer of territory from Ingushetiya to Chechnya under an agreement signed in September 2018. That the longstanding leader of Ingushetiya, Yunus-bek Yevkurov, was eventually forced to resign in 2019 due to continued local protests against the agreement seemed a price worth paying, even if federal repercussions against the protesters would follow, Yevkurov himself was not blamed by the Kremlin and suffered little long-term consequence. He became Deputy Minister of Defence as the war in Ukraine intensified from 2022.

In another example, the wealthy and dominant city of Moscow was entrusted to Sergei Sobyanin, a former federal deputy premier and head of the presidential administration, with a background as Governor of energy-rich Tyumen Oblast. Sobyanin fulfilled expectations in countering the most serious political challenges to the regime during Putin's third presidential term, when he defeated prominent opposition activist Aleksei Navalnyi in the 2013 election for Mayor of Moscow, winning in the first round of voting and without excessive repression. In September 2018 Navalnyi was prohibited from standing again, owing to a criminal conviction, and Sobyanin secured re-election with 70.2% of the votes cast. In 2023 Sobyanin was re-elected with 76.9% of the vote, without any serious competitors challenging him. Official exclusion in 2018, however, would prove insufficient to silence Navalnyi, who over the following years was subject to increasingly violent attacks. In August 2020 Navalnyi was poisoned with the highly specialized nerve agent Novichok. His life was saved by swift medical intervention in Omsk and he subsequently received treatment in Germany, returning to Russia in January 2021, where he was immediately arrested for failing to attend parole hearings and subsequently sentenced to three-and-a-half years in a penal colony. By 2023, Navalnyi had received an additional sentence of 19 years' imprisonment for alleged extremism and been subjected to still-stricter prison conditions. Removing Navalnyi from the public scene did not fully pacify dissent. In the wake of Navalnyi's arrest, protests had spread across Russia, demonstrating that support for this challenger—or perhaps rather distaste for the incumbent regime—reached far beyond the middle classes of Moscow and St Petersburg. Federal and local authorities never allowed these protests to gain significant momentum and continued to profess innocence over his poisoning. In Moscow, Sobyanin now appeared in control. Yet he had found himself with a less tractable city legislature since 2019, when local elections had reduced the number of deputies who were supportive of YeR (though elected nominally as independents) to 25 (of 45 in total). This reminded the ruling party that it still needed to prevent opposition challenges, obstruct political demonstrations and events, and delay or hinder the development of political infrastructure by the opposition.

Such tactics were replicated across Russia on an ongoing basis during the annual rounds of regional and local elections in subsequent years. Navalnyi's allies, in particular, faced administrative and legal challenges, which could include bans from participating in elections as well as arrests on grounds of alleged extremism, particularly after belligerent activity in Ukraine had been stepped up in 2022. Nevertheless, political actors outside YeR did have scattered regional success. By early 2024, even after two years of ramped-up war in Ukraine and concomitant domestic political repression, the heads of 16 federal subjects were not members of YeR. Admittedly, none of these politicians had been installed since 2022 and few if any of them would stand up to the federal centre, particularly on matters of importance for the latter. Should that change, and should regional elites in any way sympathise with

INTRODUCTION

calls for genuine opposition to the system of government, the consequences could be swift. Increasingly, political subversion was used against parties other than YeR. Particularly public examples of this had come before the September 2020 regional elections in Ulyanovsk Oblast, where the Kommunisticheskaya Partiya Rossiiskoi Federatsii (KPRF—Communist Party of the Russian Federation), and indeed the electoral process, was vilified by the Protiv Vsekh (Against Everyone) movement. That movement had been sponsored by the authorities to reduce any mobilization against YeR, the brand of which had by now become badly tainted. When the elections eventually took place, YeR was mainly successful, although it lost seats in Novosibirsk, Tambov and Tomsk Oblasts. Over the following years, all major Russian political parties, including the KPRF, the nationalist Liberalno-demokraticheskaya Partiya Rossii (LDPR—Liberal Democratic Party of Russia) and Spravedlivaya Rossiya (SR—A Just Russia, known from 2021 as Spravedlivaya Rossiya—Patrioty—Za Pravdu—A Just Russia—Patriots—For Truth), became increasingly careful not to challenge the main policies promoted federally by YeR or the federal executive.

Even before 2022, overt political challenges to the Putin regime had been rare. One high-profile example had come in the city of Yekaterinburg, in Sverdlovsk Oblast, where Yevgenii Roizman became the outspoken Mayor, after his election in 2013 as a member of the Grazhdanskaya Platforma (Civic Platform) party. Roizman did not succeed in securing the governorship of Sverdlovsk Oblast in the elections of 2017, however, as his candidacy was rejected. The following year the regional parliament abolished mayoral elections by popular vote in Yekaterinburg; Roizman resigned from his post in protest shortly afterwards. Roizman would later be targeted and arrested by the authorities in 2022, on charges of discrediting the Russian military, charges for which he would stand trial in 2023. Another regional leader who was imprisoned was Sergei Furgal of the LDPR who, until July 2020, had been Governor of Khabarovsk Krai. In that month Furgal was arrested by the federal authorities, being accused of involvement in murder. He was quickly replaced by the selected candidate of the federal regime, Mikhail Degtyaryov of the LDPR, on an acting basis. Furgal's downfall did not pass without broader incident, however, and demonstrated that Russian citizens angry with the federal Government did not always need an avowed civil society champion like Navalnyi to mass behind. Furgal's arrest was broadly interpreted as an act of political revenge against him by YeR, and a subsequent series of street protests alarmed the Putin administration for months. Although the Kremlin was accustomed to handling such opposition from pro-democracy demonstrators in Moscow and St Petersburg, those in Khabarovsk Krai were mainly ordinary citizens protesting against what they considered an illegitimate abuse of power by the federal authorities. Moreover, on the occasion of Russia's annual National Unity Day on 4 November, the protests even garnered solidarity elsewhere in the country from rallying Russian nationalists, a group that Putin could ill afford to alienate. Yet the authorities weathered that storm. Degtyaryov won a direct election as Governor of Khabarovsk Krai on 19 September 2021, when eight other governors who either already held their post on an acting basis or whose previous term had expired were also elected to office. While these elections only provided qualified a success for YeR and the Kremlin, the party of power clearly dominated the regional elections held in 2022 and 2023. In both years, all regional parliamentary elections were won by YeR, when control of the Irkutsk Oblast legislature was notably gained from the KPRF. Governors, too, largely remained from within YeR. Even when part of the electorates voted against YeR to express dissatisfaction with the state of national and, perhaps in particular, local affairs, no one envisioned that any other party participating in the elections could credibly fulfil a role of genuine opposition.

SECURITY DEVELOPMENTS

In 2014, Russian support to separatist insurgents in Ukraine further securitized the federal system. At the turn of the millennium, Putin had come to power as guardian of Russians' security, and continued to brand himself as their protector. He employed the military against insurgents in the North Caucasus and militarized responses to natural or man-made disasters, including through high-profile visits and harsh directives to local administrations. Moreover, nothing was more important for Putin than the fight against terrorism. Islamist suicide attacks notably took place in Volgograd in 2013 and in St Petersburg in 2017. To locate the perpetrators of these crimes and to prevent further attacks, support was required from federal and regional security agencies, who together were likely to have prevented some atrocities. By late 2019, alleged perpetrators of the St Petersburg bombing had been convicted and sentenced to lengthy sentences by a military court, albeit following credible accusations of extrajudicial investigatory methods, including torture. However, the trial largely failed to improve public trust in Russian rule of law, particularly among members of minority ethnic groups. Peoples of the North Caucasus were especially vulnerable to official harassment, although those of formerly stable regions such as Tatarstan were increasingly targeted, too. On the Crimean peninsula, the leaders of Crimean Tatar organizations had continuously suffered legal harassment and convictions since the annexation of 2014. Here, Crimean Tatars would be accused by the regional authorities of spying or otherwise acting for the Ukrainian Government. Before the renewed Russian invasion, in September 2021, Nariman Celâl (Dzhelial), the Deputy Chairman of the Qırımtatar Milly Meclisi (Crimean Tatar National Assembly—Mejlis), was among those arrested on suspicion of sabotaging a gas pipeline. Charges of association with the proscribed transnational Hizb-ut-Tahrir al-Islami (Party of Islamic Liberation) were also used to prosecute Crimean Tatars as the renewed war with Ukraine began. Yet it should be noted that accusations of terrorism and extended prison sentences did not only afflict ethnic minorities on the peninsula, where individual liberties were limited. During 2020 publicity was given to the trial of members of the Set (Network) organization, a group of young, mainly ethnic Russian men who were convicted of planning armed attacks against the state. Such legal and extra-legal assaults on the Crimean population would only increase from 2022.

The Russian security services deflected any criticism faced by highlighting threats from abroad, in particular in connection with the conflict in Ukraine. Before 2022, there seemed little risk of this conflict spilling into Russia. Occasionally, a Russian official would be accused of espionage or other subversive activity on behalf of Ukraine, particularly in the border areas; a prominent case related to a police chief in Kursk Oblast in June 2020. However, no one argued that such alleged spies were particularly successful. Furthermore, while the conflict in the Donbas regions of eastern Ukraine, which had commenced in 2014, continued with regular loss of life among combatants and civilians, before 2022 it had appeared unlikely to spread either eastwards, or southwards towards annexed Crimea. Threats to locals well-being in the occupied areas of Donetsk and Lugansk (Luhansk) appeared more likely to originate from local conditions including the local administrations and their security personnel.

INTRODUCTION

In this, as in so many contexts, the North Caucasus provided a template. Although open warfare there ended early in Putin's presidency, supporters of a caliphate long remained a recurrent threat across the region. Lawlessness also emerged within local elites. That was emphasized in 2019, when Rauf Arashukov, representing the Karachai-Cherkess Republic in the federal upper legislative chamber, the Sovet Federatsii (Federation Council), was arrested during a session of the Council on suspicion of involvement in contract killings (by late 2022, Arashukov would be sentenced to life imprisonment). Beyond the specifics of the charges faced by Arashukov, this arrest could also be interpreted as a more dramatic version of intra-elite struggles seen across Russia. The fall of Arashukov was not intended as a sign from the state that ordinary people in the North Caucasus (or elsewhere) should hold their representatives to account. Instead, local protests were repeatedly harshly repressed. In 2019 protests erupted in Ingushetiya against the local administration's decision to enter into a territorial agreement with Chechnya. Arrests followed, and in December 2021 seven people associated with these protests were sentenced to up to nine years in prison on charges of extremism and assault. Similarly, some 15 participants in an April 2020 protest in North Osetiya—Alaniya against restrictions imposed due to the COVID-19 pandemic had by that time received long prison sentences.

Even within the North Caucasus, Chechnya stood out. Here, Ramzan Kadyrov retained federal support through his ability to control Chechen society, centralizing power in the war-ravaged region. He also violently removed local competitors and repeatedly challenged federal prerogatives. Persistent rumours claimed that the 2015 assassination in Moscow of opposition leader Boris Nemtsov had been ordered by Kadyrov. While this remained unproven, the man convicted for this murder was a Chechen officer from Kadyrov's security forces. Kadyrov repeatedly offered the convicted murderer his public support. That Kadyrov might be able to order violent acts in such close proximity to the Kremlin was anathema to the principle of Russian state sovereignty. Yet President Putin allowed his Chechen protégé free reign beyond that shown to any other regional leader. When the Chechen authorities in 2019 were suspected of killing a former Chechen separatist in Germany, Putin stressed the crimes of the murdered man, Zelimkhan Khangoshvili, stating the danger that he had posed to Russia and other countries. Other exiled critics of Kadyrov's rule would find themselves pursued and sometimes attacked across Europe. Putin did not overtly support such attacks. However, by refusing to condemn them, the Kremlin made it clear that Kadyrov was an important ally. For Putin, the problem was that Kadyrov would clearly never be a servile supporter of the Russian state. Since he regularly intervened in the internal affairs of neighbouring North Caucasus regions, he might eventually cause problems to the hierarchy and cohesiveness of federal Russia. In addition, it was not clear what the Kremlin would do if Kadyrov suddenly became incapacitated or died. That problem became evident in May 2020, when he apparently suffered from COVID-19 and was taken to Moscow for treatment. Although Kadyrov recovered, relying on this 'strongman' in the long term remained a gamble for Putin. By late 2023, family members of the Chechen leader seemed to be in a position to succeed him, if need be, yet they might be even less loyal to the federal authorities than their predecessor. As shown later, a more sustainable policy by the Kremlin could be the redirection of Chechen militias towards Ukraine, which became a release valve for the politically disaffected.

ECONOMIC DEVELOPMENTS

After a brief downturn in Russian economic activity following the 2008–09 global economic crisis, from 2014 Russian growth was also hampered by the conflict in Ukraine and consequent discord with the West (which imposed numerous sanctions on Russia from 2014). Fears that this might increase public dissatisfaction prompted the Government to advance the 2016 parliamentary elections from December to September, so that pre-election debates would fall within voters' summer holidays. That strategy would be repeated at the following elections to the State Duma in 2021. While most regions witnessed a low voter turnout, the 2016 elections increased YeR's majority in the State Duma, ensuring greater central control over policymaking, including in economic matters. That political control has only increased since. However, such control also meant that the federal centre had to take public responsibility for sometimes unpopular choices. This was demonstrated in the nationwide protests against planned changes to the pension age, which engulfed Russia in 2018. There appeared trans-regional economic difficulties, too, the source of which could not easily be ascribed to a single region and its governance. Environmental challenges showed this clearly. When the River Volga ran unusually low in the summer of 2019, industries and living standards were threatened in cities such as Tolyatti (Samara Oblast) and Ulyanovsk. Mitigation required long-term investment, for which the federal authorities were unprepared. Their task was complicated further by wildfires, which devastated Siberian forests around Krasnoyarsk Krai and elsewhere, and would periodically recur, not least during the summer of 2021 when Siberia and Russia's southern regions suffered unprecedented conflagrations of forests and grasslands. The tragedies were amplified not simply by incompetence but also by machinations of local power holders. One notorious, if murky, incident occurred in Irkutsk Oblast during early 2020, when local politicians accused each other of arson. Whatever the truth in that case, forest fires had now become a regular occurrence, even reaching the outskirts of Moscow. Consequently, the economic and political impact on local and federal authorities was substantial. For his part, Putin deflected responsibility towards local administrations whenever possible. This had been characteristic of his presidency ever since he returned in 2012 and, arguably, begun with floods devastating Krasnodar Krai in 2012 and Amur Oblast in August 2013. At that time, Putin had visited the regions, ordering the provision of aid to their inhabitants and the investigation of the local authorities' inefficient response. The President's pressure on regional leaders could be expressed by subtler means, as well. His iconic and lengthy, televised public press conferences, when he would respond to questions from ordinary citizens, enabled him to challenge inadequacies in the provision of services by local administrations, leaving the latter to speedily rectify issues such as road potholes or arrears in pensions payments. Putin's response to citizens' complaints served to reinforce the image of him as the public's champion, a benevolent, all-seeing autocrat.

Yet some regional leaders were still slow to rectify problems. During 2018, for instance, demonstrations occurred in Moscow Oblast related to the local government's inability to implement its plans for refuse collection. Instead of responding to citizens' concerns, the police and the courts suppressed or intimidated protesters. This tactic continued in 2019, even after Putin that January called for a nationwide system for waste processing. Until such a system was in place, the Government could expect more protests beyond the environs of Moscow, as in Archangel (Arkhangelsk) Oblast that May, and again the following year, when local authorities in the region ceded to public pressure by finally halting the construction of a landfill site, which otherwise would have held more than 10m. tons of refuse from Moscow City. Public services were increasingly under pressure, with local challenges requiring federal assistance, especially after the intensification of the war in Ukraine. Nevertheless, Moscow City and some other population hubs had improved their image—and sometimes residents' quality of life—during Putin's tenure as President. Leaders of such cities were aware that they had to be competent even when the federal state failed. This became obvious in Moscow when its Mayor, Sobyanin, introduced measures to improve public health, amid federal inaction, adopting city-wide refuse recycling schemes. Soon afterwards, Sobyanin had the chance to demonstrate his managerial capabilities during a more acute crisis, when he became an early proponent of initiatives to contain and suppress the COVID-19 pandemic within the city.

The authorities of Moscow City, admittedly, were empowered by unique access to locally generated funds. Beyond the capital, in a few fortunate smaller cities large-scale international events had provided short-term surges in economic activity and investment. This was demonstrated by the 2014 Winter Olympics in Sochi (Krasnodar Krai) and the 2018 Football World Cup, which was hosted across the European part of Russia. Updated or new infrastructure would remain after such festivities had ended, even if it was not always clear how improved facilities would boost local economies in the long term. Russian military reforms were also accompanied by increased military production in regions previously in decline. While that process was substantially empowered after 2022, earlier initiatives had included border-crossing infrastructure projects, among them the construction during 2018–19 of road bridges from Krasnodar Krai and Amur Oblast to, respectively, Crimea and the People's Republic of China. Nevertheless, possibilities of international engagement had not always been realized. Kaliningrad Oblast, situated between Poland and Lithuania, had hoped for closer co-operation with the European Union. Sporadic progress had been made on short-term visa arrangements and investments. Nevertheless, as demonstrated during the COVID-19 pandemic in 2020, the Russian exclave remained vulnerable to closed borders and isolation, a vulnerability that would intensify during Russia's upscaled war in Ukraine from 2022. Even without such external challenges, simple economic neglect continued to haunt Russia's regions, exemplified by cases like the much publicized, deadly 2018 fire in a Kemerovo shopping centre. Neglect of the regions only became more pronounced during the COVID-19 pandemic. Although the federal authorities long insisted that Russia's relative excess mortality rates were far below those of the West, it was clear that every region struggled with insufficient health care provisions, caused by years of inattention or even corruption. By the end of 2021, when the pandemic had somewhat abated, the World Bank estimated that Russia's gross domestic product had fallen by 2.7% during 2020. (That estimate would be officially adjusted upwards subsequently, however, in part due to the increase in military production.)

The Russian economy suffered from corruption among its elites. In 2017 Navalnyi attacked premier Medvedev for owning substantial amounts of property, internationally and in Russia, acquired by dubious means. Allegations about Putin also surfaced. Following Navalnyi's arrest in January 2021, his Fond Borby s Korruptsiyei (Anti-Corruption Foundation) released an investigation on 'Putin's Palace', an enormous luxury property at the Black Sea allegedly belonging to the President. Such accusations were strenuously denied by federal elites. For their denials to be plausible, however, federal elites needed regional assistance. Regional administrations would normally be discreet concerning federal assets held within their territories. Regional administrations could help federal actors and their companies legally and politically, too, since economically centred lawsuits were often carried out in provincial courts. Legal attacks on regime-connected elites could be averted and the opponents of the state persecuted. It surprised few observers, therefore, when Navalnyi in 2017 was convicted of embezzlement in Kirov Oblast. Navalnyi's trial, like those before and afterwards of less prominent dissidents, was criticized openly at home and abroad. The federal authorities, however, cited the independence of regional courts. Regional authorities could also be useful in otherwise high-profile economic transactions, attracting less public attention than federal authorities when transferring ownership of high-earning companies and other assets.

While some regional companies had been sold abroad, others were so profitable that they had to stay under the control of the Russian state, and increasingly of the federal centre. Regions such as the Republic of Bashkortostan were economically dependent on extractive industries and consequently reluctant to relinquish these to federal control, although the acquisition in 2016–17 of a majority share in the Republic's petroleum company, Bashneft, by state monopoly Rosneft illustrated the regions' limited power. Moreover, while the federal authorities publicly financed emergency expenditure, longer-term economic investments could be difficult to secure unless a project had federal or international importance. For example, the federal centre promoted the concept of Special Economic Zones (SEZs), with consequent investments, construction, and jobs. However, results were mostly meagre. Crimea was a partial exception. Most notable was the aforementioned construction of a bridge from the Russian mainland across the Kerch Strait, while local elites had benefited for a while from federal decisions such as the July 2014 designation of the peninsula as one of the few regions in the Federation where gambling was legal. Obviously, any aspects of a leisure economy would dissipate from the peninsula after military action expanded from 2022. Other regions had to rely on local initiatives to address inhabitants' economic concerns. This was possibly the reason for the measure taken in 2016 by the Governor of Novosibirsk Oblast, Vladimir Gorodetskii, who barred immigrants from working in a range of industries, effectively closing Russia's third largest city to Central Asian immigrants. However, as with so many Russian regional economic initiatives, this policy appeared difficult to enforce and of dubious value to the economy of the Oblast overall. Regional economies remained dependant for their fortunes on federal goodwill, as well as on the competence and probity of local elites.

CULTURAL DEVELOPMENTS

Post-Soviet Russia suffered from an identity crisis, closely linked to its Soviet heritage. Yeltsin, Putin and Medvedev approached this crisis through compromise. While ethnic Russians were regarded as integral to Russia's identity, the federal centre took pride in the state's multicultural composition. For the regions, and particularly for the formally ethnocentric republics, this view of identity meant that the state could be relied on to support—at least officially—local cultural initiatives by titular ethnic groups. Republics would have compulsory education in both Russian and the titular language, while titular flags and customs were preserved. Religion had a special place in this scheme. By 1997 Russia had officially recognized four religions—Russian Orthodox Christianity, Islam, Judaism and Buddhism—as 'traditional', with defined rights including those of proselytism and property ownership. Other religious movements, which were not granted such rights, faced practical difficulties, and at times persecution. Such was

INTRODUCTION

the case for Jehovah's Witnesses, whose members were arrested in periodic campaigns across Russia on charges of extremism.

Putin officially emphasized the need for national unity following his 2012 return to the presidency. By November 2016 his call for a law to define the Russian nation could, however, be interpreted as the next step in the reduction of minority rights. Regularly, titular ethnic groups in the North Caucasus faced discrimination outside that region and were often feared by ethnic Russians and other Slavic groups. Nationalist political movements capitalized on such fears and also on growing federal suspicion of Western ideological trends and subversion. Putin himself periodically fuelled such fears through his rhetoric, yet—paradoxically—when the President loosened control over regional affairs, that could be harmful, too, to vulnerable groups. Nowhere was this more visible than in Chechnya, which promoted acts that disregarded or even contradicted Russian law. Such acts included the permission of underage marriage. Moreover, in 2022 reports continued to emerge that Chechen forces were persecuting and even abducting those suspected of homosexuality or otherwise diverging from officially sanctioned moral codes. Kadyrov's ideological reach was expanding beyond the North Caucasus. Apart from the previously mentioned violent incidents in the West, Kadyrov was also gaining ideological allies among wealthy Islamic conservatives in the Middle East.

Kadyrov was often *sui generis* among regional leaders. Viewed from a different perspective, regional minorities acted independently of the federal centre to preserve Russia's multicultural fabric. This became troubling for the federal authorities when cultural and political protests combined, as in 2019 in Buryatiya, where substantial natural resources had not prevented economic inequality and high unemployment. Local elections resulted in the victory of a YeR-backed candidate for the mayoral position in Ulan-Ude, the Republic's capital. Protests against that outcome combined with existing protests on behalf of a shaman, Aleksandr Gabyshev, who had been detained following his trek towards Moscow ostensibly to unseat Putin. Although Gabyshev was not from the Republic (but rather from Sakha—Yakutiya), to local residents his arrest became a symbol of federal-led intimidation. Over the following year Gabyshev continued to draw public attention, allegedly being subjected to psychiatric treatment on several occasions, before being released and subsequently detained again. Despite the authorities' inability to silence him completely, however, support for Gabyshev gradually diminished. Most cultural protests did not develop even as far as these had done.

Even when republics joined forces against the centre, cultural protests found it difficult to challenge the state. In July 2017 republican elites and populations complained vociferously when Putin expressed support for school pupils in the ethnic republics to be taught exclusively in Russian, while criticizing the existing system under which ethnic Russians resident in these territories were obliged to learn languages that were not their mother tongue. This might have been a minor administrative change—particularly since almost all public life throughout Russia was conducted in Russian—if Tatars and other minorities did not view language rights as one of the few areas in which their regions held a meaningful degree of sovereignty. Despite local dissatisfaction, however, the federal centre gradually forced through its policy. Thus, by the time of Putin's re-election as President in 2018 the scene was set for the victory of ethnic Russian culture in almost all of the Russian Federation. Those minority representatives who had fought to preserve their languages in the public space, such as Fail Alsynov in the Republic of Bashkortostan, the leader of the

Bashqort organization, found themselves challenged by legal threats and efforts to exclude them from government-approved minority events. Bashqort itself, for instance, was banned by the Supreme Court of Bashkortostan in May 2020 for promoting extremism, and Alsynov himself was sentenced to four years' imprisonment in January 2024 for allegedly inciting hatred. In August 2020 a prominent Bashkir activist, Airat Dilmukhametov, received a nine-year prison sentence, connected to the alleged promotion of extremism for having previously advocated greater rights for ethnic republics. In October 2021 Tatar activists had to seek assistance from the courts for permission to commemorate the fall of Tatar Kazan to Russians in 1552 (evidently not a commemoration cherished by the federal authorities); their rights for such celebrations would continue to be restricted. Furthermore, during 2021–23 the federal moves to abolish the office of President in Tatarstan were the culmination of federal–regional tensions over the self-expression of that Republic, with charges of extremism regularly used against those Tatars who complained about lack of cultural rights. As Russian culture became increasingly dominant across the country, it also become securitized, even militarized. Before 2022 this had not necessarily implied regional participation in foreign aggression—in late 2014 the image of Murmansk Oblast benefitted significantly from the official commemoration of US and British convoys sailing to the port during the Second World War. However, such opportunities for Russian regions to create peaceful foreign links would gradually vanish.

The growing emphasis by the federal centre on Soviet victory in the Second World War as a cornerstone of Russia national identity also involved pride in Soviet military accomplishments more generally. Entrepreneurial regional administrations perceived opportunities in this, for instance by stressing the role of their territories in military victories during the War. In Perm Krai, a Gulag prison camp had been converted into a museum, Perm-36, in which capacity it was one of the most damning symbolic indictments of Soviet rule. When it reopened in 2015, however, it had a new focus on the assistance by the camp system to the military victory in the Second World War. Elsewhere, in 2020 survivors of the battle of Stalingrad were approached by criminal investigators seeking further support for the narrative that the Soviet population were innocent victims of a Nazi-inspired genocide. That case had already been proven many times over the decades, yet it now again provided the Russian authorities with a focus on the past to remind citizens of the need for present state vigilance. Those stressing more discreditable aspects of the past were harassed by the authorities. An example of this came in 2019, when the Perm Oblast authorities charged members of the human rights organization Memorial with illegal logging and similar crimes, following the activists' work to preserve and restore the commemoration of victims of Stalin-era persecution. It was not clear that the federal, as opposed to regional, authorities had ordered these charges, but, as so often was the case in Putin's Russia, a context had been created within which local leaders understood how to act. Moreover, Memorial found itself increasingly targeted, as its challenge to the narrative of Soviet glory became intolerable for the federal authorities. After a Moscow court finally ordered the closure of the organization at the end of 2021, it was noticeable that repercussions against local activists spread across those regions in which Memorial's activities had long helped to disclose historical secrets and atrocities.

There was little chance that regional administrations would stand up for non-governmental organizations such as Memorial. Indeed, regional administrations mainly tried to adapt to dominant state ideologies. In a notable example of this, in 2017 the authorities in St Petersburg sought to transfer ownership of St Isaac's

INTRODUCTION

Cathedral to the Russian Orthodox Church. The Cathedral had been converted to a museum during the Soviet era but following the dissolution of the USSR was again used for religious services. Thus, the actions of the local authorities here, despite local protests, long tallied with wider support for the religious element within state-sponsored conservatism. Indeed, regional administrations found little reason to resist federal initiatives for the creation of a new, conservative, religious, securitized national image. For its part, the Moscow Patriarchate of the Russian Orthodox Church had need of state support more than ever, as it was in general turmoil over the historic, formal independence achieved by the Ukrainian Orthodox Church in early 2019. That episode had shown the Russian Orthodox Church that it must use the state to at least consolidate its position within Russia. Unfortunately for the Church, even in Russia the centre did not consistently pay attention to and intervene in religious developments in Russia's regions. Thus, following the protests over St Isaac's Cathedral in St Petersburg, its planned transfer from the state to the Russian Orthodox Church was eventually abandoned. Moreover, in another major city, Yekaterinburg, in 2019, the local authorities directly obstructed attempts to build a new church in a public park, following public protests. Much more troubling for the Kremlin were occasions when members of the Church appealed to the public against the state. Notably, during the COVID-19 crisis in 2020 a suspended abbot took over a convent in Yekaterinburg for several months, in protest against public health restrictions on church services. The abbot was eventually arrested and received a prison sentence of more than three years, yet his prominence had made clear to local authorities that cultural co-option could only be maintained when supported overtly by the federal centre.

THE IMPACT ON THE REGIONS OF THE 2022 INVASION OF UKRAINE

When Russian military forces launched a full-scale invasion of Ukraine on 24 February 2022, expectations were of a swift victory. Some regional leaders in Russia used the attack to demonstrate their loyalty to the federal centre. Chechen leader Kadyrov was at the forefront of such efforts. By March he claimed that he had travelled to Ukraine to meet Chechen forces engaged there. Kadyrov would continue to use the war in Ukraine to position himself among elites in Russia. He was not above raising the prospect of resignation that September, to underline his irreplaceability in the eyes of the federal centre. Kadyrov did stay, yet it was clear that the Russian federal centre increasingly relied on regional administrations to engender support for the war and to restrain public discord. In May the governors of five regions (Kirov, Ryazan, Saratov and Tomsk Oblasts, and the Republic of Marii-El) announced their resignations. Their replacements, all regarded as loyal supporters of Putin, were quickly installed. And, as earlier outlined, in regional elections in both 2022 and 2023 YeR retained and even amplified its regional dominance. It might appear, therefore, that Russia's intensification of hostilities in Ukraine had done little to damage federal control inside Russia itself. Indeed, on 30 September 2022 the Kremlin claimed that more regions had come under its control when Putin announced the annexation of four Ukrainian regions: the so-called 'People's Republics' established in the eastern Ukrainian cities of Donetsk and Lugansk by pro-Russian forces as long ago as 2014, and the southern Ukrainian oblasts of Kherson and Zaporizhzhya (Zaporozhye), despite Russian failing to securely control all of these territories. Few, if any, regional politicians dared to voice dissatisfaction with the war or the way in which it was being conducted. Not only did the state show increasing willingness to prosecute anyone perceived to 'insult' the military, but business and some political elites were beginning to suffer, too. During 2022 and 2023 mysterious deaths proliferated among Russia's elites. Those involved were mostly senior business officials, but in January 2023 Magomed Abdulayev, a former premier of Dagestan, died after being struck by a car, less than a month after another former Dagestani premier had been imprisoned for embezzlement.

Elites such as these had not challenged Russia's war effort directly. Even when Russia was suffering defeats on the battlefield and growing international isolation, most elites found it sensible to keep a low profile. However, while large parts of the Russian population were similarly inclined, protests did break out periodically. In order to reinforce the ranks of military servicemen, the Russian state spent the first half of 2022 raising volunteer battalions through recruitment campaigns, particularly from poor, provincial, regions. From mid-2022, however, growing casualty rates led to public calls for the recruits to return—often from their mothers or other family members, in a movement similar to that seen during the Chechen wars. By this point, Putin had repeatedly promised that no new recruits would be dispatched to the battlefield. Few believed this assertion, however, and soon federal authorities had to admit that many recruits had been deployed there—officially by mistake but in reality due to local administrations having received set quotas to fulfil. Public dissatisfaction significantly increased that September, when Putin declared a 'partial' mobilization of Russian men for the war in Ukraine—the first time that such a mobilization had been ordered by the federal Government since the Second World War. Immediately, hundreds of thousands fled to neighbouring countries, causing some regions, such as North Osetiya—Alaniya, with its access to Georgia, to be overwhelmed by the resultant cross-border traffic.

As before, socioeconomic vulnerability correlated with vulnerability to mobilization. That became an issue not least among ethnic minorities, such as in the North Caucasus where unofficial mobilizations had been proceeding since the beginning of the war. In a part of Russia where society had not healed following the violence of the 1990s and early 2000s, ordinary people had little trust in or allegiance to a Russian state which had killed people locally and effectively had installed military regimes afterwards. Mobilization now caused widespread unrest in multi-ethnic Dagestan, in particular. Local security forces clearly found it difficult to contain this, although it remained rare for local elites to agree openly with public concern. Yet exceptions existed. In October 2022 Telo Tulku Rinpoche, the Supreme Lama of the Buddhists of Kalmykiya, denounced the war. In itself such a statement was no threat to Russia. However, the longer the war continued without obvious progress for Russia the more those opposed to federal control of their community might take encouragement. Already, Chechen exiles seeking to avenge their homeland were fighting for Ukraine. Furthermore, in a Russia which increasingly stressed the ethnic identity—and ethnic supremacy—of Russians, minorities might wonder what place they had in the Federation's allegedly multicultural fabric. At the beginning of Putin's presidential tenure Russia had argued for the creation of a 'liberal empire' in Eurasia. Now it looked more like old-fashioned autocratic centralization. If Russia's war in Ukraine were to damage relations between the federal centre and its regions, it therefore appeared that such damage could become acute in places where members of ethnic minorities had ever decreasing illusions about their place in a future Russia of Putin's making.

Problems in federal-regional relations arguably increased during 2023. Putin's regime could look at the unfolding war in Ukraine with some calm, if not exactly satisfaction. Highly vaunted declarations of a Ukrainian offensive during the summer of 2023 largely went unfulfilled, at least on land. Thus, Russian control over the annexed territories in eastern Ukraine seemed secure for now, and local administrators continued to be publicly lauded by the Kremlin. The situation in Crimea was less secure. As Ukraine had some success in attacking Russian ships in the Black Sea, it also managed to target military and infrastructure installations on the peninsula, leading to protest from the Kremlin and retaliatory attacks, but seemingly no resolution.

A much bigger problem, however, was developing from 2023. Internationally recognised regions of Russia, notably Belgorod and Kursk Oblasts, found themselves repeatedly targeted by Ukrainian attacks. While most of those attacks struck military installations, civilians also got hit. And even though casualties inside Russia were vastly dwarfed by the indiscriminate bombings of Ukrainian settlements, a new insecurity now spread among ordinary Russians, for whom the war could no longer be said to be happening only 'over there'.

It remained unlikely that the Kremlin would have to worry about active protests from the vast majority of the population. Persecution of any dissent remained vigorous and vicious with activists (genuine or framed) receiving harsh penalties of several years' imprisonment, at the same time as Navalnyi—potentially the one activist who could have spearheaded coordinated rebellion—was abandoned still further into the prison system. Before Putin's anticipated re-election, scheduled for March 2024, the regime seemed satisfied with such piecemeal cruelty. Once that event had been navigated, though, it seemed possible that more organized repression would take place, particularly if ordinary economic life became more difficult and a new mobilization for the war became necessary.

Without public backing, regional elites would not be able to strike against the Kremlin, despite scattered hopes among a few ethnic minorities, in particular. However, such inactivity did not mean active support for the system, either. When militia leader Yevgenii Prigozhin rebelled against the state in the summer of 2023, the real danger to Putin did not come from the rebel himself or the, admittedly combat-trained and well-equipped forces of his private military company, the Wagner Group. The president retained control of the Russian military and, as such, Wagner would have been defeated if had Prigozhin had not accepted an ultimately fatal truce. What was ominous for the Kremlin, however, was the fact that no one outside the central state institutions had seemed motivated to challenge Prigozhin, or even warn Putin of the coming trouble. From Rostov-on-Don in the south, Wagner troops had moved seemingly unhindered many hundred kilometres to the north before being confronted by federal troops. Clearly, allegiance to the federal regime was, by now, quite thin among regional elites and populations. In a sense, perhaps, that was a consequence of the entire political system which Putin had created. From the outset, Putin had challenged the political system he encountered, by placing himself above politics. YeR was, consequently, moulded into a movement bound together not by ideology but by loyalty to the leader. As long as Putin remained popular, the system could retain control and quickly respond to challengers. However, when his popularity faltered, little would hold federal control in place. The ongoing development and potential outcome of the war in Ukraine seemed likely to show if that analysis was accurate.

Chronology of Russia

c. 862: The Viking, Rurik, founded a state based in Novgorod, which has become regarded as the first predecessor of the modern Russian state.

c. 878: Kievan Rus, the first unified state of the Eastern Slavs, was founded, with Kiev (Kyiv—now in Ukraine) as its capital. In 988 its ruler, Vladimir (Volodymyr) I 'the Great', ruler of Kievan Rus, converted to Orthodox Christianity.

1237–40: The Mongol Tatars invaded and conquered the Rus principalities.

1462–1505: Reign of Ivan III of Muscovy, who consolidated the independent Rus domains into a centralized state and who in 1480 renounced Mongol suzerainty.

1533–84: Reign of Ivan IV 'the Terrible', who began the eastern expansion of Russian territory, in 1547 being crowned 'Tsar of Muscovy and all Russia'. In 1552 the Khanate of Kazan was subjugated, as was, in 1556, that of Astrakhan.

1581: The adventurer Yermak Timofeyev pioneered Russian expansion beyond the Ural Mountains. In 1645 a Russian settlement was established on the Sea of Okhotsk, on the coast of eastern Asia.

1654: Eastern and central Ukraine came under Muscovite rule.

1679: Russian pioneers reached the Kamchatka Peninsula and the Pacific Ocean.

1682–1725: Reign of Peter (Pyotr) I 'the Great', who sought to establish Russia as a European Power and modernized the state.

1703: St Petersburg was founded, replacing Moscow as the capital from 1713.

1721: The Treaty of Nystad with Sweden ended the Great Northern War. Peter I, 'Tsar of all the Russias', proclaimed the Russian Empire.

1728: Russia annexed Transbaikal under the Treaty of Kyakhta with China.

1762–96: Reign of Catherine (Yekaterina) II 'the Great'. Parts of Belarus, Ukraine and Lithuania were incorporated into the Russian Empire, and the Khanate of Crimea was annexed.

1809: Finland became a possession of the Russian Crown.

1812: The French, under Napoleon I, unsuccessfully invaded Russia.

1853–56: The Crimean War was fought, in which the United Kingdom and France aided Türkiye (Turkey) against Russia, after it invaded the Ottoman tributaries of Moldavia and Wallachia.

1860: Russia acquired provinces on the Sea of Japan from China.

1864: Final defeat of the Circassian peoples and the confirmation of Russian hegemony in the Caucasus. In 1867 Alaska was sold to the USA.

1875: Acquisition of Sakhalin from Japan in exchange for the Kurile Islands.

1876: Subjugation of the last of the Central Asian khanates.

1881–94: Reign of Alexander III, who re-established autocratic principles of government, following the assassination of Alexander II.

1894–1917: Reign of Nicholas II, the last Tsar.

17 October 1905: After Russia was defeated in the Russo-Japanese War, unrest forced the Tsar to introduce limited political reforms, including the formation of a Duma (Parliament).

INTRODUCTION

1 August 1914: Russia entered the First World War against Austria-Hungary, Germany and the Ottoman Empire.

1917: Tsar Nicholas II abdicated on 2 March, making way for a Provisional Government led by Prince Georgii Lvov. On 9 July Prince Lvov resigned; he was replaced as Prime Minister by Aleksandr Kerenskii. On 25 October the Bolsheviks, led by Lenin (Vladimir Ulyanov), overthrew the Provisional Government; the Russian Soviet Federative Socialist Republic (RSFSR) was proclaimed. In January 1918 a Constituent Assembly, elected in November 1917, was dissolved. A civil war between the Bolshevik Red Army and 'White' anti-Communist groups continued until 1921.

3 March 1918: Treaty of Brest-Litovsk: the Bolsheviks ceded much territory to Germany, and recognized the independence of Finland and Ukraine. Belarus, Georgia, Armenia and Azerbaijan subsequently proclaimed their independence. On 9 March the Russian capital was moved from Petrograd (as St Petersburg had been renamed in 1914) to Moscow, and on 10 July the first Constitution of the RSFSR was adopted. The Allied Armistice with Germany (denied its gains at Brest-Litovsk) of 11 November ended the First World War.

30 December 1922: The Union of Soviet Socialist Republics (USSR) was formed.

21 January 1924: Death of Lenin. Stalin (Iosif Dzhugashvili) became increasingly dominant, particularly following the expulsion of Trotskii (Lev Bronstein) from the party in 1927; by 1929 Stalin was the uncontested leader of the party and state. The First Five-Year Plan, from 1928, led to the collectivization of agriculture.

1936–38: A series of mass arrests and executions (the 'Great Purge') occurred.

1939–40: The USSR signed the Treaty of Non-Aggression with Germany (the Nazi-Soviet Pact), including 'Secret Protocols' sanctioning Soviet territorial gains, on 23 August 1939. On 17 September Soviet forces invaded Poland, two weeks after Nazi Germany's invasion had precipitated the Second World War. In November the USSR invaded Finland (signing a peace treaty with that country in March 1940). In June 1940 the USSR annexed the Baltic states (Estonia, Latvia and Lithuania) and Bessarabia (now the Republic of Moldova).

1941–45: Nazi Germany invaded the USSR on 22 June 1941, precipitating extensive bloodshed and suffering. German forces surrendered at Stalingrad (now Volgograd) in February 1943. Stalin ordered the deportation of numerous peoples from the North Caucasus and Crimea. Tannu-Tuva (Tyva), a Russian protectorate since 1914, became part of the RSFSR. After Germany surrendered, most of Eastern and Central Europe came under Soviet control on 9 May 1945. On 8 August, two days after the USA exploded an atomic bomb over Hiroshima, the USSR declared war on Japan, occupying Sakhalin and the Kurile Islands. (Japan surrendered on 15 August, signing surrender documents on 2 September, ending the war.)

5 March 1953: Death of Stalin. In September, under a collective leadership, Nikita Khrushchev was elected First Secretary of the Central Committee of the ruling Kommunisticheskaya Partiya Sovetskogo Soyuza (KPSS—Communist Party of the Soviet Union), while Georgii Malenkov became premier (being succeeded by Nikolai Bulganin in 1955). In 1954 Crimea was transferred to the Ukrainian SSR.

March 1958: Khrushchev became Chairman of the Council of Ministers, in addition to First Secretary of the Central Committee of the KPSS. He was thus now the dominant political figure in the country.

October 1962: The US discovery of Soviet nuclear missiles in Cuba led to the 'Cuban Missile Crisis'; tension eased when Khrushchev ordered their withdrawal.

October 1964: Khrushchev was deposed, and replaced as KPSS First Secretary by Leonid Brezhnev (who became formal head of state in 1977).

24 December 1979: Soviet forces invaded Afghanistan (troops were withdrawn during 1986–89).

1982–84: Brezhnev died in November 1982, and was succeeded as General Secretary by Yurii Andropov, who died in February 1984 and was succeeded by Konstantin Chernenko.

10 March 1985: Death of Chernenko; he was succeeded by Mikhail Gorbachev, who proposed radical economic and political reforms and some democratization of local government.

21 October 1987: Boris Yeltsin, the reformist leader of the Moscow City Party Committee, resigned from the Political Bureau (Politburo) of the KPSS.

December 1988: The all-Union Verkhovnyi Sovet (Supreme Soviet) approved constitutional amendments creating a Congress of People's Deputies (Syezd Narodnykh Deputatov) and a full-time Supreme Soviet. In March 1989 competitive elections were held to the Congress. In May Gorbachev was elected Chairman of the USSR Supreme Soviet.

7 February 1990: The KPSS Central Committee approved proposals to end the party's monopoly of power. In March reformists made advances in elections to local and republican legislatures within Russia. The all-Union legislature elected Gorbachev to the new office of President of the USSR.

12 June 1990: The Congress adopted a declaration of Russian sovereignty, two weeks after Yeltsin was elected Chairman of the Supreme Soviet of the Russian Federation. In October the all-Union Supreme Soviet adopted legislation allowing the existence of multiple political parties and approved a programme to establish a market economy.

17 March 1991: In a referendum on the future of the USSR, some 75% of participants approved Gorbachev's concept of a 'renewed federation'.

12 June 1991: Yeltsin was elected President of the Russian Federation in direct elections, with Aleksandr Rutskoi as Vice-President. A referendum in Leningrad approved the reversion of the city's name to St Petersburg.

18–21 August 1991: Gorbachev was placed under house arrest, as a hardline communist 'State Committee for the State of Emergency' attempted a coup. On 23 August Gorbachev replaced coup supporters in the Council of Ministers and in the Committee for State Security (KGB). Yeltsin suspended the Russian branch of the KPSS, later proscribing it. On 24 August Gorbachev resigned as General Secretary of the KPSS, nationalized the party's property and dissolved the Central Committee. The Supreme Soviet of Ukraine adopted a declaration of independence, pending approval (overwhelmingly endorsed) by referendum on 1 December. By the end of the year Russia had recognized the independence of all of the other former Union Republics.

27 October 1991: An election in the eastern regions of the Checheno-Ingush Autonomous Republic (Checheno-Ingushetiya, in the Russian North Caucasus) to the presidency of the self-proclaimed separatist 'Chechen Republic' (Chechnya), was won by Gen. Dzhokhar Dudayev.

November 1991: President Yeltsin announced the formation of a new Russian Government, with himself as Chairman.

8 December 1991: The leaders of the Russian Federation, Belarus and Ukraine agreed to form a Commonwealth of Independent States (CIS) to replace the USSR, with a protocol on its formation being signed by the leaders of 11 former Union Republics of the USSR (but not Georgia or the Baltic states) on 21 December.

25 December 1991: Gorbachev resigned as Soviet President, confirming the dissolution of the USSR. The independent Russian Federation initiated a programme of radical economic reform.

31 March 1992: The leaders of the Russian administrative regions (other than Checheno-Ingushetiya and Tatarstan) signed the Russian Federation Treaty. In June the Ingush Republic was recognized as a separate republic. (It renamed itself the Republic of Ingushetiya in 1996.)

14 December 1992: Viktor Chernomyrdin was appointed premier, after the Congress rejected Yeltsin's nomination of a radical reformer, acting premier Yegor Gaidar.

20 March 1993: Amid intense tensions between the Presidency and Congress, Yeltsin commenced ruling by decree. In a referendum, held on 25 April, 57.4% of voters endorsed the President and 70.6% supported early parliamentary elections.

22 September–4 October 1993: Vice-President Aleksandr Rutskoi declared himself acting President, after Yeltsin dissolved the Supreme Soviet and scheduled elections to a new bicameral parliament, precipitating violent unrest in Moscow between supporters of Yeltsin and of Rutskoi and the dissolved Supreme Soviet. On 3 October a state of emergency was declared in Moscow after demonstrators stormed the office of the Mayor of Moscow and the Ostankino television building. Rutskoi was dismissed as Vice-President. One day later government forces shelled the parliamentary building, resulting in at least 146 deaths, before Rutskoi and parliamentary chairman Ruslan Khasbulatov surrendered.

12 December 1993: A referendum approved a new Constitution. Elections to the new Federalnoye Sobraniye (Federal Assembly)—comprising an upper chamber, the Sovet Federatsii (Federation Council)—elected, uniquely on this occasion, by direct popular vote—and a lower chamber, the Gosudarstvennaya Duma (State Duma or Duma)—were held. In the Duma elections Vladimir Zhirinovskii's extreme nationalist Liberalno-Demokraticheskaya Partiya Rossii (LDPR—Liberal Democratic Party of Russia) and the reformist Vybor Rossii (Russia's Choice) bloc each obtained 64 of the 450 seats, ahead of the reactivated Kommunisticheskaya Partiya Rossiiskoi Federatsii (KPRF—Communist Party of the Russian Federation, with 42. Ten other parties won representation, and 130 nominally independent deputies were elected. All 100 members of the Federation Council were non-partisan.

December 1994–June 1995: Yeltsin deployed 40,000 ground troops to Chechnya in December 1994 in support of an 'Interim Council' that had proclaimed itself in opposition to Dudayev. In March 1995 the Russian authorities installed a 'Government of National Revival' in Groznyi, the principal city of Chechnya. An Islamist, Shamil Basayev, took over 1,000 people hostage in a hospital in June, prompting negotiations with Chernomyrdin. Over 100 people were killed during the siege.

17 December 1995: In elections to the State Duma, the KPRF won 157 of the 450 seats, ahead of Chernomyrdin's Nash Dom—Rossiya (Our Home is Russia) bloc, with 55, the LDPR, with 51, and the liberal Yabloko party, with 45.

3 July 1996: Yeltsin was re-elected President, narrowly defeating Gennadii Zyuganov of the KPRF in the run-off poll.

31 August 1996: Following a successful attack by Chechen forces on Groznyi, a ceasefire agreement (the Khasavyurt Accords) was agreed with Col Aslan Maskhadov, the rebel military leader (Dudayev having been killed in a Russian missile attack in April); a formal resolution of the question of Chechen sovereignty was deferred. On 1 January 1997 Maskhadov was elected President of Chechnya (which renamed itself the Chechen Republic of Ichkeriya).

April–September 1998: The State Duma confirmed the appointment of Sergei Kiriyenko as premier on 24 April, following Yeltsin's dismissal of Chernomyrdin. Following a financial crisis and the Duma adopting a resolution urging Yeltsin to resign, he dismissed the Government on 23 August. The Duma rejected Chernomyrdin's nomination as premier, and on 11 September it approved the appointment of Yevgenii Primakov, a former secret services official.

12 May 1999: Yeltsin dismissed Primakov as premier; he was succeeded by Sergei Stepashin, hitherto First Deputy Prime Minister and Minister of Internal Affairs.

August–September 1999: Islamist guerrillas from Chechnya invaded neighbouring Dagestan on 7 August, prompting federal military intervention. Two days later Yeltsin dismissed Stepashin as premier, replacing him with the hitherto head of the Federal Security Service (FSB), Vladimir Putin. Putin attributed two bomb attacks in apartment blocks in Moscow in September, which killed almost 200 people, to Chechen rebels, instigating a renewed military conflict in Chechnya.

19 December 1999: At elections to the Duma, the KPRF secured 113 seats, ahead of the Yedinstvo (Unity) alliance of regional leaders, with 73, Otechestvo-Vsya Rossiya (OVR—Fatherland-All Russia), with 68, the pro-market Soyuz Pravykh Sil (SPS—Union of Rightist Forces), with 29, Yabloko, with 21 and the Blok Zhirinovskogo (Zhirinovsky Bloc—effectively the LDPR), with 17.

31 December 1999: Yeltsin resigned as President. Putin assumed the role in an acting capacity, before being elected President on 26 March 2000

May 2000: Following Putin's inauguration as President on 7 May, Mikhail Kasyanov became premier. Putin decreed that Russia no longer recognized Maskhadov as Chechen President, appointing a former rebel mufti, Akhmad Kadyrov, as republican leader. Putin issued a decree dividing Russia's constituent territories into seven Federal Okrugs (districts), each of which was to be overseen by a presidential envoy. The Duma approved legislation removing regional governors from the Federation Council, and empowering the President to dismiss them. Later in the year the State Council, a new advisory body comprising the President and the governors, was convened.

12 July 2001: New regulations required political parties to have at least 10,000 members to participate in elections.

16 January 2002: A new session of the Federation Council, now comprising the appointees of regional governors and of the chairman of regional legislatures, opened.

23–26 October 2002: Some 41 heavily armed Chechen Islamists held more than 700 people hostage in a Moscow theatre, demanding the withdrawal of Russian troops from Chechnya. When Russian special forces stormed the theatre, the rebels and at least 129 hostages were killed.

23 March 2003: Amid continuing unrest, a referendum in Chechnya overwhelmingly approved a new draft constitution defining the region as an integral part of the Russian Federation. In October Kadyrov was overwhelmingly elected republican President.

26 October 2003: Mikhail Khodorkovskii, the Chief Executive of Yukos Oil Co, and a prominent supporter of the two principal liberal parties, the SPS and Yabloko, was arrested and detained. Khodorkovskii was subsequently charged with tax evasion and fraud. In May 2005 he was sentenced to nine years' imprisonment for charges including tax evasion and embezzlement, and received further sentences, to run concurrently, in 2010.

7 December 2003: Yedinaya Rossiya (YeR—United Russia, formed by the merger of OVR and Yedinstvo) won 222 of the 450 seats in Duma elections, ahead of the KPRF, with 53, the LDPR, with 38, and the nationalist Rodina (Motherland) bloc, with 37. In February 2004 Putin dismissed the Government. Mikhail Fradkov became premier and Sergei Lavrov was appointed Minister of Foreign Affairs.

14 March 2004: Putin was re-elected President.

9 May 2004: Kadyrov was killed in a bombing in Groznyi.

24 August 2004: Two passenger planes, both flying from Moscow-Domodedovo airport, crashed, killing 89 people, as a result of attacks by Islamist suicide bombers. Five days later Maj.-Gen. Alu Alkhanov, the favoured candidate of the federal authorities, was elected President of Chechnya.

1–3 September 2004: Armed militants occupied a school in Beslan, North Osetiya—Alaniya, taking some 1,500 children, parents and teachers hostage. More then 330 hostages, including at least 150 children, were killed when special forces stormed the building, according to official reports. Following the attack, Putin announced that henceforth the President would appoint regional governors, and that all State Duma deputies were henceforth to be elected by proportional representation. In December the minimum membership required of a registered political party was increased to 50,000.

8 March 2005: Maskhadov was killed in Chechnya; he was succeeded as rebel leader by Abdul-Khalim Sadulayev.

13 October 2005: At least 130 people were killed during a series of co-ordinated attacks by Islamist fighters linked with Basayev in Nalchik, the Kabardino-Balkar Republic's capital.

14 November 2005: President Putin appointed Dmitrii Medvedev, hitherto Head of the Presidential Administration, as First Deputy Chairman of the Government. Medvedev was also Chairman of the Board of Directors of the state-controlled natural gas company, Gazprom.

1 December 2005: In the first of a series of territorial reorganizations, Perm Oblast and the Komi-Permyak Autonomous Okrug were merged to form Perm Krai.

4 March 2006: The Chechen legislature unanimously approved the nomination of Ramzan Kadyrov (the son of the former President, and leader of a controversial security force) as premier.

10 July 2006: Basayev was killed in an explosion in Ingushetiya. In June Sadulayev had also been killed; his successor as Chechen rebel leader was Doku Umarov.

1 January 2007: The Evenk and Taimyr (Dolgano-Nenets) Autonomous Okrugs were abolished and absorbed into Krasnoyarsk Krai.

15 February 2007: Putin appointed Alkhanov as a federal deputy justice minister, enabling Ramzan Kadyrov to become President of Chechnya, initially in an acting capacity.

1 July 2007: Kamchatka Oblast and the Koryak Autonomous Okrug merged to form Kamchatka Krai.

14 September 2007: The Duma approved the appointment of Viktor Zubkov as premier, succeeding Fradkov.

6 November 2007: The rebel Chechen 'parliament-in-exile' announced that Umarov's presidential status had been removed, after he proclaimed himself leader of a 'Caucasus Emirate'.

2 December 2007: At elections to the Duma, YeR obtained 315 seats, ahead of the KPRF, with 57, the LDPR, with 40, and Spravedlivaya Rossiya (SR—A Just Russia—formed by the merger of Rodina and two other parties), with 38.

1 January 2008: Irkutsk Oblast absorbed the Ust-Orda Buryat Autonomous Okrug. On 1 March Chita Oblast and the Aga-Buryat Autonomous Okrug united to form Transbaikal Krai.

2 March 2008: Medvedev was elected President, with 70.3% of votes cast. On 8 May, one day after his inauguration, he confirmed Putin (who constitutionally was prohibited from seeking a third consecutive term as President) as Chairman of the Government.

8 August 2008: Following a Georgian offensive against the separatist, Russian-allied, region of South Ossetia, Russia counter-attacked, expelling Georgian troops, attacking targets beyond the territory, and advancing into another separatist region, Abkhazia. Russia's military operations ended on 12 August, and Georgia and Russia agreed a peace plan, mediated on behalf of the EU. Russia formally recognized South Ossetia and Abkhazia as independent states on 26 August.

30 December 2008: The presidential mandate was extended from four to six years and that of State Duma deputies from four to five years. In March 2009 the Duma amended the legislation on political parties, gradually reducing the number of members required for registration from 50,000 to 40,000, with effect from 2012.

16 April 2009: Medvedev formally ended military operations in Chechnya.

22 June 2009: The President of Ingushetiya, Yunus-bek Yevkurov, was seriously injured in a suicide bomb attack. He resumed duties in August, after the Republic's construction minister was shot dead.

16 November 2009: Sergei Magnitskii, an accountant who had discovered substantial theft by senior officials, before being detained on charges of collusion of tax evasion, died in a prison in Moscow, having been beaten. The USA barred numerous Russian officials from entering the country on grounds of their suspected implication in human rights abuses.

19 January 2010: President Medvedev announced the creation of a new North Caucasus Federal Okrug, the Presidential Representative to which also become a Deputy Chairman of the federal Government.

29 March 2010: Some 40 people were killed and over 100 injured in two suicide bomb attacks on the Moscow Metro, for which Umarov claimed responsibility. Two days later unauthorized demonstrations demanding that Putin resign took place nationwide, with particularly large demonstrations occurring in Kaliningrad and Vladivostok.

INTRODUCTION

28 September 2010: Medvedev dismissed Yurii Luzhkov, Mayor of Moscow since 1992. He was succeeded by Sergei Sobyanin, a former Governor of Tyumen Oblast and federal deputy premier.

31 December 2010: Boris Nemtsov, a Deputy Chairman of the Government in 1997–98, and subsequently a prominent critic of Putin, was among those detained during an anti-Government rally in Moscow; he was sentenced to 15 days' imprisonment.

24 January 2011: A suicide bomb attack at Moscow-Domodedovo airport, organized by supporters of Umarov, killed 37 people and injured a further 180.

24 September 2011: Putin announced that he would contest the presidential election of 2012, and intended to nominate Medvedev as his premier.

4 December 2011: At State Duma elections, YeR won 49.3% of the votes cast and 238 seats. The KPRF received 92 seats, SR 64, and the LDPR 56. Protests against alleged electoral fraud took place in Moscow and other cities. One day later anti-corruption campaigner Aleksei Navalnyi was arrested; he was sentenced to 14 days' detention for disobeying police instructions. On 21 December Sergei Naryshkin, hitherto head of the presidential administration, was elected Chairman of the State Duma.

4 February 2012: A further mass demonstration, attended by more than 100,000 supporters (according to opposition estimates), was staged in Moscow to protest against Putin's anticipated return to the presidency.

March–May 2012: Putin was elected President on 4 March, with 63.6% of votes cast. Demonstrations against Putin's election in Moscow and St Petersburg were violently dispersed, and more than 500 protesters were arrested. On 3 April the number of members required of a political party was reduced from 40,000 to 500, and on 2 May Medvedev signed legislation reintroducing direct popular gubernatorial elections. Putin was inaugurated as President on 7 May, and a new Government, led by Medvedev, was appointed two weeks later.

1 July 2012: The territory of Moscow City was substantially expanded, to incorporate a number of districts from Moscow Oblast.

14 October 2012: The first gubernatorial elections since 2005 were conducted in five territories; in each case the pro-Government incumbent was returned to office.

6 November 2012: Sergei Shoigu, a former longserving Minister of Civil Defence, Emergencies and Disaster Relief was appointed Minister of Defence, replacing Anatolii Serdyukov, who had been dismissed after criminal investigations into corruption against him began.

1 January 2013: Electoral reforms entered into effect, reducing the threshold for a party to obtain representation in the State Duma from 7% to 5%. Representatives of regional legislatures in the Federation Council were required to be a member of the respective assembly, and their appointment was to require the endorsement of the regional governor.

28 January 2013: Putin dismissed the President of Dagestan, Magomedsalam Magomedov, following an intensification of Islamic sectarian violence in the territory.

1 March 2013: Putin submitted amendments to electoral legislation, under which one-half of the Duma seats would henceforth be elected in single-member constituencies. In April Putin signed into force legislation that permitted regions to permit their regional legislature to elect the governor from three candidates nominated by the President in place of direct popular voting. (Dagestan became the first federal subject to adopt these measures; a few other regions followed.)

18 July 2013: A court in Kirov sentenced Navalnyi to five years' imprisonment for embezzlement. One day later, however, he was released, pending an appeal: he was, moreover, to be permitted to contest the Moscow mayoral election in September.

8 September 2013: Legislative, gubernatorial and local elections were held in numerous territories. YeR remained the strongest party, but with lower support. Sobyanin was re-elected as Mayor of Moscow, receiving 51.4% of the vote, narrowly avoiding a run-off against Navalnyi, with 27.2%. Notably, the YeR mayoral candidate in the Urals city of Yekaterinburg, Sverdlovsk Oblast, was defeated.

16 October 2013: A court suspended Navalnyi's prison sentence, although he was to be prohibited indefinitely from seeking public office.

4 November 2013: New legislation reduced the minimum share of deputies in regional assemblies required to be elected from party lists from 50% to 25%. Party list requirements were removed entirely in elections to the city assemblies of Moscow and St Petersburg.

18 December 2013: Russia announced that it had stationed short-range ballistic missiles in its Baltic exclave, Kaliningrad Oblast.

20 December 2013: Putin pardoned Khodorkovskii; several other prisoners were also to benefit from an amnesty. (However, in 2015 Russia issued an international arrest warrant for Khodorkovskii, who had left Russia for Switzerland, in association with the killing of the Mayor of Nefteyugansk, in the Khanty-Mansii Autonomous Okrug—Yugra, in 1998.)

25 February 2014: Popular demonstrations in Sevastopol, Crimea, Ukraine, led the city council, meeting in emergency session, to appoint a Russian citizen (hence ineligible to hold public office there), Aleksei Chalyi, as Mayor, while checkpoints were set up around the city to prevent supporters of the Ukrainian authorities reaching the city. These developments occurred three days after the Ukrainian President, Viktor Yanukovych (an ally of the Russian authorities), had fled from office following months of protests. On 27 February unidentified armed men seized control of the Crimean Supreme Council in Simferopol. The Council went on to elect a deputy of the Russkoye Yedinstvo (Russian Unity) party (holding three of the 100 seats), Sergei Aksyonov, as Crimean premier. On 6 March the Crimean Supreme Council voted in favour of the territory joining Russia and announced that a referendum to seek endorsement of the decision would be held.

16 March 2014: Referendums in Crimea and Sevastopol overwhelmingly supported the admission of both territories to the Russian Federation. They were formally incorporated into the country on 21 March, three days after Putin and the two territorial heads signed a treaty to that end.

18 March 2014: The Caucasus Emirate organization announced that Umarov had been killed.

25 March 2014: The G8 (Group of Eight) suspended Russia's membership, in response to its annexation of Crimea. Meanwhile, the EU, the USA and Canada imposed the first of a number of rounds of asset freezes and visa restrictions against senior Russian officials.

7 April 2014: In Donetsk, Ukraine, rebels seized the regional council buildings, proclaiming a 'Donetsk People's Republic' (DNR). Russian support for forces in the

DNR and the neighbouring Lugansk People's Republic (LNR), while officially denied, subsequently became evident.

12 May 2014: A federal Ministry of North Caucasus Affairs was created. (A Ministry of Crimean Affairs had been created in March, but this was abolished in July 2015.)

17 July 2014: Following the shooting down, seemingly by pro-Russian rebels, of a Malaysian passenger plane, which resulted in 298 deaths, amid continuing unrest in the Donbas region of eastern Ukraine, the US forbade commercial transactions with two major Russian energy companies and with two banks. In August Russia prohibited the import of many food products from the EU, the USA, Australia, Canada and Norway (further countries were subsequently made subject to similar sanctions).

5 September 2014: The Minsk Protocol, providing for an immediate ceasefire, was signed by representatives of Ukraine, Russia, and the DNR and the LNR in Minsk, Belarus, although it was not generally observed.

14 September 2014: Elections were held to regional legislatures and gubernatorial positions in many federal subjects. In the overwhelming majority of cases the candidates supported by the federal authorities were successful. Shortly after the elections, security forces conducted a search operation of the Crimean Tatar Mejlis (Assembly) building in Simferopol. The organization was subsequently expelled from its office, and its property and assets frozen by court order.

22 September 2014: Several thousand people participated in rallies in Moscow, demonstrating against the conflict in the Donbas, in which the covert use of Russian forces had been reported on numerous occasions.

4 December 2014: Gun battles, instigated by Islamist militants, broke out in Groznyi. At least 15 security officials and 11 Islamist militants were killed, in the largest outbreak of violence in the Chechen capital for several years.

30 December 2014: A court in Moscow sentenced Navalnyi to a suspended term of three-and-a-half years (and placing him under house arrest) for fraud.

12 February 2015: A new peace agreement, Minsk II, was signed by the leaders of Russia, Ukraine, France, Germany and the DNR and LNR. The terms of this agreement were endorsed on 17 February by a UN Security Council resolution, drafted by Russia. While violence abated, ceasefire violations continued subsequently.

27 February 2015: Nemtsov was shot dead in Moscow, two days before he was to have participated in a protest against Russian involvement in Ukraine. The rally, on 1 March, expressed outrage at his murder. In early March five Chechens, including a former senior police official, Zaur Dadayev, were detained on suspicion of involvement. Putin awarded Kadyrov the state Order of Honour on 9 March, shortly after Kadyrov had commended Dadayev.

13 April 2016: The Crimean Prosecutor-General suspended the activities of the Crimean Tatar Mejlis, pending a court investigation on the body's proscription.

28 July 2016: The Crimean Federal Okrug (established in 2014) was abolished, and its territories incorporated into the Southern Federal Okrug. On the same day Putin dismissed Nikita Belykh, a former leader of the SPS, as Governor of Kirov Oblast, shortly after he had been charged with receiving bribes from a company associated with Navalnyi.

18 September 2016: In elections to the State Duma, held under a reintroduced mixed system of voting, YeR increased its representation to 343 of the 450 seats, having obtained 54.2% of the votes cast to the 225 seats allocated on a proportional basis. The KPRF was second, with 42 seats, ahead of the LDPR, with 39, and SR, with 23.

3 October 2016: The trial of the five Chechens accused of involvement in Nemtsov's murder commenced at a military court in Moscow. (All five were awarded custodial sentences in 2017.) Associates of Nemtsov expressed scepticism that the real organizers of the murder had been identified.

5 October 2016: Vyacheslav Volodin (erstwhile First Deputy Chairman of the Presidential Administration) became Chairman of the State Duma, succeeding Sergei Naryshkin, now Director of the Foreign Intelligence Service.

15 November 2016: Putin dismissed Aleksei Ulyukayev as Minister of Economic Development, following his arrest and detention on suspicion of receiving illicit payments. (In December 2017 he was sentenced to eight years' imprisonment.)

7 February 2017: After the Federal Supreme Court overturned the 2013 ruling that had allowed Navalnyi's release, a court in Kirov, having retried the case, imposed a five-year suspended sentence and a financial penalty on Navalnyi; the sentence also barred Navalnyi from seeking public office.

26 March 2017: Large-scale anti-corruption protests in Moscow and other major cities took place, organized by Navalnyi, which resulted in at least 500 arrests in the capital alone, including that of Navalnyi himself. He was also one of at least 1,500 people arrested following demonstrations held on 12 June, when he was sentenced to 30 days detention.

3 April 2017: A bomb attack on the St Petersburg Metro, which coincided with a visit to the city by Putin, killed 16 people; an Islamist group connected with the al-Qa'ida network claimed responsibility for the attack.

4 March 2018: A former Russian military agent (and former British double agent), Sergei Skripal, and his daughter, Yuliya, were poisoned by a nerve agent developed by the Russian state, near their residence in Salisbury, England. (A British citizen subsequently died after inadvertently being contaminated by the nerve agent.) After the UK determined that it was probable that Russia had been responsible for the attack, a total of 107 Russian diplomats were expelled from some 25 Western countries in response.

18 March 2018: Putin was re-elected to the presidency with 76.7% of the votes cast.

1 April 2018: The longest serving regional governor in the Federation (in post, with a short interlude in 2001, since 1997), Aman-Geldy Tuleyev, resigned as Governor of Kemerovo Oblast (renamed Kemerovo Oblast—Kuzbass in 2019).

7 May 2018: Putin was inaugurated to a further six-year presidential term. Shortly afterwards he proposed the reappointment of Medvedev as premier. Two days earlier around 1,600 people had been detained nationwide during protests against Putin's continued rule, organized by Navalnyi. Several of the principal office-holders in the outgoing administration were reappointed to the new Government that was approved later in May.

9 September 2018: Although it remained, by far, the dominant party in elections held to the executive leadership of 22 federal territories, and to the legislative assemblies of 16 territories, support for YeR dropped sharply, largely owing to hostility to proposed pensions reforms.

INTRODUCTION

3 November 2018: A presidential decree provided for the transfer of the Republic of Buryatiya and Transbaikal Krai from the Siberian to the Far Eastern Federal Okrug. In the following month it was announced that the administrative centre of the Far Eastern Federal Okrug was to be relocated from Khabarovsk to Vladivostok (in Maritime Krai); this entered into effect in 2020.

7 November 2018: Aleksandr Gutsan assumed office as Presidential Representative to the North-Western Federal Okrug, replacing Aleksandr Beglov, whom Putin had appointed Acting Governor of St Petersburg (Beglov was formally elected to the post in September 2019).

25 November 2018: Russian maritime border guards seized three Ukrainian navy gunboats and a tugboat which had attempted to pass through the Kerch Strait (over which Russia had constructed bridges linking Crimea to its mainland) to the Sea of Azov. The 24 captured Ukrainian sailors were subsequently transferred to prison in Moscow, and were charged with illegally crossing Russia's maritime border; they were released in September 2019.

18 March 2019: New legislation enabling the authorities to impose penalties on outlets or individuals, and to block websites for the publication of what was deemed to be 'fake news', or 'insults to the authorities, state symbols or Russian society' entered into effect.

26 March 2019: Mikhail Abyzov, a former Minister without Portfolio, was detained on charges of large-scale embezzlement. Two days later, Viktor Ishayev, a former Minister of the Development of the Russian Far East, Presidential Representative to the Far Eastern Federal Okrug, and Governor of Khabarovsk Krai, was arrested on suspicion of defrauding Rosneft; both Abyzov and Ishayev were subsequently found guilty of the charges against them.

10 August 2019: Up to 60,000 people gathered at a protest demonstration in Moscow against the denial of registration to numerous independent opposition representatives who wished to contest elections to the city Duma scheduled for 8 September. Over 1,500 people were arrested during a series of related demonstrations.

8 September 2019: Direct elections were held to the leadership of 16 federal territories, and to 13 regional parliaments. Support for YeR again fell, with the party's representatives standing as independent candidates in some territories, notably in the elections to Moscow City Duma.

15 January 2020: Putin proposed several constitutional changes, which were to be presented for approval at a national referendum, while appointing Medvedev to the new post of Deputy Chairman of the Security Council. One day later Mikhail Mishustin, hitherto Director of the Federal Tax Service, succeeded him as Prime Minister. His Government was confirmed in office on 21 January. The Ministry of North Caucasus Affairs was abolished, reflecting the general abatement in unrest across the region.

10 February 2020: Seven left-wing activists were sentenced by a military court in the city of Penza to prison terms of up to 18 years on various charges connected to an alleged terrorist organization known as Set (Network), which, according to the authorities, had plotted to overthrow the Government. Four of the prisoners claimed that they had confessed after being tortured in custody.

18 February 2020: A longstanding close adviser of Putin, Vladislav Surkov, was dismissed.

10 March 2020: The Duma approved further proposed constitutional amendments that would, by 'resetting' when presidential terms began, permit Putin to seek a further two terms in office. Other significant aspects of the amendments included the assertion of the domestic primacy of Russian constitutional law over the terms of international treaties deemed to violate it, the commitment of support to those resident in other countries who claim Russian cultural identity and who are deemed to be under threat, and the introduction of new restrictions prohibiting many senior officials from holding citizenship or permanent residency of a foreign country, and restricting their usage of foreign banks. The powers of the presidency over judicial appointments were to be increased.

25 March 2020: Following the introduction of a number of containment measures imposed in response to the escalating pandemic of COVID-19. Putin announced the postponement of the constitutional referendum that had been scheduled for 22 April; on 30 March a lockdown (requiring all non-essential workers to stay in their homes) was imposed in Moscow City and Moscow Oblast; most other federal regions imposed similar measures subsequently.

4 July 2020: The amendments to the Constitution approved by the State Duma earlier in the year entered into effect, after 77.9% of the votes cast in a popular vote (formally consultative in character) held between 25 June and 1 July endorsed the reforms. Only in one federal territory, the Nenets Autonomous Okrug, did a majority of those voting express opposition to the amendments.

20 August 2020: Navalnyi became seriously ill and fell into a coma while on an aeroplane, and was hospitalized in Omsk; after several days the Russian authorities permitted his evacuation to Germany, where he remained in hospital; the German Government subsequently stated that it had found 'unequivocal proof' that Navalnyi had been poisoned by a nerve agent. Navalnyi remained in Germany following his discharge from hospital on 22 September.

13 September 2020: Elections to 11 regional legislatures and to 18 regional leaderships were held. Additionally, in two regions in which the governor is not directly elected, indirect elections to that post were held in the respective local legislature. A further downturn in support for YeR was evident in the election results, although all the incumbent governors and acting governors were re-elected or elected, respectively, to office.

10 November 2020: A government reorganization was implemented. In accordance with the revised Constitution, the new ministerial appointments required the State Duma's approval.

5 December 2020: Russia commenced a programme of mass public vaccinations against COVID-19, using its domestically developed Sputnik V vaccine.

22 December 2020: Legislation granting lifetime immunity from criminal prosecution to Russian Presidents and their family members, and empowering the President to appoint up to 30 members of the Federation Council, and to enable a former President to become a lifetime member of the chamber, entered into effect.

17 January 2021: Navalnyi returned by plane from Germany to Moscow, where he was immediately detained on charges of having violated the conditions of his parole. Demonstrations against his arrest were staged nationwide on 23 January, with those in Moscow reportedly attended by as many as 40,000 supporters (although official figures reported an attendance of 4,000). Some rallies were violently dispersed by police.

INTRODUCTION

2 February 2021: Navalnyi was sentenced to two years and eight months' imprisonment for violating the terms of his 2014 suspended sentence, prompting protests in Moscow. A ruling by the European Court of Human Rights on 16 February that the Government should release Navalnyi, since it was unable to safeguard his health, was dismissed by the Minister of Justice, and on 20 February a Moscow appeals court upheld the prison sentence against him. Another court on the same day fined Navalnyi 850,000 roubles for defaming a Second World War veteran who had promoted the new constitutional amendments. By that time more than 10,000 protesters had been arrested and hundreds of them had received short prison sentences.

13 March 2021: Police raided an opposition conference in Moscow, detaining some 200 people, including prominent opposition figures, claiming that it had been organized by the banned Otkrytaya Rossiya (Open Russia) organization established by Khodorkovskii.

22 April 2021: Following a period of several weeks during which a significant mobilization of Russian troops near the border with Ukraine had prompted international expressions of concern, it was announced that most of the Russian military units on exercise in the area would return to base; the return of around 300,000 troops to their permanent bases was reported later in the month.

8 September 2021: The Minister of Civil Defence, Emergencies and Disaster Relief, Yevgenii Zinichev, died in an accident.

19 September 2021: In elections to the State Duma, the representation of YeR decreased to 324 of the 450 seats; the party had received 49.8% of the proportional vote. The KPRF was second, with 57 seats and 18.9% of the vote, ahead of SR (which had merged with two smaller nationalist parties—Za Pravdu (For Truth) and Patrioty Rossii (Patriots of Russia)—renaming itself SR—Patrioty—Za Pravdu (SR—Patriots—For Truth—earlier in the year), with 27 seats, the LDPR, with 21 seats, and a recently founded centre-right party, the Partiya Novyye Lyudi (New People Party), with 13 seats. An official voter turnout of 51.6% was recorded. In regional elections, 12 incumbent governors or acting governors were returned to office (in nine cases by direct vote, and in three cases by vote of the regional legislature, with the vote in Dagestan taking place on 14 October). YeR remained the dominant party in concurrent elections to 39 regional legislatures.

6 October 2021: Following a number of diplomatic expulsions involving Russia and NATO states, NATO expelled eight members of the Russian delegation to the Alliance, who were accused of being undeclared intelligence officers; in response, Russia recalled its remaining accredited diplomats and ordered NATO to close its liaison office in Moscow. After President Putin accused NATO of responsibility for escalating tensions with Ukraine by supplying its Government with advanced weaponry and staging exercises near Russia's borders, on 17 December Russia presented a number of security guarantees to be met by NATO in order to end the crisis. Negotiations on the Russian demands began in Geneva in January 2022, continuing with a meeting of the NATO-Russia Council in Brussels, Belgium. However, Russia quickly declared that the security discussions had been unsuccessful and accused Western powers of ignoring Russia's security concerns. From November 2021 a renewed build-up of Russian military forces had commenced near the border with Ukraine, prompting renewed international concern, amounting to around 100,000 troops by the end of December.

28 December 2021: The Supreme Court ordered the closure of prominent and longstanding human rights group Memorial International (which had gathered information on victims of the Stalin regime). One day later a Moscow court ordered the dissolution of the associated Memorial Human Rights Centre.

10 February 2022: Joint military exercises in Belarus's western and southern border regions began, after Russia had deployed at least 30,000 troops to the country. Belarusian President Alyaksandr Lukashenka visited Moscow to discuss 'further activities' with Putin on 18 February.

21 February 2022: President Putin signed two decrees formally recognizing the DNR and the LNR, ordering troops to enter the territories for 'peacekeeping operations'; he announced his decision in a televised address during which he denied the legitimacy of Ukrainian statehood. On the following day both legislative chambers ratified Putin's decrees, together with friendship and co-operation treaties signed with the heads of the DNR and the LNR, which included provisions allowing Russia to establish military infrastructure in the territories. The Federation Council also authorized a request by Putin to use military force outside the country.

24 February 2022: Putin announced the start of a 'special military operation' in Ukraine, declaring the 'demilitarization and denazification' of the country to be one of its objectives. Shortly afterwards, regulatory agency Roskomnadzor ordered media outlets only to use the terms and information provided by Russian official sources when reporting on the conflict (notably prohibiting the use of numerous terms, including 'war' and 'invasion'). New legislation, which was approved by both parliamentary chambers and signed into force by Putin on 4 March, introduced penalties for the dissemination of 'false information about the Russian military' or support for sanctions against Russia. On the same day Roskomnadzor blocked access to many online foreign news outlets. Russia launched air and land attacks from its border with Belarus, from its western frontier and from Crimea in the south; forces from the Chechen Republic answerable to that region's leader, Kadyrov, were also dispatched to Ukraine, as were forces from the Russian-allied separatist 'Republic of South Ossetia' within Georgia. Russian forces rapidly reached the outskirts of Kyiv, but their efforts to capture major cities were repelled by the Ukrainian military, and by early April Russian activity was concentrated in the Donbas and in the south of Ukraine. In response to the invasion, numerous countries, including the USA, and also the EU, expanded sanctions regimes in force against Russia, causing many Western companies to suspend or terminate their operations there. Numerous NATO countries also subsequently supplied heavy weaponry to Ukraine. On 25 February 2022 Russia vetoed a draft UN Security Council resolution condemning its invasion of Ukraine. An ensuing emergency special session of the UN General Assembly, convened on 2 March, adopted a resolution demanding a full Russian withdrawal from Ukrainian territory.

25 May 2022: Aleksandr Kurenkov was appointed as Minister of Civil Defence, Emergencies and Disaster Relief.

15 July 2022: Denis Manturov, Minister of Industry and Trade was additionally appointed as a Deputy Chairman of the Government, replacing Yurii Borisov in that capacity.

11 September 2022: Direct popular elections were held to the leadership of 15 federal subjects, as well as to six regional legislatures. (In Adygeya, the newly elected legislature subsequently voted for the Head of the Republic.). In each of the gubernatorial elections, the incumbent was either re-elected or the acting incumbent elected to a full term, in all cases by a substantial margin over other candidates. Some 13 of the 15 executive heads directly elected were representatives of YeR, other than in the Republic of Marii-El and Yaroslavl Oblasts, where nominally independent candidates, both of whom had been appointed as acting governors, were confirmed in office.

30 September 2022: As conflict in Ukraine continued, particularly in southern regions, Russia announced the annexation of four territories, including, in addition to the DNR and the LNR, two territories in the south of Ukraine—Kherson Oblast (neighbouring and providing direct land access to Crimea, and including a part of neighbouring Nikolayev—Mykolayiv Oblast) and Zaporozhye (Zaporizhzhya) Oblast, thereby granting Russia full control of the Sea of Azov littoral. The formal borders of the territories, none of which were fully controlled by Russia, were not defined, although it was understood that the territories based in Donetsk and Lugansk (Luhansk) were intended to encompass the full extent of the oblasts formally based in those cities prior to the commencement of the conflict there in 2014. However, in practice, Ukraine maintained control of extensive parts of the territories, including the city of Zaporizhzhya itself (the pro-Russian administration being based instead in Melitopol).

19 October 2022: Martial law was introduced in the territories that had recently been annexed, while President Putin declared a 'medium level of response' in eight other territories (including the annexed Republic of Crimea and Sevastopol) bordering the Russian-occupied parts of Ukraine; under this regime, the regional authorities concerned were granted powers to undertake 'economic mobilization' for the provision of supplies to the Russian armed forces in Ukraine, as well as to increase security measures and introduce restrictions on freedom of movement to and from the territory.

11 November 2022: A Ukrainian military counteroffensive led to the country regaining control (lost since March) of the city of Kherson; the pro-Russian authorities in the Oblast relocated to a smaller city, Genichesk (Henichesk), strategically located at an access point to Crimea.

11 January 2023: Chief of the General Staff Valerii Gerasimov was appointed as the most senior commander of the war in Ukraine. The paramilitary Wagner Group attracted domestic and international controversy by its recruitment of large numbers of prisoners to fight in Ukraine; after clashing with Russia's military leadership, in February Wagner's leader, Yevgenii Prigozhin, announced an end to the recruitment programme. In March it was reported that more than 5,000 former criminals who had fought under contracts with the Wagner Group had been pardoned.

14 April 2023: New legislation facilitated conscription procedures and further strengthened measures against evasion. Three days later journalist and opposition activist Vladimir Kara-Murza, who had denounced Russia's invasion of Ukraine in the USA, was sentenced to 25 years in prison on charges of treason, spreading 'false information' about the Russian military and affiliation with an 'undesirable organization'.

26 May 2023: The Supreme Court ordered the dissolution of the liberal Partiya Narodnoi Svobody (Party of People's Freedom), originally registered in 1991 as the Respublikanskaya Partiya Rossiiskoi Federatsii (Republican Party of the Russian

Federation). The party's leader, former premier Kasyanov, had left Russia in 2022 after opposing the invasion of Ukraine.

24 June 2023: Heavily armed troops affiliated with the Wagner Group took control of a number of public buildings, including the headquarters of the Southern Military District, in Rostov-on-Don, near the Ukrainian border, meeting negligible resistance, before proceeding to commence a march towards Moscow, around 1,000 km away; Prigozhin had accused the Russian Ministry of Defence and what he termed 'the oligarchic clan that rules Russia' of having invaded Ukraine, in effect, for their own benefit, and also had opposed a recent command that the Wagner forces be fully incorporated into the Russian military by 1 July. However, later that day Prigozhin ordered his troops to end their rebellion, after negotiations had concluded between the Russian and Belarusian leaderships had taken place, providing for Prigozhin and the Wagner troops to relocate to Belarus, and pledging that participants in the rebellion would not be punished for their actions.

21 July 2023: FSB agents arrested a prominent former commander of Russian-allied forces in the DNR, Igor Girkin ('Strelkov') who had been increasingly critical of the Russian management of the conflict in Ukraine; he was charged with extremism, shortly after he had called for Putin to be removed from office.

4 August 2023: Navalnyi received a further custodial sentence, of 19 years, to be spent in a 'special regime' camp, for charges that included extremist activity and 'rehabilitating Nazi ideology'. In December it was reported that he had been transferred to such a camp, located in the Arctic region of the Yamalo-Nenets Autonomous Okrug.

23 August 2023: Prigozhin and other senior members of Wagner were killed in a plane crash near Tver.

10 September 2023: Direct popular elections were held to the leadership of 21 federal subjects and to 16 regional legislatures. (In the Yamalo-Nenets Autonomous Okrug, the legislature voted for the district Governor.). In each of the gubernatorial elections, the incumbent was either re-elected or the acting incumbent elected to a full term. Of the 21 executive heads directly elected all but two were representatives of YeR; in Khakasiya and Oryol Oblast the KPRF incumbents were re-elected. The regional legislative elections were generally characterized by an upturn in support for YeR, particularly in areas of Siberia and the Far East in which it had not previously held a legislative majority, but in most cases this was accompanied by low participation rates, in several cases of well below 30% of the electorate.

Statistics

MAJOR DEMOGRAPHIC AND ECONOMIC INDICATORS

Note: Except where otherwise stated, data for the federal okrugs refer to their boundaries at January 2023.

Federal Okrug and Territory	Area ('000 sq km)	Population at 1 January 2023 (official estimate, '000)	Population density, January 2023 (official estimate, per sq km)	Average annual change in population, 2000–23 (%)[1]	Male life expectancy at birth, 2022 (years)
Central	650.2	40,240.3	61.9	0.22	69.1
Moscow City	2.5	13,104.2	5,220.8	1.18[2]	74.4
Belgorod Oblast	27.1	1,514.5	55.8	0.04	67.7
Bryansk Oblast	34.9	1,152.5	33.1	−0.91	65.2
Ivanovo Oblast	21.4	914.7	42.7	−1.15	64.8
Kaluga Oblast	29.8	1,070.9	36.0	0.00	67.4
Kostroma Oblast	60.2	571.9	9.5	−1.24	63.6
Kursk Oblast	30.0	1,067.0	35.6	−0.79	65.8
Lipetsk Oblast	24.0	1,126.3	46.8	−0.40	66.9
Moscow Oblast	44.4	8,591.7	193.6	1.18[2]	69.7
Oryol Oblast	24.7	700.3	28.4	−1.01	65.3
Ryazan Oblast	39.6	1,088.9	27.5	−0.68	66.3
Smolensk Oblast	49.8	873.0	17.5	−1.00	64.5
Tambov Oblast	34.5	966.3	28.0	−1.05	66.6
Tula Oblast	25.7	1,481.5	57.7	−0.71	66.5
Tver Oblast	84.2	1,211.2	14.4	−1.05	64.5
Vladimir Oblast	29.1	1,325.5	45.6	−0.75	65.0
Voronezh Oblast	52.2	2,285.3	43.8	−0.29	67.0
Yaroslavl Oblast	36.2	1,194.6	33.0	−0.71	65.8
North-Western	1,687.0	13,867.3	8.2	−0.14	68.0
St Petersburg City	1.4	5,600.0	3,891.6	0.73	71.4
Republic of Kareliya	180.5	527.9	2.9	−1.43	63.1
Republic of Komi	416.8	726.4	1.7	−1.62	64.4
Archangel Oblast	589.9	1,005.7	1.7	−1.40	65.3
Nenets Autonomous Okrug	176.8	41.4	0.2	0.02	64.8
Kaliningrad Oblast	15.1	1,032.3	68.3	0.32	68.5
Leningrad Oblast	83.9	2,023.8	24.1	0.80	68.7
Murmansk Oblast	144.9	658.7	4.5	−1.54	64.4
Novgorod Oblast	54.5	575.9	10.6	−0.96	64.4
Pskov Oblast	55.4	587.8	10.6	−1.29	63.1
Vologda Oblast	144.5	1,128.8	7.8	−0.61	65.9

[1] According to official estimates of population at 1 January.
[2] Figure refers to change of population of Moscow City and Moscow Oblast combined.

Female life expectancy at birth, 2022 (years)	Gross regional product (GRP), 2021 (m. roubles)	GRP per head, 2021 (roubles)	Rate of un-employment, 2022 (%)	Average monthly wage, 2022 (roubles)	Federal Okrug and Territory
78.6	41,685,337	1,064,007	3.0	83,126	**Central**
81.6	24,471,160	1,935,205	2.2	125,638	Moscow City
78.4	1,354,811	881,701	3.7	47,638	Belgorod Oblast
77.3	468,666	398,619	3.2	40,804	Bryansk Oblast
76.1	300,626	306,145	3.1	36,380	Ivanovo Oblast
77.7	664,150	659,591	3.9	53,910	Kaluga Oblast
76.5	241,530	386,695	3.4	40,242	Kostroma Oblast
77.3	683,802	627,321	3.0	46,059	Kursk Oblast
77.7	843,982	752,926	3.7	46,711	Lipetsk Oblast
77.9	6,832,298	882,876	3.1	70,705	Moscow Oblast
76.1	336,688	468,019	4.0	40,843	Oryol Oblast
77.8	531,962	487,276	2.9	45,770	Ryazan Oblast
76.1	421,673	460,597	3.5	41,717	Smolensk Oblast
77.5	429,268	434,613	3.3	39,346	Tambov Oblast
77.1	867,817	602,298	3.6	51,218	Tula Oblast
75.3	555,098	448,418	3.8	45,732	Tver Oblast
76.6	736,830	552,811	2.6	45,677	Vladimir Oblast
78.0	1,254,722	546,329	3.5	46,277	Voronezh Oblast
77.0	690,253	559,180	5.0	47,388	Yaroslavl Oblast
77.8	16,611,895	1,193,254	3.2	72,465	**North-Western**
79.4	9,440,411	1,754,423	1.8	86,630	St Petersburg City
75.0	447,147	737,782	5.8	56,458	Republic of Kareliya
75.5	857,013	1,059,960	6.7	68,790	Republic of Komi
76.6	1,055,421	941,763	5.6	67,835	Archangel Oblast
76.9	406,838	9,149,623	7.4	106,949	Nenets Autonomous Okrug
77.6	675,001	659,727	3.1	47,349	Kaliningrad Oblast
78.0	1,481,188	778,692	3.3	60,008	Leningrad Oblast
75.7	1,083,779	1,487,364	4.8	87,326	Murmansk Oblast
76.2	342,070	580,495	3.1	45,247	Novgorod Oblast
75.0	219,949	356,595	4.0	38,966	Pskov Oblast
77.1	1,009,918	881,816	3.4	53,580	Vologda Oblast

INTRODUCTION

Major Demographic and Economic Indicators (continued)

Federal Okrug and Territory	Area ('000 sq km)	Population at 1 January 2023 (official estimate, '000)	Population density, January 2023 (official estimate, per sq km)	Average annual change in population, 2000–23 (%)[1]	Male life expectancy at birth, 2022 (years)
Southern	447.9	16,642.1	37.2	0.02[2]	67.7
Sevastopol City . . .	0.9	558.3	646.1	n.a.	70.0
Republic of Adygeya . . .	7.8	498.0	63.9	0.45	69.0
Republic of Crimea . . .	26.1	1,916.8	73.5	n.a.	66.9
Republic of Kalmykiya .	74.7	264.5	3.5	−0.66	68.2
Krasnodar Krai . . .	75.5	5,819.3	77.1	0.55	68.2
Astrakhan Oblast . .	49.0	950.6	19.4	−0.27	66.8
Rostov Oblast	101.0	4,164.5	41.2	−0.29	66.8
Volgograd Oblast . . .	112.9	2,470.1	21.9	−0.45	68.3
North Caucasus . . .	170.4	10,205.7	59.9	0.72	72.1
Chechen Republic . . .	15.6	1,533.2	98.0	1.41	71.8
Republic of Dagestan .	50.3	3,209.8	63.9	1.19	75.3
Republic of Ingushetiya .	3.6	519.1	143.1	1.86	76.3
Kabardino-Balkar Republic.	12.5	903.3	72.4	0.12	71.5
Karachai-Cherkess Republic	14.3	468.4	32.8	0.27	70.9
Republic of North Osetiya—Alaniya	8.0	680.7	85.2	−0.08	69.7
Stavropol Krai	66.2	2,891.2	43.7	0.23	69.9
Volga	1,037.0	28,693.9	27.7	−0.43	66.8
Republic of Bashkortostan .	142.9	4,077.6	28.5	−0.04	67.8
Chuvash Republic . . .	18.3	1,178.5	64.3	−0.54	66.3
Republic of Marii-El .	23.4	672.3	28.8	−0.44	65.7
Republic of Mordoviya .	26.1	771.4	29.5	−0.76	67.5
Republic of Tatarstan . .	67.8	4,001.6	59.0	0.24	69.8
Udmurt Republic . . .	42.1	1,442.3	34.3	−0.44	65.6
Perm Krai	160.2	2,508.4	15.7	−0.60	64.9
Kirov Oblast	120.4	1,138.1	9.5	−1.34	65.4
Nizhnii Novgorod Oblast .	76.6	3,081.8	40.2	−0.71	65.6
Orenburg Oblast . . .	123.7	1,841.4	14.9	−0.79	65.6
Penza Oblast	43.4	1,246.6	28.8	−0.80	66.3
Samara Oblast	53.6	3,142.7	58.7	−0.20	66.9
Saratov Oblast	101.2	2,404.9	23.8	−0.52	68.1
Ulyanovsk Oblast . . .	37.2	1,186.3	31.9	−0.80	65.5

[1] According to official estimates of population at 1 January.
[2] Excluding Sevastopol City and the Republic of Crimea.

Statistics

Female life expectancy at birth, 2022 (years)	Gross regional product (GRP), 2021 (m. roubles)	GRP per head, 2021 (roubles)	Rate of un-employment, 2022 (%)	Average monthly wage, 2022 (roubles)	Federal Okrug and Territory
77.6	7,952,017	483,150	4.1	46,231	**Southern**
79.2	168,574	326,677	3.9	43,112	Sevastopol City
78.1	170,793	366,702	7.1	40,231	Republic of Adygeya
77.0	586,498	308,848	5.0	41,986	Republic of Crimea
78.8	100,008	371,956	8.1	36,349	Republic of Kalmykiya
77.7	3,200,607	562,926	3.5	50,252	Krasnodar Krai
76.8	657,016	661,245	7.0	47,780	Astrakhan Oblast
77.3	2,017,007	483,970	3.5	44,767	Rostov Oblast
78.3	1,051,515	427,069	3.5	44,242	Volgograd Oblast
79.4	2,695,611	270,039	10.3	37,361	**North Caucasus**
77.5	268,069	177,860	11.0	33,700	Chechen Republic
81.1	814,427	259,076	12.1	35,082	Republic of Dagestan
80.4	77,237	148,587	28.5	32,801	Republic of Ingushetiya
79.3	199,326	229,153	10.0	35,251	Kabardino-Balkar Republic
79.6	109,390	235,355	9.8	35,463	Karachai-Cherkess Republic
79.5	202,602	293,366	11.9	36,360	Republic of North Osetiya—Alaniya
78.6	1,024,560	367,687	4.3	41,402	Stavropol Krai
77.9	16,878,415	582,868	3.3	47,299	**Volga**
78.3	2,000,038	499,045	3.4	49,460	Republic of Bashkortostan
78.8	392,958	326,607	3.2	41,527	Chuvash Republic
78.3	221,991	329,660	3.6	40,713	Republic of Marii-El
78.9	298,023	384,636	3.6	39,538	Republic of Mordoviya
79.8	3,454,700	888,039	2.3	52,274	Republic of Tatarstan
78.6	841,936	565,472	2.9	45,811	Udmurt Republic
76.8	1,740,525	677,760	3.4	53,234	Perm Krai
77.4	481,407	387,458	3.8	40,833	Kirov Oblast
77.2	1,888,121	597,431	4.1	48,368	Nizhnii Novgorod Oblast
77.0	1,394,280	721,025	3.5	43,540	Orenburg Oblast
77.8	537,290	418,946	3.7	41,307	Penza Oblast
77.2	2,122,537	675,335	2.7	48,874	Samara Oblast
77.5	1,005,801	422,955	3.4	42,917	Saratov Oblast
77.2	498,806	411,847	4.2	41,523	Ulyanovsk Oblast

INTRODUCTION

Major Demographic and Economic Indicators (continued)

Federal Okrug and Territory	Area ('000 sq km)	Population at 1 January 2023 (official estimate, '000)	Population density, January 2023 (official estimate, per sq km)	Average annual change in population, 2000–23 (%)[1]	Male life expectancy at birth, 2022 (years)
Urals	1,818.5	12,259.1	6.7	−0.09	66.8
Chelyabinsk Oblast	88.5	3,407.1	38.5	−0.31	66.4
Kurgan Oblast	71.5	761.6	10.7	−1.43	63.3
Sverdlovsk Oblast	194.3	4,239.2	21.8	−0.33	65.6
Tyumen Oblast	1,464.2	3,851.2	2.6	0.78	69.6
Khanty-Mansii Autonomous Okrug—Yugra	534.8	1,730.4	3.2	1.05	70.9
Yamalo-Nenets Autonomous Okrug	769.3	512.4	0.7	0.14	70.5
Siberian	4,361.7	16,645.8	3.8	−0.40	64.8
Republic of Altai	92.9	210.8	2.3	0.18	62.5
Republic of Khakasiya	61.6	530.2	8.6	−0.22	65.2
Republic of Tyva	168.6	337.3	2.0	0.42	61.4
Altai Krai	168.0	2,131.0	12.7	−0.95	64.1
Krasnoyarsk Krai	2,366.8	2,845.5	1.2	−0.26	65.2
Irkutsk Oblast	774.8	2,344.4	3.0	−0.52	63.3
Kemerovo Oblast—Kuzbass	95.7	2,568.2	26.8	−0.62	64.0
Novosibirsk Oblast	177.8	2,794.3	15.7	0.11	65.7
Omsk Oblast	141.1	1,832.1	13.0	−0.67	66.0
Tomsk Oblast	314.4	1,052.1	3.3	−0.02	67.0
Far Eastern	6,952.6	7,903.9	1.1	−0.62	64.1
Republic of Buryatiya	351.3	974.6	2.8	−0.13	63.0
Republic of Sakha (Yakutiya)	3,083.5	997.6	0.3	0.16	67.7
Kamchatka Krai	464.3	288.7	0.6	−1.10	63.4
Khabarovsk Krai	787.6	1,284.1	1.6	−0.60	64.7
Maritime (Primorskii) Krai	164.7	1,820.1	11.!	−0.70	64.4
Transbaikal Krai	431.9	992.4	2.3	−0.80	62.0
Amur Oblast	361.9	756.2	2.1	−0.92	62.6
Magadan Oblast	462.5	134.3	0.3	−1.76	62.9
Sakhalin Oblast	87.1	460.5	5.3	−0.92	65.5
Jewish Autonomous Oblast	36.3	147.5	4.1	−1.21	61.9
Chukot Autonomous Okrug	721.5	47.8	0.1	−1.09	61.4
Russian Federation	17,125.2	146,458.1	8.6	−0.09[2]	67.6

[1] According to official estimates of population at 1 January.
[2] Excluding Sevastopol City and the Republic of Crimea.

Source: Federal Service of State Statistics, Moscow.

Statistics

Female life expectancy at birth, 2022 (years)	Gross regional product (GRP), 2021 (m. roubles)	GRP per head, 2021 (roubles)	Rate of unemployment, 2022 (%)	Average monthly wage, 2022 (roubles)	Federal Okrug and Territory
77.8	16,698,970	1,356,291	3.3	68,084	**Urals**
77.7	2,042,593	595,385	3.1	50,104	Chelyabinsk Oblast
76.9	268,495	330,642	6.5	41,792	Kurgan Oblast
77.0	3,038,443	710,381	3.5	55,308	Sverdlovsk Oblast
79.3	11,349,439	2,992,775	2.7	94,962	Tyumen Oblast
79.6	5,651,897	3,334,557	2.0	97,562	Khanty-Mansii Autonomous Okrug—Yugra
79.2	4,161,530	7,572,420	1.7	131,516	Yamalo-Nenets Autonomous Okrug
76.0	11,287,168	666,041	4.4	57,203	**Siberian**
74.7	71,336	322,413	9.8	43,974	Republic of Altai
75.8	307,517	580,016	3.3	54,522	Republic of Khakasiya
72.7	88,771	267,795	9.5	51,782	Republic of Tyva
75.8	845,430	370,434	3.7	39,270	Altai Krai
75.9	3,064,832	1,074,424	2.7	71,728	Krasnoyarsk Krai
75.2	1,924,361	813,312	5.0	64,635	Irkutsk Oblast
75.2	1,807,387	690,143	4.1	57,653	Kemerovo Oblast—Kuzbass
77.1	1,617,011	581,018	4.7	53,757	Novosibirsk Oblast
76.8	854,133	451,537	5.3	46,952	Omsk Oblast
77.7	706,392	660,598	5.2	57,879	Tomsk Oblast
75.3	7,373,575	909,459	4.8	74,799	**Far Eastern**
76.0	342,185	347,738	7.4	53,495	Republic of Buryatiya
77.6	1,615,527	1,636,734	6.5	96,728	Republic of Sakha (Yakutiya)
75.0	337,505	1,081,102	2.9	103,540	Kamchatka Krai
75.4	987,187	759,344	2.6	65,897	Khabarovsk Krai
75.3	1,308,884	699,778	3.4	63,589	Maritime (Primorskii) Krai
73.9	487,423	464,887	8.7	59,413	Transbaikal Krai
74.2	530,948	683,168	4.2	65,864	Amur Oblast
74.7	314,708	2,273,882	4.1	121,462	Magadan Oblast
75.7	1,234,355	2,545,593	4.2	102,684	Sakhalin Oblast
73.8	78,702	507,212	5.2	56,957	Jewish Autonomous Oblast
71.3	136,152	2,734,863	1.9	140,602	Chukot Autonomous Okrug
77.8	121,182,988	830,793	3.9	65,338	**Russian Federation**

INTRODUCTION

RUSSIAN CURRENCY AND EXCHANGE RATES
Monetary Units
  100 kopeks = 1 Russian rouble (rubl or ruble).

Sterling, Dollar and Euro Equivalents (31 December 2023)
  £1 sterling = 114.532 roubles;
  US $1 = 89.688 roubles;
  €1 = 99.192 roubles;
  1,000 roubles = £8.73 = $11.15 = €10.08.

Average Exchange Rate (roubles per US dollar)
  2021   73.669
  2022   68.352
  2023   85.812

RUSSIAN INFLATION
The annual percentage increase in consumer prices in the Russian Federation as a whole, according to official figures, for the year to December was:
  2021   8.4
  2022   11.9
  2023   7.4

The Government of the Russian Federation

According to its Constitution, the Russian Federation is a democratic, federative, multi-ethnic state. The President is elected for a term of six years by universal direct suffrage, for no more than two consecutive terms (constitutional reforms enacted in 2020 'reset' this arrangement with regard to the incumbent President, Vladimir Putin). The President appoints the Chairman of the Government (Prime Minister) and certain key ministers, but the legislature must approve the appointment of other cabinet members. Supreme legislative power is vested in a bicameral Federal Assembly, comprising a directly elected State Duma and an appointed Federation Council.

The status of the federal subjects, as the territories are formally known, began to be regularized by the Federation Treaty of March 1992. A programme of territorial mergers was implemented in the 2000s, as a number of autonomous okrugs (districts) were merged into the larger territories of which they formed a part; between 2005 and 2008 the number of territories was reduced from 89 to 83. In March 2014 Russia annexed two territories internationally recognized as constituting parts of Ukraine—the Republic of Crimea and Sevastopol City—bringing the de facto membership of the Federation to 85 territories. Including the two territories on the Crimean peninsula, the 85 territories comprise 22 republics, nine krais (provinces), 46 oblasts (regions), three cities of federal status (Moscow, St Petersburg and Sevastopol), one autonomous oblast and four autonomous okrugs. Of these, the republics, autonomous okrugs and the autonomous oblast are (sometimes nominally) ethnically defined. The federal subjects are grouped into eight federal okrugs (districts).

In September 2022, amid its ongoing military conflict in Ukraine, Russia announced the annexation of a further four territories within that country—the Donetsk and Lugansk (Luhansk) People's Republics (established by pro-Russian forces in 2014) and Kherson and Zaporozhye (Zaporizhzhya) Oblasts. However, these annexations were, like those of Crimea and Sevastopol, not internationally recognized, and moreover substantial regions of these territories remained outside Russian control. By early 2024 none of these territories had been incorporated into the system of federal okrugs; a transitional period, due to end in 2026, prior to their intended full integration into the Russian Federation had been announced.

The republics each have their own governments and ministries. The other federal units are, in most cases, governed by a local administration and a representative assembly. The federal legislature created the post of governor in August 1991. After President Boris Yeltsin secured an agreement that governors be appointed, in many regions conflict arose between the executive and legislative bodies. Where a vote of no confidence in the governor was approved by regional assemblies, elections were permitted. From September 1993, heads of the federal subjects were appointed and dismissed by presidential decree. However, from December 1995 elected governors became the norm. In September 2004 Yeltsin's successor as President, Putin, announced that, henceforth, governors of all federal subjects would be appointed by the federal authorities, subject to their approval by regional legislatures. In 2012 new legislation again providing for the election of governors entered into effect. In practice these elections appeared to be subject to rather greater state control than had been the case in the 1990s and early 2000s. In 2013 territories were permitted, alternatively, to allow their legislatures to elect a governor from a list of candidates presented by the federal authorities; several republics in the North Caucasus implemented such a system later that year, and similar arrangements were subsequently introduced in the two autonomous okrugs within Tyumen Oblast.

Yeltsin strongly advocated decentralization within the Russian Federation, granting the republics wide-ranging powers, specifically over the use of natural resources and land. From 1995 the undertaking of bilateral treaties to delineate powers between the federal Government and regional authorities became commonplace. This decentralization was largely reversed by Putin, who sought to consolidate what he termed an arrangement of 'vertical power' by establishing the Federal Okrugs in 2000, each of which was headed by a presidential appointee. A series of presidential decrees ruled that laws specific to certain regions were unconstitutional; the regional power-sharing treaties were gradually annulled. A new consultative body, the State Council of the Russian Federation, comprising the heads of the federal subjects, was created by presidential decree in September 2000. The Council's presidium is chaired by the Russian President, and its membership (which was expanded further in 2012—see below) is rotated approximately every six months. The presidium initially included the leaders of one federal subject from each of the Federal Okrugs, but was expanded in size in 2020. According to its founding decree, the body was to advise the President mainly on issues concerning the relationship between the central and regional administrations.

HEAD OF STATE

President: VLADIMIR V. PUTIN (elected 4 March 2012, inaugurated 7 May; re-elected 18 March 2018).

Head of the Presidential Administration: ANTON E. VAINO.

PRESIDENTIAL ADMINISTRATION

Office of the President: 103132 Moscow, ul. Ilinka 23/16; tel. (495) 606-36-02; e-mail accredit@gov.ru; internet www.kremlin.ru.

THE GOVERNMENT
(January 2024)

Chairman: MIKHAIL V. MISHUSTIN.

First Deputy Chairman: ANDREI R. BELOUSOV.

Deputy Chairman, Head of the Government Administration: DMITRII YU. GRIGORENKO.

Deputy Chairman, Presidential Representative to the Far Eastern Federal Okrug: YURII P. TRUTNEV.

Deputy Chairman, Minister of Industry and Trade: DENIS V. MANTUROV.

Deputy Chairmen: VIKTORIYA V. ABRAMCHENKO, DMITRII N. CHERNYSHENKO, TATYANA A. GOLIKOVA, MARAT SH. KHUSNULLIN, ALEKSANDR V. NOVAK, ALEKSEI L. OVERCHUK.

Minister of Agriculture: DMITRII N. PATRUSHEV.

Minister of Civil Defence, Emergencies and Disaster Relief: Lt-Gen. ALEKSANDR V. KURENKOV.
Minister of Construction, Housing and Utilities: IREK E. FAIZULLIN.
Minister of Culture: OLGA B. LYUBIMOVA.
Minister of Defence: Col-Gen. SERGEI K. SHOIGU.
Minister of Development of the Russian Far East and the Arctic: ALEKSEI O. CHEKUNKOV.
Minister of Digital Development, Communications and the Mass Media: MAKSUT I. SHADAYEV.
Minister of Economic Development: MAKSIM G. RESHETNIKOV.
Minister of Education: SERGEI S. KRAVTSOV.
Minister of Energy: NIKOLAI G. SHULGINOV.
Minister of Finance: ANTON G. SILUANOV.
Minister of Foreign Affairs: SERGEI V. LAVROV.
Minister of Health Care: MIKHAIL A. MURASHKO.
Minister of Internal Affairs: Lt-Gen. VLADIMIR A. KOLOKOLTSEV.
Minister of Justice: KONSTANTIN A. CHUICHENKO.
Minister of Labour and Social Protection: ANTON O. KOTYAKOV.
Minister of Natural Resources and Ecology: ALEKSANDR A. KOZLOV.
Minister of Science and Higher Education: VALERII N. FALKOV.
Minister of Sport: OLEG V. MATYTSIN.
Minister of Transport: VITALII G. SAVELYEV.

MINISTRIES

Office of the Government: 103274 Moscow, Krasnopresnenskaya nab. 2; tel. (495) 985-42-80; fax (495) 605-53-62; e-mail duty_press@aprf.gov.ru; internet government.ru.

Ministry of Agriculture: 107139 Moscow, Orlikov per. 1/11; tel. (495) 607-80-00; e-mail info@mcx.ru; internet www.mcx.ru.

Ministry of Civil Defence, Emergencies and Disaster Relief: 109012 Moscow, Teatralnyi prozeyd 3; tel. and fax (495) 624-19-46; e-mail info@mchs.gov.ru; internet www.mchs.gov.ru.

Ministry of Construction, Housing and Utilities: 119435 Moscow, ul. B. Pirogovskaya 23; tel. (495) 647-15-80; e-mail pressa@minstroyrf.ru; internet minstroyrf.ru.

Ministry of Culture: 125993 Moscow, M. Gnezdnikovskii per. 7/6, Bldgs 1, 2; tel. (495) 629-10-10; e-mail mail@culture.ru; internet mkrf.ru.

Ministry of Defence: 119160 Moscow, Frunzenskaya nab. 22/2; tel. (495) 498-01-84; fax (495) 498-12-07; e-mail press@mil.ru; internet mil.ru.

Ministry of Development of the Russian Far East and the Arctic: 109544 Moscow, ul. Shkolnaya 25; tel. (495) 531-06-44; e-mail pr.ministr@minvr.ru; internet minvr.ru.

Ministry of Digital Development, Communications and the Mass Media: 123112 Moscow, Presnenskaya nab. 10/2; tel. (495) 771-81-00; e-mail office@digital.gov.ru; internet minsvyaz.ru.

Ministry of Economic Development: 123112 Moscow, Presnenskaya nab. 10, Bldg 2; tel. (495) 870-29-21; fax (499) 870-70-06; e-mail mineconom@economy.gov.ru; internet economy.gov.ru.

Ministry of Education: 127006 Moscow, ul. Karetnyi Ryad 2; tel. (495) 539-55-19; e-mail info@edu.gov.ru; internet edu.gov.ru.

Ministry of Energy: 107996 Moscow, ul. Shchepkina 42; tel. (495) 631-98-58; fax (495) 631-83-64; e-mail minenergo@minenergo.gov.ru; internet minenergo.gov.ru.

Ministry of Finance: 109097 Moscow, ul. Ilinka 9; tel. (495) 913-55-55; fax (495) 625-08-89; e-mail pr@minfin.ru; internet minfin.ru.

Ministry of Foreign Affairs: 119200 Moscow, Smolenskaya-Sennaya pl. 32/34; tel. (499) 244-16-06; fax (499) 244-91-57; e-mail ministry@mid.ru; internet www.mid.ru.

Ministry of Health Care: 127994 Moscow, Rakhmanovskii per. 3; tel. (495) 627-24-00; e-mail info@rosminzdrav.ru; internet www.rosminzdrav.ru.

Ministry of Industry and Trade: 123317 Moscow, Presnenskaya nab. 10/2; tel. (495) 547-88-88; fax (495) 647-74-04; e-mail info_admin@minprom.gov.ru; internet minpromtorg.gov.ru.

Ministry of Internal Affairs: 119049 Moscow, ul. Zhitnaya 16; tel. (495) 667-72-64; e-mail pr@mvd.gov.ru; internet www.mvd.ru.

Ministry of Justice: 119991 Moscow, ul. Zhitnaya 14, Bldg 1; tel. (800) 303-30-03; e-mail info@minjust.gov.ru; internet minjust.gov.ru.

Ministry of Labour and Social Protection: 127994 Moscow, ul. Ilinka 21; tel. (495) 870-67-00; e-mail mintrud@mintrud.gov.ru; internet mintrud.gov.ru.

Ministry of Natural Resources and Ecology: 123993 Moscow, ul. B. Gruzinskaya 4/6; tel. (499) 254-25-55; fax (499) 254-66-10; e-mail pr@mnr.gov.ru; internet www.mnr.gov.ru.

Ministry of Science and Higher Education: 125993 Moscow, Tverskaya ul. 11; tel. (495) 547-13-16; e-mail press@minobrnauki.gov.ru; internet www.minobrnauki.gov.ru.

Ministry of Sport: 105064 Moscow, ul. Kazakova 18, Bldg 3; tel. (495) 720-53-80; e-mail info@minsport.gov.ru; internet minsport.gov.ru.

Ministry of Transport: 109992 Moscow, ul. Rozhdestvenka 1/1; tel. (495) 495-00-00; fax (495) 495-00-10; internet mintrans.ru.

THE LEGISLATURE

The Federal Assembly (Federalnoye Sobraniye) is the bicameral federal parliament. Its upper chamber, the Federation Council (Sovet Federatsii), comprises two senators appointed from each federal unit, representing the executive and legislative branches of power in the territory. The lower chamber is the State Duma (Gosudarstvennaya Duma), with 450 deputies elected for a five-year term.

Federation Council
(Sovet Federatsii)

103426 Moscow, ul. B. Dmitrovka 26; tel. (495) 629-70-09; fax (495) 629-67-43; e-mail post_sf@gov.ru; internet council.gov.ru.

The Federation Council is the upper chamber of the Federal Assembly. It comprises two deputies appointed from each of the constituent members (federal territorial units) of the Russian Federation, representing the legislative and executive branches of power in each republic and region.

Chairman: VALENTINA I. MATVIYENKO (Representative of the executive branch of St Petersburg City).

First Deputy Chairmen: ANDREI A. TURCHAK (Representative of the legislative-representative branch of Pskov Oblast), ANDREI V. YATSKIN (Representative of the executive branch of Rostov Oblast).

Deputy Chairmen: KONSTANTIN I. KOSACHEV (Representative of the executive branch of the Republic of Mari El), INNA YU. SVYATENKO (Representative of the legislative-representative branch of Moscow City), YURII L. VOROBYEV (Representative of the legislative-representative branch of Vologda Oblast), NIKOLAI A. ZHURAVLEV (Representative of the executive branch of Kostroma Oblast).

State Duma
(Gosudarstvennaya Duma)

103265 Moscow, Okhotnyi ryad 1; tel. (495) 692-62-66; fax (495) 697-42-58; e-mail stateduma@duma.gov.ru; internet duma.gov.ru.

Note: for the expansion of the acronyms referring to political parties, see the Principal Political Organizations section, below.

Chairman: VYACHESLAV V. VOLODIN (YeR).

First Deputy Chairmen: IVAN I. MELNIKOV (KPRF), ALEKSANDR D. ZHUKOV (YeR).

Deputy Chairmen: ALEKSANDR M. BABAKOV (SR), BORIS A. CHERNYSHOV (LDPR), VLADISVLAV A. DAVANKOV (NL), ALEKSEI V. GORDEYEV (YeR), SHOLBAN V. KARA-OOL (YeR), ANNA YU. KUZNETSOVA (YeR), SERGEI I. NEVEROV (YeR), PYOTR O. TOLSTOI (YeR), IRINA A. YAROVAYA (YeR).

General Election, 19 September 2021

Parties	% of votes*	A†	B†	Total
YeR	49.82	126	198	324
KPRF	18.93	48	9	57
SR	7.55	19	2	27
LDPR	7.46	19	8	21
NL	5.32	13	—	13
Rodina	0.80	—	1	1
ROST	0.52	—	1	1
GP	0.15	—	1	1
Other parties	7.38	—	—	—
Independents	—	—	5	5
Total	100.00‡	225	225	450

* Percentage refers to share of the votes cast to those seats elected by proportional representation.
† Of the 450 seats in the State Duma, 225 (A) are awarded according to proportional representation on the basis of party lists, and 225 (B) are elected in single-mandate constituencies.
‡ Including invalid votes (equivalent to 2.08% of the total).

INTRODUCTION

Parliamentary factions at January 2024: YeR 324, KPRF 57, SR 27, LDPR 23, NL 15, not members of any faction 2, vacant 2.

THE STATE COUNCIL

The State Council (Gosudarstvennyi Sovet) is a consultative body, established in September 2000, and intended to improve co-ordination between federal and regional government, and to strengthen federal control in the regions. Until 2012 the membership of the Council comprised the leaders of the federal subjects and the President of the Russian Federation, who chairs the Council. In June 2012 President Vladimir Putin announced that, henceforth, the Chairmen of the two chambers of the federal legislature would also be members of the State Council, as would be the leaders of factions in the State Duma, while former heads of regional executive bodies would also be eligible for appointment. In August Putin additionally appointed the Presidential Representatives to the Federal Okrugs to the Council. The President also granted himself the authority to appoint 'people with extensive experience of public (state and social) activities' as members of the council. The President appoints a presidium, who serve for a period of approximately six months. The presidium appointed to serve from 12 December 2023 comprised the Secretary of the State Council and 30 officials, including 27 regional leaders.

Secretary: IGOR YE. LEVITAN.

PRESIDENTIAL REPRESENTATIVES TO THE FEDERAL OKRUGS

Note: the identity of, and contact details for, the Presidential Representative to each Federal Okrug is given at the start of the appropriate sub-section of Part Two of this volume.

POLITICAL ORGANIZATIONS

At January 2024 a total of 27 parties were officially registered with the Ministry of Justice. The following were among the most important:

Grazhdanskaya Initsiativa (GranI) (Civic Initiative): 108841 Moscow, Troitsk, Mikrorayon B, dom 52, pom. VII., kom 15,17,18; tel. (926) 876-15-57; e-mail partygrani@gmail.com; internet grazhdan-in.ru; liberal; Chair. ANDREI A. NECHAYEV.

Grazhdanskaya Platforma (GP) (Civic Platform): 123001 Moscow, Blagoveshenskii per. 3, Bldg 1; tel. (985) 100-22-26; e-mail info@ppgprf.ru; internet bit.ly/3aWFJF0; f. 2012; Leader, Chair., Political Cttee RIFAT SHAYKHUTDINOV.

Kommunisticheskaya Partiya Rossiiskoi Federatsii (KPRF) (Communist Party of the Russian Federation): 127051 Moscow, per. M. Sukharevskii 3/1; tel. (495) 692-11-65; e-mail press-sluzhba@kprf.ru; internet kprf.ru; f. 1993; Chair. of Cen. Cttee GENNADII A. ZYUGANOV; 162,173 mems (2016).

Kommunisty Rossii (KR) (Communists of Russia): 125167 Moscow, Leningradskii pr. 47, Bldg. 1/132; tel. and fax (499) 963-01-11; e-mail komros@bk.ru; internet komros.info; f. 2012; Marxist-Leninist; Chair. of Cen. Cttee SERGEI A. MALINKOVICH.

Liberalno-demokraticheskaya Partiya Rossii (LDPR) (Liberal Democratic Party of Russia): 107078 Moscow, 1-y Basmannii per. 3, Bldg 1; tel. (495) 530-62-62; e-mail info@ldpr.ru; internet ldpr.ru; f. 1988; nationalist; Chair. LEONID E. SLUTSKII.

Partiya Novyye Lyudi (NL) (New People Party): 123376 Moscow, B. Tryokhgornyi per. 11, Bldg 2; tel. (800) 550-10-39; e-mail info@newpeople.ru; internet newpeople.ru; f. 2020; centre-right, represents small business interests; Chair. ALEKSEI G. NECHAYEV.

Partiya Rosta (ROST) (Party of Growth): 119072 Moscow, per. Bersenevskii 2, Bldg 1/405; tel. (495) 967-07-92; e-mail mail@partrost.ru; internet rost.ru; f. 2009 as Pravoye Delo (The Right Cause); present name adopted 2016; liberal, pro-market; Chair. BORIS YU. TITOV.

Rodina (Motherland): 125284 Moscow, ul. Polikarpova 27/3; tel. (495) 788-38-87; e-mail mail@rodina.ru; internet rodina.ru; f. 2012 as revival of fmr party absorbed into SR in 2006; nationalist; Chair. ALEKSEI A. ZHURAVLEV.

Rossiiskaya Ekologicheskaya Partiya 'Zelyonyye' (Greens—Russian Ecological Party): 111000 Moscow, Luchnikov per. 4, Bldg 1; tel. (925) 820-25-25; e-mail party@greens.ru; internet greens.ru; f. 1992; present name adopted 2002; Chair. ANDREI NAGIBIN.

Rossiiskaya Partiya Pensionerov za Spravedlivost—Partiya Pensionerov (RPPS) (Russian Party of Pensioners for Justice—Party of Pensioners): 129090 Moscow, pr. Mira 7, Bldg 2; tel. (495) 665-90-75; e-mail info@pensioner.party; internet pensioner.party; f. 2012 as revival of Rossiiskaya Partiya Pensionerov (Russian Party of Pensioners) previously absorbed into SR; Chair. VLADIMIR YU. BURAKOV.

Rossiyskaya Partiya Svobody i Spravedlivosti (RPSS) (Russian Party of Freedom and Justice): 27287 Moscow, ul. Poltava 18; tel. 495) 611-30-11; e-mail kpssrf@mail.ru; f. 2012; fmrly Kommunisticheskaya Partiya Sotsialnoi Spravedlivosti (Communist Party of Social Justice); present name adopted 2021; Leader MAKSIM SHEVCHENKO.

Spravedlivaya Rossiya—Patrioty—Za Pravdu (SR) (A Just Russia—Patriots—For Truth): 115230 Moscow, Varshavskoye shosse 47/4; tel. (495) 787-85-15; e-mail info@spravedlivo.ru; internet spravedlivo.ru; f. 2021 by merger of Spravedlivaya Rossiya (A Just Russia, f. 2006), Patrioty Rossii (Patriots of Russia, f. 2005) and Za Pravdu (For Truth, f. 2020); statist, socialist, nationalist; Chair. SERGEI M. MIRONOV.

Yabloko: 119017 Moscow, ul. Pyatnitskaya 31, Bldg 2; tel. (495) 780-30-10; e-mail yabloko@yabloko.ru; internet yabloko.ru; f. 1993; liberal; Chair. NIKOLAI I. RYBAKOV; 28,000 mems (2021).

Yedinaya Rossiya (YeR) (United Russia): 121170 Moscow, Kutuzovskii per. 39; tel. and fax (495) 786-82-89; e-mail priem.pp@edinros.ru; internet er.ru; f. 2001 as Yedinstvo i Otechestvo—Yedinaya Rossiya (Unity and Fatherland—United Russia); Chair. DMITRII A. MEDVEDEV; Chair., Supreme Council BORIS V. GRYZLOV; Sec., Gen. Council ANDREI A. TURCHAK.

Zelyonaya Alternativa (Green Alternative): 129090 Moscow, per. Dokuchayev 17, Bldg. 11; tel. (929) 117-81-88; e-mail info@zaecology.ru; internet zaecology.ru; f. 2020; ecologist; Chair. RUSLAN KHVOSTOV.

INTRODUCTION

Disputed and Annexed Territories

In 2014 Russia annexed two territories internationally recognized as constituting part of Ukraine—Sevastopol City and what became known as the Republic of Crimea (having been designated the Autonomous Republic of Crimea under Ukrainian rule). Details of the recent political developments and the economy of these two territories are included in the main section of this publication.

Following the full-scale invasion of Ukraine by Russia that commenced in February 2022, four further territories were formally annexed by Russia on 30 September. Two of these territories—the Donetsk People's Republic and the Lugansk People's Republic—had been formed by pro-Russian and Russian-backed elements in Ukraine in 2014; under the terms decreed by Russia upon their annexation in 2022, these territories were designated as including the entire expanse of the Donetsk and Luhansk (Lugansk) Oblasts of Ukraine, despite substantial proportions of both territories, and in particular of Donetsk Oblast, remaining under Ukrainian control. Both of the other territories that Russia annexed in October 2022—Kherson Oblast and Zaporozhye (Zaporzhzhiya) Oblast—were also zones of active conflict, and in neither case was Russian control of these territories complete or assured; indeed, Kherson itself, the administrative centre of Kherson Oblast, which had been captured and occupied by Russian forces in March, was regained by Ukraine on 11 November, with the pro-Russian administration being forced to relocate to a smaller city, Genichesk (Henichesk). A section of Nikolayev (Mykolayiv) Oblast was also included in this territory. Meanwhile, Zaporozhye (Zaporzhzhiya), the administrative centre of the eponymous oblast, remained under Ukrainian control, with the pro-Russian administration being based at Melitopol. In December 2022, for the first time, the pro-Russian executive and legislative bodies established in Donetsk and Lugansk appointed representatives to the Federation Council, as did the newly established executive bodies of Kherson and Zaporozhye Oblasts. Elections to the regional legislatures of these four territories were reported to have been held in September 2023. Details of the pro-Russian administrations (which are recognized solely by the Russian state) in these territories are listed below:

THE REPUBLIC OF CRIMEA AND SEVASTOPOL

For details of these territories, see the section on the Southern Federal Okrug in Part Two.

DONETSK PEOPLE'S REPUBLIC

Head of the Republic: DENIS V. PUSHILIN.

Office of the Head of the Republic: 283050 Donetsk, pl. Sovetskaya 1; tel. (71) 300-58-66; e-mail info@dnronline.su; internet denis-pushilin.ru; internet xn--80ahqgjaddr.xn--p1ai.

Chairman of the Council of Ministers: YEVGENII A. SOLNTSEV.

Office of the Chairman of the Council of Ministers: 283050 Donetsk, bul. Pushkina 34; e-mail info@pravdnr.ru; internet pravdnr.ru.

Narodnyi Sovet (People's Council): 283000 Donetsk, ul. Pushkina 34; tel. (63) 430-04-60; e-mail press@dnrsovet.su; internet dnrsovet.su; Chair. ARTYOM V. ZHOGA.

Representatives in the Federation Council: Natalya Yu. Nikonorova, Aleksandr V. Voloshin.

LUGANSK PEOPLE'S REPUBLIC

Head of the Republic: Leonid I. Pasechnik.

Office of the Head of the Republic: 291000 Lugansk; tel. (642) 59-19-88; internet xn--80aafc4bdoy.xn--p1ai.

Chairman of the Council of Ministers: Sergei I. Kozlov.

Office of the Chairman of the Council of Ministers: 291000 Lugansk, pl. Geroyev VOV 3/220; tel. (642) 58-56-13; fax (642) 58-58-88; internet sovminlnr.ru.

Narodnyi Sovet (People's Council): 291000 Lugansk, pl. Geroyev VOV 9; tel. (642) 58-55-16; e-mail press@nslnr.su; Chair. Denis N. Miroshnichenko.

Representatives in the Federation Council: Olga Ye. Bas, Darya S. Lantratova.

KHERSON OBLAST (RUSSIAN ADMINISTRATION)

Governor: Vladimir V. Saldo.

Office of the Governor: 275501 Kherson obl., Genichesk; tel. (800) 301-99-99; e-mail info@khogov.ru; internet khogov.ru.

Oblast Duma: 275501 Kherson obl., Genichesk; Chair. Tatyana Yu. Tomilina.

Representatives in the Federation Council: Konstantin V. Basyuk, Igor Yu. Kastyukevich.

ZAPOROZHYE OBLAST (RUSSIAN ADMINISTRATION)

Head of the Administration, Governor: Yevgenii V. Balitskii.

Deputy Governor, Chairman of the Council of Ministers of the Military-Civilian Administration: Anton V. Koltsov.

Office of the Governor: 272301 Zaporozhye obl., Melitopol; e-mail info@zo.gov.ru; internet zo.gov.ru.

Legislative Assembly: 272301 Zaporozhye obl., Melitopol; Chair. Viktor A. Yemelyanenko.

Representatives in the Federation Council: Dmitrii N. Vorona, Dmitrii O. Rogozin.

PART TWO
Territorial Surveys

EUROPEAN RUSSIA

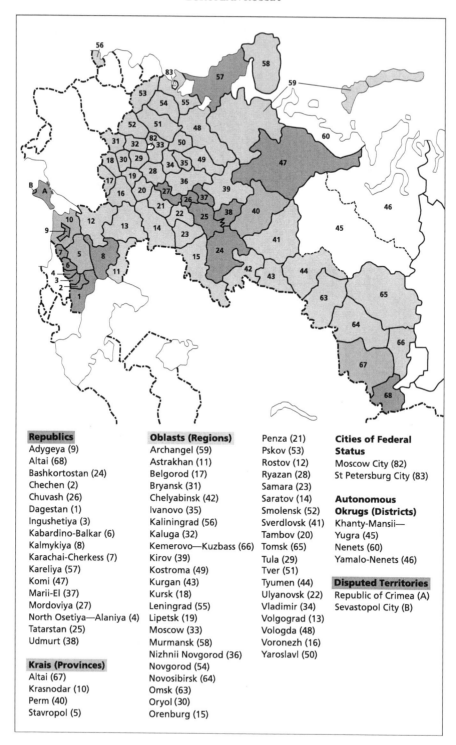

Republics
Adygeya (9)
Altai (68)
Bashkortostan (24)
Chechen (2)
Chuvash (26)
Dagestan (1)
Ingushetiya (3)
Kabardino-Balkar (6)
Kalmykiya (8)
Karachai-Cherkess (7)
Kareliya (57)
Komi (47)
Marii-El (37)
Mordoviya (27)
North Osetiya—Alaniya (4)
Tatarstan (25)
Udmurt (38)

Krais (Provinces)
Altai (67)
Krasnodar (10)
Perm (40)
Stavropol (5)

Oblasts (Regions)
Archangel (59)
Astrakhan (11)
Belgorod (17)
Bryansk (31)
Chelyabinsk (42)
Ivanovo (35)
Kaliningrad (56)
Kaluga (32)
Kemerovo—Kuzbass (66)
Kirov (39)
Kostroma (49)
Kurgan (43)
Kursk (18)
Leningrad (55)
Lipetsk (19)
Moscow (33)
Murmansk (58)
Nizhnii Novgorod (36)
Novgorod (54)
Novosibirsk (64)
Omsk (63)
Oryol (30)
Orenburg (15)
Penza (21)
Pskov (53)
Rostov (12)
Ryazan (28)
Samara (23)
Saratov (14)
Smolensk (52)
Sverdlovsk (41)
Tambov (20)
Tomsk (65)
Tula (29)
Tver (51)
Tyumen (44)
Ulyanovsk (22)
Vladimir (34)
Volgograd (13)
Vologda (48)
Voronezh (16)
Yaroslavl (50)

Cities of Federal Status
Moscow City (82)
St Petersburg City (83)

Autonomous Okrugs (Districts)
Khanty-Mansii—Yugra (45)
Nenets (60)
Yamalo-Nenets (46)

Disputed Territories
Republic of Crimea (A)
Sevastopol City (B)

ASIAN RUSSIA

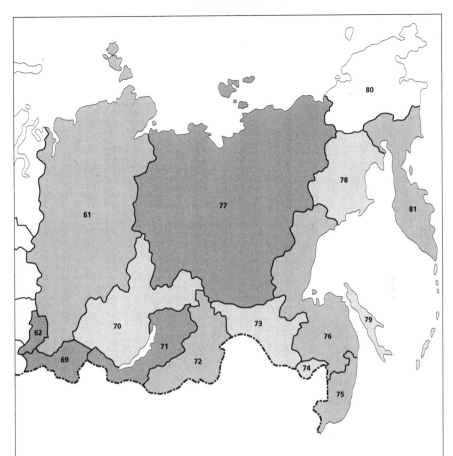

Republics
Buryatiya (71)
Khakasiya (62)
Tyva (69)
Sakha (Yakutiya) (77)

Krais (Provinces)
Kamchatka (81)
Khabarovsk (76)
Krasnoyarsk (61)
Maritime (Primorskii) (75)
Transbaikal (72)

Oblasts (Regions)
Amur (73)
Irkutsk (70)
Magadan (78)
Sakhalin (79)

Autonomous Oblast
Jewish (74)

Autonomous Okrug (District)
Chukot (80)

Notes

The maps distinguish between international borders (dots and dashes), borders between separate federal units (bold unbroken lines) and borders of units that are formally part of another territory (dashed lines).

Maps of European and Asian Russia are included on the two preceding pages.

The territorial surveys are ordered by Federal Okrug, starting with the Central Federal Okrug, based in Moscow, and continuing according to the order conventionally used in Russian statistical publications, which broadly runs from west to east across the Federation. Within each Federal Okrug the surveys are ordered according to the status of the territory concerned, as follows: Cities of Federal Status; Republics; Krais; Oblasts; Autonomous Oblast; Autonomous Okrugs. Territories of identical status are listed in English alphabetical order.

Acronyms of Political Parties used in the Territorial Surveys

In the territorial surveys, the following abbreviations are used to refer to the principal current or former political parties.

GP: Grazhdanskaya Platforma (Civic Platform)

KPRF: Kommunisticheskaya Partiya Rossiiskoi Federatsii (Communist Party of the Russian Federation)

KR: Kommunisty Rossii (Communists of Russia)

LDPR: Liberalno-demokraticheskaya Partiya Rossii (Liberal Democratic Party of Russia)

NL: Partiya Novyye Lyudi (New People Party)

PR: Patrioty Rossii (Patriots of Russia)

RPPS: Rossiiskaya Partiya Pensionerov za Spravedlivosti—Partiya Pensionerov (Russian Party of Pensioners for Social Justice—Party of Pensioners)

SPS: Soyuz Pravykh Sil (Union of Rightist Forces)

SR: Spravedlivaya Rossiya (A Just Russia), known as **Spravedlivaya Rossiya—Patrioty—Za Pravdu** (A Just Russia—Patriots—For Truth) from 2021

YeO-YeR: Yedinstvo i Otechestvo-Yedinaya Rossiya (Unity and Fatherland-United Russia)

YeR: Yedinaya Rossiya (United Russia)

CENTRAL FEDERAL OKRUG

Presidential Representative to the Central Federal Okrug: IGOR O. SHCHYOGOLEV, 103132 Moscow, Nikolskii per. 6; tel. (495) 206-12-76; e-mail malakhov_dm@gov.ru; internet cfo.gov.ru.

Moscow City

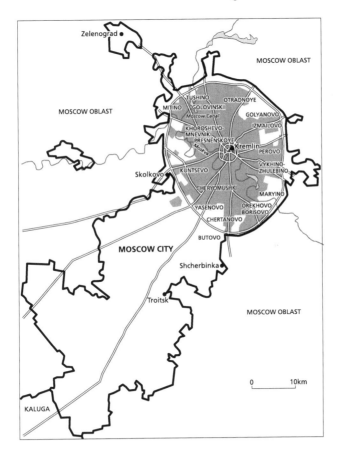

Moscow (Moskva) is located in the west of European Russia, on the River Moskva. It is connected to the Volga river system by the Moscow–Volga Canal. The city's total area is 2,511 sq km (970 sq miles). According to official estimates, at January 2023 Moscow City had a total population of 13,104,177, all of which was urban, and a population density of 5,220.8 per sq km. The city has a south-western boundary with Kaluga

Oblast; it is surrounded to the north-west, north and south-east by Moscow Oblast. Of residents who stated their ethnicity at the census of 2021, 90.2% were Russian, 0.8% were Tatar, and 0.7% were Armenian. The city is in the time zone UTC+3.

HISTORY

Moscow city was founded in about 1147. In 1325 it became the seat of the Eastern Orthodox Metropolitan of Rus (in 1589–1721 and after 1917 the Patriarch of Moscow and all Rus). The steadily expanding Muscovite state became the foundation for the Russian Empire, although the capital city was moved to St Petersburg between 1712 and 1918.

In the 1990s reformists enjoyed considerable support. Reformist mayor Gaveiil Popov, elected one year earlier, resigned in June 1992, when President Boris Yeltsin appointed Yurii Luzhkov as head of the City Government; in 1996 Luzhkov was overwhelmingly elected Mayor and in 1998 signed a power-sharing treaty with the federal authorities. A series of bomb attacks in the city in 1999, attributed to Chechen militants, killed more than 200 people.

Luzhkov was re-elected Mayor in 1999 and 2003. In Municipal Duma elections in 2001, YeO-YeR, formed by the merger of Luzhkov's Otechestvo (Fatherland) movement with another centrist group, Yedinstvo (Unity), and later renamed YeR, secured the largest number of seats. Further attacks conducted by Chechen Islamist militants in Moscow included the besieging of a theatre in October 2002, as a result of which at least 129 hostages died.

In June 2007 the Municipal Duma confirmed Luzhkov's re-appointment as Mayor. In elections to the State Duma held in December. YeR secured 54.2% of the votes cast in Moscow, one of its lowest levels of support recorded across the Federation.

At elections to the Municipal Duma held in October 2009, YeR secured 66.3% of the votes cast on a proportional basis. The rate of participation was just 34.4%. YeR controlled 32 of the 45 seats in the chamber overall and the KPRF (the only other party to obtain representation) three.

On 28 September 2010 President Dmitrii Medvedev dismissed Luzhkov, nominating Sergei Sobyanin (a Deputy Chairman of the federal Government and Head of the Government Staff, and a former Governor of Tyumen Oblast) as Mayor; he was inaugurated on 21 October, after the Municipal Duma endorsed his candidacy.

On 11 December 2010 several thousand extreme nationalists clashed with police in Moscow during protests against the recent killing of a football supporter by a group of men from the North Caucasus. During ensuing disturbances at least two people were killed, and on 15 December around 800 people were arrested during a rally. On 31 December liberal opposition leader Boris Nemtsov was among some 60 people to be arrested in the city during an anti-Government rally. On 24 January 2011 a suicide bombing at Domodedovo international airport by Islamist militants killed at least 36 people.

As part of measures intended to encourage major companies to establish their headquarters outside the congested city centre, substantial parts of the south-west of Moscow Oblast were absorbed into the city from 1 July 2012.

Following elections to the State Duma in December 2011, large protests ensued against alleged electoral malpractice. Permission was granted for a demonstration of some 30,000 people to be held on the opposite bank of the Moscow River from the Kremlin; opposition sources estimated an attendance of 50,000.

At the presidential election of 4 March 2012, Moscow City was the only federal subject in which Putin was recorded as having received under one-half of the votes cast, with 47.0%, and was also the only territory in which the independent, Mikhail Prokhorov, was placed second, with 20.5% of the votes cast (he obtained 8.0% nationwide).

In the mayoral poll of 8 September 2013, Sobyanin was re-elected with 51.4% of the votes cast, narrowly in excess of the 50% required to avoid a run-off election. His principal challenger, an anti-corruption activist supported by liberals and nationalists, Aleksei Navalnyi, obtained 27.2%. Despite having been sentenced to five years' imprisonment for embezzlement in July, Navalnyi had been released pending an appeal and permitted to participate in the election, although in October he was prohibited from seeking public office.

In October 2013 protests against the killing several days earlier of an ethnic Russian, reportedly by an Azerbaijani citizen, developed into riots in the south of the city, resulting in some 400 arrests. One day later, the police detained around 1,200 migrant workers from the North Caucasus and Central Asia at a local market, apparently to investigate if they were involved in any illegal activity.

Elections to the Municipal Duma were held on 14 September 2014, with all 45 deputies now being elected in single-mandate constituencies. Some 28 of those elected were representatives of YeR, while five represented the KPRF. The LDPR and Rodina (Motherland) each obtained one representative. The remaining 10 non-partisan deputies formed the Moya Moskva (My Moscow) faction. On 30 December a court in Moscow imposed a suspended sentence of three-and-a-half years (during which period he was to remain under house arrest) on Navalnyi, finding him guilty of further charges of fraud. Several thousand demonstrators assembled in Moscow to protest against the ruling.

In February 2015, shortly before he had been due to speak at a rally against Russian military support for separatists in eastern Ukraine, Nemtsov was shot dead near the Kremlin. (Five Chechen men received custodial sentences for their involvement in his murder in June 2017.) Meanwhile, in place of the rally at which Nemtsov had been due to speak, tens of thousands of demonstrators instead commemorated his life.

In March 2017 some 500 people were arrested in Moscow, following large-scale anti-corruption protests organized by Navalnyi. At a further such demonstration in June, at least 1,500 arrests were reported; Navalnyi was again among those detained.

On 9 September 2018 Sobyanin was re-elected to a further term of office as Mayor, with 70.2% of the votes cast. A participation rate of only 30.9% was recorded. Public protests against planned pensions reforms proceeded in central Moscow and other major cities on that day.

The decision of the Moscow City Election Commission in mid-2019 to refuse the registration of many prospective opposition candidates for forthcoming muncipal Duma elections, on the grounds of alleged irregularities, precipitated protest rallies from 14 July. An unauthorized demonstration (attended by an estimated 20,000 people) was staged on 27 July; following violent clashes, as many as 1,300 were arrested. Further mass opposition rallies staged weekly were attended by as many as 60,000 (the largest protest demonstrations in Russia since 2011), according to independent monitors, and thousands of arrests were made.

The elections to the Municipal Duma were duly held on 8 September 2019. When it convened later in the month, 19 of the 45 deputies were members of the YeR parliamentary faction (reflecting a significant loss of support for the party), 13 that of the KPRF, three that of SR, and five that of Moya Moskva. Five deputies were not affiliated with any faction. All the candidates of YeR had contested the election as independents, while the Moya Moskva deputies were also independents backed by YeR. A project supported by Navalnyi to promote tactical voting to defeat YeR-supported candidates, Umnoye Golosovaniye (Intelligent Voting), had supported all the successful KPRF and SR deputies, and also the four (non-faction) Yabloko members elected. The official participation rate was only 21.8%.

Following the onset of the COVID-19 pandemic in 2020, on 16 March Sobyanin banned all public events of more than 50 people. Following the gradual closure of public facilities, on 29 March Sobyanin announced the imposition of a quarantine (requiring all non-essential workers to stay in their homes), and a digital pass system was introduced to enforce the restrictions from 13 April. Sobyanin announced the staged lifting of lockdown restrictions from 1 June.

Some 65.3% of voters in Moscow City supported proposals for constitutional reforms, including a provision permitting President Putin to seek two further terms of office, in a popular vote held between 25 June and 1 July 2020, according to the official results, compared with 77.9% of voters Federation-wide; the rate of participation in the city, at 55.2%, was more than 12 percentage points lower than the national average. In December a Yabloko member of the Municipal Duma, received a two-year suspended sentence for repeatedly organizing unsanctioned protests against the new provisions.

Following a renewed surge in COVID-19 cases from late September 2020, some restrictions were reintroduced, and subsequently extended in the capital. Distribution of the domestically developed Sputnik V vaccine commenced in Moscow City on 5 December (marking the beginning of Russia's mass COVID-19 immunization programme). Sobyanin announced the easing of some restrictions later that month; schools were reopened on 18 January 2021, followed by colleges and cultural facilities such as museums on 22 January. However, after the spread of COVID-19 accelerated in mid-2021, Sobyanin reintroduced wide-ranging restrictions and ordered mandatory vaccination for residents of the capital working in public-facing roles.

Meanwhile, by-elections to the Municipal Duma were held on 19 September 2021 to replace two KPRF deputies (including Oleg Sheremetyev, who had received a four-year suspended prison sentence for embezzlement). Vladimir Ryzhkov, a former leader of the opposition Partiya Narodnoi Svobody (Party of People's Freedom), representing Yabloko, was narrowly elected in one constituency and a YeR candidate was successful in the other.

A series of demonstrations and rallies were staged in Moscow and other major cities in protest against the Russian invasion of Ukraine that commenced on 24 February 2022; they were violently dispersed by police with ensuing mass arrests (numbering 5,000 on 6 March alone). Sobyanin declared that attempts by 'provocateurs' to create disorder would be prevented, and addressed a state rally in support of the war on 18 March, which was attended by some 200,000 people. The municipal authorities lifted the requirement for the wearing of masks in public places and other pandemic-related restrictions in Moscow from mid-March, although the ban on public gatherings and demonstrations introduced in 2020 was maintained. The large anti-war protests had subsided by late March, although numerous one-person protests that did not require official permission continued. After large numbers of Western companies suspended operations in Russia (under international sanctions imposed against Russia), in April Sobyanin announced the approval of a programme to support more than 58,000 people who had consequently become unemployed in the capital by providing training and involvement in temporary public works projects. In June Sobyanin pledged assistance to the Russian-allied 'Donetsk People's Republic' and 'Lugansk People's Republic' (LNR) territories in eastern Ukraine (which Russia later annexed) for the reconstruction of their cities, and visited Lugansk (Luhansk), where he signed a declaration with the head of the LNR administration establishing 'brotherly' ties between Moscow and Lugansk. Later that month a street outside the US embassy in Moscow was renamed 'Donetsk People's Republic Square'.

In July 2022 a Moscow City municipal council deputy, Aleksei Gorinov, who had publicly opposed the invasion of Ukraine became the first elected official in Russia to be convicted for 'distributing false information', and was sentenced to seven years in prison. The detention or emigration of prominent anti-war activists, and the suspension of political activity by others reduced the range of candidates contesting elections to Moscow's municipal councils, held on 11 September. YeR candidates won around 1,160 of the 1,502 contested seats (around the same number as in 2017), and pro-Government candidates grouped under the newly created Moi Raion (My District) movement, led by Sobyanin, secured a further 134 seats. The number of elected Yabloko candidates declined from 176 to only three. Nevertheless, around 73 candidates were reportedly elected under the Umnoye Golosovaniye initiative. A participation rate of 34% was reported (more than double that of 2017), which was attributed to the adoption of a new electronic voting system. The highest number of electoral violations among the federal subjects was reported in Moscow City, together with numerous arrests and assaults of election observers. An order by Putin shortly afterwards, on 21 September, for the partial mobilization of military reservists precipitated small-scale protests in major cities nationwide; at least 537 arrests were reported in Moscow City on that day. In December Ketevan Kharaidze, a Yabloko municipal deputy who had been re-elected in September, was sentenced to four years' imprisonment on charges of extortion.

Amid continued drone strikes in Russian regions close to Ukraine, on 3 May 2023 Russia accused Ukraine of attempting to assassinate President Putin, claiming that two Ukrainian drones had been shot down above the Kremlin in Moscow. Ukraine strongly denied any involvement. At the end of that month the Russian defence ministry announced that a total of eight drones had been shot down over Moscow, near an area in the western suburbs where a private residence of Putin and luxury housing owned by other senior officials were located; unconfirmed reports on social media suggested that up to 32 drones had reached Moscow and surrounding areas. On 24 July two drone attacks damaged business offices in Moscow, one of them near the defence ministry's headquarters. At the end of July and in early August an office complex in the Moscow City business district, in which employees of three federal ministries were based, was damaged in drone attacks.

On 10 September 2023 Sobyanin was elected for a further mayoral term of office by 76.4% of the votes cast, contesting the poll as the candidate of YeR (having previously participated as a nominal independent); of the four other candidates, Leonid Zyuganov of the KPRF (a grandson of party leader Gennadii Zyuganov) was placed second, with 8.1% of the vote. A higher turnout of 42.5% was recorded. In November supporters of Gorinov announced that he was to be charged additionally with justifying terrorism, and in December more than 70 regional deputies urged President Putin and the presidential council on human rights to provide him with urgent medical assistance.

ECONOMY

In 2021 Moscow City's gross regional product (GRP) amounted to 24,471,160m. roubles (20.2% of the gross domestic product of the Russian Federation in that year), equivalent to an estimated 1,935,205 roubles per head. There are nine railway termini in the city and 11 electrified radial lines. The metro system included 18 lines (including a 'light metro' line, a monorail, and an orbital suburban, ground level, railway line) and 300 stations, and extended 526 km at late 2023; further expansion of the network was under way. The metro system carries more than 6.5m. passengers per day. Moscow's waterways connect with the Baltic, White, Caspian and Black Seas. There are two international airports located within the federal city, at Vnukovo and Ostafyevo.

There is a small agriculture sector in the federal city, employing 0.2% of the workforce and contributing a negligible share of GRP in 2021. Moscow's industry consists primarily of mechanical engineering, metal working, electricity production, the production of chemicals and petrochemicals, petroleum refining and food processing. Industry employed around 23.4% of the workforce and contributed 23.3% of GRP in 2021, when manufacturing employed 9.0% of the workforce and contributed 15.6% of GRP. As the capital city, Moscow is the site of a large number of government offices, and a centre for major businesses and financial companies. In 2005 one of six special economic zones supported by the federal authorities, specializing in microelectronics, was established in the north-western Zelenograd district.

In 2022 the economically active population numbered 7,099,978, when the rate of unemployment, at 2.2%, was the fifth lowest in the Federation, while the average monthly wage was 125,638 roubles. There was a budgetary deficit of 109,297.8m. roubles in 2021. In that year international trade amounted to US $207,285m. in exports and $128,980m. in imports, by far the highest level of any federal subject; only 10.1% of export trade and 8.0% of import trade was with countries of the CIS.

DIRECTORY

Mayor: Sergei S. Sobyanin.

Office of the Mayor: 125032 Moscow, ul. Tverskaya 13; tel. (495) 777-77-77; fax (495) 232-18-74; e-mail mayor@mos.ru; internet mos.ru.

Municipal Duma: 127994 Moscow, ul. Petrovka 22; tel. (495) 623-50-80; fax (495) 957-03-31; e-mail spravka@duma.mos.ru; internet duma.mos.ru; Chair. Aleksei V. Shaposhnikov.

State Duma Representatives (15): Timofei T. Bazhenov (YeR), Yevgenii G. Popov (YeR), Galina P. Khovanskaya (SR), Pyotr O. Tolstoi (YeR), Dmitrii A. Pevtsov (NL), Svetlana V. Razvorotneva (YeR), Dmitrii V. Sablin (YeR), Yevgenii O. Nifantyev (YeR), Tatyana V. Butskaya (YeR), Anatolii A. Vasserman (SR), Aleksandr G. Mazhuga (YeR), Irina V. Belykh (YeR), Oleg Yu. Leonov (NL), Aleksandr G. Rumyantsev (YeR), Roman Yu. Romanenko (YeR).

Federation Council Representatives: Vladimir I. Kozhin, Inna Yu. Svyatenko.

Belgorod Oblast

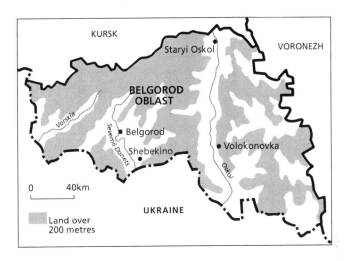

Belgorod Oblast is situated in the south-west of the Central Russian Highlands. Kursk Oblast lies to the north and Voronezh to the east. To the south, the Oblast lies on the international border with Ukraine, including territories to the south-east outside Ukrainian state control, of which Russia announced the annexation, as the Lugansk People's Republic, in 2022. Belgorod Oblast's main rivers are the Severnii Donets, the Vorskla and the Oskol. The territory occupies 27,134 sq km (10,476 sq miles). According to official estimates, at January 2023 the Oblast had a total population of 1,514,527 and a population density of 55.8 per sq km. Some 65.4% of the population was urban in 2023. The Oblast's administrative centre is at Belgorod, which had an estimated 333,931 inhabitants at January 2023. A further major city is Staryi Oskol (218,340). Of residents who stated their ethnicity at the 2021 census, 95.3% were Russian and 1.2% were Ukrainian. Belgorod Oblast is in the time zone UTC+3.

HISTORY

The Belgorod region was part of Lithuania until 1503, when it was annexed by the Muscovite state. The city of Belgorod was founded in 1593. In 1943, outside the city, the Red Army defeated the Germans in the largest single tank battle of the Second World War. Belgorod Oblast was established on 6 January 1954.

In October 1993 President Boris Yeltsin dismissed the region's Governor, Viktor Berestovoi, and called elections to a new Regional Duma. Communists enjoyed a majority in this body, and there was constant conflict with the administration headed by Yeltsin's appointee, Yevgenii Savchenko, who was elected Governor in 1995, 1999 and 2003. The Regional Duma approved his appointment to a further term in 2007.

In 2012 Savchenko was overwhelmingly elected Governor by direct popular vote. He was re-elected in September 2017, with 69.3% of the vote.

Elections to the Regional Duma were held on 13 September 2020. YeR obtained 64.0% of the votes cast on the basis of proportional representation, ahead of the KPRF, with 13.2%, the LDPR, with 6.6%, and the RPPS, with 5.1%. In total, the newly elected

50-member legislature comprised four factions: 44 deputies were members of the YeR faction, four of that of the KPRF, while the LDPR and RPPS factions each had one member.

On 17 September 2020 Savchenko (the final head of a federal subject to have held the post since the 1990s) resigned as Governor; several days later he became one of the Oblast's two representatives in the Federation Council. Vyacheslav Gladkov, previously a Deputy Chairman of the Government of Stavropol Krai, was appointed Acting Governor by President Vladimir Putin on 18 September. He was confirmed in the post of Governor on 19 September 2021, securing 78.8% of votes cast in a direct election. Gladkov assumed office on 27 September.

Belgorod Oblast was one of the staging areas for Russia's invasion of Ukraine which was launched on 24 February 2022. At the beginning of April two Ukrainian helicopters reportedly attacked an oil storage depot owned by the state–owned oil company Rosneft in Belgorod (40 km from the international border), causing a fire at the facility. A high terrorist threat level was declared in the Oblast on 11 April and was subsequently extended. Local officials reported further strikes as Ukrainian forces regained control of territory near the border. In early July the Russian defence ministry announced that three Ukrainian missiles had been fired at Belgorod, following an explosion in the city in which at least five civilians were killed. On 19 August Governor Gladkov reported that the residents of two villages had been evacuated after a fire erupted at a munitions depot near the border with Ukraine. On 19 October 2022 President Putin declared a 'medium level of response' in Belgorod Oblast and seven other regions (including the annexed Republic of Crimea and Sevastopol) bordering Russian-occupied parts of Ukraine where martial law was introduced; under this regime, the regional authorities were granted powers to undertake 'economic mobilization' for the provision of supplies to the Russian armed forces in Ukraine, as well as to increase security measures and introduce restrictions on freedom of movement to and from the territory. The shelling of Belgorod, particularly targeting essential infrastructure, continued late that year: an explosion occurred at an electric sub-station in the town of Shebekino, around 5 km from the border, in October; at least three people were killed in attacks on border villages in mid-November; and on 18 December one person was killed and several injured during further strikes around the capital. In December Gladkov announced the creation of self-defence battalions comprising local residents. The regional authorities reported further attacks during early 2023, including the shelling of Shebekino in February.

On 22 May 2023 a military incursion staged from the territory of Ukraine, together with explosions and drone attacks, entered the south-western border Grayvoron district. Paramilitary groups affiliated with a Russian nationalist dissident group, the Russkii Dobrovolcheskii Korpus (Russian Volunteer Corps) and with the Ukrainian-based anti-Putin organization, the Legion 'Svoboda Rossii' (Freedom to Russia Legion), announced that they had (despite their ideological differences) taken control of the villages of Kozinka, Gora-Podol and Glotovo before reaching the district administrative centre at Grayvoron, claiming to be creating a demilitarized zone. Gladkov temporarily imposed counter-terrorism restrictions on the civilian population and border villages were evacuated. On the following day the federal Ministry of Defence announced that the attacks had been repelled, and insisted that the insurgents were Ukrainians. A further military raid by two groups, supported by a Belarusian volunteer battalion, was staged near Shebekino on 1 June; at least nine civilians were injured, and a further two were killed in an artillery strike two days later. Sporadic insurgent activity in border areas continued, and on 16 July Gladkov reported further shelling of Shebekino and two other towns, during which one civilian was killed.

On 30 December 2023, according to an announcement by Gladkov, at least 24 people were killed and 108 injured in a Ukrainian missile and drone attack on central Belgorod (one day after Russia had launched a large-scale air bombardment across Ukraine which killed around 40 people). The federal Government announced that a large number of Ukrainian drones had been shot down over Belgorod and other regions, and requested an emergency meeting of the UN Security Council. At the session on the same day, the Russian envoy to the UN accused Ukraine of using 'cluster munitions' in the cross-border strike (which was one of the largest since Russia's invasion of Ukraine in February 2022).

ECONOMY

In 2021 Belgorod Oblast's gross regional product (GRP) amounted to 1,354,811m. roubles, or 881,701 roubles per head. The main industrial centres are at Belgorod and Shebekino. At the end of 2021 there were 700 km of railway lines in the Oblast.

Belgorod Oblast became one of the leading agricultural regions of Russia in the late 2000s. Its principal crops are grain, sugar beet, sunflower seeds and essential-oil plants. Horticulture, animal husbandry and beekeeping are also important. Agriculture employed 12.5% of the labour force and contributed 15.5% of GRP in 2021. The Oblast has substantial reserves of bauxite, iron ore and apatites. Its main industries are iron ore mining, the production of electricity, mechanical engineering, metal working, chemicals, the manufacture of building materials and food processing. Industry employed 30.0% of the workforce and contributed 51.0% of GRP in 2021, when manufacturing employed 15.5% of the workforce and contributed 14.2% of GRP.

The economically active population numbered 794,721 in 2022, when 3.7% of the labour force were unemployed, and the average monthly wage was 47,638 roubles. There was a budgetary surplus of 32,930.1m. roubles in 2021. Export trade amounted to US $5,053m. in that year (21.4% of which was with CIS countries), while import trade amounted to $1,479m. (of which 54.5% was with CIS countries).

DIRECTORY

Governor: Vyacheslav V. Gladkov.

Office of the Governor: 308005 Belgorod, pl. Sobornaya 4; tel. (4722) 22-42-47; fax (4722) 22-33-43; e-mail boss@beladm.bel.ru; internet belregion.ru.

Regional Duma: 308005 Belgorod, pl. Sobornaya 4; tel. and fax (4722) 32-38-63; e-mail info@belduma.ru; internet belduma.ru; Chair. Yurii N. Klepikov.

State Duma Representatives (2): Valerii S. Skrug (YeR), Andrei V. Skoch (YeR).

Federation Council Representatives: Yevgenii S. Savchenko, Zhanna Yu. Chefranova.

Bryansk Oblast

Bryansk Oblast is situated in the Central Russian Highlands. It borders Belarus to the west and Ukraine to the south; Kursk and Oryol Oblasts lie to the east, Kaluga to the north-east and Smolensk to the north-west. The main river is the Desna. The Oblast occupies 34,857 sq km (13,458 sq miles). According to official estimates, at January 2023 the region had a total population of 1,152,505 and a population density of 33.1 per sq km. Some 69.6% of the population was urban in 2023. The administrative centre, Bryansk, had an estimated 375,669 inhabitants at January 2023. Of residents who stated their ethnicity at the 2021 census, 95.9% were Russian. Bryansk Oblast is in the time zone UTC+3.

HISTORY

Bryansk, an early Orthodox bishopric, was part of the principality of Novgorod-Seversk until 1356. The Muscovite state acquired Bryansk from Lithuania in the 16th century. Bryansk Oblast was founded on 5 July 1944.

In late 1993 Yurii Lodkin, the communist-backed Governor elected in 1992, was dismissed, and a new Regional Duma formed. Lodkin was again elected Governor in 1996 and in 2000, despite obtaining only 29% of the vote. In 2004 a court prohibited Lodkin's candidacy to a further term, and the YeR candidate, Nikolai Denin, was elected. The Regional Duma confirmed Denin to a further term in 2007.

Denin was one of four candidates initially registered to contest a direct gubernatorial election scheduled for 14 October 2012. In early October the candidates representing Yabloko and the LDPR withdrew from the poll, urging support for Denin and objecting to the candidacy of the KPRF candidate, Vadim Potomskii. On 5 October a regional court, responding to a case brought by Pomotskii, suspended Denin's participation in the election while alleged irregularities in his campaign were investigated; the federal Supreme Court quickly overturned this ruling. In the election, Denin obtained 65.2%

of the votes cast, defeating Potomskii (the only other remaining candidate), with 30.8%; Potomskii subsequently became Governor of Oryol Oblast. At elections to the Regional Duma, held on 14 September 2014, YeR obtained 71.9% of the votes cast on the basis of proportional representation; the KPRF obtained 9.1%.

Meanwhile, on 9 September 2014 President Vladimir Putin dismissed Denin as Governor. The Acting Governor appointed thereafter, Aleksandr Bogomaz, hitherto a State Duma deputy, was elected to the post on 13 September 2015.

Elections to the Regional Duma were held on 8 September 2019. YeR won 63.7% of the votes cast on the basis of proportional representation, ahead of the LDPR, with 12.9%, and the KPRF, with 12.3%. When it convened later in the month, 45 of the 60 deputies joined the YeR parliamentary faction, five that of the LDPR, four that of the KPRF, and two that of SR.

Bogomaz of YeR was one of five candidates to contest a gubernatorial election on 13 September 2020, when he was re-elected with 71.7% of the votes cast; Andrei Arkhitskii of the KPRF was second, with 10.1%.

Bryansk Oblast was one of the border regions where Russian military units and equipment were amassed prior to the invasion of Ukraine on 24 February 2022. A high 'terrorist threat level' was declared by the authorities in the Oblast on 11 April. Three days later a state of emergency was declared in the south-western Klimovo district, after eight people were injured in shelling of the settlement of Klimovo, by Ukrainian forces, according to the regional authorities. Further repeated incidents of cross-border shelling were reported, particularly centred on a military base in the town of Klintsy, 46 km from the border. On 14 June the village of Zaimishche, near Klintsy, was bombarded, injuring six people. On 19 October President Putin declared a 'medium level of response' in Bryansk Oblast and seven other regions (including the annexed Republic of Crimea and Sevastopol) bordering Russian-occupied parts of Ukraine where martial law was introduced; under this regime, the regional authorities concerned were granted powers to undertake 'economic mobilization' for the provision of supplies to the Russian armed forces in Ukraine, as well as to increase security measures and introduce restrictions on freedom of movement to and from the territory. A Ukrainian drone attack caused a large fire at an oil storage facility in the Surazh district at the end of November, and further explosions occurred in Klintsy and Klimovo on 13 December.

On 2 March 2023 a paramilitary unit launched a cross-border raid from Ukraine, attacked two villages in Klimovo district and opened fire on civilians, killing two, before being repelled by Federal Security Service (FSB) forces. The federal Government denounced the incident as a terrorist attack by Ukrainian saboteurs, although a Russian extreme nationalist group opposed to the Putin regime claimed responsibility and Ukraine denied involvement. At the beginning of May Governor Bogomaz announced two incidents in which goods trains had been derailed by explosive devices, and several drone attacks against military targets in the Oblast were reported during that month. Further drone attacks were reported to have been thwarted in the region on 30 August.

On 30 December 2023 (one day after Russia had launched a large-scale air bombardment across Ukraine) Bogomaz announced that a child had been killed in a Ukrainian shelling of two villages, and that six Ukrainian drones had been shot down over the Oblast. In addition, local media reported a fire caused by a drone strike at the Kremniy El enterprise near Bryansk, a major supplier of microelectronics to the Russian military.

ECONOMY

Bryansk Oblast's gross regional product (GRP) was 468,666m. roubles in 2021, equivalent to 398,619 roubles per head. Its main industrial centres are at Bryansk and Klintsy. At the end of 2021 there were 1,041 km of railways in the Oblast.

The agricultural sector, which employed 9.5% of the workforce and contributed 20.3% of GRP in 2021, consists mainly of grain, sugar beet and potato production, and animal husbandry. The main industries are mechanical engineering, food processing, electrical energy and the manufacture of building materials. Industry employed 25.6% of the workforce and contributed 23.6% of GRP in 2021, when manufacturing employed 16.1% of the workforce and contributed 16.4% of GRP.

The economically active population numbered 561,918 in 2022, when 3.2% of the labour force were unemployed, while the average monthly wage was 40,804 roubles. There was a regional budgetary surplus of 3,897.5m. roubles in 2021. In that year international trade comprised US $415m. of exports (64.9% of which was with countries of the CIS) and $785m. of imports (63.6% of which was with CIS countries).

DIRECTORY

Governor: ALEKSANDR V. BOGOMAZ.

Office of the Governor: 241002 Bryansk, pr. Lenina 33; tel. (4832) 66-26-11; fax (4832) 41-13-10; e-mail gubernator@bryanskobl.ru; internet bryanskobl.ru.

Regional Duma: 241050 Bryansk, pl. K. Marksa 2; tel. (4832) 66-36-91; fax (4832) 74-31-95; e-mail ipriem@duma32.ru; internet duma32.ru; Chair. VALENTIN V. SUBBOT.

State Duma Representatives (2): NIKOLAI S. VALUYEV (YeR), NIKOLAI N. ALEKSEYENKO (YeR).

Federation Council Representatives: GALINA N. SOLODUN, VADIM YE. DENGIN.

Ivanovo Oblast

Ivanovo Oblast is situated in the central part of the Eastern European Plain. It neighbours the Oblasts of Kostroma (to the north), Nizhnii Novgorod (east), Vladimir (south) and Yaroslavl (north-west). The main river is the Volga, and one-half of the territory is forested. The Oblast covers an area of 21,437 sq km (8,277 sq miles). At January 2023 the Oblast's population was an estimated 914,725 and the population density 42.7 per sq km. Some 82.1% of the population was urban in 2023. The city of Ivanovo had an estimated 360,687 inhabitants at January 2023. Of residents who stated their ethnicity at the 2021 census, 96.0% were Russian. Ivanovo Oblast is in the time zone UTC+3.

HISTORY

The city of Ivanovo-Voznesensk (later Ivanovo) was founded in 1871. Ivanovo Oblast was founded on 20 July 1918.

In 1996 Vladislav Tikhomirov was elected Governor. Following elections in 2000 he was succeeded by Vladimir Tikhonov of the KPRF. In 2005 the regional legislature approved the nomination of Mikhail Men, hitherto Deputy Mayor of Moscow, as Governor. In 2006 the editor of *Kursiv*, an online publication based in the region, Vladimir Rakhmankov, was brought to trial and fined 20,000 roubles for insulting a public official, after he published an article that had satirized President Vladimir Putin's annual address to the federal legislature. On 22 October 2010 the Regional Duma voted to appoint Men to a second term as Governor.

In elections to the Regional Duma on 8 September 2013, YeR obtained 55.8% of the votes cast to seats elected on the basis of party lists, ahead of the KPRF, with 14.6%, and the LDPR, with 7.0%. On 16 October Men resigned as Governor, stating that he had fulfilled his role as a 'crisis manager' in the Oblast. On 14 September 2014 Pavel Konkov, the Acting Governor, a local businessman, was elected to office, receiving 80.3% of the vote.

TERRITORIAL SURVEYS

On 10 October 2017 Konkov resigned as Governor. He was succeeded in an acting capacity by Stanislav Voskresenskii, an erstwhile federal Deputy Minister of Economic Development. Both the gubernatorial election and polls to the Regional Duma were held on 9 September 2018, when Voskresenskii was elected Governor, defeating four other candidates, with 65.7% of the votes cast. In the concurrent legislative elections, YeR won 34.1% of the votes cast to seats on a proportional basis, ahead of the KPRF, with 26.9%, the LDPR, with 16.3%, and SR, with 8.2%. A total of 15 of the 26 deputies had joined the YeR parliamentary faction by the end of the year.

On 10 September 2023 Voskresenskii, the candidate of YeR, was overwhelmingly re-elected Governor with 82.5% of the votes cast, defeating four other candidates. Shortly afterwards, Voskresenskii appointed a former head of the Federal Customs Service, Vladimir Bulavin, as a representative of Ivanovo Oblast in the Federation Council. Following concurrent elections to the Regional Duma, YeR held 27 of the 30 seats in the expanded chamber, substantially increasing its representation there, although the rate of participation was only 33.9%.

ECONOMY

In 2021 Ivanovo Oblast's gross regional product (GRP) amounted to 300,626m. roubles, equivalent to 306,145 roubles per head. The main industrial centres are at Ivanovo, Shuya, Vichuga and Furmanov. There are well-developed land and river transport networks, and an international airport. At the end of 2021 there were 345 km of railways in the Oblast.

Ivanovo Oblast was the historic centre of Russia's cotton-milling industry. Flax production is an important agricultural activity, as are grain and vegetable production and animal husbandry. Agriculture employed 3.6% of the workforce and contributed 2.8% of GRP in 2021. The main industries are light manufacturing, electrical energy, mechanical engineering and metal working, and food processing. Industry employed 32.6% of the workforce and contributed 32.5% of GRP in 2021, when manufacturing employed 21.3% of the workforce and contributed 22.7% of GRP.

The economically active population numbered 501,327 in 2022, while 3.1% of the labour force were unemployed, and the average monthly wage was 36,380 roubles. There was a budgetary surplus of 5,611.3m. roubles in 2021, when export trade amounted to US $273m. (41.0% of which was with CIS countries), while import trade amounted to $796m. (of which 49.6% was with CIS countries).

DIRECTORY

Governor: STANISLAV S. VOSKRESENSKII.

Office of the Governor: 153000 Ivanovo, ul. Pushkina 9; tel. (4932) 47-17-19; e-mail aio@adminet.ivanovo.ru; internet ivanovoobl.ru.

Regional Duma: 153000 Ivanovo, ul. Baturina 5; tel. (4932) 41-60-68; fax (4932) 41-92-21; e-mail zsio@ivanovo.zsio.ru; internet ivoblduma.ru; Chair. MARINA A. DMITRIYEVA.

State Duma Representatives (2): VIKTOR V. SMIRNOV (YeR), MIKHAIL V KUZEYEV (YeR).

Federation Council Representatives: VALERII N. VASILYEV, VLADIMIR I. BULAVIN.

Kaluga Oblast

Kaluga Oblast is situated in the central part of the Eastern European Plain. Tula and Oryol Oblasts lie to the south-east, Bryansk to the south-west, Moscow Oblast and Moscow City lie to the north-east and Smolensk to the north-west. The Oblast occupies 29,777 sq km (11,497 sq miles). At January 2023 its population was an estimated 1,070,853 and the population density 36.0 per sq km. Some 74.9% of the population was urban in 2023. The administrative centre, Kaluga, a river-port on the Oka river, had an estimated 333,954 inhabitants at January 2023. Other major cities in the Oblast include Obninsk (129,584). Of residents who stated their ethnicity at the 2021 census, 90.4% were Russian, 1.9% were Tajik, 1.2% were Armenian, 1.2% were Uzbek, and 0.9% were Ukrainian. Kaluga Oblast is in the time zone UTC+3.

HISTORY

The city of Kaluga, first mentioned in 1371, was founded as a Muscovite outpost. Kaluga Oblast was founded on 5 July 1944.

Valerii Sudarenkov, the Governor from 1996, did not stand for re-election in 2000; his former deputy, Anatolii Artamonov, was elected to succeed him and was re-elected in 2004. In 2005 and 2010 the Legislative Assembly voted to confirm Artamonov to further terms of office.

On 13 September 2015 Artamonov was elected Governor by direct popular vote. In concurrent elections to the Legislative Assembly YeR obtained 57.0% of the votes cast on a proportional basis; 32 of the 40 deputies subsequently joined the YeR faction.

President Putin accepted the resignation of Artamonov as Governor on 13 February 2020 and appointed Vladislav Shapsha, hitherto the Mayor of Obninsk, to succeed him in an acting capacity. Artamonov became a representative of the Oblast in the Federation Council.

On 13 September 2020 Shapsha was elected as Governor, securing 71.2% of the votes cast. In concurrent elections to the Legislative Assembly, the share of the vote cast for YeR on a proportional basis decreased to 42.4%. The KPRF was second, with 12.9%, ahead of the LPDR, with 8.6%, the recently formed centre-right NL, with 8.1%, SR (8.0%) and the RPPS (7.8%). By late December 28 of the 40 deputies had joined the YeR faction, three that of the KPRF, three that of SR, two that of the LDPR, two that of NL, and one that of the RPPS.

ECONOMY

In 2021 Kaluga Oblast's gross regional product (GRP) amounted to 664,150m. roubles, equivalent to an estimated 659,591 roubles per head. The major industrial centres are at Kaluga, Lyudinovo, Kirov and Maloyaroslavets. At the end of 2021 there were 860 km of railway track in the Oblast.

Certain areas of the Oblast contain fertile black earth (*chernozyom*). Agriculture employed 4.8% of the workforce and contributed 5.4% of GRP in 2021. The Oblast's main industries are mechanical engineering, food processing, and timber and timber processing. Industry employed 37.2% of the workforce and contributed 50.4% of GRP in 2021, when manufacturing employed 23.3% of the workforce and contributed 42.9% of GRP. In 2007 the German automobile manufacturer Volkswagen opened a plant in Kaluga Oblast, to assemble automobiles of the VW Polo and Škoda brands; in 2018 it produced over 140,000 vehicles. Operations at the plant ceased in 2022, in association with the imposition of international sanctions following the Russian invasion of Ukraine; in May 2023 Volkswagen sold the plant to the US-based Art-Finance Partners company.

The economically active population numbered 516,220 in 2022, when the unemployment rate was 3.9%, while the average monthly wage was 53,910 roubles. There was a budgetary deficit of 2,200.7m. roubles in 2021, when export trade amounted to US $1,513m. (of which 38.6% was with countries of the CIS), and imports to $7,532m. (of which 1.6% was with CIS countries).

DIRECTORY

Governor: Vladislav V. Shapsha.

Office of the Governor: 248600 Kaluga, pl. Staryi Torg 2; tel. (4842) 56-23-57; fax (4842) 53-13-09; e-mail admgub@adm.kaluga.ru; internet bit.ly/39fCCs0.

Legislative Assembly: 248600 Kaluga, pl. Staryi Torg 2; tel. (4842) 77-82-01; fax (4842) 59-15-63; e-mail zsko@adm.kaluga.ru; internet zskaluga.ru; Chair. Gennadii S. Novoseltsev.

State Duma Representatives (2): Olga V. Korobova (YeR), Gennadii I. Sklyar (YeR).

Federation Council Representatives: Anatolii D. Artamonov, Aleksandr A. Savin.

Office of the Government: 305002 Kursk, Krasnaya pl. 1; tel. (4712) 55-68-29; e-mail zam.priem@rkursk.ru; internet kursk.ru/region/control/page-193917.

Regional Duma: 305001 Kursk, ul. S. Perovskoi 24; tel. (4712) 54-86-54; fax (4712) 54-86-50; e-mail oblduma@kursknet.ru; internet kurskduma.ru; Chair. YURII M. AMEREV.

State Duma Representatives (2): YEKATERINA V. KHARCHENKO (YeR), OLGA G. GERMANOVA (YeR).

Federation Council Representatives: GRIGORII A. RAPOTA, ALEKSANDR YU. BRYKSIN.

Lipetsk Oblast

Lipetsk Oblast is situated in the Central Russian Highlands. It borders the Oblasts of Voronezh and Kursk to the south, Oryol (west), Tula (north-west), Ryazan (north) and Tambov (east). It occupies 24,047 sq km (9,285 sq miles). At January 2023 it had an estimated population of 1,126,263 and a population density of 46.8 per sq km. Some 63.0% of the population was urban in 2023. The administrative centre, Lipetsk, had an estimated 490,428 inhabitants at January 2023. Of residents who stated their ethnicity at the 2021 census, 96.7% were Russian. Lipetsk Oblast is in the time zone UTC+3.

HISTORY

Lipetsk city was founded in the 13th century. Lipetsk Oblast was formed on 6 January 1954. In 1993 a left-wing candidate, Mikhail Narolin, was elected as Governor (Head of the Administration). In 1998 the Chairman of the oblast legislature, Oleg Korolyov, who was supported by both the KPRF and Yabloko, defeated Narolin in a gubernatorial election. Korolyov was re-elected in 2002. In 2005 and 2010 the regional legislature endorsed his nomination to further terms of office. At elections to the Regional Council of Deputies, held on 4 December 2011, YeR was the most successful party, but its share of the votes cast was only 38.8%, ahead of the KPRF, with 23.5%, SR, with 18.4%, and the LDPR, with 16.5%. On 14 September 2014, in a direct popular election contested by five candidates, Korolyov was elected Governor, obtaining 81.8% of the votes cast.

YeR obtained some 53.9% of the votes cast on a proportional basis at elections to the Regional Council of Deputies held on 18 September 2016; the KPRF received 13.7%, the LDPR 12.1% and SR 7.2%. By the end of the year, 46 of the 56 deputies had joined the YeR parliamentary faction. Korolyov resigned as Governor on 2 October; in the following month he was appointed as a representative of the Oblast to the Federation Council; he remained in this post until June 2021. Meanwhile, Putin appointed Igor Artamonov, a banker, as Acting Governor. On 8 September 2019 Artamanov was duly elected, receiving 67.3% of the votes cast. The second-placed candidate was Sergei Tokarev of the KPRF, with 20.0%.

ECONOMY

In 2021 Lipetsk Oblast's gross regional product (GRP) amounted to 843,982m. roubles, or 752,926 roubles per head. Its main industrial centres are at Lipetsk, Yelets and Dankov. At the end of 2021 there were 757 km of railway lines in the Oblast.

The region's agriculture consists mainly of animal husbandry, and the production of grain, sugar beet and sunflower seeds. Agriculture employed 10.2% of the workforce and contributed 8.6% of GRP in 2021. The Oblast's main industries include ferrous metallurgy, mechanical engineering and metal working. NLKM (Novolipetsk Steel), one of Russia's major industrial companies, is based in the region. Industry employed 30.1% of the workforce and contributed 56.5% of GRP in 2021, when manufacturing employed 17.8% of the workforce and contributed 48.9% of GRP (a higher proportion than in any other federal subject).

A partnership with the Italian Marche Region resulted in the establishment in the Oblast of a subsidiary of the Merloni Elettrodomestici (later Indesit, now Whirlpool, of the USA) household appliances company. Merloni acquired the refrigerator-manufacturing subsidiary of NLKM in 2002, and opened two further plants in the region to manufacture domestic washing machines; the Oblast became a principal producer of refrigerators and washing machines in the Russian Federation. In June 2022 Whirlpool sold its entire Russian operations and interests to Arçelik AŞ of Türkiye (Turkey).

The economically active population amounted to 574,080 in 2022. In 2022 3.7% of the labour force were unemployed, while the average monthly wage was 46,711 roubles. There was a budgetary surplus of 36,354.9m. roubles in 2021, when export trade amounted to US $6,824m. (of which only 6.5% was with countries of the CIS), and import trade amounted to $1,375m. (of which 12.2% was with CIS countries).

DIRECTORY

Head of the Administration: IGOR G. ARTAMONOV.

Office of the Head of the Administration: 398014 Lipetsk, pl. Lenina-Sobornaya 1; tel. (4742) 25-08-24; fax (4742) 72-24-26; e-mail office@admlr.lipetsk.ru; internet bit.ly/2TkVyz6.

Regional Council of Deputies: 398014 Lipetsk, pl. Lenina-Sobornaya 1; tel. (4742) 27-14-29; fax (4742) 72-24-15; e-mail info@oblsovet.ru; internet oblsovet.ru; Chair. VLADIMIR V. SERIKOV.

State Duma Representatives (2): DMITRII L. AVEROV (YeR), MIKHAIL V. TARASENKO (YeR).

Federation Council Representatives: MAKSIM G. KAVDZHARADZE, OKSANA V. KHLYARKINA.

Moscow Oblast

Moscow Oblast is situated in the centre of the Eastern European Plain. The region is surrounded by seven other oblasts: Tver to the north, Yaroslavl to the north-east, Vladimir to the east, Ryazan to the south-east, Tula to the south, Kaluga to the south and south-west and Smolensk to the west. Moscow City is largely surrounded by the Oblast. The main rivers are the Moskva and the Oka. The Oblast covers 44,379 sq km (17,135 sq miles). At January 2023 the Oblast had an estimated population of 8,591,736 and a population density of 193.6 per sq km. Some 78.3% of the population was urban in 2023. The Oblast's administrative centre is Moscow, which does not itself form part of the Oblast. Large cities (estimated population figures at January 2023) include Balashikha (526,851), Podolsk (312,400), Mytishchi (266,436), Khimki (257,006), Lyubertsy (230,134), Korolyov (226,936), Krasnogorsk (188,850), Odintsovo (186,172), Domodedovo (155,421), Elektrostal (143,182), Shchyolkovo (135,509), Serpukhov (133,646), Kolomna (133,019), Dolgoprudnyi (119,957), Ramenskoye (114,000), Reutov (113,140), Pushkino (111,738), Zhukovskii (110,507), Orekhovo-Zuyevo (105,542), Vidnoye (103,957) and Noginsk

(102,205). Of residents who stated their ethnicity at the 2021 census, 92.1% were Russian, 0.9% were Armenian, and 0.7% were Ukrainian. Moscow Oblast is in the time zone UTC+3.

HISTORY

The region, an important trade route between the Baltic and Black or Caspian Seas, became industrialized in the early 18th century, with the development of the textiles industry. Invading German forces reached Moscow Oblast (which was formed on 14 January 1929) in 1941, although by 1942 they had been driven from the region.

Col-Gen. Boris Gromov, a former member of the State Duma and a Deputy Minister of Defence, was elected as Governor in January 2000. He was re-elected in December 2003. At elections to the Regional Duma held in March 2007, YeR attracted 49.5% of the votes cast; the KPRF was second, with 18.6%. The rate of participation was only 29.8%. In May the Regional Duma approved Gromov's nomination to a third gubernatorial term.

In June 2011 President Dmitrii Medvedev proposed that the territory of Moscow City be expanded, partly with the intention of encouraging major companies to establish their headquarters outside the congested city centre. A proposal, presented in August by the Governments of Moscow City and Moscow Oblast, provided for the incorporation of large areas of the south-west of Moscow Oblast into the city, including the towns of Vnukovo, Shcherbinka and Troitsk, and the federal centre of technological innovation at Skolkovo. Following their approval by the federal legislature, the new boundaries took effect from 1 July 2012. Meanwhile, at elections to the Regional Duma, held on 4 December 2011, YeR was again the most successful party, although its support decreased to 33.5% of the votes cast, only narrowly ahead of the KPRF, with 27.2%, and both SR and the LDPR obtained over 15%.

In April 2012 the Regional Duma approved the nomination of Sergei Shoigu, hitherto the federal Minister of Civil Defence, Emergencies and Disaster Relief, and a senior member of YeR, as Gromov's successor as Governor; he assumed office on 11 May. However, in November Shoigu was appointed Minister of Defence. Two days later Andrei Vorobyov, a former YeR State Duma deputy, was appointed Acting Governor of Moscow Oblast. On 8 September 2013 Vorobyov was elected Governor, receiving 78.9% of the votes cast.

YeR obtained 43.2% of the votes cast on a proportional basis in elections to the Regional Duma held in September 2016, ahead of the KPRF, with 15.9%, and the LDPR, with 14.4%. Thirty-seven of the 50 deputies had joined the YeR parliamentary faction by the end of the year. Repeated demonstrations against the regional authorities' failure to implement reforms in the collection and processing of household waste occurred in the Oblast throughout 2018–19.

Meanwhile, on 9 September 2018 Vorobyov was re-elected Governor, with 62.5% of the votes cast, defeating five other candidates; the second-placed candidate was Konstantin Cheremisov of the KPRF, with 13.0%.

In May 2021 Vorobyov announced the separation of the positions of Governor and head of government, and appointed the hitherto First Vice-Governor, Ildar Gabrakhmanov, as Chairman of the Government. At elections to the Regional Duma held on 19 September, YeR secured 45.2% of the votes cast on the basis of proportional representation, ahead of the KPRF, with 19.5%. By the end of the year 35 of the 49 deputies had joined the YeR faction.

In December 2022 Vorobyov was among the Russian officials to be subject to targeted sanctions imposed by the European Union (EU) in connection with the ongoing Russian war in Ukraine. On 10 September 2023 he was re-elected to a third term in office with 83.7% of the votes cast. On 20 September Gabrakhmanov was again appointed First Vice-Governor, while retaining his incumbent position.

ECONOMY

In 2021 Moscow Oblast's gross regional product (GRP) amounted to 6,832,298m. roubles, or 882,876 roubles per head. The main industrial centres include Podolsk, Lyubertsy, Kolomna, Mytishchi, Odintsovo, and Noginsk. At the end of 2021 there were 2,171 km of railways in Moscow Oblast and Moscow City combined. Moscow-Sheremetyevo and Moscow-Domodedovo international airports are located in the Oblast.

Agriculture, which employed 2.5% of the region's workforce and contributed 1.5% of GRP in 2021, consists mainly of the production of vegetables and animal husbandry. Heavy industry is the dominant industrial sector, although major industries include mechanical engineering, radio electronics, chemicals, light manufacturing, textiles, ferrous and non-ferrous metallurgy, metal working, the manufacture of building materials, wood working and handicrafts. The region's military-industrial complex is also important. Industry employed 30.7% of the workforce and contributed 28.5% of GRP in 2021, when manufacturing employed 17.0% of the workforce and contributed 20.1% of GRP. The construction of a special economic zone at Dubna, to specialize in the development of nuclear technology, commenced in 2007. By 2024 more than 160 companies were operating in the zone.

The economically active population was 4,021,447 in 2022, when 3.1% of the labour force were unemployed, and the average monthly wage was 70,705 roubles. There was a budgetary surplus of 20,795.6m. roubles in 2021, when export trade amounted to US $11,413m. (of which 47.8% was with countries of the CIS), and import trade to $33,562m. (of which 10.0% was with CIS countries).

DIRECTORY

Governor: ANDREI YU. VOROBYOV.

Chairman of the Government, First Vice-Governor: ILDAR N. GABDRAKHMANOV.

Office of the Governor: 103070 Moscow, pl. Staraya 6; tel. (495) 623-24-13; fax (495) 628-98-12; e-mail amo@mosreg.ru; internet mosreg.ru.

Regional Duma: 129063 Moscow, pr. Mira 72; tel. (495) 988-69-69; fax (495) 988-69-70; e-mail info@mosoblduma.ru; internet mosoblduma.ru; Chair. IGOR YU. BRYNTSALOV.

State Duma Representatives (11): VYACHESLAV V. FOMICHEV (YeR), IRINA K. RODNINA (YeR), NIKITA YU. CHAPLIN (YeR), SERGEI V. KOLUNOV (YeR), ROMAN I. TERYUSHKOV (YeR), DENIS V. MAIDANOV (YeR), GENNADII O. PANIN (YeR), VYACHESLAV A. FETISOV (YeR), SERGEI A. PAKHOMOV (YeR), ALEKSANDR B. KOGAN (YeR), ALEKSANDR R. TOLMACHYOV (YeR).

Federation Council Representatives: OLGA S. ZABRALOVA, ALEKSANDR V. DVOINYKH.

Oryol Oblast

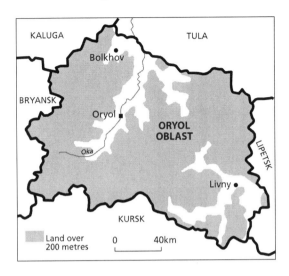

Oryol Oblast is situated in the Eastern European Plain, in the Central Russian Highlands. It neighbours five other oblasts: Kursk (to the south), Bryansk (west), Kaluga (north-west), Tula (north-east) and Lipetsk (east). Oryol Oblast covers some 24,652 sq km (9,518 sq miles). At January 2023 the population was estimated at 700,276 and the population density at 28.4 per sq km. Some 66.6% of the population was urban in 2023. The administrative centre is at Oryol, with an estimated 296,633 inhabitants at January 2023. Of residents who stated their ethnicity at the 2021 census, 95.3% were Russian. Oryol Oblast is in the time zone UTC+3.

HISTORY

Oryol was founded as a fortress in 1566, later becoming a place of exile and detention. Oryol Oblast was formed on 27 September 1937. Yegor Stroyev was elected Governor in 1993, and re-elected, on both occasions receiving over 90% of the vote, in 1997 and 2001. (Stroyev was also Chairman of the upper chamber of the federal legislature, the Federation Council, in 1996–2001.) In 2005 the regional legislature voted to appoint Stroyev to a further term.

In February 2009 President Dmitrii Medvedev approved Stroyev's resignation as Governor; the regional legislature approved the nomination of Aleksandr Kozlov, a deputy minister in the federal Ministry of Agriculture, as his successor. At elections to the regional legislature on 4 December 2011 YeR obtained 40.6% of the votes cast; the KPRF obtained some 32.4%. In the concurrent elections to the State Duma the KPRF obtained 32.0% of the votes cast in Oryol Oblast, more than in any other federal subject, compared with the 39.0% awarded to YeR. The level of support (29.1%) awarded to the KPRF leader (who originated from the Oblast), Gennadii Zyuganov, at the presidential election conducted on 4 March 2012 was also the highest recorded in any federal subject, reflecting the territory's continuing status as a stronghold of Communist support.

TERRITORIAL SURVEYS

Following the expiry of Kozlov's gubernatorial mandate, on 26 February 2014 President Vladimir Putin appointed Vadim Potomskii, hitherto a KPRF State Duma deputy, as Acting Governor. On 14 September Potomskii was elected Governor, with 89.2% of the vote.

YeR obtained 46.0% of the votes cast on the basis of proportional representation at elections to the Regional Council of People's Deputies on 18 September 2016; the KPRF was second, with 23.1%. 34 of the 50 deputies subsequently joined the YeR parliamentary faction. On 5 October 2017 Potomskii resigned as Governor. On the same day President Putin appointed Andrei Klychkov, a senior KPRF official and hitherto a Moscow City Duma deputy, to succeed him in an acting capacity. On 9 September 2018 Klychkov was elected Governor, obtaining 83.6% of the votes cast.

On 10 September 2023 Klychkov was re-elected Governor with 82.1% of the votes cast, defeating two other candidates.

ECONOMY

Oryol Oblast's gross regional product (GRP) amounted to 336,688m. roubles in 2021, equivalent to 468,019 roubles per head. The principal industrial centres in the region are at Oryol, Livny and Mtsensk. Oryol lies on the Moscow–Crimea highway and is an important railway junction. At the end of 2021 there were 596 km of railway track in the Oblast.

Agriculture, which employed 8.7% of the workforce and contributed 28.0% of GRP in 2021, consists mainly of the cultivation of grain and sugar beet. There is a source of iron ore at Novoyaltinskoye. The Oblast's main industries are mechanical engineering, metal working, the production of building materials and food processing. Industry employed 26.2% of the workforce and contributed 21.6% of GRP in 2021, when manufacturing employed 16.0% of the workforce and contributed 14.8% of GRP.

The economically active population numbered 329,977 in 2022, when 4.0% of the labour force were unemployed, while the average monthly wage was 40,843 roubles. There was a budgetary surplus of 4,076.9m. roubles in 2021. In that year export trade amounted to US $419m. (of which 32.9% was with CIS countries), and import trade to $396m. (of which 30.1% was with CIS countries).

DIRECTORY

Governor: ANDREI YE. KLYCHKOV.

Office of the Governor: 302021 Oryol, pl. Lenina 1; tel. (4862) 41-63-13; fax (4862) 41-25-30; e-mail post@adm.orel.ru; internet orel-region.ru.

Regional Council of People's Deputies: 302021 Oryol, pl. Lenina 1; tel. (4862) 41-58-53; fax (4862) 59-80-95; e-mail mail@oreloblsovet.ru; internet oreloblsovet.ru; Chair. LEONID S. MUZALEVSKII.

State Duma Representative (1): OLGA V. PILIPENKO (YeR).

Federation Council Representatives: VASILII N. IKONNIKOV, VADIM V. SOKOLOV.

Ryazan Oblast

Ryazan Oblast is situated in the Eastern European Plain. The region neighbours the Oblasts of Moscow (to the north-west), Vladimir (north), Nizhnii Novgorod (north-east), Penza (south-east), Tambov and Lipetsk (south), and Tula (west). Mordoviya lies to the east. The Oblast occupies 39,605 sq km (15,292 sq miles). At January 2023 the population was an estimated 1,088,918 and the population density 27.5 per sq km. Some 71.4% of the population was urban in 2023. The Oblast's principal city, Ryazan, had an estimated 523,203 inhabitants at January 2023. Of residents who stated their ethnicity at the 2021 census, 94.6% were Russian. Ryazan Oblast is in the time zone UTC+3.

HISTORY

Ryazan city was an early Orthodox Christian bishopric. The Oblast was formed on 26 September 1937. In December 1996 Vyacheslav Lyubimov, the KPRF-affiliated candidate, was elected Governor; he was re-elected in 2000, but in an election in 2004 was defeated by Georgii Shpak of the Rodina (Motherland) bloc, a former Commander-General of the Air Force.

To replace Shpak, the regional legislature unanimously approved the nomination of Oleg Kovalyov, a YeR State Duma deputy, as Governor on 13 March 2008. In October 2012 Kovalyov was elected Governor in a popular election. In elections to the Regional Duma, held on 13 September 2015, YeR obtained 62.7% of the proportional vote, recording a substantial increase in support.

On 14 February 2017 Kovalyov resigned as Governor. His successor, initially in an acting capacity, was Nikolai Lyubimov, previously a Deputy Governor of Kaluga Oblast and a State Duma deputy. On 10 September he was elected to the post.

In elections to the Regional Duma, held on 13 September 2020, support for YeR declined; the party obtained 47.7% of the proportional vote. The LDPR was second, with 12.0%, ahead of the KPRF, with 9.1%, the recently formed nationalist party (later absorbed into SR) Za Pravdu (For Truth), with 6.9%, the recently formed centre-right

NL, with 5.7%, SR, also with 5.7%, and the RPPS, with 5.4%. Some 29 deputies joined the YeR parliamentary faction when the new chamber convened.

President Vladimir Putin appointed Pavel Malkov, hitherto the head of the Federal Service of State Statistics, as Acting Governor on 10 May 2022, after Lyubimov announced that he would not seek a further gubernatorial term. Malkov was overwhelmingly elected Governor on 11 September, securing 84.6% of the votes cast, defeating Denis Sidorov of the KPRF (who obtained only 5.7%) and three other candidates; he assumed office on 21 September.

ECONOMY

In 2021 Ryazan Oblast's gross regional product (GRP) amounted to 531,962m. roubles, or 487,276 roubles per head. The Oblast's industrial centres are at Ryazan, Skopin and Kasimov. At the end of 2021 there were 941 km of railways in the region.

The Oblast's warm, moist climate is conducive to agriculture, which consists mainly of production of grain, vegetables, fruit, potatoes and sugar beet, and animal husbandry. Agriculture employed 5.7% of the workforce and contributed 10.9% of GRP in 2021. There are substantial reserves of timber, brown coal and peat in the region. The Oblast's main industries are mechanical engineering, metal working, the generation of electrical energy, petroleum processing, the production of building materials, light manufacturing and food processing. Industry employed 31.6% of the workforce and contributed 33.7% of GRP in 2021, when manufacturing employed 19.5% of the workforce and contributed 25.1% of GRP.

The economically active population numbered 511,491 in 2022, with 2.9% of the labour force were unemployed, while the average monthly wage was 45,770 roubles. There was a budgetary surplus of 2,271.1m. roubles in 2021. In that year export trade amounted to US $1,561m. (of which 16.4% was with countries of the CIS), while import trade amounted to $917m. (of which 9.0% was with CIS countries).

DIRECTORY

Governor: Pavel V. Malkov.

Office of the Governor: 390000 Ryazan, ul. Lenina 30; tel. (4912) 29-04-04; e-mail syo@adm1.ryazan.su; internet ryazangov.ru/governor.

Regional Duma: 390000 Ryazan, ul. Pochtovaya 50/57; tel. (4912) 25-48-82; fax (4912) 21-64-22; e-mail post@duma.ryazan.ru; internet rznoblduma.ru; Chair. Arkadii V. Fomin.

State Duma Representatives (2): Andrei L. Krasov (YeR), Dmitrii A. Khubezov (YeR).

Federation Council Representatives: Nikolai V. Lyubimov, (one vacancy).

Smolensk Oblast

Smolensk Oblast is situated in the central part of the Eastern European Plain. Belarus lies to the south-west, the Oblasts of Pskov and Tver to the north, Moscow to the north-east, and Kaluga and Bryansk to the south-east. The Oblast covers 49,779 sq km (19,220 sq miles). At January 2023 the population was an estimated 873,041 and the population density 17.5 per sq km. Some 72.7% of the population was urban in 2023. The administrative centre is at Smolensk, a river-port on the Dnepr (Dnieper), with an estimated 312,896 inhabitants at January 2023. Of residents who stated their ethnicity at the 2021 census, 94.7% were Russian, and 0.7% were Belarusian. Smolensk Oblast is in the time zone UTC+3.

HISTORY

Smolensk was first documented in 863, as the chief settlement of the Krivichi tribe. It became an Orthodox Christian bishopric in 1128, achieving prosperity from the 14th century due to its location on a Hanseatic trade route. It was the site of a major battle in 1812 between the Russian army and the forces of Napoleon I of France. Smolensk Oblast was formed in 1937.

In a 1998 election Aleksandr Prokhorov of the KPRF, the Mayor of Smolensk, defeated the incumbent Governor, Anatolii Glushenkov. In 2002 Viktor Maslov, a Federal Security Service (FSB) general, narrowly defeated Prokhurov. In 2005 the Regional Duma endorsed Maslov's nomination to a further term.

In December 2007 the Regional Duma voted to confirm the appointment of Sergei Antufyev, a former Chairman of the chamber, as Governor. Following Antufyev's resignation in 2012, the Regional Duma endorsed the appointment of Sergei Ostrovskii, an LDPR State Duma deputy, as Governor, before his direct election in September 2015.

Elections to the Regional Duma were held in September 2018. YeR won 36.3% of the proportional vote, ahead of the KPRF, with 22.9% and the LDPR, with 19.8%.

On 13 September 2020 Ostrovskii was re-elected Governor with 56.5% of the votes cast; the second-placed candidate, Andrei Mitrofanenkov of the KPRF, received 25.8%. On 17 March 2023 Ostrovskii resigned as Governor; his acting successor, appointed by President Vladimir Putin, was Vasilii Anokhin, a federal civil servant.

In July 2023 Anokhin was placed under US sanctions, in association with his support for the ongoing Russian war in Ukraine. Meanwhile, in June Anokhin announced that an oil refinery of the state-owned Transneft company and a gas distribution station had been targeted by Ukrainian drone attacks. A military aircraft factory in the Oblast was attacked on two occasions in October and November.

On 10 September 2023 Anokhin, the YeR candidate, was overwhelmingly elected Governor with 86.6% of votes cast. Following concurrent elections to the Regional Duma, YeR held 41 of the 48 seats in the expanded chamber, substantially increasing its representation there, although the rate of participation was only 33.7%.

ECONOMY

In 2021 Smolensk Oblast's gross regional product (GRP) amounted to 421,673m. roubles, or 460,597 roubles per head. Its major industrial centres are at Smolensk, Safonovo and Vyazma. At the end of 2021 there were 1,121 km of railway lines in the Oblast.

Agriculture, which employed 4.7% of the workforce and contributed 4.3% of GRP in 2021, mainly consists of animal husbandry, beekeeping, and the production of flax, potatoes, fruit and vegetables, grain and sugar beet. The Oblast's main industries are mechanical engineering, metal working, chemicals and petrochemicals, food processing, and electrical energy production. Industry employed 30.5% of the workforce and contributed 36.1% of GRP in 2021, when manufacturing employed 18.0% of the workforce and contributed 22.1% of GRP.

The economically active population numbered 464,503 in 2022, when 3.5% of the labour force were unemployed, while the average monthly wage was 41,717 roubles. There was a budgetary surplus of 7,754.1m. roubles in 2021, when export trade amounted to US $1,488m. (of which 49.2% was with countries of the CIS), and import trade to $2,391m. (of which 77.0% was with CIS countries).

DIRECTORY

Head of the Administration (Governor): Vasilii N. Anokhin.

Office of the Governor: 214008 Smolensk, pl. Lenina 1; tel. and fax (4812) 38-61-65; e-mail region@admin-smolensk.ru; internet admin-smolensk.ru.

Regional Duma: 214008 Smolensk, pl. Lenina 1; tel. (4812) 38-67-00; fax (4812) 38-71-85; e-mail duma@smoloblduma.ru; internet smoloblduma.ru; Chair. Igor V. Lyakhov.

State Duma Representatives (2): Sergei I. Neverov (YeR), Sergei D. Leonov (LDPR).

Federation Council Representatives: Ruslan V. Smashnev, Artyom S. Malashchenkov.

Tambov Oblast

Tambov Oblast is situated in the central Oka-Don plain. The Oblasts of Penza and Saratov lie to the east, Voronezh to the south, Lipetsk to the west and Ryazan to the north. Its major river is the Tsna. It occupies 34,462 sq km (13,306 sq miles). At January 2023 its population was an estimated 966,250 and its population density 28.0 per sq km. Some 60.4% of the population was urban in 2023. The administrative centre is Tambov, with an estimated 258,546 inhabitants at January 2023. Of residents who stated their ethnicity at the 2021 census, 95.6% were Russian. Tambov Oblast is in the time zone UTC+3.

HISTORY

Tambov city was founded in 1636 as a Muscovite fort. The region was the scene of an army mutiny during the anti-tsarist uprising of 1905. Numerous peasant revolts against the Bolsheviks were brutally suppressed in the region in the early 1920s. Tambov Oblast was formed on 27 September 1937.

Having appointed Oleg Betin as Head of the Administration (Governor) in March 1995, President Boris Yeltsin permitted a gubernatorial election nine months later. After Betin lost to the KPRF candidate, Aleksandr Ryabov, he was appointed as presidential representative to the region, before being elected Head of the Administration in 1999 and re-elected in 2003. The Regional Duma approved Betin's appointment to further terms of office in 2005 and 2010. On 25 May 2015 President Vladimir Putin appointed Aleksandr Nikitin, hitherto Chairman of the Regional Duma, as Acting Governor. On 13 September Nikitin was elected Governor, obtaining 85.5% of the votes cast; he was re-elected on 13 September 2020, with 79.3% of the vote.

At elections to the Regional Duma held on 19 September 2021, YeR secured 57.9% of the votes cast on a proportional basis; the KPRF obtained 15.6%, Rodina (Motherland) 12.7%, SR 6.6% and the LDPR 5.3%. By the end of the year 42 of the 50 deputies had joined the YeR faction, three that of the KPRF and three that of Rodina; the factions of SR and the LDPR each comprised one deputy.

Meanwhile, on 4 October 2021 Nikitin submitted his resignation; President Putin appointed the Secretary of the regional branch of YeR, Maksim Yegorov, as acting Head of the Administration. Three days later the new Regional Duma elected Nikitin as its representative in the Federation Council, the upper chamber of the federal legislature. On 11 September 2022 Yegorov was overwhelmingly elected as Head of the Administration, with 85.0% of the votes cast, defeating four other candidates.

ECONOMY

In 2021 Tambov Oblast's gross regional product (GRP) amounted to 429,268m. roubles, equivalent to 434,613 roubles per head. The region's industrial centres are at Tambov, Michurinsk and Morshansk. At the end of 2021 there were 738 km of railway lines in the region.

Agriculture, which employed 21.1% of the workforce (the second highest proportion among federal subjects) and contributed 35.4% of GRP in 2021, consists mainly of the production of grain, sugar beet, sunflower seeds and potatoes. The principal industries are mechanical engineering, metal working, chemicals and petrochemicals, the production of electrical energy, light manufacturing and food processing. Industry employed 22.2% of the workforce and contributed 19.1% of GRP in 2021, when manufacturing employed 14.1% of the workforce and contributed 12.9% of GRP.

The economically active population numbered 486,327 in 2022, when 3.3% of the labour force were unemployed, while the average monthly wage was 39,346 roubles. There was a budgetary surplus of 4,110.6m. roubles in 2021, when export trade amounted to US $426m. (of which 42.4% was with countries of the CIS), while import trade amounted to $236m. (of which 36.0% was with CIS countries).

DIRECTORY

Head of the Administration: Maksim B. Yegorov.

Office of the Head of the Administration: 392017 Tambov, ul. Internatsionalnaya 14; tel. (4752) 72-10-61; fax (4752) 72-25-18; e-mail post@tambov.gov.ru; internet tambov.gov.ru.

Regional Duma: 392017 Tambov, ul. Internatsionalnaya 14; tel. (4752) 71-23-70; fax (4752) 71-11-38; e-mail regduma@duma.tambov.gov.ru; internet duma.tmbreg.ru; Chair. Yevgenii A. Matushkin.

State Duma Representatives (2): Aleksei A. Zhuravlev (LDPR), Aleksandr A. Polyakov (YeR).

Federation Council Representatives: Aleksandr V. Nikitin, Mikhail V. Belousov.

Tula Oblast

Tula Oblast is situated in the northern section of the Central Russian Highlands. It is bordered by the Oblasts of Ryazan to the east, Lipetsk to the south-east, Oryol to the south-west, Kaluga to the north-west, and Moscow to the north. The Oblast covers 25,679 sq km (9,915 sq miles). At January 2023 it had an estimated population of 1,481,471 and a population density of 57.7 per sq km. Some 73.2% of the population was urban in 2023. The administrative centre, Tula, had an estimated 466,609 inhabitants at January 2023. The second largest city is Novomoskovsk (118,066). Of residents that stated their ethnicity at the 2021 census, 94.1% were Russian, and 0.7% were Armenian. Tula Oblast is in the time zone UTC+3.

HISTORY

The city of Tula was founded in the 12th century. The Imperial Small Arms Factory was constructed in the city in 1712. Tula Oblast was founded on 26 September 1937.

Vasilii Starodubtsev, a prominent KPRF member, and a participant in the attempted coup in Moscow in August 1991, was elected Governor in 1997 and re-elected in 2001. In March 2005 the Regional Duma voted to appoint President Vladimir Putin's nominee, Vyacheslav Dudka, as Governor. In April 2010 it confirmed his appointment to a further term. In July 2011 President Dmitrii Medvedev dismissed Dudka as Governor, nominating Vladimir Gruzdev of YeR, a former State Duma deputy and founder of a prominent supermarket chain, as his successor. The Regional Duma confirmed this appointment on 18 August. A criminal investigation commenced, and in July 2013 Dudka was sentenced to nine-and-a-half years' detention and fined 900,000 roubles for having accepted bribes.

On 2 February 2016 President Putin appointed Lt-Gen. Aleksei Dyumin, a former commander of the Russian Special Operations Forces, as Acting Governor, after Gruzdev resigned. On 18 September Dyumin was elected Governor by 84.2% of votes cast, defeating three other candidates.

Elections were held to the Regional Duma on 8 September 2019. YeR obtained 50.3% of the votes cast on the basis of proportional representation, ahead of the KPRF, with 14.5%. When the Duma convened later in the month, 28 of the 36 deputies joined the faction of YeR.

On 19 September 2021 Dyumin was re-elected as Governor, with 83.6% of votes cast, defeating Vladimir Isakov of the KPRF (who received 9.0% of the vote) and two other candidates. On 10 October 2022 an erstwhile Deputy Governor, Vyacheslav Fyodorishchev, was appointed as First Deputy Governor, Chairman of the Government following the departure of his predecessor, Valerii Sherin, for a post in a state corporation.

ECONOMY

In 2021 Tula Oblast's gross regional product (GRP) amounted to 867,817m. roubles, or 602,298 roubles per head. The principal industrial centres are Tula, Novomoskovsk and Shchyokino. At the end of 2021 there were 931 km of railway lines in the Oblast.

Agriculture, which employed 5.3% of the workforce and contributed 7.5% of GRP in 2021, consists primarily of the production of grain, potatoes, fruit and vegetables, and sugar beet, as well as animal husbandry. The main industries are mechanical engineering, metal working, chemicals and petrochemicals, ferrous metallurgy, food processing, the production of brown coal (lignite) the generation of electricity, and the production of fabrics. Industry employed 34.5% of the workforce and contributed 52.6% of GRP in 2021, when manufacturing employed 22.3% of the workforce and contributed 42.8% of GRP.

The economically active population numbered 761,729 in 2022, when 3.6% of the labour force were unemployed, while the average monthly wage was 51,218 roubles. There was a budgetary surplus of 4,584.4m. roubles in 2021, when export trade amounted to US $3,953m. (of which 17.7% was with countries of the CIS), and import trade to $1,797m. (of which 6.7% was with CIS countries).

DIRECTORY

Governor: Lt-Gen. ALEKSEI G. DYUMIN.

First Deputy Governor, Chairman of the Government: VYACHESLAV A. FYODOR-ISHCHEV.

Office of the Governor and of the Government: 300041 Tula, pl. Lenina 2; tel. (4872) 27-84-36; fax (4872) 20-63-26; e-mail admin@region.tula.ru; internet gubernator.tularegion.ru.

Regional Duma: 300041 Tula, pl. Lenina 2; tel. (4872) 20-50-24; fax (4872) 36-49-84; e-mail 71@tulaoblduma.ru; internet tulaoblduma.ru; Chair. NIKOLAI YU. VOROBYOV.

State Duma Representatives (2): VIKTOR V. DZYUBA (YeR), NADEZHDA V. SHKOLKINA (YeR).

Federation Council Representatives: DMITRII V. SAVELYEV, MARINA V. LEVINA.

Tver Oblast

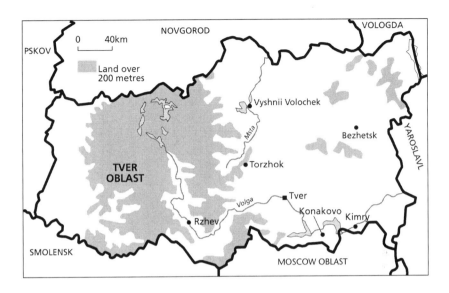

Tver Oblast is situated in the central Eastern European Plain. The Oblasts of Moscow and Smolensk lie to the south, Pskov to the west, Novgorod and Vologda to the north, and Yaroslavl to the east. The Oblast occupies 84,201 sq km (32,510 sq miles). At January 2023 the Oblast had an estimated 1,211,183 inhabitants and a population density of 14.4 per sq km. Some 76.3% of the population was urban in 2023. The administrative centre is at Tver, a river-port, with an estimated 414,756 inhabitants at January 2023. Of residents who stated their ethnicity at the 2021 census, 94.2% were Russian, and 0.7% were Tajik. Tver Oblast is in the time zone UTC+3.

HISTORY

Tver was founded as a fortress in 1135, and its princes rivalled those of Moscow in the 14th and 15th centuries. The Oblast was formed in January 1935 as Kalinin Oblast. Tver city was named Kalinin in 1931–90.

An elected Legislative Assembly, dominated by the KPRF, replaced the oblast Soviet in 1994. In 1995 Vladimir Platov of the KPRF defeated the incumbent, Vladimir Suslov, in a gubernatorial election. Platov was re-elected in 2000 but was defeated at elections in 2003 by Dmitrii Zelenin of YeR. In 2005 Platov was sentenced to five years' imprisonment for abuse of office. On 10 July 2007 the Legislative Assembly endorsed the nomination of Zelenin for a further term of office.

In elections to the Legislative Assembly held on 13 March 2011, YeR obtained 39.8% of the votes cast on a proportional basis; both the KPRF and SR obtained over 20% of the vote. On 16 June President Dmitrii Medvedev dismissed Zelenin as Governor, and nominated the erstwhile First Deputy Governor of Ryazan Oblast, Andrei Shevelyov, as his successor; the Legislative Assembly approved his appointment on 7 July. In February 2016 Shevelyov resigned, amid social unrest in the Oblast. Igor Rudenya, a former federal Deputy Minister of Agriculture, was appointed Acting

Governor by President Putin on 2 March. Rudenya was elected Governor by 72.1% of votes cast on 18 September, defeating two other candidates. YeR secured some 46.5% of the votes cast on the basis of proportional representation at elections to the Legislative Assembly held on the same day, ahead of the LDPR, with 17.8% and the KPRF, with 16.2%. A total of 30 of the 40 deputies had joined the YeR parliamentary faction by the end of the year.

At elections to the regional Legislative Assembly on 19 September 2021, YeR secured 35.4% of the votes cast on a proportional basis (representing a fall of more than 10 percentage points compared with the 2016 elections), while the KPRF received 21.5% of the vote, the LDPR and SR 11.2% each, and the RPPS 6.0%. Rudenya was re-elected as Governor on the same day, although his share of the vote fell to 52.3%; he defeated Lyudmila Vorobyova of the KPRF (with 20.1%) and three other candidates. By the end of the year 29 of the 40 regional deputies had joined the YeR faction, five that of the KPRF, three that of the LDPR, two that of SR, and one that of the RPPS.

ECONOMY

In 2021 Tver Oblast's gross regional product (GRP) amounted to 555,098m. roubles, equivalent to 448,418 roubles per head. The principal industrial centres are Tver, Vyshnii Volochyok and Rzhev. At the end of 2021 there were 1,807 km of railways in the Oblast.

Agriculture, which employed 7.3% of the workforce and contributed 5.5% of GRP in 2021, consists mainly of the production of vegetables, potatoes and flax, and animal husbandry. The major industries are mechanical engineering, metal-working, electricity generation, food processing and light manufacturing. Industry employed 29.3% of the workforce and contributed 32.8% of GRP in 2021, when manufacturing employed 18.2% of the workforce and contributed 20.6% of GRP.

The economically active population numbered 611,462 in 2022, when 3.8% of the labour force were unemployed, while the average monthly wage was 45,732 roubles. There was a budgetary surplus of 3,928.4m. roubles in 2021, when export trade amounted to US $606m. (of which 35.0% was with countries of the CIS), and import trade to $678m. (of which 14.7% was with CIS countries).

DIRECTORY

Governor: Igor M. Rudenya.

Office of the Governor: 170100 Tver, pl. M. Tverskogo 1; tel. (4822) 35-37-77; fax (4822) 35-55-08; e-mail region@tverreg.ru; internet bit.ly/38cJBzZ.

Legislative Assembly: 170100 Tver, ul. Sovetskaya 33; tel. (4822) 32-10-11; fax (4822) 34-10-15; e-mail zsto@zsto.ru; internet zsto.ru; Chair. Sergei A. Golubev.

State Duma Representatives (2): Yuliya V. Saranova (YeR), Vladimir A. Vasilyev (YeR).

Federation Council Representatives: Andrei N. Yepishin, Lyudmila N. Skakovskaya.

Vladimir Oblast

Vladimir Oblast is situated in the centre of the Eastern European Plain. It borders Ryazan and Moscow Oblasts to the south-west, Yaroslavl and Ivanovo to the north and Nizhnii Novgorod to the east. The Oblast's main rivers are the Oka and the Klyazma. It occupies 29,084 sq km (11,229 sq miles) and at January 2023 had an estimated population of 1,325,510 and a population density of 45.6 per sq km. Some 77.6% of the population was urban in 2023. The administrative centre is Vladimir, with an estimated 346,771 inhabitants at January 2023. Other major cities are Kovrov (130,327) and Murom (105,995). Of residents who stated their ethnicity at the 2021 census, 95.8% were Russian. Vladimir Oblast is in the time zone UTC+3.

HISTORY

Founded in 1108 as a frontier fortress by Prince Vladimir Monomakh, after the disintegration of Kyivan Rus, Vladimir was the seat of the principality of Vladimir-Suzdal. It fell under the rule of Muscovy in 1364 and was subsequently supplanted as the seat of the Russian Orthodox patriarch by Moscow. Vladimir Oblast was formed on 14 August 1944.

Nikolai Vinogradov of the KPRF was elected Governor in 1996. An oblast flag, controversially incorporating the Soviet hammer and sickle symbol, was adopted in 1999. Vinogradov was re-elected in 2000, and in 2005 the Legislative Assembly approved his appointment to a further term. At elections to the regional legislature on 20 March, YeR obtained only 20.5% of the votes cast, only slightly more than the KPRF, with 20.3%, and the option to vote 'against all candidates' (17.9%). In February 2009 the Legislative Assembly approved the re-appointment of Vinogradov. At elections to the Legislative Assembly on 1 March, YeR increased its share of the votes cast substantially, to 51.3%, after the option to vote against all candidates was abolished.

Vinogradov's term as Governor expired on 24 March 2013. On 8 September Svetlana Orlova, a former YeR member of the Federation Council, who had served as

Acting Governor in the interim, was elected to the post, receiving 74.7% of the vote. Only 27.7% of the electorate participated. At the concurrent elections to the Legislative Assembly, YeR obtained 44.3% of the proportional vote; the KPRF were second, with 13.5%.

In elections to the Legislative Assembly held in September 2018 YeR won 29.6% of the votes cast to seats on a proportional basis, ahead of the KPRF, with 23.7%, the LDPR, with 20.8%, and SR, with 10.2%. By the end of the year 22 of the 38 deputies had joined the YeR parliamentary faction. Later in the month Vladimir Sipyagin defeated Orlova in a run-off poll with 57.0% of the vote, thereby replacing her as Governor.

Sipyagin resigned as Governor on 29 September 2021, having been elected to the State Duma as an LDPR representative. He was succeeded in an acting capacity, by Aleksandr Avdeyev, a former YeR State Duma deputy, who was overwhelmingly elected as Governor, with 83.7% of the votes cast, on 11 September 2022. He took office on 16 September.

Following elections to the Legislative Assembly held on 10 September 2023, YeR held 35 of the 40 seats in the expanded chamber, substantially increasing its representation there, although the rate of participation was only 24.8%.

ECONOMY

Vladimir Oblast's gross regional product (GRP) in 2021 was 736,830m. roubles, or 552,811 roubles per head. The Oblast's main industrial centres are at Vladimir, Kovrov, Murom, Aleksandrov, Kolchugino and Gus-Khrustalnyi. At the end of 2021 there were 921 km of railway track in the Oblast.

Agriculture, which employed 4.7% of the workforce and contributed 3.0% of GRP in 2021, consists mainly of animal husbandry, vegetable production and horticulture. The region is rich in peat deposits and timber reserves. The main industries are mechanical engineering, metal working, food processing, the production of electrical energy, light manufacturing, chemicals, glass-making and handicrafts. Industry employed 36.2% of the workforce and contributed 50.4% of GRP in 2021, when manufacturing employed 24.3% of the workforce and contributed 43.4% of GRP.

The economically active population numbered 696,191 in 2022, when 2.6% of the labour force were unemployed, while the average monthly wage was 45,677 roubles. There was a budgetary surplus of 10,810.7m. roubles in 2021, when export trade amounted to US $1,138m. (of which 55.3% was with countries of the CIS), and import trade to $1,760m. (of which 6.5% was with CIS countries).

DIRECTORY

Governor: Aleksandr A. Avdeyev.

Office of the Governor: 600000 Vladimir, Oktyabrskii pr. 21; tel. (4922) 33-15-52; fax (4922) 25-34-45; e-mail post@avo.ru; internet gubernator33.ru.

Legislative Assembly: 600000 Vladimir, Oktyabrskii pr. 21; tel. (4922) 33-27-28; e-mail zsvo@zsvo.ru; internet zsvo.ru; Chair. Olga N. Kokhlova.

State Duma Representatives (2): Igor N. Igoshin (YeR), Grigorii V. Anikeyev (YeR).

Federation Council Representatives: Andrei S. Shokhin, Vladimir N. Kiselev.

Voronezh Oblast

Voronezh Oblast is situated in the centre of the Eastern European Plain. The Oblasts of Belgorod and Kursk to the west, Lipetsk and Tambov to the north, Saratov to the north-east, Volgograd to the east and Rostov to the south-east. Ukraine lies to the south, although the annexation of these neighbouring territories, as the Lugansk People's Republic, was announced by Russia in 2022. The main rivers are the Don, the Khoper and the Bityug. The Oblast occupies 52,216 sq km (20,161 sq miles). At January 2023 the population was an estimated 2,285,282 and the population density 43.8 per sq km. Some 68.5% of the population was urban in 2023. The region's administrative centre is Voronezh, which had an estimated 1,051,995 inhabitants at January 2023. Of residents who stated their ethnicity at the 2021 census, 95.6% were Russian. Voronezh Oblast is in the time zone UTC+3.

HISTORY

Voronezh city was founded in 1586 as a fortress. The centre of a fertile region, the city began to industrialize in the tsarist period. Voronezh Oblast was formed in June 1934.

Ivan Shabonov of the KPRF was elected Governor in 1996. At an election held in December 2000 he was defeated by Vladimir Kulakov, a Federal Security Service (FSB) general; he was re-elected in 2004.

On 12 March 2009 Aleksei Gordeyev, hitherto the federal Minister of Agriculture, assumed office as Governor, following his endorsement by the Regional Duma. He was elected Governor by popular vote in September 2014. YeR obtained 73.8% of the votes cast on the basis of proportional representation in elections to the Regional Duma held in September 2015, representing a substantial increase in support. Following Gordeyev's appointment, in December 2017, as Presidential Representative to the Central Federal Okrug, he was succeeded as Governor, initially in an acting capacity, by the erstwhile Mayor of Voronezh, Aleksandr Gusev, who was elected to the post on 9 September 2018 with 72.5% of the vote.

In elections to the Regional Duma, held on 13 September 2020, support for YeR declined to 61.5% of the votes cast on a proportional basis. The KPRF was second, with 14.5%. Some 47 of the 54 deputies had joined the YeR faction by late December.

Following Russia's invasion of Ukraine on 24 February 2022, the oblast authorities declared a high level of 'terrorist threat' in two border districts. Later that month Gusev reported that a surveillance drone had been destroyed by the air defence system near Voronezh. The threat level was lifted in May. On 19 October President Putin declared a 'medium level of response' in Voronezh Oblast and seven other territories bordering Russian-occupied parts of Ukraine, in which martial law was imposed. In November FSB officers shot dead three alleged Ukrainian saboteurs reportedly planning to attack energy facilities in the region; local media outlets later reported that the suspects were video game players who had been mistakenly identified as Ukrainian agents.

In early June 2023 Gusev announced that a drone attack had damaged a residential building in Voronezh, injuring three people. After the state-funded paramilitary Wagner Group launched a mutiny from Rostov-on-Don, in the Southern Federal Okrug, on 23 June, a convoy of its forces advanced through Voronezh Oblast, where they were attacked by federal military helicopters. During the clashes a missile struck an oil depot in Voronezh, causing a fire, and it was reported that Wagner combatants had seized control of military facilities in the city. Following a negotiated agreement with the head of the Wagner Group, Yevgenii Prigozhin (who was killed in August), on 25 June Wagner forces began a complete withdrawal from the Oblast, prior to their relocation to Belarus at the invitation of that country's President, Alyaksandr Lukashenka.

On 10 September 2023 Gusev, the candidate of YeR, was re-elected Governor with 76.8% of the votes cast, defeating four other candidates. In December saboteurs associated with a Ukrainian-based anti-Putin organization, the Legion 'Svoboda Rossii' (Freedom to Russia Legion), claimed responsibility for the destruction of a fuel depot owned by the state–owned oil company Rosneft in the Oblast.

ECONOMY

In 2021 Voronezh Oblast's gross regional product (GRP) amounted to 1,254,722m. roubles, equivalent to 546,329 roubles per head. The important industrial centres in the Oblast are at Voronezh, Borisoglebsk and Rossosh. At the end of 2021 the territory contained 1,194 km of railway track.

Agriculture consists mainly of the production of grain, sugar beet, sunflower seeds, potatoes and vegetables. Animal husbandry is important. Agriculture employed 11.4% of the workforce and contributed 16.3% of GRP in 2021. The main industries are mechanical engineering, metal working, chemicals and petrochemicals, electricity production, the manufacture of building materials, and food processing. Industry employed 25.0% of the workforce and contributed 27.1% of GRP in 2021, when manufacturing employed 13.7% of the workforce and contributed 17.7% of GRP.

The economically active population numbered 1,145,403 in 2022, when 3.5% of the labour force were unemployed, while the average monthly wage was 46,277 roubles. There was a budgetary surplus of 22,066.6m. roubles in 2021, when export trade amounted to US $1,509m. (of which 46.8% was with countries of the CIS), and import trade to $1,221m. (of which 22.5% was with CIS countries).

DIRECTORY

Governor: ALEKSANDR V. GUSEV.

Office of the Governor: 394018 Voronezh, pl. Lenina 1; tel. (473) 212-66-04; e-mail reference@govvrn.ru; internet govvrn.ru.

Regional Duma: 394018 Voronezh, ul. Kirova 2; tel. (473) 277-93-13; fax (473) 252-09-22; e-mail postoffice@vrnoblduma.ru; internet vrnoblduma.ru; Chair. VLADIMIR I. NETYOSOV.

State Duma Representatives (4): ARKADII N. PONOMAROV (YeR), SERGEI V. CHIZHOV (YeR), ANDREI P. MARKOV (YeR), ALEKSEI V. GORDEYEV (YeR).

Federation Council Representatives: SERGEI N. LUKIN, GALINA N. KARELOVA.

Yaroslavl Oblast

Yaroslavl Oblast is situated in the Eastern European Plain. It borders six oblasts: Ivanovo (to the south-east); Vladimir and Moscow (south); Tver (west); Vologda (north); and Kostroma (east). It covers 36,177 sq km (13,968 sq miles). At January 2023 the Oblast's population was an estimated 1,194,605 and the population density 33.0 per sq km. Some 81.0% of the population was urban in 2023. The Oblast's administrative centre, Yaroslavl, had an estimated 570,824 inhabitants at January 2023. The second largest city is Rybinsk (173,910). Of residents who stated their ethnicity at the 2021 census, 96.5% were Russian. Yaroslavl Oblast is in the time zone UTC+3.

HISTORY

Yaroslavl city was founded in c. 1024. The Muscovite state acquired the region during the reign of Ivan III (1462–1505). The Oblast was formed in March 1936.

In 1995 Anatolii Lisitsyn, the incumbent Governor, was elected to the post. He was re-elected in 1999 and 2003, and in 2006 the Regional Duma approved his nomination to a further term. In December 2007 Lisitsyn resigned. Shortly afterwards, the Regional Duma confirmed the appointment of Sergei Vakhrukov, the Oblast's former representative in the Federation Council, as Governor. In May 2012, following Vakhrukov's resignation, the Regional Duma endorsed the appointment of the erstwhile First Deputy Mayor of Yaroslavl, Sergei Yastrebov, as Governor.

President Vladimir Putin dismissed Yastrebov in July 2016, appointing former federal deputy interior minister Dmitrii Mironov as his acting successor. On 10 September 2017 Mironov was elected Governor, receiving 79.3% of the votes cast. In elections to the Regional Duma, held on 9 September 2018, YeR won 38.4% of the votes cast to seats elected by proportional representation (reflecting the relative lack of support for the party in the region), ahead of the KPRF, with 24.0%. By the end of the year 32 of the 50 deputies had joined the YeR parliamentary faction.

On 12 October 2021 Putin appointed Mironov as a presidential aide; he was succeeded as acting Governor, pending an election, by Mikhail Yevrayev, a former federal deputy minister and member of Yabloko. On 11 September 2022 Yevrayev, contesting the poll as an independent candidate, was overwhelmingly elected as Governor, with 82.3% of the votes cast, defeating Mikhail Paramonov of the KPRF (who obtained 6.1%) and three others.

Following elections to the Legislative Assembly held on 10 September 2023, YeR held 38 of the 46 seats in a smaller chamber, although the rate of participation was only 27.4%.

ECONOMY

In 2021 Yaroslavl Oblast's gross regional product (GRP) amounted to 690,253m. roubles, equivalent to 559,180 roubles per head. The major industrial centres are at Yaroslavl, Rybinsk and Pereslavl-Zalesskii. There are river-ports at Yaroslavl, Rybinsk and Uglich. At the end of 2021 there were 652 km of railways in the region.

Agriculture, which employed 6.7% of the workforce and contributed 4.0% of GRP in 2021, comprises the production of vegetables, fruit and flax, and animal husbandry. The main industries are mechanical engineering, chemicals and petrochemicals, petroleum refining, peat production and the production of electricity. Industry employed 30.9% of the workforce and contributed 36.5% of GRP in 2021, when manufacturing employed 20.6% of the workforce and contributed 27.9% of GRP.

The economically active population numbered 610,720 in 2022, when the rate of unemployment was 5.0%, while the average monthly wage was 47,388 roubles. There was a budgetary surplus of 4,247.2m. roubles in 2021. In that year export trade amounted to US $1,134m. (of which 27.8% was with countries of the CIS), while import trade amounted to $855m. (of which 10.1% was with CIS countries).

DIRECTORY

Governor: MIKHAIL YA. YEVRAYEV.

Office of the Governor: 150000 Yaroslavl, Sovetskaya pl. 3; tel. (4852) 72-81-28; fax (4852) 73-05-65; e-mail gubern@adm.yar.ru; internet yarregion.ru.

Regional Duma: 150000 Yaroslavl, Sovetskaya pl. 1/19; tel. (4852) 40-18-13; fax (4852) 32-77-75; e-mail duma@duma.yar.ru; internet yarduma.ru; Chair. MIKHAIL V. BOROVITSKII.

State Duma Representatives (2): ANATOLII I. LISITSYN (SR), ANATOLII N. GRESHNEVIKOV (SR).

Federation Council Representatives: NATALIYA V. KOSIKHINA, ALEKSANDR I. RUSAKOV.

NORTH-WESTERN FEDERAL OKRUG

Presidential Representative to the North-Western Federal Okrug: ALEKSANDR V. GUTSAN, 199004 St Petersburg, Vasilyevskii ostrov, 3-ya liniya 12; tel. (812) 323-07-74; internet szfo.gov.ru.

St Petersburg City

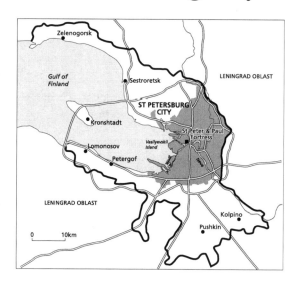

St Petersburg (Sankt-Peterburg) is a seaport at the mouth of the River Neva, which drains into the Gulf of Finland, in the Baltic Sea. The territory, including 42 islands, occupies an area of 1,439 sq km (556 sq miles). According to official estimates, at January 2023 the city's population was 5,600,044 (all of which was urban) and the population density 3,891.6 per sq km. Of residents who stated their ethnicity at the 2021 census, 90.6% were Russian. St Petersburg is in the time zone UTC+3.

HISTORY

St Petersburg was founded by Tsar Peter (Pyotr) I 'the Great' in 1703, becoming the Russian capital in 1712. In 1914 the city was renamed Petrograd. Following the Bolshevik Revolution, in 1918 Moscow became the capital. Troops led by Trotskii (Lev Bronstein) quashed a revolt at the naval base of Kronshtadt in 1921. German troops besieged the city (renamed Leningrad in 1924) between November 1941 and January 1944.

In June 1991 a reformist, Anatolii Sobchak, was elected Mayor; in October the city name reverted to St Petersburg. In 1994–96 the future President, Vladimir Putin, was

First Deputy Chairman of the City Government. A liberal, Vladimir Yakovlev, was elected to the renamed post of Governor in 1996 and 2000.

In June 2003 Putin appointed Yakovlev as a Deputy Chairman of the federal Government. In the subsequent gubernatorial election, Valentina Matviyenko, the Presidential Representative to the North-Western Federal Okrug, despite obtaining the support of Putin, YeR, the pro-market SPS, Yabloko and the KPRF, as well as of Yakovlev, was only elected after two rounds of voting. The rate of participation in both rounds was less than 30%. In 2006 the Legislative Assembly endorsed Matviyenko's nomination to a second term.

In August 2011 Matviyenko resigned as Governor, shortly afterwards becoming a member (and subsequently Chairman) of the Federation Council, the upper chamber of the federal parliament. Her successor, Georgii Poltavchenko, hitherto the Presidential Representative to the Central Federal Okrug, as Governor was appointed later that month and was elected to the post by popular vote in September 2014.

On 3 April 2017 a bomb attack on the St Petersburg Metro, which coincided with a visit by President Putin to the city, killed 16 people; an Islamist group connected with the al-Qa'ida network subsequently claimed responsibility for the attack.

On 3 October 2018 Putin dismissed Poltavchenko as Governor, appointing Aleksandr Beglov, hitherto Presidential Representative to the North-Western Federal Okrug, as his acting successor. On 8 September 2019 Beglov, who, despite his longstanding membership of YeR, contested the election as an independent, was elected Governor, winning 64.4% of the vote.

Beglov introduced initial measures intended to curb the spread of the pandemic of COVID-19, largely comprising restrictions on travel, on 13 March 2020. He ordered the closure of public facilities from 28 March, and banned gatherings of more than 50 people. The lockdown restrictions were gradually lifted from June. After a resurgence in COVID-19 infections, Beglov introduced renewed restrictions in December. In November 2021 vaccination against COVID-19 was mandated for all residents of St Petersburg aged over 60 years and with certain illnesses.

Meanwhile, at elections to the Legislative Assembly held on 19 September 2021, YeR secured 33.3% of the votes cast on a proportional basis, while the KPRF obtained 17.5% of the vote, SR 12.7%, the recently formed centre-right NL 10.1%, Yabloko 9.2% and the LDPR 7.9%. By the end of the year 30 of the 50 deputies had joined the YeR faction, seven that of the KPRF, five that of SR, three that of the LDPR, three that of NL, and two that of Yabloko.

Following Russia's invasion of Ukraine on 24 February 2022, the annual St Petersburg International Economic Forum in June took place with reduced international participation; it was officially opened by Governor Beglov and the Head of the Russian-allied 'Donetsk People's Republic' in eastern Ukraine (which Russia later annexed), Denis Pushilin, and was addressed by President Putin. Beglov became a vocal supporter of Russia's war in Ukraine. In late May St Petersburg officially adopted the Ukrainian port city of Mariupol, which had been largely destroyed by Russian forces before they captured it, as a 'sister city', together with a programme to assist in its reconstruction. Beglov visited Mariupol in early June, signing an agreement with its Russian-installed Mayor. An order by Putin, issued on 21 September, for the partial mobilization of military reservists precipitated small-scale protests in major cities nationwide; at least 480 arrests were reported in St Petersburg on that day.

In late 2022 an intensifying dispute was reported between Beglov and a controversial businessman born in the city, Yevgenii Prigozhin, who was linked to President

Putin and had founded a private paramilitary organization known as the Wagner Group that operated internationally (notably in Africa) in support of Russian interests. Prigozhin accused the Office of the Governor of repeatedly obstructing infrastructure and development projects he sought to implement in St Petersburg, and in October submitted a criminal complaint to the federal Office of the Prosecutor-General demanding that Beglov be investigated for corruption. Following delays in obtaining a permit, in December a business centre funded by Prigozhin was opened in the city and renamed the PMC Wagner Center, becoming the first official headquarters of the organization. In the same month a student was arrested and charged with discrediting the Russian armed forces, after she allegedly wrote an anti-war comment on an installation symbolizing the 'friendship' between St Petersburg and Mariupol. Following the development of the Levashovo military airfield located in the north of St Petersburg, on 27 December it was officially opened as a new airport, providing services for both military and civil aircraft. In January 2023 a prominent Yabloko deputy in the Legislative Assembly, Boris Vishnevskii, and his deputy were charged with discrediting the Russian army, after signing an open letter demanding an investigation into a massacre of civilians that took place in Ukraine in March 2022.

On 2 April 2023 a prominent pro-war blogger known as Vladlen Tatarskii was killed in a bomb explosion in a cafe in St Petersburg; at least 24 other people were injured. A main suspect was arrested on terrorism charges on the following day.

As the antagonism between Prigozhin and Beglov continued, in early April 2023 Prigozhin again urged the Prosecutor-General to initiate a criminal investigation against the Governor, accusing him of responsibility for the neglect of more than 850 culturally significant monuments in St Petersburg. After leading an abortive insurrection by Wagner Group personnel on 23 June, Prigozhin fled to Belarus under a negotiated agreement with the Russian Government. However, he subsequently returned to St Petersburg, attending a two-day Russia-Africa summit hosted in the city in late July. Prigozhin was killed when an plane travelling from Moscow to St Petersburg crashed under unclear circumstances on 23 August, and the Wagner Group effectively ceased to exist.

ECONOMY

In 2021 St Petersburg's gross regional product (GRP) amounted to 9,440,411m. roubles, or 1,754,423 roubles per head. At the end of 2021 there were 432 km of railway lines in the city. The metro system includes five lines and 72 stations and extended 125 km in 2022.

There is a small agricultural sector, employing 0.6% of the workforce and contributing 0.1% of GRP in 2021. Industry consists mainly of mechanical engineering, metal working and food processing. Other important areas are ferrous and non-ferrous metallurgy, electricity generation, the manufacture of chemicals and petrochemicals, rubber production, light manufacturing, the manufacture of building materials, timber processing and printing. There is also a significant defence sector industry. General Motors of the USA opened an automobile factory in the city in 2008, the first such project in Russia that was not part of a joint venture with a Russian company. The plant suspended operations in July 2015 and was sold to Hyundai of the Republic of Korea in 2020. An automobile factory, belonging to Nissan of Japan, was opened in 2009, and produced 56,000 vehicles in 2018, while another factory belonging to Hyundai opened in 2010; it produced 235,000 vehicles in 2018. Both the Nissan and Hyundai plants suspended operations in March 2022, following the Russian invasion of Ukraine. In late 2022 Hyundai announced a programme of redundancies at the plant, which had not resumed operations, while it was announced that all Russian assets of Nissan were effectively to be nationalized by their transfer to the state-owned AvtoVAZ company. In December 2023 Hyundai accounced that it was to sell its plant to the US-based Art-Finance Partners company. Industry employed 26.8% of the workforce and contributed 14.8% of GRP in 2021. Manufacturing employed 14.6.3% of the workforce and contributed 10.6% of GRP in 2021. The city is an important centre for service industries, such as tourism, financial services and leisure activities.

The economically active population amounted to 3,038,524 in 2022, when 1.8% of the workforce were unemployed, the lowest rate in the Federation, while the average monthly wage was 86,630 roubles. There was a budgetary surplus of 46,327.9m. roubles in 2021, when export trade amounted to US $29,910 m. (of which 12.4% was with countries of the CIS), and import trade to $26,625m. (of which only 6.0% was with CIS countries).

DIRECTORY

Governor: ALEKSANDR D. BEGLOV.

Office of the Governor: 191060 St Petersburg, Smolnyi; tel. (812) 576-45-01; fax (812) 576-78-27; e-mail gubernator@gov.spb.ru; internet gov.spb.ru.

Legislative Assembly: 190107 St Petersburg, Isaakiyevskaya pl. 6; tel. (812) 310-00-00; fax (812) 570-30-01; e-mail vtulpanov@assembly.spb.ru; internet assembly.spb.ru; Chair. ALEKSANDR N. BELSKII.

State Duma Representatives (8): MIKHAIL V. ROMANOV (YeR), ALEKSANDR P. TETERDINKO (YeR), YEVGENII YE. MARCHENKO (non-faction), YELENA G. DRAPENKO (SR), NIKOLAI G. TSED (YeR), SERGEI A. SOLOVYEV (YeR), OKSANA G. DMITRIYEVA (non-faction), VITALII V. MILONOV (YeR).

Federation Council Representatives: VALENTINA I. MATVIYENKO, ANDREI V. KUTEPOV.

Republic of Kareliya

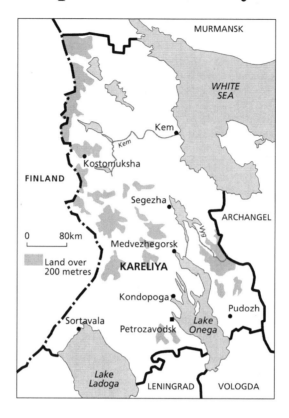

The Republic of Kareliya is situated in the north-west of Russia. It is bordered by Finland to the west and by Murmansk Oblast to the north, and the White Sea to the north-east. The Oblasts of Archangel, Vologda and Leningrad lie to the east, south-east and south, respectively. Kareliya contains some 83,000 km (51,540 miles) of waterways. The Ladoga and the Onega are the largest and second largest lakes in Europe, respectively. The 225-km White Sea–Baltic Canal connects the port of Belomorsk to St Petersburg. Kareliya occupies 180,520 sq km (69,699 sq miles). At January 2023 it had an estimated population of 527,880 and a population density of 2.9 per sq km. Some 79.7% of the population was urban in 2023. The capital is Petrozavodsk, with an estimated 235,793 inhabitants at January 2023. Of residents who stated their ethnicity at the 2021 census, 86.4% were Russian, 5.5% were Kareliyan, 2.0% were Belarusian, 1.2% were Ukrainian, and 0.7% were Finnish. The dominant religion is Orthodox Christianity. The Kareliyan language comprises three dialects of Finnish—Livvi, Karjala and Lyydiki. Kareliya is in the time zone UTC+3.

HISTORY

Kareliya was formerly an independent, Finnish-dominated state. In the 16th century the area came under Swedish hegemony. It was annexed by Russia in 1721 and became an Autonomous Soviet Socialist Republic (ASSR) within the Russian Soviet Federative Socialist Republic (RSFSR) in 1923. A Karelo-Finnish Soviet Socialist Republic, including territory annexed from Finland, was created in 1940. Some territory was ceded to the RSFSR in 1946, and in 1956 Kareliya resumed the status of an ASSR within the RSFSR.

The Republic declared sovereignty on 9 August 1990. Following the adoption of a Constitution, in 1994 elections took place to a bicameral Legislative Assembly. In 1998 the Mayor of Petrozavodsk, Sergei Katanandov, defeated Viktor Stepanov, the incumbent, in popular elections to the premiership (Head of the Republic). In 2001 the Constitution was amended, to establish an executive presidency and a unicameral legislature. Katanandov was elected to the reconstituted post of Head of the Republic in 2002, and was reappointed in 2006.

In June 2010 Katanandov resigned as Head of the Republic; his successor was Andrei Nelidov, formerly a representative of Kareliya in the Federation Council, the upper chamber of the federal legislature. At elections to the Legislative Assembly held in December 2011, YeR obtained only 30.1% of the votes cast on a proportional basis; SR, the KPRF and the LDPR each obtained between 18% and 23%, and YeR lacked a majority in the Assembly.

Nelidov resigned as Head of the Republic in May 2012. Shortly afterwards the Legislative Assembly voted to endorse the appointment of the recently appointed Chairman of the Legislative Assembly of Leningrad Oblast, Aleksandr Khudilainen, as his successor.

In February 2016 President Putin reprimanded Khudilainen in connection with his failure to implement a federal programme on the resettlement of citizens from dilapidated housing; the Republic's authorities were fined 133m. roubles. On 21 April the Legislative Assembly approved the appointment of Oleg Telnov, previously the First Deputy Head of the Republic, to the reinstated post of Prime Minister.

YeR secured 33.2% of the votes cast on a proportional basis in elections to the Legislative Assembly held on 18 September 2016; the LDPR obtained 18.9%, SR 15.5%, the KPRF 14.4% and Yabloko 9.9%. Some 23 of the 35 deputies had joined the YeR parliamentary faction by the end of the year.

On 15 February 2017 Khudilainen resigned as Head of the Republic. Putin appointed Artur Parfenchikov, hitherto a federal judicial official, as his acting successor. In March Aleksandr Chepik, formerly a banking official, succeeded Telnov as Prime Minister. On 10 September Parfenchikov was elected Governor, receiving 61.3% of the votes cast; the SR candidate, Irina Petelyayeva, was second, with 18.1%.

At elections to the republican Legislative Assembly held on 19 September 2021, YeR secured only 29.0% of the votes cast on the basis of proportional representation, narrowly ahead of the KPRF, with 16.9%; SR obtained 12.8%, the LDPR 9.9%, Yabloko 8.5%, the recently established centre-right NL 6.4%, and the RPPS 5.6%. By the end of the year 22 of the 36 deputies had joined the YeR faction, four that of SR, four that of the KPRF, two that of the LDPR, and two that of Yabloko. The factions of NL and the RPPS each comprised one deputy.

Parfenchikov was re-elected as Governor on 11 September 2022, with 69.2% of the votes cast, defeating Andrei Rogalevich of SR (who obtained 13.4% of the votes), Yevgenii Ulyanov of the KPRF (12.6%) and two other candidates.

ECONOMY

In 2021 Kareliya's gross regional product (GRP) was 447,147m. roubles, equivalent to 737,782 roubles per head. Its major industrial centres include Petrozavodsk, Sortavala and Kem. At the end of 2021 there were 2,226 km of railway lines in the Republic. Kareliya's main port is at Petrozavodsk.

The economy is largely based on the timber industry, and the Republic is a leading Russian producer of rosin and turpentine. Agriculture (including forestry) employed 4.8% of the workforce and contributed 5.5% of GRP in 2021. The Republic has important mineral reserves. The main industries, apart from the processing of forestry products, are food processing, ferrous metallurgy, the production of electrical energy, and the extraction of iron ore and muscovite (mica). The Republic's major enterprise, the Segezha Pulp and Paper Mill, is one of the world's largest pulp and paper manufacturers. Industry employed 27.7% of the workforce and contributed 52.1% of GRP in 2021, when manufacturing employed 12.3% of the workforce and contributed 15.2% of GRP.

The economically active population amounted to 276,356 in 2022, when the rate of unemployment was 5.8%, while the average monthly wage was 56,458 roubles. There was a budgetary surplus of 3,509.2m. roubles in 2021, when export trade amounted to US $1,232m. (of which 4.5% was with countries of the CIS), and import trade to $405m. (of which 19.9% was with CIS countries).

DIRECTORY

Head of the Republic: Artur O. Parfenchikov.

First Deputy Head of the Republic, Prime Minister: Aleksandr Ye. Chepik.

Office of the Government: 185028 Kareliya, Petrozavodsk, pr. Lenina 19; tel. (8142) 79-93-09; fax (8142) 79-93-91; e-mail government@karelia.ru; internet gov.karelia.ru.

Legislative Assembly: 185910 Kareliya, Petrozavodsk, ul. Kuibysheva 5; tel. (8142) 79-00-04; fax (8142) 79-69-69; e-mail inbox@zsrk.onego.ru; internet karelia-zs.ru; Chair. Elissan V. Shandalovich.

State Duma Representative (1): Valentina N. Pivnenko (YeR).

Federation Council Representatives: Igor D. Zubarev, Vladimir A. Chizhov.

Republic of Komi

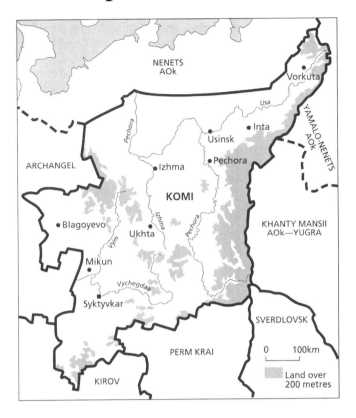

The Republic of Komi is situated in the north-east of European Russia. Mountains of the Northern, Circumpolar and Polar Urals occupy the eastern part of the Republic. Its major rivers are the Pechora and the Vychegda. Komi is bordered to the north and west by Archangel Oblast (including the Nenets Autonomous Okrug), and to the east by Tyumen Oblast (including the Khanty-Mansii Autonomous Okrug—Yugra and the Yamalo-Nenets Autonomous Okrug). To the south there are borders with Kirov Oblast, Perm Krai and Sverdlovsk Oblast. Some 90% of the territory is taiga (forested marshland), while the extreme north-east of the Republic is Arctic tundra. The Republic occupies an area of 416,774 sq km (160,917 sq miles). At January 2023 it had an estimated population of 726,434 and a population density of 1.7 per sq km. Some 77.7% of the population was urban in 2023. Komi's capital is Syktyvkar, with an estimated 220,042 inhabitants at January 2023. Of residents who stated their ethnicity at the 2021 census, 69.7% were Russian, 22.1% were Komi (including 0.8% who were Izhma Komi), 1.9% were Ukrainian, and 0.7% were Tatar. The predominant religion in the region is Orthodox Christianity, although among the Komi this faith is combined with strong animist traditions. The language of the Komi population belongs to the Finnic branch of the Uralo-Altaic family. The Republic of Komi is in the time zone UTC+3.

HISTORY

The Komi (known historically as the Zyryans or the Permyaks) are descended from inhabitants of the Volga, Kama, Pechora and Vychegda river basins. From the 12th century Russian settlers began to inhabit territory along the Vychegda and Vym rivers. The Vym subsequently acquired a strategic significance as the main route of the Russian advance to Siberia. The city of Ust-Sysolsk (now Syktyvkar) was founded in 1586, the territory having been annexed in 1478. The region acquired importance as a centre of mining and metallurgy after the discovery of copper and silver ores. In 1697 petroleum was discovered in the region, and a primitive refinery was constructed in 1745. The Komi Autonomous Oblast, established in 1921, became an Autonomous Soviet Socialist Republic in 1931.

The territory declared its sovereignty in August 1990. A Constitution adopted in February 1994 established a quasi-presidential premiership and a new legislature, the State Council. Vladimir Torlopov, hitherto Chairman of the republican legislature, was elected republican President in 2001 with the support of the liberal Yabloko party, narrowly defeating the incumbent, Yurii Spiridonov. In December 2005 the State Council approved Torlopov's appointment to a further term of office.

In January 2010 the State Council approved the nomination of a former banker and the erstwhile First Deputy Head of the Republic, Vyacheslav Gaizer, as Head of the Republic. In September 2014 he was directly elected to a new term of office. Shortly afterwards, Gaizer appointed Vladimir Tukmakov as premier. In elections to the State Council held in September 2015, YeR obtained 58.1% of the votes cast on a proportional basis; 26 of the 30 deputies joined the YeR legislative faction when the State Council convened.

In September 2015 Gaizer and 18 associates were arrested on charges of involvement in large-scale criminal activity, including fraud. (In June 2019 Gaizer was sentenced to 11 years' detention and fined 160,000m. roubles.) President Vladimir Putin dismissed Gaizer as Head of the Republic on 30 September 2015, appointing Sergei Gaplikov, a former premier of the Chuvash Republic, as his acting successor. On 10 March 2016 Gaplikov dismissed Tukmakov's Government, after investigations concluded that Tukmakov had undeclared income of 5m. roubles, and had implicated him and other senior officials in substantial bribe taking. Later in March Gaplikov additionally assumed the responsibilities of Chairman of the Government, that post effectively being abolished. Gaplikov was elected Head of the Republic by 62.2% of the votes cast in an election held on 18 September.

In June 2019 some 5,300 people attended a KPRF-led rally in Syktyvkar, in protest against the construction of a major site for municipal waste from Moscow City in Shiyes, Archangel Oblast, 100km north-west of Syktyvkar. Construction of the site was subsequently abandoned.

On 2 April 2020 President Putin accepted the resignation of Gaplikov, following reports that an outbreak of COVID-19 at a hospital in Syktyvkar had been spread by an infected medical worker. On the same day Putin appointed Vladimir Uiba, federal Deputy Minister of Health since January, as Acting Head of the Republic. On 13 September Uiba was elected as Head of the Republic with 73.2% of the votes cast. In concurrent polls to the State Council, support for YeR, as measured by its share of the proportional vote, decreased substantially, to 28.6%. The KPRF was second, with 14.8%, ahead of the LDPR, with 14.5%, the Zelyonaya Alternativa (Green Alternative), with 10.0%, Rodina (Motherland), with 9.8%, and SR, with 8.6%. By late

December 20 deputies had joined the YeR faction, four that of the KPRF, and three that of the LDPR.

ECONOMY

In 2021 Komi's gross regional product (GRP) was 857,013m. roubles, equivalent to 1,059,960 roubles per head. Komi's major industrial centres are at Syktyvkar, Ukhta and Sosnogorsk. At the end of 2021 the Republic contained 1,690 km of railway lines.

Komi's agriculture consists principally of animal husbandry, especially reindeer breeding. Agriculture employed 4.3% of the workforce and contributed 1.6% of GRP in 2021. Industry is based on the production and processing of petroleum and natural gas, the production of coal and electrical energy, and the processing of forestry products. The Republic contains the Vorgashorskaya coal mine, one of the largest in Europe; additionally, two new coal mines opened in the 2010s. Ore mining has been developed since the 1990s: Komi contains Russia's largest reserves of bauxite, titanium, manganese and chromium ore, and also has significant reserves of petroleum and natural gas. Industry employed 26.9% of the workforce and contributed 64.7% of GRP in 2021, when manufacturing employed 8.7% of the workforce and contributed 9.8% of GRP.

The economically active population numbered 374,044 in 2022, when the rate of unemployment was 6.7%, while the average monthly wage was 68,790 roubles. There was a budgetary surplus of 2,681.3m. roubles in 2021, when export trade amounted to US $1,281 m. (of which 11.8% was with countries of the CIS), and import trade to $129m. (of which 7.1% was with CIS countries).

DIRECTORY

Head of the Republic: VLADIMIR V. UIBA.

Office of the Head of the Republic: 167000 Komi, Syktyvkar, ul. Kommunisticheskaya 9; tel. (8212) 28-51-05; fax (8212) 21-43-84; e-mail glava@rkomi.ru; internet rkomi.ru.

State Council: 167000 Komi, Syktyvkar, ul. Kommunisticheskaya 8; tel. (8212) 28-55-28; fax (8212) 24-44-90; e-mail gossovet@gs.rkomi.ru; internet gsrk.ru; Chair. SERGEI A. USACHYOV.

State Duma Representative (1): OLEG A. MIKHAILOV (KPRF).

Federation Council Representatives: OLGA N. YEPIFINOVA, YELENA B. SHUMILOVA.

Archangel Oblast

Archangel Oblast is situated in the north of the Eastern European Plain. It lies on the White, Barents and Kara Seas (parts of the Arctic Ocean) and includes the northern archipelago of Franz-Josef Land and the Novaya Zemlya islands. In the east the Nenets Autonomous Okrug, a constituent part of the Oblast, runs along the coast to end in a border with the Yamalo-Nenets Autonomous Okrug (within Tyumen Oblast). Komi lies to the east of the Oblast. Kirov and Vologda Oblasts to the south, and Kareliya to the west. The Kola Peninsula and Murmansk Oblast lie north-west, across the White Sea, while to the north there is access to the Barents Sea. The Oblast contains several large rivers, including the Onega, the Severnaya Dvina and the Pechora, and some 2,500 lakes. Around 40% of its area is forested and almost 25% is reindeer pasture. The Oblast occupies an area of 589,913 sq km (227,767 sq miles). It spans three climatic zones: arctic, sub-arctic and continental. At January 2023 the population was an estimated 1,005,687 and the population density 1.7 per sq km. Some 77.7% of the population was urban in 2023. The administrative centre is Archangel (Arkhangelsk), with an estimated 298,617 inhabitants at January 2023. The Oblast's second city is Severodvinsk (156,056). Of residents who stated their ethnicity at the 2021 census,

96.2% were Russian, and 0.8% were Nenets (over 95% of whom lived in the Nenets Autonomous Oblast). Archangel Oblast is in the time zone UTC+3.

HISTORY

The city of Archangel was founded in the 16th century to further Muscovite trade. It was the first Russian seaport. The port played a major role in the attack by the British and French navies against the Red Army in 1918, and was an important supply route for the Allied Powers during the Second World War. Archangel Oblast was founded on 23 September 1937.

On 13 October 1993 the regional Soviet transferred its responsibilities to the regional administration. Communist candidates initially formed the largest single group elected to the Regional Assembly of Deputies. The regional Governor appointed in September 1991, Pavel Balakshin, was dismissed in February 1996, after an inquiry into alleged corruption was opened against him. Anatolii Yefremov, previously a regional official, was confirmed as Governor in a popular election in 1996; he was re-elected in 2000 but was defeated in an election in 2004 by dairy owner Nikolai Kiselyov.

In March 2008 the Regional Assembly of Deputies voted to confirm President Vladimir Putin's nomination of Ilya Mikhalchuk, the former Mayor of Yakutsk in Sakha (Yakutiya), in the Russian Far East, to succeed Kiselyov as Governor. President Dmitrii Medvedev removed Mikhalchuk from office in January 2012, appointing the former director-general of a shipyard in Kaliningrad, Igor Orlov, as Acting Governor.

YeR was placed first, with 40.7% of the proportional vote, in elections to the Regional Assembly of Deputies in September 2013; the KPRF, the LDPR and SR each obtained more than 10%, but 45 of the 60 deputies subsequently joined the YeR legislative faction. On 13 September 2015 Orlov was elected Governor, winning 53.3% of the popular vote; his nearest rival was Olga Ositsyna of the LDPR, with 19.2%.

In elections to a smaller Regional Assembly of Deputies, held on 9 September 2018, YeR won only 31.6% of the proportional vote. The LDPR was second, with 23.5%, ahead of the KPRF, with 18.8%, and SR, with 15.1%. By the end of the year 25 of the 47 deputies had joined the YeR parliamentary faction, nine that of the LDPR, seven that of the KPRF, and five that of SR.

On 2 April 2020 Orlov, who had become increasingly unpopular with the electorate, tendered his resignation. Putin appointed Aleksandr Tsybulskii, hitherto the Governor of the Nenets Autonomous Okrug, to replace him in an acting capacity. On 13 May Tsybulskii and the new Acting Governor of the Nenets Autonomous Okrug, Yurii Bezdudnyi, signed a memorandum of intent on the merger of the two regions into a single federal subject in order to strengthen the response to a severe regional economic crisis. However, the proposal that a referendum on the planned unification be conducted in September was met with protests in the Nenets Autonomous Okrug. Later in May the referendum was postponed, and in July the proposals were abandoned.

On 13 September 2020 Tsybulskii was elected as Governor, receiving 69.6% of the votes cast; he was inaugurated to office on 8 October. Following elections to the Legislative Assembly held on 10 September 2023, YeR held 36 of the 47 seats in the expanded chamber, substantially increasing its representation there, although the rate of participation was only 28.1%.

ECONOMY

All figures in this survey incorporate data for the Nenets Autonomous Okrug, which is also treated separately. Archangel Oblast's gross regional product (GRP) amounted to 1,055,421m. roubles, or 941,763 roubles per head, in 2021. The Oblast's main industrial centres are at Archangel, Severodvinsk, Novodvinsk and, in the south-east, Kotlas. At the end of 2021 there were 1,767 km of railways in the Oblast. Its main ports are Archangel, Onega, Mezen and, in the Nenets Autonomous Okrug, Naryan-Mar.

Agriculture consists mainly of potato and vegetable production, animal husbandry (livestock and reindeer) and hunting. Agriculture employed 4.7% of the workforce and contributed 3.8% of GRP in 2021. Industry is based on timber, timber processing and wood working, and petroleum and natural gas production. Other important areas include the extraction of minerals (in particular, bauxite), electrical energy, mechanical engineering and metal working, and the processing of fish products. Diamonds are also mined in the Oblast, although legal disputes have inhibited the growth of the sector. Industry employed 29.4% of the workforce and contributed 59.3% of GRP in 2021, when manufacturing employed 17.5% of the workforce and contributed 16.9% of GRP.

The Oblast's economically active population numbered 516,491 in 2022, when the rate of unemployment was 5.6%, while the average monthly wage was 67,835 roubles. There was a budgetary deficit of 4,306.5m. roubles in 2021. Export trade amounted to US $3,207m. in that year (of which 4.5% was with countries of the CIS), while import trade amounted to $374m. (of which 3.3% was with CIS countries).

DIRECTORY

Governor: ALEKSANDR V. TSYBULSKII.

Office of the Governor: 163004 Archangel, pr. Troitskii 49; tel. (8182) 28-81-01; e-mail webmaster@dvinaland.ru; internet dvinaland.ru.

Regional Assembly of Deputies: 163000 Archangel, pl. Lenina 1; tel. (8182) 21-56-13; fax (8182) 20-03-43; e-mail duma@aosd.ru; internet aosd.ru; Chair. YEKATERINA V. PROKOPYEVA.

State Duma Representatives (2): ALEKSANDR YU. SPIRIDONOV (YeR), YELENA A. VTORYGINA (YeR).

Federation Council Representatives: ALEKSANDR N. NEKRASOV, IVAN V. NOVIKOV.

Kaliningrad Oblast

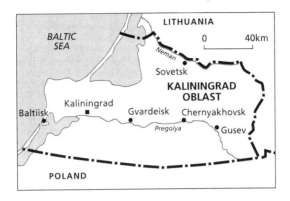

Kaliningrad Oblast is a Russian exclave on the Baltic coast with land borders with Lithuania to the north and east and Poland to the south. The city of Kaliningrad is sited at the mouth of the River Pregolya, where it flows into the Vistula Lagoon, an inlet of the Baltic Sea. The other main river is the Neman. The Oblast occupies 15,125 sq km (5,840 sq miles), of which 13,300 sq km are dry land; the rest of the territory comprises the freshwater Curonian Lagoon and the Vistula Lagoon. The coastline is 140 km (87 miles) long. At January 2023 the Oblast had a population of an estimated 1,032,343 and a population density of 68.3 per sq km. Some 76.6% of the population was urban in 2023. The administrative centre is Kaliningrad, with an estimated 489,735 inhabitants at January 2023. Of residents who stated their ethnicity at the 2021 census, 91.3% were Russian, 1.4% were Ukrainian, and 1.3% were Belarusian. The Oblast is in the time zone UTC+2.

HISTORY

The city of Kaliningrad was founded in 1255, as Königsberg. The chief city of East Prussia, it was the original royal capital of the Hohenzollern dynasty (from 1871 the German emperors). The USSR annexed it after the Second World War, rebuilding and renaming the almost completely destroyed city; the German population was deported. On 7 April 1946 the region joined the Russian Federation.

In 1993 Kaliningrad Oblast unsuccessfully sought republican status. The regional Soviet was disbanded; it was replaced by a Regional Duma. In January 1996 Governor Yurii Matochkin signed a power-sharing agreement between the Oblast and the federal Government. Leonid Gorbenko, an independent, was elected Governor in October. In the gubernatorial election of November 2000, he was defeated by Adm. Vladimir Yegorov, the former Commander of the Baltic Fleet.

As the European Union (EU) prepared to admit neighbouring Lithuania and Poland in 2004, the status of Kaliningrad became an increasing source of contention; in particular, Russia objected to the requirement for oblast residents to possess EU visas to transit through Lithuania en route to metropolitan Russia. In November 2002 simplified visa arrangements were agreed, with effect from July 2003.

TERRITORIAL SURVEYS

In September 2005 the Regional Duma approved President Vladimir Putin's nomination of Georgii Boos, hitherto a Deputy Chairman of the State Duma, as Governor.

In 2010 Kaliningrad was one of the principal centres of demonstrations (which occurred nationwide) against economic and other policies of the federal Government: in January around 12,000 people demonstrated in the city. In March, in an illegal protest, more than 5,000 demonstrators demanded the resignation of Boos as Governor and of Putin as federal premier (which position he held in 2008–12). In August 2012 the Regional Duma voted to approve the appointment of Nikolai Tsukanov of YeR to succeed Boos as Governor, with effect from September.

In December 2011 the foreign ministers of Russia and Poland signed an agreement (recently approved by the EU) that permitted residents of Kaliningrad Oblast visa-free travel for up to 30 consecutive days to neighbouring regions of Poland, with reciprocal access to the Oblast to be granted to residents of those Polish regions. (A passport and special permit would, however, be required to cross the border.)

At the presidential election held on 4 March 2012, only Moscow City awarded Putin a lower share of the votes cast than did Kaliningrad Oblast (52.6%).

Tsukanov was elected Governor on 13 September 2015, obtaining 70.4% of the popular vote. In July 2016 he was appointed Presidential Representative to the North-Western Federal Okrug. Yevgenii Zinichev, hitherto head of the regional branch of the Federal Security Service (FSB) and a former member of the presidential security service, was appointed as Acting Governor. However, Zinichev resigned on 6 October, following controversy about his educational and professional qualifications; he was succeeded as Acting Governor by Anton Alikhanov, the recently appointed Chairman of the Oblast Government and a former federal official. Meanwhile, in July Poland suspended visa-free access from Kaliningrad Oblast, citing security concerns, prompting reciprocal action from Russia. Meanwhile, in October nuclear-capable Iskander-M missiles were relocated from metropolitan Russia to Kaliningrad Oblast, serving to heighten tensions between Russia and the West.

Meanwhile, YeR secured some 41.2% of the votes cast on a proportional basis in elections to the Regional Duma held on 18 September 2016; the LDPR and the KPRF each obtained 16.7% of the votes. On 10 September 2017 Alikhanov was elected Governor, receiving 81.1% of the votes cast.

A large military training event, the Zapad-2021 Joint Strategic Exercise, was staged by the Russian and Belarusian armed forces in September 2021, concentrated in Kaliningrad, Belarus and the western districts of metropolitan Russia.

At elections to the Regional Duma held on 19 September 2021, YeR secured 39.0% of the votes cast on a proportional basis, ahead of the KPRF, with 19.0%, SR, with 11.3%, the LDPR, with 11.2% and the RPPS, with 6.4%. By the end of the year 29 of the 40 deputies had joined the YeR faction, six that of the KPRF, two that of the LDPR, two that of SR, and one that of the RPPS.

Under EU economic sanctions imposed against Russia in response to the invasion of Ukraine on 24 February 2022, in mid-June Lithuania imposed a ban on the transit of goods from metropolitan Russia to Kaliningrad Oblast by both road and rail. Following strong protests from the federal Government, in late July, in accordance with a decision by the European Commission, Lithuania lifted the ban on the rail transport of goods to Kaliningrad, although the restrictions on road transit were retained. However, Alikhanov protested in early August that the annual transit quota agreed by the EU of some 500,000 tons of goods had already been reached. Meanwhile, it was reported in

August that the federal defence ministry had deployed three warplanes equipped with hypersonic missiles to Kaliningrad Oblast.

Alikhanov was overwhelmingly re-elected as Governor on 11 September 2022, securing 80.2% of the votes cast, defeating Yevgenii Mishin of the LDPR (with 6.4%) and four other candidates.

In response to concerns that the Russian authorities planned to orchestrate a new and illicit influx of migrants from the Middle East and North Africa into the European Union via Kaliningrad, in November 2022 the Polish Government ordered the construction of a razor-wire fence extending along all of Poland's border with the exclave; a further reinforcement of the fence was announced in April 2023. In early May, following a recommendation by the Polish Commission on the Standardization of Geographical Names, the Polish Government announced its decision to refer to the city of Kaliningrad as Królewiec in official documents (as it had been known when ruled by the Kingdom of Poland in the 15th and 16th centuries), prompting denunciations from Russian officials.

In November 2023 the British Ministry of Defence announced that recent intelligence on Russian transport movements indicated that the country's strategic air defence systems had most likely been relocated away from Kaliningrad Oblast, with their anticipated new location being in the conflict in Ukraine.

ECONOMY

In 2021 Kaliningrad Oblast's gross regional product (GRP) was 675,001m. roubles, or 659,727 roubles per head. Its main industrial centres are at Kaliningrad, Gusev and Sovetsk. There are rail services to Lithuania and Poland. A rail cargo ferry operates between Baltiisk, in the Oblast, and Ust-Luga (Leningrad Oblast). At the end of 2021 there were 668 km of railways in the Oblast.

The Oblast's agricultural sector consists mainly of animal husbandry, including fur-farming, and vegetable-growing and fishing. Agriculture employed 4.4 of the workforce and contributed 6.6% of GRP in 2021. The Oblast has substantial reserves of petroleum, peat deposits and coal. The main industries are mechanical engineering and metal working, the processing of fishing and forestry products, electrical energy, and the production and processing of amber (of which the Oblast contains more than 90% of the world's known reserves). The Oblast is a major producer of television sets and of automobiles. The Avtodor factory, founded in 1996, previously manufactured vehicles on behalf of, in succession, General Motors (of the USA), Chery (of the People's Republic of China), and, until the imposition of international sanctions against Russia in 2022 following its invasion of Ukraine, BMW (of Germany) and Hyundai (of the Republic of Korea). None the less, in late 2022 Avtodor announced its intention of resuming and expanding automobile production at the plant, with a focus on electric vehicles. An offshore economic zone in the territory, with a preferential tax regime commenced operations in 2018. Industry employed 28.4% of the workforce and contributed 29.5% of GRP in 2021, when manufacturing employed 14.6% of the workforce and contributed 16.5% of GRP.

The economically active population numbered 528,288 in 2022, when the rate of unemployment was 3.1%, while the average monthly wage was 47,349 roubles. There was a budgetary surplus of 5,772.4m. roubles in 2021, when export trade amounted to US $2,385m. (of which 15.3% was with countries of the CIS), and import trade to $8,765m. (of which 6.3% was with CIS countries).

DIRECTORY

Governor: ANTON A. ALIKHANOV.

Office of the Governor: 236007 Kaliningrad, ul. D. Donskogo 1; tel. (4012) 59-90-01; fax (4012) 59-90-02; e-mail first@gov.39.ru; internet gov39.ru.

Regional Duma: 236000 Kaliningrad, ul. Kirova 17; tel. (4012) 91-84-38; e-mail letters@duma39.ru; internet duma39.ru; Chair. ANDREI M. KROPOTKIN.

State Duma Representatives (2): ANDREI I. KOLESNIK (YeR), MARINA E. ORGEYEVA (YeR).

Federation Council Representatives: ALEKSANDR G. YAROSHUK, ALEKSANDR V. SHENDERYUK-ZHIDKOV.

Leningrad Oblast

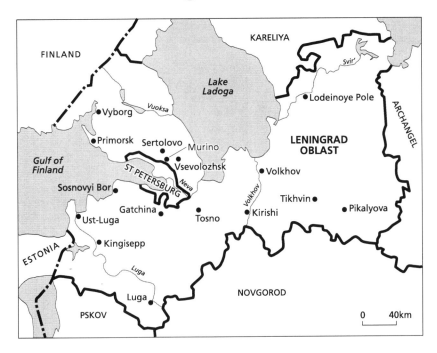

Leningrad Oblast is situated in the Eastern European Plain, on the Gulf of Finland, an inlet of the Baltic Sea. The Republic of Kareliya lies to the north, Vologda Oblast to the east and Novgorod and Pskov Oblasts to the south. Estonia lies to the west and Finland to the north-west. The Oblast occupies 83,908 sq km (32,397 sq miles). At January 2023 its population was an estimated 2,023,767 and the population density 24.1 per sq km. Some 67.1% of the population of the Oblast was urban in 2023. The administrative centre is St Petersburg, which does not form part of the Oblast. The largest city is Murino, located on the border with St Petersburg, with an estimated 104,611 inhabitants at January 2023. Of residents who stated their ethnicity at the 2021 census, 93.7% were Russian, and 0.7% were Ukrainian. Leningrad Oblast is in the time zone UTC+3.

HISTORY

Leningrad Oblast, which was formed on 1 August 1927, was heavily industrialized during the Soviet period.

An independent, Vadim Gustov, was elected Governor in 1996. He resigned in 1998 and was succeeded, following an election in 1999, by Valerii Serdyukov, who was re-elected in 2003. In July 2007 the regional legislature endorsed Serdyukov's nomination to a further term.

In May 2012 Serdyukov resigned as Governor, having lost the support of YeR. Shortly afterwards, the regional legislature voted to approve the appointment of Aleksandr Drozdenko, Serdyukov's deputy since 2002, as his successor. Drozdenko was elected Governor in a popular vote held on 13 September 2015, obtaining 82.1% of the vote.

YeR secured some 51.3% of the votes cast on a proportional basis in elections to the regional legislature on 18 September 2016. By the end of the year 39 of the 50 deputies had joined the YeR parliamentary faction.

Drozdenko was one of four candidates to contest a gubernatorial election on 13 September 2020; he was re-elected with 83.6% of the votes cast.

At elections to the Regional Legislative Assembly held on 19 September 2021, YeR secured 46.4% of the votes cast on the basis of proportional representation; the KPRF obtained 20.7%, SR 15.2% and the LDPR 10.6%. By the end of the year 35 of the 50 deputies had joined the YeR faction, seven that of the KPRF, five that of SR, and three that of the LDPR.

ECONOMY

Leningrad Oblast's gross regional product (GRP) was 1,481,188m. roubles, or 778,692 roubles per head, in 2021. The main industrial centres are at Vyborg, a major seaport and Kingisepp. A railway ferry service provides a direct link between metropolitan Russia (at Ust-Luga) and the exclave of Kaliningrad. At the end of 2021 Leningrad Oblast contained 2,550 km of railways. One station of the St Petersburg metro is located in the Oblast, as is St Petersburg-Pulkovo international airport.

The agricultural sector consists mainly of animal husbandry and vegetable production. It employed 7.8% of the workforce and contributed 5.0% of GRP in 2021. Timber reserves are estimated to cover 6.1m. ha. The major industries are the processing of forestry and agricultural products, petroleum refining and the production of electrical energy and automobiles. Industry employed 34.1% of the workforce and contributed 46.2% of GRP in 2021, when manufacturing employed 17.7% of the workforce and contributed 30.8% of GRP.

The economically active population numbered 1,021,718 in 2022, when the rate of unemployment was 3.1%, while the average monthly wage was 60,008 roubles. There was a budgetary deficit of 4,032.7m. roubles in 2021, when export trade amounted to US $8,370m. (of which 9.9% was with countries of the CIS), and import trade to $4,353m. (of which 5.1% was with CIS countries).

DIRECTORY

Governor: ALEKSANDR YU. DROZDENKO.

Office of the Governor: 191311 St Petersburg, Suvorovskii pr. 67; tel. (812) 274-42-42; fax (812) 274-67-33; e-mail lenobl@lenobl.ru; internet lenobl.ru.

Regional Legislative Assembly: 191311 St Petersburg, Suvorovskii pr. 67; tel. (812) 710-25-18; fax (812) 274-85-39; e-mail mail@lenoblzaks.ru; internet lenoblzaks.ru; Chair. SERGEI M. BEBENIN.

State Duma Representatives (3): SVETLANA S. ZHUROVA (YeR), SERGEI V. YAKHNYUK (YeR), SERGEI V. PETROV (YeR).

Federation Council Representatives: DMITRII YU. VASILENKO, SERGEI N. PERMINOV.

Murmansk Oblast

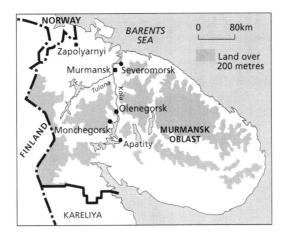

Murmansk Oblast occupies the Kola Peninsula, bordering the Barents Sea to the north and the White Sea to the south-east. The Oblast has international borders with Norway and Finland to the west. The Republic of Kareliya lies to the south. Much of its territory lies within the Arctic Circle. The Oblast covers 144,902 sq km (55,947 sq miles). The climate is severe and changeable. At January 2023 its population was an estimated 658,698 and its population density 4.5 per sq km. Some 93.0% of the population was urban in 2023. Its administrative centre is Murmansk, a major seaport, with an estimated 267,422 inhabitants at January 2023. Of residents who stated their ethnicity at the 2021 census, 89.9% were Russian, 2.3% were Ukrainian, and 0.8% were Belarusian. Murmansk Oblast is in the time zone UTC+3.

HISTORY

The city of Romanov-on-Murman was founded in 1916. Following the Bolshevik Revolution of 1917 (after which the city was renamed Murmansk), the region was a centre of anti-communist resistance. Murmansk Oblast was formed on 28 May 1938.

Yurii Yevdokimov was elected Governor, with the support of the LDPR, in 1996. He was re-elected in 2000 and 2004. In 2007 the Regional Duma endorsed his nomination to a further term. In March 2009 Yevdokimov resigned. The Regional Duma approved President Dmitrii Medvedev's nominee, Dmitrii Dmitriyenko, as Governor on 25 March.

In April 2012 the Regional Duma voted to endorse the appointment of Medvedev's nominee, Marina Kovtun, as Governor, after Dmitriyenko resigned. In September 2014 Kovtun was directly elected Governor, with 64.7% of the vote.

YeR secured 39.2% of the votes cast on the basis of proportional representation at elections to the Regional Duma held on 18 September 2016, ahead of the LDPR, with 21.0%. None the less, by the end of the year 25 of the 32 deputies had joined the YeR parliamentary faction.

In 2017 several senior regional officials, including Deputy Governor Igor Babenko, were arrested on charges of involvement in large-scale corruption. After Kovtun was implicated during trial proceedings, on 21 March 2019 Putin accepted her resignation. He appointed Andrei Chibis, hitherto the federal Deputy Minister of Construction, Housing and Utilities, as Acting Governor. On 8 September Chibis was elected Governor, obtaining 60.1% of the votes cast.

At elections to the Regional Duma held on 19 September 2021, YeR secured 36.0% of the votes cast on the basis of proportional representation; the KPRF obtained 19.6%, SR 17.0%, the LDPR 13.3% and the RPPS 10.7%. By the end of the year 24 of the 32 deputies had joined the YeR faction, and two that of the KPRF.

ECONOMY

In 2021 Murmansk Oblast's gross regional product (GRP) was 1,083,779m. roubles, or 1,487,364 roubles per head. The principal industrial centres are at Murmansk, Zapolyarnyi and Apatity. At the end of 2021 there were 870 km of railways in the Oblast. Murmansk is Russia's sole all-weather Northern port, through which some 12m. metric tons of cargo pass annually, and which is the base for the world's only nuclear icebreaker fleet, the Northern Fleet. There is an international airport at Murmansk.

The Oblast's agricultural sector consists mainly of fishing. The sector employed 2.9% of the workforce and contributed 11.5% of GRP in 2021. The region is rich in natural resources and a major producer of apatites, nickel, copper and iron concentrates. In 1985 exploitation of the Shtokman gas condensate deposit began on the continental shelf of the Barents Sea. In 1999 LUKoil, the domestic petroleum producer, signed an agreement that made Murmansk a base for exploration of the Barents Sea, in association with the state-controlled gas producer Gazprom. The city is a centre for the export of petroleum products. Industry employed 29.4% of the workforce and contributed 54.5% of GRP in 2021, when manufacturing employed 11.6% of the workforce and contributed 33.6% of GRP.

The region's economically active population numbered 376,801 in 2022, when the rate of unemployment was 4.8%, while the average monthly wage was 87,326 roubles. There was a budgetary surplus of 18,258.8m. roubles in 2021, when export trade amounted to US $4,669m. (of which less than 0.1% was with CIS countries), and import trade to $543m. (of which 1.2% was with CIS countries).

DIRECTORY

Governor: ANDREI V. CHIBIS.

Office of the Governor: 183006 Murmansk, pr. Lenina 75; tel. (8152) 48-62-01; fax (8152) 47-65-03; e-mail pgov@gov-murman.ru; internet gov-murman.ru.

Regional Duma: 183016 Murmansk, ul. S. Perovskoi 2; tel. (8152) 40-16-00; fax (8152) 45-97-79; e-mail post@duma-murman.ru; internet duma-murman.ru; Chair. SERGEI M. DUBOVOI.

State Duma Representative (1): TATYANA A. KUSAIKO (YeR).

Federation Council Representatives: KONSTANTIN K. DOLGOV, TATYANA A. SAKHAROVA.

Novgorod Oblast

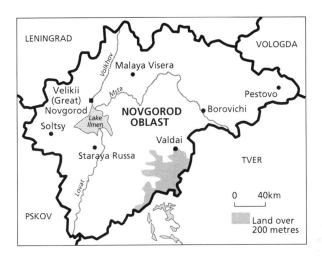

Novgorod Oblast is situated in the north-west of the Eastern European Plain. Tver Oblast lies to the south-east, Pskov Oblast to the south-west, and Leningrad and Vologda Oblasts lie to the north. The Oblast covers 54,501 sq km (21,043 sq miles). At January 2023 its population was an estimated 575,926 and its population density 10.6 per sq km. Some 73.1% of the population was urban in 2023. The region's administrative centre is Velikii (Great) Novgorod (also known as Novgorod), with an estimated 223,191 inhabitants at January 2023. Of residents who stated their ethnicity at the 2021 census, 95.4% were Russian. Novgorod Oblast is in the time zone UTC+3.

HISTORY

One of the oldest Russian cities, Novgorod remained a powerful principality after the dissolution of Kievan Rus. In 1478 Ivan III 'the Great', prince of Muscovy and the first Tsar of All Russia, destroyed the Republic of Novgorod. The wealth and importance of the city declined after the foundation of St Petersburg in the 18th century. Novgorod Oblast was formed on 5 July 1944.

In the mid-1990s the region displayed a high level of support for reformists. Mikhail Prusak, the incumbent appointed in 1991, was elected Governor in 1995 and was re-elected in 1999 and 2003.

In August 2007 Prusak resigned as Governor, following official criticism of corruption in the Oblast. The Regional Duma approved the appointment of Sergei Mitin as his successor. At elections to the Regional Duma, held in December 2011, YeR obtained 37.0% of the vote, ahead of SR, with 27.2% and the KPRF, with 21.2%.

A direct election to the post of Governor was held on 14 October 2012. Mitin was one of three registered candidates: four other applicants, including those from SR and the KPRF, were disqualified. Mitin, the YeR candidate, was duly elected, obtaining 76.0% of the votes cast.

YeR secured 38.9% of the votes cast on the basis of proportional representation at elections to the Regional Duma held on 18 September 2016. Some 21 of the 32 deputies had joined the YeR parliamentary faction by the end of the year.

On 13 February 2017 Mitin submitted his resignation to President Putin, who appointed Andrei Nikitin, hitherto a federal economic official, as Acting Governor. On 10 September Nikitin was elected Governor, receiving 68.0% of the votes cast.

At elections to the Regional Duma held on 19 September 2021, YeR secured 29.5% of the votes cast on the basis of proportional representation; the KPRF obtained 19.8%, SR 15.8%, the LDPR 9.0%, the recently established centre-right NL 8.4% and the RPSS 5.8%. By the end of the year 22 of the 31 deputies had joined the YeR faction, two that of the KPRF and two that of SR.

On 11 September 2022 Nikitin was re-elected as Governor with 77.0% of the votes cast, defeating four other candidates.

ECONOMY

In 2021 Novgorod Oblast's gross regional product (GRP) was 342,070m. roubles, or 580,495 roubles per head. The Oblast's major industrial centres are at Velikii Novgorod and Staraya Russa, a resort town famed for its mineral and radon springs. At the end of 2021 there were 1,144 km of railways in the Oblast.

Agriculture, which employed 7.4% of the workforce and contributed 6.3% of GRP in 2021, comprises mainly flax production and animal husbandry. The region's major industries include mechanical engineering and metal working, chemicals and petrochemicals, the production of mineral fertilizers, wood working, the processing of forestry and agricultural products, and electricity production. Industry employed 31.8% of the workforce and contributed 49.7% of GRP in 2021, when manufacturing employed 20.4% of the workforce and contributed 41.3% of GRP.

The economically active population amounted to 278,223 in 2022, when the rate of unemployment was 3.1%, while the average monthly wage was 45,247 roubles. There was a budgetary surplus of 7,383.4m. roubles in 2021, when export trade amounted to US $2,550 m. (of which 5.3% was with CIS countries), while import trade amounted to $566m. (of which 5.9% was with CIS countries).

DIRECTORY

Governor: ANDREI S. NIKITIN.

Office of the Governor: 173005 Novgorod obl., Velikii Novgorod, pl. Pobedy-Sofiiskaya 1; tel. (8162) 73-25-22; fax (8162) 73-13-30; e-mail niac@novreg.ru; internet novreg.ru.

Regional Duma: 173005 Novgorod obl., Velikii Novgorod, pl. Pobedy-Sofiiskaya 1; tel. (8162) 73-25-14; fax (8162) 77-63-55; e-mail inform@novreg.ru; internet novoblduma.ru; Chair. YURII I. BOBRYSHEV.

State Duma Representative (1): ARTYOM YU. KIRYANOV (YeR).

Federation Council Representatives: YELENA V. PISAREVA, SERGEI G. MITIN.

Pskov Oblast

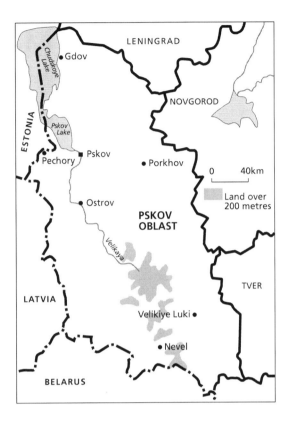

Pskov Oblast is situated on the Eastern European Plain. It has borders with Belarus to the south and Latvia and Estonia to the west, with the Oblasts of Smolensk in the south-east, Tver and Novgorod in the east and Leningrad in the north-east. Around two-fifths of the Oblast's territory is forested. On its border with Estonia lie the Pskov (Pihkva) and Chudskoye (Peipsi) lakes. Pskov Oblast covers an area of 55,399 sq km (21,390 sq miles). At January 2023 its population was an estimated 587,786 and the population density 10.6 per sq km. Some 70.9% of the population was urban in 2023. The administrative centre is Pskov, with an estimated 189,315 inhabitants at January 2023. Of residents who stated their ethnicity at the 2021 census, 95.8% were Russian. Pskov Oblast is in the time zone UTC+3.

HISTORY

Pskov city was founded in 903. In 1242 the Muscovite Prince Aleksandr Nevskii defeated an army of Teutonic Knights in the region. The Muscovite state finally acquired the region in 1510. The Oblast was created on 23 August 1944. Some formerly Estonian territory to the south of Lake Pskov was transferred to Pskov Oblast in 1945, remaining a cause for dispute in the early 1990s.

The Oblast was a bastion of support for the nationalist LDPR in the 1990s. Yevgenii Mikhailov, a LDPR deputy, was elected Governor in 1996, and re-elected in 2000. In December 2004 a former deputy of the federal State Duma, Mikhail Kuznetsov, was elected Governor, defeating Mikhailov. In November 2006 security forces dispersed nationalist groups assembled outside the Estonian consulate in Pskov, who were protesting against the relocation of a Soviet war memorial in the Estonian capital, Tallinn.

In February 2009 Kuznetsov resigned as Governor; he was succeeded by a presidential nominee, Andrei Turchak, hitherto a representative of Pskov Oblast in the Federation Council, the upper chamber of the federal legislative, and a senior member of YeR. Turchak was elected Governor by popular vote in September 2014.

On 24 September 2015 the Pskov Regional Assembly of Deputies voted to remove the legislative mandate of a Yabloko deputy, Lev Shlosberg, an outspoken critic of the federal authorities, who had published photographs purporting to show the funerals of Russian military personnel from Pskov who had, he stated, been killed in the conflict in eastern Ukraine, despite official denials of direct Russian military participation therein. (Shlosberg had been assaulted and hospitalized in August 2014, shortly after starting to publish such photographs.) Earlier in September 2015 audio recordings had emerged that appeared to implicate Turchak in ordering the severe assault, in November 2010 in Moscow, of a prominent opposition journalist, Oleg Kashin.

YeR secured some 44.1% of the votes cast on a proportional basis at elections to the Regional Assembly of Deputies held on 18 September 2016. The KPRF was second, with 20.1%. Some 32 of the 42 deputies had joined the YeR parliamentary faction by the end of the year.

Turchak stepped down as Governor in October 2017, in order to become the Secretary of the General Council of YeR. In November the Regional Assembly of Deputies appointed Turchak as its representative to the Federation Council; later in the month he became a Deputy Chairman of that body (in 2020 becoming First Deputy Chairman). Meanwhile, Putin appointed Mikhail Vedernikov, hitherto the Deputy Presidential Representative to the North-Western Federal Okrug, as Acting Governor. On 9 September 2018 he was elected Governor, with 70.7% of the votes cast.

At elections to the Regional Assembly of Deputies held on 19 September 2021, YeR secured 39.6% of the votes cast on a proportional basis; the KPRF obtained 20.7%, SR 9.1%, the LDPR 8.9%, while the recently established centre-right NL and Yabloko each obtained 6.2%. By the end of the year 19 of the 26 deputies had joined the YeR faction, and three that of the KPRF.

In Governor Vedernikov filed a lawsuit in response to an anonymous report published on online messaging service Telegram, which criticized him for acclaiming Russia's recent ongoing invasion of Ukraine while announcing the death of soldiers from the region. Police subsequently searched the homes of several politicians, activists and journalists in the Oblast, including the leader of the regional branch of Yabloko, Shlosberg, and the chief editor of a local newspaper, as part of the investigations. Ukraine's Ministry of Defence reported at the end of October that three Russian attack helicopters had been destroyed at an airfield near Pskov, in what was described as a sabotage operation by Ukrainian agents. Vedernikov announced on 29 May 2023 that two drone attacks had damaged the administrative building of the operator of an oil pipeline near the village of Litvinovo. In June the federal Ministry of Justice designated Shlosberg as a 'foreign agent', and Yabloko's regional headquarters in Pskov were raided by police in July. Two military transport aircraft were destroyed and a further two damaged in a drone attack against an airbase in the Oblast on 30 August.

On 10 September 2023 Vedernikov, the candidate of YeR, was overwhelmingly re-elected Governor with 86.3% of votes cast, defeating three other candidates. Later that month Vedernikov appointed Aleksei Naumets, previously a Russian air force commander, as a representative of the Oblast in the Federation Council.

ECONOMY

Pskov Oblast's gross regional product (GRP) amounted to 219,949m. roubles, or 356,595 roubles per head in 2021—the latter figure by far the lowest in the North-Western Federal Okrug. The Oblast's principal industrial centres are at Pskov and Velikiye Luki. At the end of 2020 there were 1,089 km of railway track in the Oblast. There is an international airport at Pskov.

Agricultural activity consists mainly of animal husbandry, and the production of flax. A major project to improve the agricultural infrastructure of the region was implemented in the mid-1990s. Fishing is an important source of income in the north of the territory. The agricultural sector employed 10.1% of the workforce and contributed 11.3% of GRP in 2021. The Oblast's major industries are the production of electricity, mechanical engineering and metal working, and food processing. Industry employed 29.1% of the workforce and contributed 26.2% of GRP in 2021, when manufacturing employed 16.9% of the workforce and contributed 16.6% of GRP.

The Oblast's economically active population numbered 295,555 in 2022, when the rate of unemployment was 4.0%, while the average monthly wage was 38,966 roubles. There was a budgetary surplus of 537.9m. roubles in 2021, when export trade amounted to US $256m. (of which 45.7% was with countries of the CIS), and import trade to $473m. (of which 10.6% was with CIS countries).

DIRECTORY

Governor: MIKHAIL YU. VEDERNIKOV.

Office of the Governor: 180001 Pskov, ul. Nekrasova 23; tel. (8112) 29-97-50; fax (8112) 16-03-90; e-mail governor@obladmin.pskov.ru; internet pskov.ru.

Regional Assembly of Deputies: 180001 Pskov, ul. Nekrasova 23; tel. (8112) 69-98-43; fax (8112) 69-98-46; e-mail press@pskovsobranie.ru; internet sobranie.pskov.ru; Chair. ALEKSANDR A. KOTOV.

State Duma Representative (1): ALEKSANDR N. KOZLOVSKII (YeR).

Federation Council Representatives: ANDREI A. TURCHAK, ALEKSEI V. NAUMETS.

Vologda Oblast

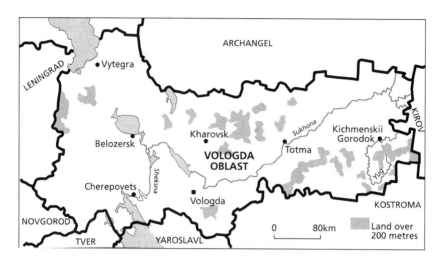

Vologda Oblast is situated in the north-west of the Eastern European Plain. It has a short north-western border with the Republic of Kareliya, including the southern tip of Lake Onega. Leningrad Oblast lies to the west, Novgorod Oblast to the south-west, and Tver, Yaroslavl and Kostroma Oblasts to the south. Kirov Oblast lies to the east and Archangel Oblast to the north. Vologda Oblast occupies 144,527 sq km (55,802 sq miles). At January 2023 its population was an estimated 1,128,782 and the population density 7.8 per sq km. Some 72.5% of the total population was urban in 2023. The Oblast's administrative centre is at Vologda, which had an estimated 311,628 inhabitants at January 2023. The second largest city is Cherepovets (301,040). Of residents who stated their ethnicity at the 2021 census, 96.7% were Russian. Vologda Oblast is in the time zone UTC+3.

HISTORY

Muscovy annexed the Vologda province in the 14th century. Vologda Oblast was formed on 23 September 1937. In October 1991 the Russian President, Boris Yeltsin, appointed Nikolai Podgornov as head of the regional administration. There was a high level of support for the LDPR for much of the 1990s. In 1996 President Yeltsin dismissed Podgornov, who was subsequently imprisoned on charges of corruption. His successor as Governor, Vyacheslav Pozgalyov, overwhelmingly won a direct elections in 1996, 1999 and 2003. In 2007 the Legislative Assembly approved Pozgalyov's nomination to a fourth gubernatorial term. He resigned in 2011. The Legislative Assembly approved the nomination of the erstwhile Mayor of Cherepovets, Oleg Kuvshinnikov, as Governor in December.

In 2014, in a direct popular election, Kuvshinnikov was elected Governor, receiving 63.0% of the vote. YeR secured 37.3% of the votes cast on the basis of proportional representation at elections to the Legislative Assembly held in September 2016, ahead of the LDPR, with 21.8%. A total of 25 of the 34 deputies had joined the YeR parliamentary faction by the end of the year. On 8 September 2019 Kuvshinnikov was re-elected as Governor, obtaining 60.8% of the votes cast.

At elections to the regional Legislative Assembly held on 19 September 2021, YeR secured 35.7% of the votes cast on a proportional basis, ahead of the KPRF, with 24.4%. By the end of the year 24 of the 34 deputies had joined the YeR faction. In November 2022 the post of Chairman of the Government was abolished, and its functions assumed by the Governor.

On 31 October 2023 Putin accepted the resignation of Kuvshinnikov and appointed Georgii Filimonov, hitherto Deputy Chairman of the Government of Moscow Oblast, as Acting Governor, pending an election in September 2024. On 20 November 2023 Filimonov announced that Aleksandr Mordvinov, previously Deputy Chairman of the Government of Samara Oblast, had been appointed to the reinstated post of Chairman of the Government.

ECONOMY

In 2021 Vologda Oblast's gross regional product (GRP) was 1,009,918m. roubles, or 881,816 roubles per head. The main industrial centres are at Vologda and Cherepovets. At the end of 2021 there were 765 km of railways in the Oblast.

Agriculture in Vologda Oblast consists mainly of animal husbandry and the production of flax and vegetables. Agriculture employed 6.7% of the workforce and contributed 4.2% of GRP in 2021. The main industry is ferrous metallurgy; the region produces around one-sixth of each of Russia's iron, rolled stock and steel, as well as significant quantities of textiles and chemicals, including mineral fertilizers. Severstal, the steel manufacturer, is a major employer. Industry employed 30.8% of the workforce and contributed 61.8% of GRP in 2021, when manufacturing employed 19.9% of the workforce and contributed 54.6% of GRP.

The Oblast's economically active population numbered 532,473 in 2022, when the rate of unemployment was 3.4%, while the average monthly wage was 53,580 roubles. There was a budgetary surplus of 34,200.3m. roubles in 2021, when export trade amounted to US $7,166m. (of which 10.4% was with countries of the CIS), and import trade to $631m. (of which 28.4% was with CIS countries).

DIRECTORY

Acting Governor: GEORGII YU. FILIMONOV.

Chairman of the Government: ALEKSANDR MORDVINOV.

Office of the Governor: 160000 Vologda, ul. Gertsena 2; tel. (8172) 72-99-90; fax (8172) 72-87-22; internet vologda-oblast.ru.

Office of the Government: 160000 Vologda, ul. Gertsena 2; tel. and fax (8172) 23-00-03; e-mail government@pvo.gov35.ru; internet vologda-oblast.ru.

Legislative Assembly: 160000 Vologda, ul. Pushkinskaya 25; tel. (8172) 59-51-10; fax (8172) 21-11-33; e-mail sobranie@vologdazso.ru; internet vologdazso.ru; Chair. ANDREI N. LUTSENKO.

State Duma Representatives (2): VALENTINA N. ARTAMONOVA (YeR), ALEKSEI V. KANAYEV (YeR).

Federation Council Representatives: YURII L. VOROBYEV, OLEG A. KUVSHINNIKOV.

Nenets Autonomous Okrug

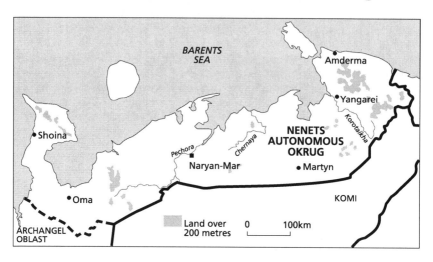

The Nenets Autonomous Okrug is part of Archangel Oblast. It is situated in north-eastern European Russia, its coastline lying, from west to east, on the White, Barents and Kara Seas, parts of the Arctic Ocean. Most of the territory lies within the Arctic Circle. Archangel proper lies to the south-west, but most of the southern border is with the Republic of Komi. At its eastern extremity, the district touches the Yamalo-Nenets Autonomous Okrug (in Tyumen Oblast). The territory occupies 176,810 sq km (68,267 sq miles). At January 2023 its population was an estimated 41,383, and the population density 0.2 per sq km. Some 74.5% of the population was urban in 2023. The administrative centre is Naryan-Mar, with an estimated 23,579 inhabitants at January 2023. Of residents who stated their ethnicity at the 2021 census, 69.6% were Russian, 17.9% were Nenets, 6.5% were Komi, and 1.3% were Ukrainian. The language spoken by the Nenets belongs to the Samoyedic group of Uralian languages, which is part of the Uralo-Altaic linguistic group. The Nenets Autonomous Okrug is in the time zone UTC+3.

HISTORY

The Nenets were traditionally concerned with herding and breeding reindeer. They broke away from other Finno-Ugrian groups in around 3000 BCE and migrated east, where, in about 200 BCE, they began to mix with Turkic-Altaic people. By the 17th century CE their territory was entirely under the control of the Muscovite state.

The Nenets National Okrug was formed on 15 July 1929, becoming an Autonomous Okrug in 1977. During the Soviet period collectivization of the Nenets' economic activity, together with the exploitation of petroleum and natural gas, was accompanied by the mass migration of ethnic Russians to the region.

In 1994 President Boris Yeltsin suspended a resolution by the district administration that had ordered a referendum on the formation of a 'Nenets Republic'. A businessman, Vladimir Butov, was elected as head of the district administration in 1996; he was re-elected in 2001. Arrest warrants for Butov were issued in 2002 and 2003, for abuse of office and the assault of a police officer in St Petersburg, respectively. The petroleum company LUKoil was a prominent source of opposition to Butov, as it objected to the preferential treatment granted in the Autonomous Okrug to the Nenets Oil Company (NNK), which Butov controlled.

In January 2005 the federal Supreme Court ruled against Butov being permitted to seek a further term of office. Aleksei Barinov, the former head of a subsidiary of LUKoil, was elected Governor in February, receiving 48.5% of the votes cast. A federal investigation into Barinov was subsequently opened on charges of embezzlement and the misuse of budgetary funds. After Barinov was arrested, in June 2006 President Vladimir Putin suspended him from office, formally dismissing him in July. The district legislature endorsed Putin's nomination of Valerii Potapenko, hitherto Chief Federal Inspector for the territory, as Governor in August. In September 2007 an Archangel court imposed a three-year suspended sentence on Barinov for financial malpractice and abuse of office.

In February 2009 President Dmitrii Medvedev formally accepted Potapenko's resignation as Governor, nominating Igor Fyodorov, hitherto an official in the Archangel Oblast administration, as his successor; his appointment was confirmed by the district legislature shortly afterwards.

Following the expiry of Fyodorov's gubernatorial mandate, in February 2014 Putin (again President) appointed Igor Koshin, the leader of the district branch of YeR and hitherto a representative of the region in the upper chamber of the federal legislature, the Federation Council, as Acting Governor. In a popular election held on 14 September 2014, Koshin became Governor, obtaining 76.7% of the votes cast. At concurrent elections to the district Assembly of Deputies, which was expanded from 11 to 19 deputies, YeR obtained 45.6% of the proportional vote; the KPRF was again second, with 19.3%.

In September 2017 Putin dismissed Koshin as Governor; his position had become increasingly untenable after he introduced unpopular economic reforms. Koshin was succeeded, in an acting capacity, by Aleksandr Tsybulskii, hitherto an official in the federal Ministry of Economic Development. Elections to the Assembly of Deputies were held on 9 September 2018: YeR won 39.0% of the votes cast to seats on a proportional basis, ahead of the KPRF, with 23.8%, and the LDPR, with 17.4%; 11 of the 19 deputies had joined the YeR parliamentary faction by the end of the year. Meanwhile, on 1 October the new Assembly of Deputies elected Tsybulskii as Governor, direct elections to the post having been abolished.

On 2 April 2020 Tsybulskii was transferred to the post of Acting Governor of Archangel Oblast, and Yurii Bezdudnyi, hitherto the Deputy Governor of the Nenets Autonomous Okrug, succeeded him in an acting capacity. On 13 May Bezdudnyi and Tsybulskii signed a memorandum of intent on the merger of the two regions into a single federal entity in order to strengthen the response to a severe regional economic crisis. However, their proposal that a referendum on the planned unification be conducted in September prompted a public outcry and a campaign of protests in the Autonomous Okrug, and later in May the referendum was postponed to 2021. On 2 July 2020 Bezdudnyi announced an end to the plans, shortly after the Autonomous Okrug became the only federal subject in which a majority of residents (55.3%) had rejected the adoption of extensive amendments to the federal Constitution in a popular vote (only 43.8% voted in support of the proposal, almost 15 percentage points lower than the support it obtained in any other territory).

On 13 September 2020 the Assembly of Deputies elected Bezdudnyi as Governor from a list of three candidates presented by Putin. He was inaugurated to office on the same day.

Following elections to the Assembly of Deputies held on 10 September 2023, YeR increased its representation to 13 of the 19 seats in the chamber.

ECONOMY

In 2021 the Nenets Autonomous Okrug's gross regional product (GRP) amounted to 406,838m. roubles, or 9,149,623 roubles per head. There are no railway lines in the Autonomous Okrug. The major ports are at Naryan-Mar and Amderma.

The territory's agriculture consists mainly of fishing, reindeer-breeding, hunting and fur-farming. Agriculture employed 4.0% of the workforce and contributed 0.4% of GRP in 2021. There are substantial reserves of petroleum, natural gas and gas condensate. Petroleum deposits in the region were developed only slowly, and a sea terminal for petroleum transportation, served by a fleet of ice-breaking tankers, was opened at Varandei in 2000. Other sectors of the district's industry included the processing of agricultural products and the generation of electricity. Industry employed 40.8% of the workforce and contributed 90.8% of GRP in 2021, when manufacturing engaged 1.9% of the workforce and contributed 0.1% of GRP.

The economically active population numbered 22,522 in 2022, when the rate of unemployment was 7.4%, while the average monthly wage was 106,949 roubles. There was a budgetary surplus of 2,503.9m. roubles in 2021, when export trade amounted to US $1,120m. (all of which was with countries outside the CIS) and import trade was negligible.

DIRECTORY

Governor: YURII V. BEZDUDNYI.

Office of the Governor: 166000 Archangel obl., Nenets AO, Naryan-Mar, ul. Smidovicha 20; tel. (81853) 4-21-13; fax (81853) 4-22-69; e-mail priem@adm-nao.ru; internet bit.ly/36iHcVV.

Assembly of Deputies: 166000 Archangel obl., Nenets AO, Naryan-Mar, ul. Smidovicha 20; tel. and fax (81853) 4-20-11; e-mail parlament@sdnao.ru; internet sdnao.ru; Chair. ALEKSANDR P. CHURSANOV.

State Duma Representative (1): SERGEI N. KOTKIN (YeR).

Federation Council Representatives: DENIS V. GUSEV, ALEKSANDR I. LUTOVINOV.

SOUTHERN FEDERAL OKRUG

Presidential Representative to the Southern Federal Okrug: VLADIMIR V. USTINOV, 344006 Rostov-on-Don, ul. Bolshaya Sadovaya 73; tel. (863) 244-16-16; e-mail pppufo@ufo.gov.ru; internet ufo.gov.ru.

Sevastopol City

Note: The territories of the Crimean peninsula, comprising Sevastopol City and the Republic of Crimea, remained internationally recognized as constituting part of Ukraine, following their annexation by Russia in March 2014.

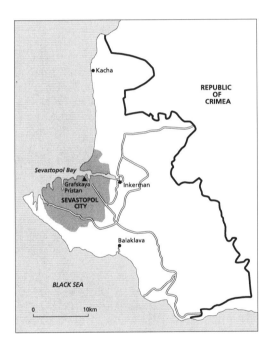

Sevastopol City is situated at the south-western tip of the Crimean Peninsula. The Black Sea lies to the west and the Republic of Crimea to the east. The territory's major river is the Chorna. The territory occupies 864 sq km (334 sq miles) and incorporates numerous towns, villages and rural areas. At January 2023 it had an estimated population of 558,273 and a population density of 646.1 per sq km. Some 92.5% of the population was urban in 2023. Of residents who stated their ethnicity at the 2021 census, 90.1% were Russian, and 5.6% were Ukrainian. Sevastopol City is in the time zone UTC+3.

HISTORY

Sevastopol City is located on the site of the ancient Greek city of Chersonesus, near which Prince Vladimir (Volodymyr) was baptized in 988, marking the adoption of Christianity by Kievan (Kyivan) Rus. The modern city was founded in 1783 by Catherine 'the Great', shortly after the territory had been incorporated into the Russian Empire, and became an important trading centre and naval base. The city was besieged for 349 days in 1854–55 during the Crimean War. Sevastopol was a stronghold of support for the Bolsheviks during the civil war after the revolutions of 1917. The city suffered greatly during the Second World War, and was besieged for eight months before being captured by Nazi Germany in 1942. Sevastopol, a separate administrative unit, with the rest of the Crimean peninsula, was transferred from Russian to Ukrainian jurisdiction in 1954.

Following the disintegration of the USSR in 1991, Sevastopol became the principal centre of support for Russian nationalism in Ukraine. The question of the division of the Black Sea Fleet, stationed at several ports in the city, and of basing rights for Russian troops and vessels, represented a major strain in relations between Ukraine and Russia. A new City Administration was established in April 1992. In a direct mayoral election, held in June 1994, Viktor Semyonov defeated a strongly pro-Russian candidate. A 1997 treaty between Russia and Ukraine provided for the division of the Fleet and permitted the lease of bases in Sevastopol to Russia until 2017.

At elections to the City Council held in 2006, 45 of the 75 deputies elected were representatives of the Partiya Rehioniv (PRe—Party of the Regions). In association with pro-Russian and far left groupings, the party established a majority administration, chaired by Valerii Saratov. In June a centrist, Sergei Kunitsyn, a former Chairman of the Council of Ministers of the Autonomous Republic of Crimea, was appointed Chairman of the City Administration (Mayor).

The election of Viktor Yanukovych of the PRe as President of Ukraine in February 2010 brought about a more conciliatory approach towards Russia. In April an agreement was reached to extend Russia's lease on the naval base until 2042. Moreover, units of the Russian Federal Security Service (FSB), expelled several years earlier, were to be permitted to return. In April 2010 Saratov was appointed Mayor. Yanukovych dismissed him in June 2011, appointing Vladimir Yatsuba as his successor. At elections to the City Duma held on 30 October 2010, the PRe won 46 of the 76 seats.

On 25 February 2014, shortly after Yanukovych had fled Kyiv, the Ukrainian capital, following several months of protests, popular demonstrations in Sevastopol led the City Council, illegally, to appoint a Russian citizen, Aleksei Chalyi, as Mayor; checkpoints were established to prevent Ukrainian state forces from reaching the city. On 16 March a referendum in Sevastopol endorsed territorial union with Russia. On 18 March Russian President Vladimir Putin signed a treaty with Chalyi on the admission of the city to the Russian Federation, with effect from 21 March. On 11 April a new city charter was approved, reducing the membership of the City Legislative Assembly (as the City Duma was renamed) from 76 to 25 members. Chalyi resigned as Mayor on 14 April; he was succeeded by Sergei Menyaylo, a former deputy commander of the Black Sea Fleet.

At elections to the Legislative Assembly held on 14 September 2014, the de facto ruling party of Russia, YeR, obtained 76.7% of the votes cast on a proportional basis, and 22 of the 24 deputies. Chalyi became its Chairman (remaining in this position until March 2016). On 9 October 2014 the Legislative Assembly voted to confirm Menyaylo as Governor (as the head of the territory was henceforth styled). On 28 July 2016 Putin appointed Menyaylo as Presidential Representative to the Siberian Federal Okrug, nominating Dmitrii Ovsyannikov, hitherto federal Deputy Minister of Industry and Trade, as Acting Governor, Chairman of the Government.

In November 2016 the City Legislative Assembly introduced legislation providing for direct popular gubernatorial elections. On 10 September 2017 Ovsyannikov was elected Governor, receiving 71.1% of the votes cast in a poll contested by four other candidates.

Ovsyannikov provoked controversy in 2017–18 by seeking to redistribute budget funds in favour of the City Government rather than the Legislative Assembly. In early 2018 antagonism increased between Ovsyannikov and the City Prosecutor (who subsequently resigned), after the City Government launched a campaign to confiscate several thousand land plots that had been issued under Ukrainian rule.

On 11 July 2019 Putin accepted the resignation of Ovsyannikov, and appointed Mikhail Razvozhayev of YeR, a former federal Deputy Minister of North Caucasus Affairs, as Acting Governor.

Elections to the City Legislative Assembly were held on 8 September 2019. YeR was placed first in proportional voting, with 38.5%, ahead of the KPRF, with 18.7%, the LDPR, with 18.6%, SR, with 8.8%, and the RPPS, with 6.9%. By January 2020 a total of 14 of the 24 deputies had joined the parliamentary faction of YeR, three that of the KPRF, three that of the LDPR, one that of SR, and one that of the RPPS.

On 26 July 2020 a naval parade of Black Sea Fleet units was conducted in Sevastopol; a subsequent formal note of protest from Ukraine was returned unopened by the Russian authorities. At the end of that month a Russian Black Sea Fleet serviceman was detained by the FSB in Sevastopol on charges of passing state secrets to the Ukrainian intelligence services.

On 13 September 2020 Razvozhayev was one of six candidates to contest a gubernatorial poll; he was overwhelmingly elected with 85.7% of the votes cast. Razvozhayev was inaugurated as Governor on 2 October.

On 19 October 2022 Putin declared a 'medium level of response' in Sevastopol, Crimea, and six other regions bordering Russian-occupied parts of Ukraine where martial law was introduced; under this regime, the regional authorities concerned were granted powers to undertake 'economic mobilization' such as the requisitioning of civilian infrastructure for the provision of supplies to assist the Russian armed forces, as well as to increase security measures and introduce restrictions on freedom of movement. Numerous drone attacks attributed to Ukraine occurred in the city. Notably in late October several Russian ships in Sevastopol Naval Base were damaged in an attack by a number of drones. Another drone attack on the base occurred in September 2023; in the same month the headquarters of the Russian Black Sea Fleet in the city were attacked, when, according to the Ukrainian military, 34 Russian officers were killed and more than 100 other personnel injured. It was reported in October that much of the Black Sea Fleet had been relocated from Sevastopol to the port of Feodosiya, in the Republic of Crimea, and to Novorossiisk, in Krasnodar Krai.

ECONOMY

In 2023 Sevastopol City's gross regional product (GRP) was 168,574m. roubles, or 326,677 roubles per head. There are no railways.

Agriculture, which principally comprises animal husbandry, poultry farming, and the cultivation of cereals and vegetables, and includes a small fishing industry, employed 2.0% of the workforce and contributed 2.7% of GRP in 2021. Construction and manufacturing are the most important industrial sub-sectors. Industry employed 22.2% of the workforce and contributed 16.4% of GRP in 2021, when manufacturing employed 8.6% of the workforce and contributed 5.3% of GRP. The economy of Sevastopol is dominated by the services sector, particularly trade, real estate, and transport and communications.

The economically active population numbered 253,932 in 2022, when 3.9% of the labour force was unemployed, while the average monthly wage was 43,112 roubles. There was a budgetary deficit of 2,390.1m. roubles in 2021, when export trade amounted to US $6m. (78.2% of which was with CIS countries), and import trade to $5m. (34.7% of which was with CIS countries).

DIRECTORY

Governor: MIKHAIL V. RAZVOZHAYEV.

Office of the Governor: 299001 Sevastopol, ul. Lenina 2; tel. (692) 54-42-14; fax (692) 54-20-53; e-mail pravitelstvo@sevastopol.gov.ru; internet sev.gov.ru.

City Legislative Assembly: 299011 Sevastopol, ul. Lenina 3; tel. (692) 54-05-38; fax (692) 54-03-53; e-mail pressa@sevzaksobranie.ru; internet sevzakon.ru; Chair. VLADIMIR V. NEMTSEV.

State Duma Representative (1): TATYANA G. LOBACH (YeR).

Federation Council Representatives: YEKATERINA B. ALTABAYEVA, SERGEI N. KOLBIN.

Republic of Adygeya

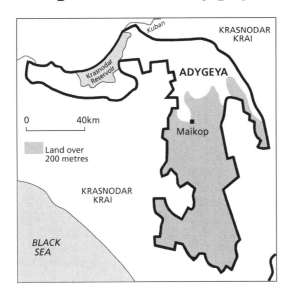

The Republic of Adygeya is situated in the foothills of the Greater Caucasus, a landlocked region in the basin of the Kuban river, surrounded by Krasnodar Krai. The Republic is characterized by open grassland and fertile soil and covers 7,792 sq km (3,009 sq miles). At January 2023 it had an estimated 497,985 inhabitants and a population density of 63.9 per sq km. Only 49.0% of the population was urban in 2023. The administrative centre is Maikop, with an estimated 139,687 inhabitants at January 2023. Of residents who stated their ethnicity at the 2021 census, 64.4% were Russian, 22.0% were Adyge, 3.6% were Cherkess, 3.3% were Armenian, 1.2% were Kurdish, and 0.7% were Gypsy (Roma). Almost all of the Adyge population speak Adyge (part of the Abkhazo-Adyge group of Caucasian languages) as their native language. The dominant religion in Adygeya, owing to the preponderance of ethnic Russians, is Orthodox Christianity, but the traditional religion of the Adyges is Islam. The Republic is in the time zone UTC+3.

HISTORY

The Adyges, a Circassian people, were traditionally renowned for their horsemanship and marksmanship. They emerged as a distinct ethnic group in the 13th century, when they inhabited much of the area between the Don river and the Black Sea. They were conquered by the Mongol Empire in the 13th century. In 1557 the Adyges entered into an alliance with the Russian Empire as protection against the Tatar Khanate of Crimea and against Turkic groups such as the Karachai, the Kumyks and the Nogai, which had retreated into the Caucasus to evade the Mongol forces of Temujin (Chinghiz or Genghis Khan).

Russian settlers subsequently moved into the Don and Kuban regions, causing unrest among the Adyges and other Circassian peoples, many of whom supported the Ottoman Empire against Russia in the Crimean War of 1853–56. The Circassians were finally defeated by the Russians in 1864. Most were forced either to emigrate or to move to the plains under Russian control.

A Kuban-Black Sea Soviet Republic was established in 1918, but anti-communist forces soon occupied the region. Eventually, the Red Army prevailed. The Adyge Autonomous Oblast was established on 27 July 1922. From August 1922 until August 1928 it was known as the Adyge (Circassian) Autonomous Oblast. The Oblast was ruled from Stavropol until 1937, when it was placed in Krasnodar Krai.

In the mid-1980s the Adyge Khase Movement, which sought the formation of a national legislative council for Adyges and other Circassian peoples, notably the Cherkess and the Kabardins, emerged. Adygeya declared its sovereignty on 28 June 1991; an inter-parliamentary council was subsequently formed between Adygeya and the Kabardino-Balkar and Karachai-Cherkess Republics. A Constitution, providing for the existence of Adygeya as a republic, separate from Krasnodar Krai, was adopted on 10 March 1995.

In an election held in January 2002, the republican President, Aslan Dzharimov, was conclusively defeated; he was succeeded by Khazrat Sovmen, the owner of a gold mining co-operative. In 2003 the bicameral legislature, the Khase (State Council), approved constitutional changes providing for its reconstitution on a unicameral basis, with effect from 2006. A large demonstration was staged in Maikop in 2005 to protest against proposals, advanced locally by the Soyuz Slavyan Adygei (Union of Slavs of Adygeya) and the KPRF, for the reunification of Adygeya with Krasnodar Krai. In February 2006 the leaders of Adygeya and Krasnodar Krai declared that no political merger of the two territories was planned, although various state administrative agencies in the two territories were combined subsequently.

In April 2006 reports that Sovmen had announced his resignation to the Khase prompted rallies in his support and against any potential change to the status of Adygeya. Sovmen, who stated that his decision was motivated by the imposition of pressure from the federal authorities to assent to the territory's reabsorption into Krasnodar Krai, met federal President Vladimir Putin in Moscow on 17 April, and tendered his resignation. This, however, was rejected, and he remained in office.

The Khase voted to approve Aslan Tkhakushinov (who had won only 2.1% of the votes cast in the Republic's presidential election in 2002) as candidate for republican President in October 2006. Despite a strenuous campaign waged by Sovmen for his appointment to a further term, Tkhakushinov was inaugurated in January 2007. Shortly afterwards, he signed an agreement providing for closer co-operation with Krasnodar Krai. In November the Khase formally protested to the federal Government that plans to abolish the republican branches of several federal agencies were unconstitutional. After the Chairman of the Khase was elected to the State Duma in December, the selection of a new candidate to the post, traditionally reserved for an Adyge, proved contentious, and it was not until April 2008 that the Khase approved the appointment of Anatolii Ivanov, an ethnic Russian, as its Chairman. Tkhakushinov formally appointed his nephew, Murat Kumpilov, as Prime Minister in May. An extraordinary congress of the Adyge Khase organization, held in November, adopted a resolution demanding the unification of those parts of Adygeya, the Kabardino-Balkar Republic and the Karachai-Cherkess Republic where Circassian peoples constituted a demographic majority. (The Kabardin chapter of the organization subsequently rejected this proposal.)

With effect from May 2011, the title of President of Adygeya was changed to Head of the Republic. In December the Khase elected Tkhakushinov to a further term of office. In that month the Khase adopted a resolution requesting the assistance of the federal authorities in resettling Circassians from the Syrian Arab Republic to the territories in Russia in which their ancestors had resided prior to the 1860s, following the onset of civil unrest in Syria. By mid-2015 around 700 Syrian citizens of Circassian descent were believed to have resettled in Adygeya. Additionally, in August 2014 it was reported that around 2,500 ethnic Russian refugees from the unrest that had recently commenced in the eastern Donetsk and Luhansk (Lugansk) oblasts of Ukraine had taken up residency in the Republic. In March 2016 the Khase approved legislation ensuring that future governors would continue to be elected by parliamentary deputies.

At elections to the Khase held on 18 September 2016, YeR obtained 58.3% of votes cast on a proportional basis, ahead of the KPRF, with 15.3%, the LDPR, with 14.1%, and SR, with 7.2%. By the end of the year 40 of the 50 deputies had joined the YeR parliamentary faction. Following his election to the Khase (of which he was appointed Chairman in October), Kumpilov resigned as Prime Minister; he was succeeded in an acting capacity by Natalya Shirokova. On 12 January 2017, following the expiry of Tkhakushinov's mandate, Putin appointed Kumpilov as Acting Head of the Republic. On 10 September the Khase voted unanimously to confirm Kumpilov as Head of the Republic, and on 29 September it voted to approve the appointment of Aleksandr Narolin, the Mayor of Maikop since 2013, as Prime Minister.

On 14 September 2020 Kumpilov appointed Gennadii Mitrofanov, hitherto the Republic's First Deputy Minister of Economic Development and Trade, as Prime Minister, replacing Narolin; he was confirmed in office on 23 September.

At elections to the Khase held on 19 September 2021, YeR secured 66.7% of the votes cast on the basis of proportional representation; the KPRF obtained 17.7%, the LDPR 7.7% and SR 6.1%. By the end of the year 40 of the 49 deputies had joined the YeR faction, five that of the KPRF and three that of the LDPR.

On 11 September 2022 the Khase unanimously elected Kumpilov (who had been nominated by YeR) for a second term as Governor.

ECONOMY

In 2021 the gross regional product (GRP) of Adygeya was 170,793m. roubles, or 366,702 roubles per head. At the end of 2021 there were 160 km of railways in Adygeya.

Agricultural production consists mainly of animal husbandry, grain, sunflowers, sugar beet, tobacco, vegetables, cucurbit (gourds and melons) and viniculture (Adygeya is one of Russia's principal centres for the production of grape wine). Agriculture employed 11.5% of the workforce and contributed 13.2% of GRP in 2021. There is some extraction of natural gas. Food processing is an important industrial activity, and timber processing, mechanical engineering and metal working are also significant. Adygeya lies along the route of the Blue Stream pipeline, completed in 2002, which delivers gas to Türkiye (Turkey) via the Black Sea ports of Novorossiisk and Tuapse (both in Krasnodar Krai). The largest wind farm in Russia, comprising 60 wind turbines, with a combined annual average output of 354m. kWh, commenced operations in Adygeya in early 2020. Industry employed 23.7% of the workforce and contributed 21.0% of GRP in 2021, when manufacturing employed 11.3% of the workforce and contributed 12.5% of GRP.

The economically active population numbered 188,065 in 2022, when 7.1% of the labour force were unemployed, while the average monthly wage was 40,231 roubles.

There was a budgetary surplus of 2,244.6m. roubles in 2021. Export trade amounted to US $38m. in that year (of which 35.2% was with countries of the CIS), while import trade amounted to $68m. (of which 7.3% was with CIS countries).

DIRECTORY

Head of the Republic: Murat K. Kumpilov.

Office of the Head of the Republic: 385000 Adygeya, Maikop, ul. Zhukovskogo 22; tel. (8772) 57-07-15; fax (8772) 52-27-17; e-mail president@adygheya.ru; internet adygheya.ru.

Prime Minister: Gennadii A. Mitrofanov.

Office of the Prime Minister: 385000 Adygeya, Maikop, ul. Pionerskaya 199; tel. (8772) 57-00-22; fax (8772) 52-27-17; e-mail premier@adygheya.ru; internet bit.ly/32m3iF2.

State Council (Khase): 385000 Adygeya, Maikop, ul. Zhukovskogo 22; tel. (8772) 52-19-02; fax (8772) 57-11-94; e-mail info@gshra.ru; internet gshra.ru; Chair. Vladimir I. Narozhnyi.

State Duma Representative (1): Vladislav M. Reznik (YeR).

Federation Council Representatives: Murat K.-G. Khapsirokov, Aleksandr V. Narolin.

Republic of Crimea

Note: The territories of the Crimean peninsula, comprising Sevastopol City and the Republic of Crimea, remained internationally recognized as constituting part of Ukraine, following their annexation by Russia in March 2014.

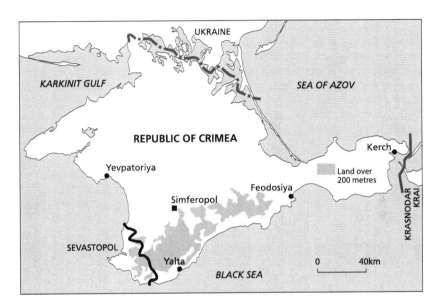

The Republic of Crimea constitutes most of the Crimean peninsula. It is joined to mainland Ukraine (Kherson Oblast, of which Russia announced the annexation in September 2022) by the Perekop Isthmus to the north-west, the Arabat Spit to the north-east, and a road and railway bridge at the Crimean Tup-Dzhankoi peninsula to the north. The Republic covers 26,081 sq km, much of which is dry steppeland, with mountains to the south-west. Sevastopol City lies to the south-west, the Black Sea to the west and south, and the Sea of Azov to the north-east. In the east, the Kirch Strait separates Crimea from Krasnodar Krai; a bridge linking the territories opened in 2018. At January 2023 the Republic had an estimated population of 1,916,805 and a population density of 73.5 per sq km. Only 50.3% of the population was urban in 2023. The administrative centre is Simferopol, with an estimated 337,730 inhabitants in January 2023. The other principal cities are Kerch, in the east, with a population of 152,683, and Yevpatoriya (106,763), in the west. Of residents who stated their ethnicity at the 2021 census, 72.9% were Russian, 14.1% were Crimean Tatar, 8.2% were Ukrainian, and 1.6% were Tatar. The Republic of Crimea is in the time zone UTC+3.

HISTORY

The Crimean peninsula was colonized by Greeks in the seventh century BCE. It was subsequently invaded by Goths, Huns, Khazars, Eastern Roman, or Byzantine, Greeks, Kipchaks, Mongol Tatars and Ottoman Turks. A Crimean Khanate, founded in 1475 CE, survived until its annexation by the Russian Empire in 1783, when much of the

Tatar population fled. The Russians were defeated in the Crimean War (1854–55) by the Western Powers (France, the Kingdom of Sardinia and the United Kingdom) and the Ottoman Turks. Crimea formed part of the Republic of Taurida founded in 1918. On 18 October 1921 the Crimean Autonomous Soviet Socialist Republic (ASSR) was created within the Russian Soviet Federative Socialist Republic, which in 1922 became part of the USSR. Almost all of Crimea was occupied by Axis (Nazi German and Romanian) troops during the Second World War in 1941–44. Following their recapture of the territory, the Soviet authorities deported the entire 200,000-strong Crimean Tatar population to Central Asia; a substantial proportion of them died en route or during their initial exile. The Crimean ASSR was abolished on 30 June 1945, becoming an oblast (region), and the immigration of ethnic Russians was promoted. In 1954 Crimea was transferred to the Ukrainian Soviet Socialist Republic (SSR).

Following a referendum in January 1991, Crimea claimed the status of an Autonomous Republic within the Ukrainian SSR. In June Crimean Tatars (who had begun to return to the peninsula) established 'parallel' institutions to those of the state, including the Qurultay (Assembly) and an executive body, the Qırımtatar Milly Meclisi (Crimean Tatar National Assembly—Mejlis). In December Crimea voted in support of Ukrainian independence from the USSR at a referendum, with 54.2% of the votes cast in favour (compared with the 90.3% support for independence recorded overall). In February 1992 the Crimean Supreme Council (legislature) voted to transform the region into the Republic of Crimea. Although Ukraine offered the region greater self-government, on 5 May the Supreme Council declared independence. The Ukrainian Verkhovna Rada (legislature) annulled this declaration, and in June Ukraine recognized Crimea as an Autonomous Republic.

In January 1994 a Russian nationalist, Yurii Meshkov, won elections to the new presidency of Crimea. Elections to the republican legislature in March demonstrated substantial support for pro-Russian parties, and a referendum supported greater autonomy. In May the Supreme Council voted to restore the 1992 Constitution, effectively renewing the declaration of independence. In March 1995 the Verkhovna Rada voted to abolish the 1992 Constitution and the Crimean presidency. Two weeks later Ukrainian President Leonid Kuchma assumed direct control over Crimea (which continued until August) and ordered the restoration of Anatolii Franchuk (recently dismissed by the Supreme Council) as republican premier.

In October 1995 the Supreme Council adopted a new Constitution, which the Ukrainian authorities recognized in April 1996. It defined Crimea as an Autonomous Republic within Ukraine. The new Constitution of Ukraine, adopted in June, described Ukraine as a unitary state, including the Autonomous Republic of Crimea.

At elections in March 1998, the Komunistychna Partiya Ukrainy (KPU—Communist Party of Ukraine) obtained 40 of the 100 seats in the Supreme Council; 44 independent candidates were elected. Leonid Grach, the local KPU leader, became Chairman of the Supreme Council. In October the process of naturalization of Tatars was simplified, and by 2002 some 90% of Crimean Tatars resident on the peninsula held Ukrainian citizenship. In May 1998 a new Council of Ministers was appointed, under the leadership of the centrist, Sergei Kunitsyn. On 12 January 1999 a new Crimean Constitution came into effect, granting Crimea the right to draft a budget and manage its own property. In May 2000 some 20,000 Crimean Tatars held a demonstration in Simferopol to demand greater autonomy.

In July 2001 the Supreme Council dismissed Kunitsyn as premier. Although Kuchma had refused to recognize two previous dismissals, he expressed support for the new premier elected by the Supreme Council, Valerii Gorbatov. Elections to the Crimean Supreme Council on 31 March 2002 demonstrated a shift in support towards the Komanda Kunitsyna (Kunitsyn Team), which received 39 of the 100 seats. The KPU and its allies won 28 seats; 29 independent candidates were elected. The new Supreme Council voted to reappoint Kunitsyn as Prime Minister.

At the 2004 Ukrainian presidential election, Crimea's Russian-speaking majority strongly supported Viktor Yanukovych, while the Crimean Tatar minority voted principally for the winning candidate, Viktor Yushchenko. In April 2005 Kunitsyn resigned; he was succeeded as Crimean premier by Yushchenko's nominee, Anatolii Matviyenko. In September Matviyenko was replaced by Anatolii Burdyugov.

In elections to the Supreme Council in 2006, the Za Yanukovycha (For Yanukovych) bloc, dominated by the Partiya Rehioniv (PRe—Party of the Regions), won 44 of the 100 seats, far more than any other party. On 2 June the Supreme Council approved the formation of a new Government, chaired by Viktor Plakida, an ally of Yanukovych. Meanwhile, in May the proposed staging of North Atlantic Treaty Organization (NATO) military exercises off the Crimean coast was abandoned, following protests by Russian nationalists.

Russia's invasion of Georgia in August 2008, and its ensuing recognition of the statehood of the separatist territories of South Ossetia and Abkhazia, increased concerns about a similar conflict potentially emerging in Crimea, particularly since Russia had commenced issuing passports to residents of Crimea (as they had in South Ossetia). In September the Supreme Council urged Ukraine to recognize the independence of Abkhazia and South Ossetia.

In January 2009 the Mejlis, chaired by Mustafa Cemil (Dzhemilev), expressed concern that the authorities were planning to demolish a Tatar-occupied district in Simferopol, comprising land owned by the Ministry of Defence. Around 2,000 Tatar activists staged a protest in March, demanding the provision of land to returnees. In April 2009 the Supreme Council voted in support of a motion attempting to stop Black Sea naval exercises off the coast of Crimea that would have involved US forces. The planned exercises were subsequently cancelled. Meanwhile, on 18 May some 20,000 Tatars attended a commemoration in Simferopol marking the 65th anniversary of their deportation.

Pro-Russian elements in Crimea were strengthened by the election of Yanukovych as President of Ukraine in February 2010; in that month the Supreme Council voted to adopt the Russian variant of its name as its official designation. In March members of the PRe, Vladimir Konstantinov and Vasil Dzharty, became, respectively, Chairman of the Supreme Council and Crimean Prime Minister.

Elections to the Supreme Council were conducted on 31 October 2010, under a new mixed voting system. The PRe obtained 48.9% of the votes cast on a proportional basis and 80 of the 100 seats. Konstantinov was re-elected legislative Chairman.

Dzharty died in August 2011. In November Yanukovych appointed Anatolii Mogilyov of the PRe, hitherto the Minister of Internal Affairs of Ukraine (and a former chief of police in Crimea, in which capacity he had endorsed the use of force against Tatar demonstrators), as Prime Minister of Crimea.

In January 2013 a presidential decree ordered reforms to the membership of an official consultative Council of Representatives of Crimean Tatars. Members of the Mejlis and the Qurultay refused to recognize the legitimacy of the reformed Council. In March Cemil stated that any attempts to abolish the Mejlis would provoke a violent response. Tensions were heightened further when the Crimean Government announced that members of the Mejlis would be excluded from the organization of official commemorations to mark the anniversary in May of the 1944 deportation. In October Refat Çubarov succeeded Cemil as Chairman of the Mejlis.

The removal from office of President Yanukovych on 21–22 February 2014 immediately precipitated unrest on the Crimean peninsula. On 27 February unidentified armed men seized control of the Supreme Council building in Simferopol. The Council approved a vote of no confidence in the new interim Ukrainian Government, and elected a deputy of the Russkoye Yedinstvo (Russian Unity) party (which held three of the 100 seats), Sergei Aksyonov, as Chairman of the Council of Ministers. It called a referendum on increased territorial autonomy for 25 May (subsequently brought forward to 30 March). On 5 March Ukraine issued a warrant for Aksyonov's arrest.

Meanwhile, unidentified 'self-defence' forces blockaded Ukrainian military bases across Crimea. On 6 March 2014 the Supreme Council voted in favour of Crimea joining Russia and announced that a referendum to seek endorsement of this would be held on 16 March. The plebiscite proceeded; 96.7% of votes were reported to have supported the territory joining Russia as a federal subject (the only alternative option provided was a return to the 1992–95 Constitution of Crimea). After the Crimean parliament (which had reconstituted itself as the State Council) formally applied to join Russia, on 18 March 2014 a treaty was signed by Russian President Vladimir Putin and Aksyonov on the admission of the Republic of Crimea (as the territory was renamed) to the Russian Federation; this entered into effect on 21 March. On 24 March all Ukrainian troops withdrew from Crimea; at least five deaths had occurred in clashes.

Following the Russian annexation many Crimean Tatars were reported to have suffered adverse discrimination from the Crimean authorities, particularly after they refused to register for Russian passports; in April 2014 Cemil was prohibited from entering Russian territory (including Crimea) for five years. Meanwhile, the authorities imposed a ban on the annual rally to commemorate the 1944 deportation; an unauthorized rally was held, instead, on the outskirts of Simferopol, in May 2014. In July Çubarov was prevented from entering Crimea following a meeting of the Mejlis in Ukraine, and was subsequently barred from entering Russian territory until 2019.

Elections were held to the State Council on 14 September 2014. A boycott of the polls urged by Crimean Tatar representatives was observed, while pro-Ukrainian groups also declined to participate. YeR won 70 seats in the reconstituted 75-member State Council; the LDPR obtained the remaining five. An overall participation rate of 53.6% was recorded.

Shortly after the elections, the Mejlis was expelled from its office, after its property and assets had been frozen under a court order. Meanwhile, Crimea suffered severe water and electricity shortages, after Ukraine suspended most supplies. On 9 October 2014 the State Council unanimously voted to confirm the appointment of Aksyonov as Head of the Republic. He was to remain Chairman of the Council of Ministers.

The construction of a 19-km, road and rail bridge to link Kerch, in eastern Crimea, with Krasnodar Krai commenced in May 2015. Putin made a three-day visit to the peninsula in August, when he discouraged the Crimean Tatar community from seeking special status. Later that month a Russian military court sentenced a Crimean-born film director, Oleh Sentsov, to 20 years' imprisonment and another activist, Oleksandr Kolchenko, to a term of 10 years for planning terrorist acts in Crimea in early 2014.

In September 2015 Çubarov announced that a blockade of supplies entering Crimea at the three crossing points with mainland Ukraine would be imposed unless Russia acceded to several demands, including the lifting of the ban on entry imposed against Crimean Tatar leaders and activists. By that time up to 15,000 of the 300,000-strong Crimean Tatar community in Crimea resident there in early 2014 were estimated to have left the peninsula. The ensuing imposition of the blockade on 20 September 2015 was endorsed by Ukraine. In November electricity supplies from Ukraine to the peninsula were suspended, following a series of explosions that damaged pylon lines in southern Ukraine. A state of emergency was declared later in the month, and alternative power supplies were arranged. In early 2016 Crimean officials announced that the import of electricity supplies from Ukraine would be abandoned totally, and in May the construction of a new power line from Russia was completed. Meanwhile, a court in Simferopol issued a warrant for the arrest of Cemil in January 2016. In April the activities of the Mejlis were suspended.

On 28 July 2016 the Crimean Federal Okrug (comprising the two territories on the peninsula) that had been established in 2014 was abolished and absorbed into the Southern Federal Okrug. On the same day Russian Minister of Defence Sergei Shoigu announced that a 'self-sufficient' contingent of troops had been deployed in Crimea, and a military build-up near the de facto border with Ukraine, in addition to the temporary closure of the border crossing, was reported. Tensions escalated in August, when Putin accused Ukraine of orchestrating subversive activities in Crimea.

On 29 September 2016 Russia's Supreme Court upheld the ban that had been imposed against the operations of the Mejlis; the Mejlis subsequently challenged the ban at the European Court of Human Rights.

In July 2017 the German company Siemens filed a case at the Moscow Arbitration Court against its Russian-based affiliate and the Russian state-owned Tekhnopromeksport corporation, in an effort to prevent the use in the Crimean peninsula, in contravention of sanctions, of four turbine sets that it had manufactured.

In January 2018 Russia deployed units of an S-400 air defence system to south-western Crimea, outside Sevastopol, following the setting up of a similar system near Feodosiya in the previous year. In May 2019 a senior Ukrainian reconnaissance officer was convicted of planning acts of sabotage against the electricity infrastructure in Crimea and sentenced to eight years' imprisonment by a Crimean court.

Tensions increased over navigation in the Sea of Azov, after the Ukrainian authorities detained a Crimean fishing vessel in March 2018. In May Putin officially opened the road section of the bridge over the Kerch Strait (the railway section was inaugurated in December 2019). The EU imposed asset freezes on an additional six Russian companies for their involvement in the construction of the bridge in July 2018.

On 25 November 2018 Russian maritime border guards seized three Ukrainian navy gunboats and a tugboat which had attempted to pass through the Kerch Strait to the Sea of Azov. Putin subsequently insisted that the Ukrainian vessels had entered Russian territorial waters illegally, while Ukraine denounced the incident as a violation of a 2003 bilateral treaty on the status of the Kerch Strait. In response, Ukraine imposed martial law along the border with Russia and along the Black Sea littoral (with effect until 26 December). Shortly afterwards, the 24 captured Ukrainian sailors were transferred to pre-trial detention in Moscow. On 28 December the FSB announced that it had completed the construction of a 60-km security fence separating the peninsula from mainland Ukraine. (In September 2019 the 24 Ukrainian sailors held in detention in Russia were released, as part of a prisoner exchange between Russia and Ukraine.)

Elections to the State Council were held on 8 September 2019. YeR obtained 54.7% of the proportional vote, ahead of the LDPR, with 16.8%, and the KPRF, with 8.2%.

TERRITORIAL SURVEYS

When the new Council convened later in the month, 60 deputies joined the YeR faction, 10 that of the LDPR, and five that of the KPRF. On 1 October the State Council voted to appoint Yurii Gotsanyuk as Chairman of the Council of Ministers.

Amid the escalating COVID-19 pandemic, Putin made a visit to the Crimean peninsula on 18–19 March 2020, during which he attended ceremonies to inaugurate thermal power stations, and met Aksyonov for discussions. Meanwhile, on 18 March the FSB largely closed Crimea's administrative border with Ukraine. Quarantine requirements (introduced in March) for visitors were lifted in mid-June, and the tourism sector was officially reopened on 1 July.

Meanwhile, on 20 March 2020 President Putin signed a decree prohibiting non-Russian citizens from owning land in most parts of the Crimean peninsula, requiring them to acquire Russian citizenship or to sell their property within one year. In early July the FSB announced that it had detained seven Crimean Tatar activists, who were accused of being members of the proscribed Hizb-ut-Tahrir al-Islami (Party of Islamic Liberation). Putin visited Kerch to attend an inauguration ceremony for new warships on 20 July, prompting a further protest from Ukraine.

As tensions between Russia and Ukraine intensified further, in September 2021, Nariman Celâl (Dzhelial), Deputy Chairman of the Mejlis, was detained, together with two other Crimean Tatar activists, on suspicion of involvement in the sabotage of a gas pipeline. In April 2022 Cemil was found guilty *in absentia* on charges including illegal entry to Crimea, but two associated prison sentences and three fines that were imposed against him were immediately waived owing to the expiry of the statute of limitations. Crimea's Supreme Court on 21 September sentenced Celâl to 17 years' imprisonment for sabotage; the other two defendants received terms of 15 and 13 years, respectively.

Meanwhile, following Russia's invasion of Ukraine on 24 February 2022, on 11 April a high level of terrorist threat was declared in northern and eastern areas of Crimea. On 7 June the federal Ministry of Defence announced that it had opened a new land corridor between Russia and Crimea through eastern Ukrainian territory by the Sea of Azov now under its control, and that water supplies to the peninsula through the North Crimean Canal, which had been suspended by Ukraine in 2014, had been restored. In July a bus service between the Crimean peninsula and neighbouring Kherson Oblast, in southern Ukraine (now under de facto Russian occupation), resumed, after an eight-year suspension.

As Ukrainian forces launched a counter-offensive to regain control of territory in the south of the country, at the end of July 2022 annual Navy Day celebrations were cancelled in Sevastopol, following a drone attack against the Black Sea Fleet headquarters in which six people were injured. On 9 August Aksyonov confirmed that one person had been killed and 14 injured in an Ukrainian strike against a military airbase in the Saki district, west of Simferopol. The incident was reported to have severely damaged the airbase, destroyed nine fighter aircraft and precipitated the flight of tourists from the peninsula. On 16 August explosions at an ammunition depot in the Dzhankoi district in northern Crimea caused a severe fire. A drone attack was staged near the Belbek military airport outside Sevastopol on 18 August, followed by a further strike targeting the Black Sea Fleet headquarters two days later.

Following continued drone attacks, on 8 October 2022 an explosion near the road section of the Kerch bridge resulted in a severe fire, killing four people and causing significant damage. The FSB arrested at least eight people suspected of involvement of the incident, which Putin denounced as an 'act of terrorism' by the Ukrainian special services. In response, Russia launched mass missile attacks against targets in Ukraine.

On 19 October Putin declared a 'medium level of response' in Crimea, Sevastopol and six other regions bordering Russian-occupied parts of Ukraine where martial law was introduced; under this regime, the regional authorities concerned were granted powers to undertake 'economic mobilization' such as the requisitioning of civilian infrastructure for the provision of supplies to assist the Russian armed forces, as well as to increase security measures and introduce restrictions on freedom of movement. Road traffic was fully restored on the Kerch bridge in early December. Meanwhile, the FSB announced the arrest of two residents of Crimea on charges of high treason.

On 17 July 2023 the road section of the Kerch bridge was again damaged by two explosions, which killed two people and injured one. The Ukrainian Government subsequently admitted responsibility for the attack, which had been conducted by maritime drones. The bridge was partly reopened on the following day; however, on 22 July a drone attack on an ammunition depot in the central Krasnogvardeiskoye district of Crimea necessitated civilian evacuations. In early August Russian oil tankers in the Black Sea were attacked by naval drones near the Crimean peninsula, while the Chonhar road bridge linking mainland Ukraine to Crimea and a smaller bridge were damaged in a missile strike. It was reported in October that much of the Black Sea Fleet had been relocated from Sevastopol City to Feodosiya, in the east of Crimea, and to Novorossiisk, Krasnodar Krai, after major Ukrainian missile strikes against the Fleet's base and headquarters in Sevastopol had occurred in September. In November US newspaper *The Washington Post*, citing intercepted e-mails provided by Ukrainian officials, reported that a Russian-Chinese consortium had been established to construct an underwater tunnel connecting Crimea with Krasnodar Krai, due to increasing Russian concerns over the security of the Kerch bridge.

The FSB announced on 11 December 2023 that 18 people had been arrested on suspicion of planning the assassination of Russian-installed officials in Crimea, including Aksyonov and Konstantinov. Shortly afterwards, police detained a Crimean Tatar religious leader, Ismail Yurdamov, after searching his residence. On 26 December the Ukrainian military announced that a Russian major landing ship had been destroyed in a missile attack against Feodosiya, in which at least one person was killed and four injured.

ECONOMY

In 2021 the gross regional product (GRP) of the Republic of Crimea amounted to 586,498m. roubles, or 308,848 roubles per head. The longest trolleybus route in the world links the capital, Simferopol, with the coastal resorts of Alushta and Yalta; the latter, a major tourism resort, is situated some 86 km from Simferopol. In association with the construction of a bridge across the Kerch Strait to link the Crimean peninsula with Krasnodar Krai and mainland Russia, a trans-Crimean highway, linking Kerch with Feodosiya, Simferopol and Sevastopol, was opened in 2020. At the end of 2021 there were 668 km of railways in the Republic.

Agriculture, which principally comprises animal husbandry, poultry farming, beekeeping, and the cultivation of cereals, sunflowers, fruit and vegetables, employed 10.1% of the workforce and contributed 7.4% of GRP in 2021. The main industries include chemicals and petrochemicals, mechanical engineering and food processing. Industry employed 21.7% of the workforce and contributed 25.8% of GRP in 2021, when manufacturing employed 8.5% of the workforce and contributed 8.7% of GRP. The economy is dominated by the services sector, particularly trade, health care and education. In August 2014 the Russian Government announced that 700,000m. roubles would be allocated for the economic development of the peninsula, which was to be declared a free economic zone for a period of 10 years. The Crimean authorities in early 2018 announced the construction of a gambling zone in Yalta (one of only five such areas permitted in the Federation), although the proposed opening date, initially scheduled for September 2019, was delayed until 2024.

The economically active population numbered 866,716 in 2022, when 5.8% of the labour force of the region were unemployed, while the average monthly wage was 41,986 roubles. There was a budgetary deficit of 5,347.5m. roubles in 2021, when export trade amounted to US $37m. (of which 83.9% was with CIS countries) and import trade to $32m. (of which 77.6% was with CIS countries).

DIRECTORY

Head of the Republic: SERGEI V. AKSYONOV.

Office of the Head of the Republic: 295005 Crimea, Simferopol, pr. Kirova 13; tel. (652) 27-42-10; e-mail sovmin@rk.gov.ru; internet glava.rk.gov.ru.

Chairman of the Council of Ministers: YURII M. GOTSANYUK.

Office of the Chairman of the Council of Ministers: 295005 Crimea, Simferopol, pr. Kirova 13; tel. (652) 27-63-77; e-mail sovmin@rk.gov.ru; internet rk.gov.ru.

State Council: 295000 Crimea, Simferopol, ul. K. Marksa 18; tel. (652) 54-43-01; fax (652) 27-25-81; e-mail odk_svr@rada.crimea.ua; internet crimea.gov.ru; Chair. VLADIMIR A. KONSTANTINOV.

State Duma Representatives (3): YURII YU. NESTERENKO (YeR), KONSTANTIN M. BAKHAREV (YeR), LEONID I. BABASHOV (YeR).

Federation Council Representatives: SERGEI P. TSEKOV, OLGA F. KOVITIDI.

Republic of Kalmykiya

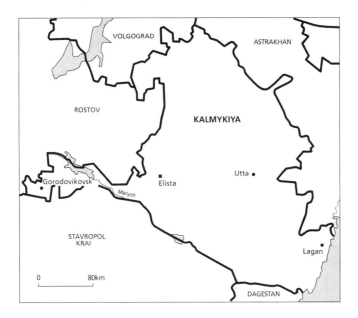

The Republic of Kalmykiya is situated in the north-western part of the Caspian lowlands. There is a south-eastern border with the Caspian Sea. Dagestan lies to the south and Stavropol Krai to the south-west, while Rostov, Volgograd and Astrakhan Oblasts are to the west, north-west and north-east, respectively. The Republic occupies 74,731 sq km (28,854 sq miles), one-half of which is desert. At January 2023 it had an estimated population of 264,483 and a population density of 3.5 per sq km. Only 47.0% of the population was urban in 2023. The capital is Elista, with an estimated 102,428 inhabitants at January 2023. Of residents who stated their ethnicity at the 2021 census, 62.5% were Kalmyk, 25.7% were Russian, 2.8% were Dargin, 1.7% were Kazakh, 1.6% were Turks, 1.1% were Chechen, and 1.0% were Avar. The dominant religion among the Kalmyks is Lamaism (Tibetan Buddhism). Some 90% of the indigenous population speak the Kalmyk language, which is from the Mongol division of the Uralo-Altaic family. Kalmykiya is in the time zone UTC+3.

HISTORY

The Kalmyks (Oirots), a semi-nomadic Mongol-speaking people, originated in Eastern Turkestan (Dzungaria, mostly in the People's Republic of China). Displaced by the Han Chinese, they migrated westwards, in 1608 reaching the Volga basin, under Russian control since 1556. The region became the Kalmyk Khanate, until its dissolution in 1771. By this time many Kalmyks had been slaughtered during a mass migration eastwards; those who remained were dispersed. Ethnic Russians and Germans settled in Kalmykiya during the 18th century. A Kalmyk Autonomous Oblast was established on 4 November 1920. Its status was upgraded to that of an Autonomous Soviet Socialist Republic (ASSR) in 1935. In 1943 the Kalmyks were deported to Central Asia, and the Republic was dissolved. A Kalmyk Autonomous Oblast was reconstituted in 1957, regaining the status of an ASSR in 1958. In the late 1990s a territorial dispute between Kalmykiya and Astrakhan Oblast resurfaced, with Kalmykiya claiming an area included in the pre-1943 Republic known as the Black Lands.

The Republic adopted a declaration of sovereignty in October 1990. It was known as the Republic of Kalmykiya-Khalmg Tangch in 1992–96. In April 1993 a business executive, Kirsan Ilyumzhinov, was elected as republican President. A new Constitution, providing for a seven-year presidential term, was adopted on 5 April 1994.

In October 1995 Ilyumzhinov was the sole candidate in a presidential election, in contravention of federal law. In that year he had also become President of the International Chess Federation (FIDE), and took steps to promote the sport in the Republic. He was re-elected President in 2002, additionally becoming Prime Minister in 2003. In December Ilyumzhinov announced the appointment of a premier, Anatolii Kozachko. Demonstrations against Ilyumzhinov took place in Elista in February and September 2004; on the latter occasion one protester was killed and several injured during the violent dispersal of a demonstration. In November the Tibetan Buddhist leader, the Dalai Lama (Tenzin Gyatso), visited Kalmykiya, precipitating criticism from the People's Republic of China, as had occurred after a previous visit in 1992.

The republican legislature confirmed the nomination of Ilyumzhinov to a further term of office in October 2005. In December 2007 Ilyumzhinov dismissed Kozachko as republican premier and appointed Vladimir Sengleyev in his place.

In April 2010 Oleg Kichikov succeeded Sengleyev as Prime Minister. On 28 September the People's Khural endorsed President Dmitrii Medvedev's nominee, Aleksei Orlov, hitherto the First Deputy Chairman of the republican government, as republican leader, to succeed Ilyumzhinov. After Orlov assumed office on 24 October, he adopted the title Head of the Republic (instead of President) and restructured the Government. In February 2011 Orlov dismissed the Government; the new premier was the erstwhile republican Deputy Prime Minister and Minister of Finance, Lyudmila Ivanova. In October 2012 Orlov again dismissed the republican Government, expressing dissatisfaction with the socioeconomic development of the Republic. On 13 November the People's Khural unanimously elected another former republican Minister of Finance, Igor Zotov, as Prime Minister.

In elections to the republican legislature, the People's Khural (Parliament), held in September 2013, YeR was again placed first, obtaining 51.3% of the votes cast on a proportional basis. The KPRF was second, with 11.4%. On 14 September 2014, in a direct popular election to the post of Head of the Republic, contested by four candidates, Orlov was elected to office, obtaining 82.9% of the vote.

In elections to the People's Khural, held on 9 September 2018, YeR won 68.5% of the proportional vote. Some 21 of the 27 deputies had joined the YeR parliamentary faction by the end of the year.

On 20 March 2019 Orlov announced his resignation as Head of the Republic. On the same day President Vladimir Putin appointed Batu Khasikov, a champion kickboxer and former representative of the Republic in the Federation Council, as Acting Head of the Republic; Orlov subsequently became a representative of Kalmykiya in the Federation Council. A new Prime Minister, Yurii Zaytsev, a former electricity sector official, was appointed in late April. On 8 September Khasikov was elected Head of the Republic, receiving 82.5% of the votes cast.

On 11 May 2022 Khasikov appointed Ochir Shurgucheyev, hitherto the first deputy premier, as acting Prime Minister, after Zaytsev was transferred by President Putin to become Acting Head of the Republic of Marii-El. On 27 September Gilyana Boskhomdzhiyeva, previously a deputy premier, was appointed as Prime Minister, replacing Shurgucheyev.

Following elections to the Legislative Assembly held on 10 September 2023, YeR held 23 of the 27 seats in the chamber.

ECONOMY

In 2021 Kalmykiya's gross regional product (GRP) amounted to 100,008m. roubles, or 371,956 roubles per head. Although primarily an agricultural territory, much of Kalmykiya's land has suffered from desertification. Kalmykiya's major industrial centres are at Elista and Kaspiiskii. At the end of 2021 there were 165 km of railways in the Republic.

Kalmykiya's agriculture consists mainly of animal husbandry. The sector employed 17.6% of the workforce and contributed 19.2% of GRP in 2021. Industry consists mainly of electricity production, the manufacture of building materials, and the production of petroleum and natural gas. The Republic has major hydrocarbons reserves, which, however, remain largely unexploited. Industry employed 16.1% of the working population (the lowest level of any federal subject) and contributed 7.4% of GRP in 2021, when manufacturing employed 4.6% of the workforce and contributed 0.8% of GRP.

The economically active population in the Republic amounted to 124,144 in 2022, when 8.1% of the labour force were unemployed, while the average monthly wage was 36,349 roubles. There was a budgetary deficit of 1,307.2m. roubles in 2021, when export trade amounted to $1m. (of which 50.0% was with countries of the CIS), while import trade amounted to less than $1m. (of which 60.0% was with CIS countries).

DIRECTORY

Head of the Republic: BATU S. KHASIKOV.

Office of the Head of the Republic: 358000 Kalmykiya, Elista, ul. Pushkina 18; tel. (84722) 3-30-88; fax (84722) 3-38-57; e-mail ap@rk.ru; internet glava.region08.ru.

Prime Minister: GILYANA G. BOSKHOMDZHIYEVA.

Office of the Prime Minister: 358000 Kalmykiya, Elista, ul. Pushkina 18; tel. (84722) 3-42-34; fax (84722) 3-42-43; e-mail ap@rk08.ru; internet kalmregion.ru.

People's Khural (Parliament): 358000 Kalmykiya, Elista, ul. Pushkina 18; tel. (84722) 4-04-97; fax (84722) 4-05-87; e-mail huralrk@huralrk.ru; internet huralrk.ru; Chair. ANATOLII V. KOZACHKO.

State Duma Representative (1): BADMA N. BASHANKAYEV (YeR).

Federation Council Representatives: ALEKSEI M. ORLOV, BAIIR E. PUTEYEV.

Krasnodar Krai

Krasnodar Krai is situated in the south of European Russia, in the north-western region of the Greater Caucasus and in the Kuban-Azov lowlands. It has a short international border with Georgia (Abkhazia) in the south, while the Karachai-Cherkess Republic and Stavropol Krai lie to the east and Rostov Oblast to the north-east. It is bounded by the Black Sea to the south-west and the Sea of Azov to the north-west. The Krai's territory encloses the Republic of Adygeya. The Kerch Strait separates the western tip of the province from Crimea (internationally recognized as Ukrainian, but annexed by Russia in 2014). Its major river is the Kuban. The Krai covers 75,485 sq km (29,145 sq miles). At January 2023 it had an estimated population of 5,819,345 and a population density of 77.1 per sq km. Some 57.1% of the population was urban in 2023. The administrative centre, Krasnodar, had an estimated 1,121,291 inhabitants at January 2023. Other large cities include Sochi (446,599), Novorossiysk (261,626) and Armavir (184,219). Of residents who stated their ethnicity at the 2021 census, 92.3% were Russian, and 3.8% were Armenian. Krasnodar Krai is in the time zone UTC+3.

HISTORY

Krasnodar city was founded as Yekaterinodar in 1793, during the campaign of Catherine (Yekaterina) II 'the Great' to win control of the Black Sea region for the

Russian Empire. The territory was dominated by the 'Whites' in the 1917–21 civil war. The Krai, then including the territory that now forms Adygeya (as a nominally autonomous oblast), was formed on 13 September 1937.

In September 1993 the communist-dominated Krai Soviet condemned President Boris Yeltsin's dissolution of the federal legislature, and the KPRF maintained a leading role in the new regional Legislative Assembly. In 1996 Nikolai Kondratenko, the communist former Chairman of the Krai Soviet, was elected Governor by a large majority. Kondratenko attracted notoriety for his incitement of inter-ethnic hostility; a voluntary Cossack militia, which he established in the late 1990s, was accused of persecuting members of minority groups. Following an election in 2000, Kondratenko was succeeded by Aleksandr Tkachyov, who also became noted for his provocative remarks, on occasion urging various minority ethnic groups to leave the region. Tkachyov was overwhelmingly re-elected Governor in March 2004.

From the late 1990s the presence of some 21,000 mostly stateless Meshketians (a Turkic people originating from Southern Georgia) in the Krai, many of whom had sought refuge in the Krai (to which other Meshketians had been exiled by Stalin— Soviet leader in 1924–53) following inter-ethnic unrest in Central Asia in 1989, was a focus for discontent. In 2002 the Krai restricted the granting of permanent residency permits to immigrants, limiting their access to housing and education. By mid-2004 almost 5,000 Meshketians had received Russian citizenship, although a larger number emigrated to the USA.

Meanwhile, in September 2003 work commenced to construct a causeway across the Kerch Strait, which separates Crimea from the Taman peninsula, ostensibly to protect part of the Krai from erosion; however, Ukraine argued that it would encroach on its territory and dispatched troops to the island of Tuzla, over which it claimed sovereignty. In October Russia agreed to halt work on the causeway, provided that Ukraine withdrew its troops. In December the Presidents of both countries signed an agreement recognizing the Sea of Azov and the Kerch Strait as inland waters of both Russia and Ukraine and pledging to co-operate in defining the international border in the area.

On 23 April 2007 the Legislative Assembly approved Tkachyov's nomination to a third gubernatorial term.

On 5 November 2010 a total of 12 people, including four children, were killed by members of a criminal group in the northern town of Kushchevskaya. The killings rapidly became a focus of attention nationwide, as did revelations concerning the close relationship between organized crime groups and the local and provincial political and security authorities. In late November a senior police officer was arrested on charges of having extorted 6,000,000m. roubles from a business executive. President Dmitrii Medvedev summoned Tkachyov to a meeting in Moscow, and demanded that the perpetrators of the massacre be brought to justice promptly, and dismissed the head of the provincial police force, while Tkachyov subsequently removed or demoted local officials deemed to have been negligent. The organizer of the killings, a prominent local figure and landowner, Sergei Tsapok, was sentenced to life imprisonment in November 2013 and ordered to pay a fine of 700,000 roubles in addition to unspecified sums of compensation. He died in prison in July 2014, having suffered a stroke.

On 16 March 2012 Medvedev appointed Tkachyov additionally to the new position of Presidential Representative to the neighbouring 'Republic of Abkhazia', which lay within Georgia but which was regarded by Russia as an independent state in its own right. Five days later the provincial Legislative Assembly voted to confirm Tkachyov to a new term as Governor. Following elections to the Legislative Assembly held on 14 October, YeR enjoyed the support of 95 of the 100 deputies, having obtained 69.5% of the proportional vote.

Following the annexation of Crimea by Russia in March 2014, the construction of a road and railway bridge (to provide the only direct land access to Crimea from Russia) linking Kerch, in the Krai, with Crimea, commenced; the road bridge opened in 2018 and the railway section in 2019.

Meanwhile, in April 2015 Tkachyov was appointed as federal Minister of Agriculture, necessitating his resignation as Governor. President Vladimir Putin appointed an aide, Veniamin Kondratyev, as Acting Governor, pending an election. On 13 September Kondratyev was elected Governor, obtaining 83.6% of the vote.

At elections to the Legislative Assembly (reduced from 100 to 70 deputies) on 10 September 2017, YeR obtained 70.8% of the votes cast to seats elected on a proportional basis. By the end of the year 64 of the 70 deputies had joined the YeR parliamentary faction.

Kondratyev was one of five candidates to contest a gubernatorial election on 13 September 2020; he was re-elected with 83.0% of the votes cast. The second-placed candidate, Aleksandr Safronov of the KPRF, obtained 8.2%. In legislative elections held on 11 September 2022 YeR obtained some 70.8% of the votes cast on a proportional basis, followed by the KPRF, with 10.8% and the LDPR, with 6.6%, and SR, with 5.8%. In the elections held in single-mandate constituencies, 41 representatives of YeR were elected, as were two of the LDPR, and one each of SR and the Partiya Rosta (Party of Growth). By the end of the year 62 deputies had joined the YeR parliamentary faction.

Meanwhile, on 19 October 2022 President Putin declared a 'medium level of response' in Krasnodar Krai and seven other regions (including the annexed Republic of Crimea and Sevastopol) bordering Russian-occupied parts of Ukraine where martial law was introduced; under this regime, the regional authorities were granted powers to undertake 'economic mobilization' for the provision of supplies to the Russian armed forces in Ukraine, as well as to increase security measures and introduce restrictions on freedom of movement to and from the territory.

It was reported in October 2022 that much of the Black Sea Fleet had been relocated from Sevastopol City to Feodosiya, in the east of Crimea, and to Novorossiisk, Krasnodar Krai, after major Ukrainian missile strikes against the Fleet's base and headquarters in Sevastopol had occurred in September.

ECONOMY

In 2021 gross regional product (GRP) in Krasnodar Krai amounted to 3,200,607m. roubles, or 562,926 roubles per head. Krasnodar is a major industrial centre, as are Armavir, Novorossiisk and Kropotkin. Novorossiisk is one of the largest seaports in Russia, while Tuapse, Yeisk and Temryuk are also important seaports. At the end of 2021 the Krai contained 2,245 km of railways.

Krasnodar Krai is a leading agriculture territory in Russia. Its principal crops are grain, sugar beet, rice, tobacco, essential oil plants, tea and hemp. Horticulture, viniculture and animal husbandry are also important. Agriculture employed 8.3% of the workforce and contributed 12.1% of GRP in 2021. There are important reserves of petroleum and natural gas, and petroleum is refined in the territory. Major oil pipelines from Baku (Bakı), Azerbaijan, and Tengiz, Kazakhstan, which opened in 1997 and

2001, respectively, terminate at Novorossiisk. The Krai's main industries are food processing, electricity generation, fuel extraction, mechanical engineering and metal working, and the production of building materials. Industry employed 23.1% of the workforce and contributed 18.1% of GRP in 2021, when manufacturing employed 10.3% of the workforce and contributed 10.0% of GRP. The tourism sector is also important, and the region's infrastructure was substantially upgraded in connection with the 2014 Winter Olympic Games, held in Sochi. The Krai contains the resort towns of Sochi, Anapa, Tuapse and Adler.

The economically active population numbered 2,689,926 in 2022, when the rate of unemployment was 3.5%, while the average monthly wage was 50,252 roubles. There was a budgetary surplus of 39,369.5m. roubles in 2021, when export trade amounted to US $7,567m. (of which 8.1% was with countries of the CIS) and import trade to $5,628m. (of which 12.0% was with CIS countries).

DIRECTORY

Head of the Administration (Governor): VENIAMIN I. KONDRATYEV.

Office of the Head of the Administration (Governor): 350014 Krasnodar, ul. Krasnaya 35; tel. (861) 262-57-16; fax (861) 268-35-42; e-mail post@krasnodar.ru; internet admkrai.krasnodar.ru.

Legislative Assembly: 350063 Krasnodar, ul. Krasnaya 3; tel. (861) 268-00-51; fax (861) 268-13-32; internet kubzsk.ru; Chair. YURII A. BURLACHKO.

State Duma Representatives (8): YEVGENII A. PERVYSHOV (YeR), DMITRII V. LAMEIKIN (YeR), IVAN I. DEMCHENKO (YeR), SERGEI V. ALTUKHOV (YeR), KONSTANTIN F. ZATULIN (YeR), ALEKSEI P. YEZUBOV (YeR), ANDREI N. DOROSHENKO (YeR), DMITRII N. LOTSMANOV (YeR).

Federation Council Representatives: ALEKSEI N. KONDRATENKO, ALEKSANDR A. TREMBITSKII.

Astrakhan Oblast

Astrakhan Oblast is situated in the Caspian lowlands. Between the Russian federal subject of Kalmykiya to the south and Kazakhstan to the east, Astrakhan Oblast flanks the River Volga as it flows out of Volgograd Oblast in the north-west towards the Caspian Sea to the south-east. The delta at the Caspian is one of the largest in the world, occupying more than 24,000 sq km (9,260 sq miles). The Oblast has 200 km (120 miles) of coastline and occupies 49,024 sq km (18,928 sq miles). At January 2023 its population was an estimated 950,557 and its population density 19.4 per sq km. Some 64.1% of the population was urban in 2023. The administrative centre is Astrakhan, with an estimated 468,842 inhabitants at January 2023. The city is 22 m (72 feet) below sea level and is protected from the waters of the Volga delta by 75 km of dykes. Of residents who stated their ethnicity at the 2021 census, 67.1% were Russian, 17.6% were Kazakh, 5.9% Tatar, 1.1% Nogai, 0.8% Chechen, 0.8% Azeri, and 0.7% were Kalmyk. Astrakhan Oblast is in the time zone UTC+4.

HISTORY

The Khanate of Astrakhan, formed in 1446 following the dissolution of the Golden Horde, was conquered by the Russians in 1556. The region subsequently became an important centre for trading in timber, grain, fish and petroleum. Astrakhan Oblast was founded on 27 December 1943. (The region had formed part of the Kazakh Soviet Socialist Republic in the early 1920s.)

There was considerable hardship in the region following the dissolution of the USSR and the economic reforms of the early 1990s. The KPRF was the pre-eminent political force in the Oblast for much of the 1990s. The Governor, Anatolii Guzhvin, initially a federal appointee, retained his post at an election in 1997 and was re-elected in 2000. Elections to the regional Representative Assembly were held in October 2001; in the following month the Assembly voted to rename itself the Regional State Duma.

On 17 August 2004 Guzhvin died, following a heart attack. On 5 December Aleksandr Zhilkin, hitherto First Deputy Governor, was elected Governor, with the support of YeR, receiving 65.3% of the votes cast. In elections to the regional legislature, held in October, YeR received 38.7% of the votes cast, Rodina (Motherland) 16.1% and the KPRF 13.6%. In December the Prosecutor's Office initiated criminal proceedings against six members of a local militant Islamist organization, who were suspected of planning an attack in the Oblast. In December 2009 the regional legislature voted to approve Zhilkin's appointment to a second term as Governor.

In elections to the Regional State Duma held in December 2011 YeR obtained 52.5% of the votes cast on a proportional basis; SR (incorporating Rodina) was second, with 15.9%, ahead of the KPRF, with 15.0%.

At an election held on 14 September 2014, contested by five candidates, Zhilkin was elected Governor, obtaining 75.3% of the vote; Oleg Shein of SR, who had led a hunger strike as part of a campaign against electoral fraud in 2012, was his closest rival, with 16.2%. In elections to the Regional State Duma on 18 September 2016, YeR obtained some 42.3% of the proportional vote, ahead of SR, with 21.5%, the KPRF, with 17.3%, and the LDPR, with 13.3%. By the end of the year 36 of the 60 deputies had joined the YeR parliamentary faction.

On 26 September 2018 Zhilkin resigned as Governor. President Vladimir Putin appointed Sergei Morozov, a state official, as Acting Governor in his place. On 5 June 2019 Morozov (who had been publicly reprimanded by Putin in May, after requesting significant federal funds for the region) resigned and was replaced by the hitherto deputy presidential envoy to the North Caucasus, Igor Babushkin. Shortly afterwards, Rasul Sultanov resigned as Chairman of the Regional Government. Sultanov was arrested, together with his acting successor, Vitalii Shvedov, in July; both were subsequently charged with abuse of office. In June 2021 Sultanov and Shvedov both received prison sentences, of five years and five-and-a-half years, respectively, for fraud in connection with taking out a loan at an inflated interest rate; in early 2023 it was announced that both men had been released on parole several months earlier. Meanwhile, Aleksandr Sharykin became the new Acting Chairman of the Government.

On 8 September 2019 Babushkin was elected Governor, obtaining 76.6% of the votes cast, defeating three other candidates.

At elections to the Regional State Duma held on 19 September 2021, YeR secured 46.8% of the votes cast on the basis of proportional representation; the KPRF obtained 18.2%, SR 16.3%, the recently established centre-right NL 5.9 and the LDPR 5.3%. By the end of the year 27 of the 43 deputies had joined the YeR faction, five that of the KPRF, five that of SR, two that of the LDPR, and one that of NL.

ECONOMY

Astrakhan Oblast's gross regional product (GRP) was 657,016m. roubles in 2021, equivalent to 661,245 roubles per head. The Oblast's main industrial centres are at Astrakhan and Akhtubinsk. At the end of 2021 there were 630 km of railways in the Oblast. In October 2003 Russia's first container terminal on the Caspian Sea opened at the port of Olya.

The Oblast remains a major producer of vegetables and cucurbits (gourds and melons). Grain production and animal husbandry are also important. Agriculture employed 12.7% of the workforce and contributed 6.0% of GRP in 2021. The Oblast is rich in natural resources, including gas and gas condensate, sulphur, petroleum and salt. Its main industries are the production of petroleum and natural gas, food processing (particularly of fish products), mechanical engineering, shipbuilding and electricity production. Industry employed 22.1% of the workforce and contributed 58.7% of GRP in 2021, when manufacturing employed 9.6% of the workforce and contributed 3.6% of GRP. Regional trade is also important to the economy. The Lakor freight company established important shipping links with Iran. Exports to Iran from the Oblast mainly comprised paper, metals, timber, mechanical equipment, fertilizers and chemical products.

Astrakhan Oblast's economically active population numbered 471,578 in 2022, when the rate of unemployment was 7.0%, while the average monthly wage was 47,780 roubles. There was a budgetary deficit of 3,119.5m. roubles in 2021, when export trade amounted to US $1,023m. (of which 22.5% was with countries of the CIS), and import trade to $139m. (of which 18.6% was with CIS countries).

DIRECTORY

Governor: Igor Yu. Babushkin.

Vice-Governor, Chairman of the Regional Government: Oleg A. Knyazev.

Office of the Governor and Regional Government: 414000 Astrakhan, ul. Sovetskaya 15; tel. (8512) 51-17-67; fax (8512) 51-05-29; e-mail gov@astrobl.ru; internet gov.astrobl.ru.

Regional State Duma: 414000 Astrakhan, ul. Volodarskogo 15; tel. (8512) 22-96-44; fax (8512) 22-22-48; e-mail gdao@astranet.ru; internet astroblduma.ru; Chair. Igor A. Martynov.

State Duma Representative (1): Leonid A. Ogul (YeR).

Federation Council Representatives: Gennadii I. Ordenov, Aleksandr D. Bashkin.

Rostov Oblast

Rostov Oblast is situated in the south of the Eastern European Plain. It lies on the Taganrog Gulf of the Sea of Azov. It borders Krasnodar and Stavropol Krais in the south, the Republic of Kalmykiya in the south-east, the Oblasts of Volgograd in the north-east and Voronezh in the north, and has an international border with Ukraine (albeit territories outside of Ukrainian state control) to the west; of those Ukrainian territories which were annexed by Russia in 2022, the Donetsk People's Republic lies to the south-west, and the Lugansk People's Republic to the west. The Oblast covers 100,967 sq km (38,984 sq miles). At January 2023 there were an estimated 4,164,547 inhabitants and a population density of 41.2 per sq km. Some 67.7% of the population was urban in 2023. The administrative centre is Rostov-on-Don (Rostov-na-Donu), with an estimated 1,135,968 inhabitants at January 2023. Other major cities are Taganrog (242,327), Shakhty (222,489), Volgodonsk (165,567), Novocherkassk (160,782), Bataisk (125,523) and Novoshakhtinsk (101,708). Of residents who stated their ethnicity at the 2021 census, 91.7% were Russian, 2.2% were Armenian, 1.0% were Turks, and 0.7% were Ukrainian. Rostov Oblast is in the time zone UTC+3.

HISTORY

The city of Rostov-on-Don was established by Cossacks in 1796. The local grain export trade increased after the completion of the Volga–Don Canal. Rostov Oblast was formed in September 1937. The region was heavily industrialized after 1946.

The incumbent Governor, Vladimir Chub, was elected to that post in 1996 and re-elected in 2001; the regional legislature confirmed him to a further term in 2005.

In the mid-2000s the Oblast became a stronghold of extremist nationalist organizations. In May 2006 members of the prohibited Natsional-Bolshevistskaya Partiya

(National Bolshevik Party) seized the Rostov office of the state savings bank, Sberbank, threatening to set the building ablaze, before being overpowered. In December 2008 a group of retired miners in the town of Zverevo began a hunger strike, in support of demands for unpaid social benefits. By February 2009 six miners had been hospitalized.

On 21 May 2010 the regional legislature voted to endorse the appointment of Vasilii Golubev, a former Deputy Governor of Moscow Oblast, to succeed Chub as Governor; he assumed office on 14 June. Golubev was re-elected in September 2015.

Rostov Oblast neighbours Donetsk Oblast, in Ukraine, the political base of that country's President in 2010–14, Viktor Yanukovych. Following his removal from office in February 2014, Yanukovych made a series of television broadcasts from Rostov, in which he described himself as the legitimate President of Ukraine. A number of military training camps used by Russian or Russian-affiliated soldiers participating in the subsequent conflict in parts of the neighbouring Donetsk and Luhansk (Lugansk) oblasts of Ukraine were established locally in 2014. A large number of official 'humanitarian convoys' ostensibly providing assistance to residents of the Russian—allied 'Donetsk People's Republic' (DNR) and 'Lugansk People's Republic' (LNR) territories in Ukraine subsequently departed from Rostov Oblast.

In July 2016 it was reported that a petition with more than 6,000 signatures had been submitted to Putin and Golubev to request the dismissal of Sergei Gorban as Mayor of Rostov. This followed a state of emergency owing to severe flooding in the centre of the city and a number of residential districts at the end of June, when one person died and at least eight others were injured. Gorban left office in October.

Elections to the Legislative Assembly were held on 9 September 2018. YeR won 57.0% of the votes cast to seats elected on a proportional basis, ahead of the KPRF, with 17.1%, the LDPR, with 9.9%, and SR, with 7.1%. Some 46 of the 60 deputies had joined the YeR parliamentary faction by the end of the year.

Golubev was one of five candidates to contest a gubernatorial election on 13 September 2020; he was re-elected with 65.5% of the votes cast. The second-placed candidate, Yevgenii Bessonov of the KPRF, obtained 17.6%.

On 19 February 2022 Golubev declared a state of emergency in the Oblast, due to the arrival of increasing numbers of refugees from neighbouring regions of Ukraine, in response to evacuation orders by the leaders of the DNR and the LNR. Following Russia's full-scale invasion of Ukraine on 24 Februay, by early March more than 149,000 people had arrived in Rostov Oblast from the DNR and the LNR since 18 February and around 100 temporary shelters had been established there. In June two drone aircraft crashed into the Novoshakhtinsk oil refinery in Rostov Oblast, on the border with Ukraine, causing an explosion and fire. On 19 October President Putin declared martial law in the DNR, the LNR and two other Russian-occupied territories of Ukraine (all of which Russia had recently annexed), while declaring a 'medium level of response' in Rostov Oblast and seven other bordering regions (including the Republic of Crimea and Sevastopol), under which the regional authorities concerned were granted powers to undertake 'economic mobilization' for the provision of supplies to assist the Russian armed forces in Ukraine, as well as to increase security measures and introduce restrictions on freedom of movement.

After launching an armed insurrection from the territories of the LNR on 23 June 2023, the head of the paramilitary Wagner Group, Yevgenii Prigozhin, announced that his fighters had occupied key military sites in Rostov, including the headquarters of the Southern Military District, a crucial command and logistical centre for the Russian army in the war against Ukraine, apparently facing only limited resistance. Wagner Group forces then advanced north towards Moscow, while Prigozhin commanded the rebellion from Rostov. However, following a negotiated agreement, on 25 June Wagner forces began to withdraw from the Oblast. (Prigozhin was killed in August.) In subsequent months Golubev periodically reported that Ukrainian drones had been shot down over the Oblast.

Following elections to the Legislative Assembly held on 10 September 2023, YeR held 54 of the 60 seats in the chamber.

ECONOMY

In 2021 Rostov Oblast's gross regional product (GRP) was 2,017,007m. roubles, or 483,970 roubles per head. The main industrial centres are at Rostov, Taganrog, Novocherkassk, Shakhty, Novoshakhtinsk and Volgodonsk. At the end of 2021 there were 1,901 km of railways in the Oblast. There are river ports at Rostov and Ust-Donetskii.

The Oblast is a major grain-producing region, and agricultural land comprises some 85% of its territory. The production of sunflower seeds, coriander, mustard, vegetables and cucurbits (gourds and melons) is also important, as are viniculture and horticulture. Agriculture employed 10.9% of the workforce and contributed 13.1% of GRP in 2021. The Oblast is rich in coal and natural gas. Its other principal industries are food processing, ferrous metallurgy, electricity generation, metal working and mechanical engineering. The largest industrial concern is the Taganrog Metallurgical Plant (TagMet). Industry employed 25.6% of the workforce and contributed 28.8% of GRP in 2021, when manufacturing employed 13.8% of the workforce and contributed 17.1% of GRP. In association with the 2018 football World Cup, a new stadium with a capacity of around 45,000 people was constructed in the city.

The economically active population numbered 2,071,218 in 2022, when the rate of unemployment was 3.5%, while the average monthly wage was 44,767 roubles. There was a budgetary surplus of 7,459.7m. roubles in 2021, when export trade amounted to US $11,569m. (of which 19.1% was with countries of the CIS), and import trade to $2,982m. (of which 28.9% was with CIS countries).

DIRECTORY

Governor: VASILII YU. GOLUBEV.

Office of the Governor: 344050 Rostov-on-Don, ul. Sotsialisticheskaya 112; tel. (863) 244-16-66; fax (863) 244-15-59; e-mail rra@donpac.ru; internet donland.ru.

Legislative Assembly: 344050 Rostov-on-Don, ul. Sotsialisticheskaya 112; tel. (863) 240-32-99; fax (863) 263-40-95; e-mail zsrnd@zsro.ru; internet zsro.ru; Chair. ALEKSANDR V. ISHCHENKO.

State Duma Representatives (7): LARISA N. TUTOVA (YeR), ANTON A. GETTA (YeR), SERGEI V. BURLAKOV (YeR), VITALII V. KUSHNAREV (YeR), NIKOLAI G. GONCHAROV (YeR), YEKATERINA P. STENYAKINA (YeR), VIKTOR YE. DEBYABKIN (YeR).

Federation Council Representatives: IRINA V. RUKAVISHNIKOVA, ANDREI V. YATSKIN.

Volgograd Oblast

Volgograd Oblast is situated in the south-east of the Eastern European Plain. It has an international border with Kazakhstan to the east. Astrakhan Oblast and the Republic of Kalmykiya lie to the south-east, and the oblasts of Rostov, Voronezh and Saratov, respectively, are to the south-west, the north-west and the north. The Oblast's main rivers are the Volga and the Don. Its terrain varies from fertile black earth (*chernozyom*) to semi-desert. The region occupies 112,877 sq km (43,582 sq miles). At January 2023 the Oblast had an estimated 2,470,057 inhabitants and a population density of 21.9 per sq km. Some 77.6% of the population was urban in 2023. The Oblast's administrative centre is Volgograd, with an estimated 1,025,662 inhabitants at January 2023. Other major cities include Volzhskii (316,544) and Kamyshin (105,471). Of residents who stated their ethnicity at the 2021 census, 92.5% were Russian, 1.7% were Kazakh, and 0.7% were Armenian. Volgograd Oblast is in the time zone UTC+3.

HISTORY

The city of Volgograd (known as Tsaritsyn until 1925 and Stalingrad in 1925–61) was founded in the 16th century, where the River Volga flows nearest to the Don (the two river systems were later connected by a canal at this point). The Oblast was formed on

10 January 1934. In 1942–43 the city was the scene of a decisive battle between Soviet and Nazi German forces in the Second World War.

The KPRF held the largest number of seats in the new Regional Duma, following elections held in 1994. The 1996 gubernatorial election was won by Nikolai Maksyuta of the KPRF. He was re-elected in 2000 and 2004. At elections to the Regional Duma held in March 2009, YeR obtained 49.5% of the votes cast; the KPRF was second, with 23.6%. Maksyuta was at this time the only member of the KPRF to head a federal subject. As the conclusion of Maksyuta's third mandate approached, in late December, President Dmitrii Medvedev announced the nomination of one of the Governor's deputies, Anatolii Brovko, as his preferred successor. The Regional Duma confirmed this appointment, and Brovko assumed office on 12 January 2010.

The conduct of elections in the Oblast to the State Duma on 4 December 2011 precipitated controversy, as several recounts of the results were required. Over 15,000 complaints about electoral processes were reportedly submitted to the regional electoral commission. None the less, the performance of YeR was relatively weak, at 35.5% of the votes cast. In January 2012 Brovko resigned as Governor; he was replaced by Sergei Bozhenov, a newly elected State Duma deputy and former Mayor of Astrakhan; the Regional Duma confirmed the appointment in February 2012.

On 21 October 2013 a suicide bomber killed seven people, injuring at least another 30, when she detonated a bomb on a bus in Volgograd. Two further Islamist suicide bombings occurred in the city in late December; 18 people were killed and at least a further 44 injured in an attack, reported to be the first suicide bombing committed by an ethnic Russian (a convert to Islam originating from the Republic of Marii-El), in the central railway station in the city, and 16 people were killed and at least 41 injured in an explosion on a trolleybus.

In February 2014 the regional branch of the KPRF led a campaign to demand Bozhenov's resignation as Governor, citing what it termed his failings to ensure security and economic stability. On 2 April Bozhenov tendered his resignation, which was accepted by President Vladimir Putin. Putin nominated Andrei Bocharov, a senior official of the YeR-linked Obshcherossiiskii Narodni Front (All-Russia National Front), who had been highly decorated for his military service in the conflict in Chechnya in 1994–96, as Acting Governor. On 14 September 2014 Bocharov was elected Governor, receiving 88.5% of the vote. At concurrent elections to the regional State Duma, YeR obtained 60.1% of the votes cast to those seats elected on a proportional basis. The KPRF was second, with 14.3%. A total of 31 of the 38 deputies subsequently joined the YeR parliamentary faction.

Elections to the Oblast's legislature and governorship were held on 8 September 2019. Bocharov was re-elected Governor with 76.8% of the votes cast. YeR obtained 48.2% of votes cast on a proportional basis in legislative polling, ahead of the KPRF, with 19.5%, the LDPR, with 14.9%, SR, with 8.4% and the RPPS, with 6.3%. By January 2020 27 of the 38 deputies had joined the parliamentary faction of YeR, five that of the KPRF, two that of SR, two that of the LDPR, and one that of the RPPS.

ECONOMY

In 2021 Volgograd Oblast's gross regional product (GRP) amounted to 1,051,515m. roubles, or 427,069 roubles per head. Its main industrial centres are at Volgograd, Volzhskii and Kamyshin. At the end of 2021 there were 1,617 km of railways in the oblast.

The region's principal agricultural products are grain, sunflower seeds, vegetables and cucurbits (gourds and melons). Horticulture, beekeeping and animal husbandry are also important. Agriculture employed 12.3% of the workforce and contributed 15.9% of GRP in 2021. The Oblast's mineral reserves include petroleum, natural gas and phosphorites. The main industries in the Oblast are petroleum refining, chemicals and petrochemicals, mechanical engineering, metal-working, ferrous metallurgy, fabric making, the production of electricity, food processing, and the production of petroleum and natural gas. Industry employed 25.3% of the workforce and contributed 30.5% of GRP in 2021, when manufacturing employed 13.3% of the workforce and contributed 18.4% of GRP.

The economically active population of the Oblast numbered 1,197,155 in 2022, when the rate of unemployment was 3.5%, while the average monthly wage was 44,242 roubles. There was a budgetary deficit of 1,537.6m. roubles in 2021. Export trade amounted to US $3,289m. in that year (of which 29.6% was with countries of the CIS), while import trade amounted to $761m. (of which 28.0% was with CIS countries).

DIRECTORY

Governor: ANDREI I. BOCHAROV.

Office of the Governor: 400098 Volgograd, pr. Lenina 9; tel. (8442) 30-70-00; e-mail kancel@volganet.ru; internet volganet.ru.

Regional Duma: 400098 Volgograd, pr. Lenina 9; tel. (8442) 30-90-00; fax (8422) 36-44-03; internet volgoduma.ru; Chair. ALEKSANDR I. BLOSHKIN.

State Duma Representatives (4): ALEKSEI A. VOLOTSKOV (YeR), ANDREI P. GIMBATOV (YeR), VLADIMIR N. PLOTNIKOV (YeR), OLEG V. SAVCHENKO (YeR).

Federation Council Representatives: NIKOLAI P. SEMISOTOV, SERGEI V. GORNYAKOV.

NORTH CAUCASUS FEDERAL OKRUG

Presidential Representative to the North Caucasus Federal Okrug: YURII YA. CHAIKA, 357501 Stavropol Krai, Pyatigorsk, pr. Kirova 26; tel. (8793) 39-44-75; internet skfo.gov.ru.

Chechen Republic

The Chechen Republic is located on the northern slopes of the Caucasus. Dagestan lies to the east, Stavropol Krai to the north-west and the Republic of North Osetiya—Alaniya and the Republic of Ingushetiya to the west. Georgia lies to the south-west. The Republic comprises lowlands in the north; mixed fields, pastures and forests in the Chechen plain; and high mountains and glaciers in the south. The Republic has an area of 15,647 sq km (6,041 sq miles). At January 2023 it had a population of 1,533,209 and a population density of 98.0 per sq km. Only 38.1% of the population was urban in 2023. The capital, Groznyi, had an estimated 331,402 inhabitants at January 2023. Of residents who stated their ethnicity at the 2021 census, 96.4% were Chechen, 1.2% were Russian, and 0.8% were Kumyk. The Chechens are closely related to the Ingush (both of whom are known collectively as Vainakhs). They are Sunni Muslims, and their language is one of the Nakh dialects of the Caucasian linguistic family. Chechnya is in the time zone UTC+3.

HISTORY

In the 18th–19th centuries the Russian, Ottoman and Persian (Iranian) Empires fought for control of the Caucasus. Chechens violently resisted the Russian forces, with the uprising of Sheikh Mansur in 1785 and in the Caucasian War of 1817–64. Russia conquered Chechnya in 1858, after the resistance led by Imam Shamil (an Avar) ended. In 1865 many Chechens were exiled to the Ottoman Empire. Russians began to settle in the lowlands, particularly after petroleum reserves were discovered in 1893. Upon the dissolution in 1922 of the Mountain People's Republic (founded initially in 1917), Chechen and Ingush Autonomous Oblasts were established; they were merged in 1934, becoming the Checheno-Ingush Autonomous Soviet Socialist Republic (ASSR) in 1936. This was dissolved in 1944, when both peoples were deported to Central Asia and Siberia; tens of thousands of people perished during the deportation. On 9 January 1957 the ASSR was reconstituted and its former population began to return.

During 1991 an All-National Congress of the Chechen People seized power and agreed with Ingush leaders to divide the Republic, with the larger part of the territory to constitute a Chechen Republic (Chechnya), which claimed independence from Russia. On 27 October Gen. Dzhokhar Dudayev was elected as President of Chechnya.

Following armed raids by Chechen rebels, and the exodus of almost the entire Russian population (24.8% of the total population of Checheno-Ingushetiya in 1989) from the Republic, in July 1994 federal President Boris Yeltsin declared his support for an Interim Council led by Umar Avturkhanov. Armed conflict broke out between this Council and Dudayev's forces. In December Russia deployed 40,000 ground troops, which obtained control of the Chechen capital, Groznyi. Chechnya was granted a special status, and in March 1995 a Government of National Revival was installed. In June more than 100 people were killed by militants allied with the Islamist Shamil Basayev, who had taken around 1,000 people hostage in a hospital in Budyonnovsk, Stavropol Krai. In November a new Government loyal to the federal authorities, headed by Doku Zavgayev, was appointed.

In April 1996 Dudayev was killed in a missile attack; he was succeeded by Zelimkhan Yandarbiyev, who agreed a ceasefire with Yeltsin in May. The truce ended after Yeltsin's re-election in July; in August rebel forces led an assault on Groznyi, prompting a new ceasefire. The ensuing agreement, the Khasavyurt Accords incorporated a five-year moratorium on discussion of Chechnya's status. All federal troops were to be withdrawn from Chechnya by January 1997, marking the end of a war in which some 100,000 people had been killed.

On 1 January 1997 Aslan Maskhadov, a former rebel chief of staff, defeated Basayev in an election to the republican presidency. The Republic renamed itself the Chechen Republic of Ickheriya. On 12 May Yeltsin and Maskhadov signed a peace treaty. Basayev served as Maskhadov's First Deputy Chairman of the Government for several months in 1997–98. During 1998, amid extreme disorder, Yeltsin's representative, Valentin Vlasov, was kidnapped and held hostage for six months, and four engineers from the United Kingdom and New Zealand were captured and killed.

Supporters of Basayev launched a series of attacks into Dagestan in August 1999, aiming to extending the jurisdiction of a 'separate Islamic territory' proclaimed there in 1998. The territory was returned to federal rule in September 1999. A series of bomb explosions in August–September in Moscow, Dagestan and Rostov Oblast, officially attributed to Chechen separatists, killed almost 300 people, prompting the redeployment of federal armed forces in Chechnya. In February 2000 federal forces, answerable to the recently appointed acting federal President, Vladimir Putin, took control of Groznyi. Akhmad Kadyrov, a former rebel leader, was inaugurated as Head of the Republican Administration in June.

In October 2022 armed rebels took captive 700 people in a Moscow theatre, demanding the withdrawal of Russian troops from Chechnya. The siege ended after three days, when elite forces stormed the theatre; the 40 rebels were killed, and at least 129 hostages died. In December at least 83 people were killed when suicide bombers detonated bombs outside the republican government headquarters in Groznyi.

According to official results, 96.0% of voters in a referendum held on 23 March 2003 endorsed a Chechen Constitution, describing the Republic as both a sovereign entity and an integral part of the Russian Federation. Suicide bombers attacked government offices in Znamenskoye in May, killing 59 people. Kadyrov inaugurated an interim appointed legislature, the State Council, in June. On 5 October he was elected President, receiving 87.7% of the votes cast.

Kadyrov and other senior officials were killed on 9 May 2004 in a bomb attack in Groznyi. Premier Sergei Abramov became Acting President, and Ramzan Kadyrov, the son of the assassinated President and the leader of the controversial presidential security service, was appointed First Deputy Chairman of the Government. On 29 August Maj.-Gen. Alu Alkhanov was elected President. The occupation of a school in Beslan, North Osetiya—Alaniya, in September, as a result of which more than 330 hostages, including 186 children, were killed, was attributed to Chechen militants.

In March 2005 Maskhadov was killed by Federal Security Service (FSB) agents. In May his successor as rebel leader, Abdul-Khalim Sadulayev stated that the expulsion of Russian forces from Chechnya would not end the conflict.

Elections were held for a new, bicameral republican legislature in November 2005; 33 of the 58 members elected represented YeR. In March 2006 the lower legislative chamber, the People's Assembly, unanimously approved Kadyrov's appointment as Chairman of the Government. Special forces killed Sadulayev in June. His successor, Doku Umarov, named Basayev his deputy. Later in the year Umarov proclaimed himself emir of a 'Caucasus Emirate', precipitating a schism between the Islamist and nationalist elements in the separatist movement. In July federal forces killed Basayev. The State Duma approved an amnesty for fighters in the North Caucasus in September; around 500 rebels surrendered.

In February 2007 Alkhanov resigned, after President Putin appointed him to a federal post. The People's Assembly endorsed the appointment of Ramzan Kadyrov as republican President in March. YeR was reported to have secured 99.4% of the votes cast in Chechnya at the elections to the State Duma held in December. A concurrent referendum approved constitutional changes, including the introduction of a unicameral legislature, the abolition of direct republican presidential elections, and the granting of the status of state language to Chechen alongside Russian. At the elections to the republican Parliament in October 2008, YeR won 37 of the 41 seats.

President Dmitrii Medvedev in April 2009 announced an end to the Russian 'counter-terrorism operations' in Chechnya, ordering the withdrawal of many federal troops from the Republic. In July the self-proclaimed 'government-in-exile', led by Akhmed Zakayev (in exile in the UK) announced the end of its armed resistance to the Chechen authorities, while in August the Chechen field commanders of the Caucasus Emirate organization withdrew their support for Umarov.

Kadyrov's title was changed to Head of the Republic in September 2010, and he was inaugurated to a new term of office in March 2011. In the presidential election held in March 2012, Putin, was attributed a far higher share of the votes cast (99.8%) in Chechnya than in any other federal subject. Kadyrov dismissed the Government of Odes Baisultanov in May; the new republican premier was Abubakar Edelgeriyev.

In July 2012 Chechen forces staged a special operation in the Ingushetiyan village of Galashki. Kadyrov criticized what he termed Ingushetiya's inability to suppress insurgent activity. In October the Chechen Parliament adopted a legislative amendment providing for the incorporation of much of the Sunzha district, disputed with Ingushetiya, into Chechnya (the Chechen section of the district was renamed Sernovodskoye in 2019). Umarov's death was announced in March 2014. His successor as leader of the Caucasus Emirate, Aliaskhab Kebekov (Ali Abu-Mukhammad), was killed by special forces in Dagestan in April 2015.

Meanwhile, at least 14 security officials and six Islamist militants were killed during gun battles in December 2014, in the largest outbreak of violence in Groznyi for several years. Kadyrov subsequently ordered that the families of militants be deported from the Republic, and that their homes be destroyed.

In March 2015 the federal authorities detained five suspects from Chechnya, including an officer of a special forces battalion under Kadyrov's command, Zaur Dadayev, following the murder of liberal opposition leader Boris Nemtsov in Moscow. On 9 March, shortly after he had publicly commended Dadayev, Kadyrov was awarded the State Order of Honour by President Putin. Dadayev and four other Chechens received custodial sentences in June 2017 for their involvement in the murder.

A dispute developed between Kadyrov and the federal Ministry of the Interior in April 2015, after a suspected militant was killed in Groznyi by police forces from Stavropol Krai. Kadyrov subsequently instructed Chechen police to fire on forces from other territories operating within Chechnya.

Kadyrov was re-elected Head of the Republic in September 2016, with 97.9% of votes cast. YeR secured 87.7% of the proportional vote at concurrent republican legislative elections. By the end of the year 34 of the 47 deputies had joined the YeR parliamentary faction. Following an escalation of hostilities in December, a total of 27 people (20 suspected militants, six security officials and one civilian) were killed in the insurgency in Chechnya during 2016, according to the news publication *Kavkazskii Uzel*, 13 more than had been killed in 2015, but substantially fewer than in other recent years.

The Russian newspaper *Novaya Gazeta* reported in April 2017 that large numbers of men believed to be homosexual had been arrested in Chechnya, that more than 100 had been detained in secret camps and tortured, and that at least three had been killed. German and French leaders both raised serious concerns over the allegations during meetings with President Putin. In June 2017 an inter-ethnic clash in the village of Leninaul, in Dagestan, during which police were reported to have assaulted nine Chechen youths, prompted a strong response in Chechnya. In July around 1,000 Chechens and Ingush entered Dagestan in a demonstration of support for the local Chechen population; however, police officers intercepted the convoy. Parliamentary Chairman Magomed Daudov and other senior officials attempted to defuse the tensions.

In December 2017 the USA included Kadyrov on its list of Russian citizens subject to US sanctions, finding him responsible for extrajudicial killings, torture and other human rights violations. The longstanding Mayor of Groznyi (and close associate of Kadyrov), Muslim Khuchiyev, became Chairman of the Government in June 2018, after Edelgeriyev became an adviser to Putin. In March 2019 the director of the Groznyi office of the Memorial human rights organization, Oyub Titiyev, was sentenced to four years' imprisonment for drug possession, but he was released from prison on parole in June; meanwhile, Kadyrov had declared that human rights activists would be prohibited from the Republic, equating them to terrorists and extremists.

Meanwhile, according to *Kavkazskii Uzel*, a total of 59 people (20 suspected militants, 13 security officials and 26 civilians) were killed in Chechnya in 2017, as a result of the insurgency. In 2018 the number of fatalities fell sharply to 26 (21 of whom were suspected militants).

The Chechen Government dismissed reports, which emerged in August 2018, of territorial infractions by Chechen construction personnel near the Ingushetiyan border village of Arshty. In September Kadyrov ordered the creation of a state commission to 'clarify' the Republic's administrative boundaries. A border demarcation agreement was signed later in the month by Kadyrov and his Ingushetiyan counterpart, Yunus-bek Yevkurov, providing for territorial exchanges between the two republics. The Chechen Parliament approved the agreement, which was highly advantageous to Chechnya, on 4 October. In December the federal Constitutional Court dismissed a ruling by Ingushetiya's Constitutional Court rejecting the agreement.

In January 2019 a court in Chechnya ruled to cancel the Republic's debt of US $135m. to a subsidiary of the state-owned natural gas corporation Gazprom, to avert potential social unrest should attempts be made to collect it. In April the US Administration imposed travel restrictions against Khuchiyev, on the grounds that he was implicated in torture. In May the US Treasury also imposed sanctions against the Chechen *Terek* special police unit, which was believed to have perpetrated extra-judicial killings.

Meanwhile, unofficial negotiations between Dagestani and Chechen officials on the demarcation of the republics' joint border during early 2019, followed by reports of the appropriation of Dagestani territory by the Chechen authorities, provoked strong public opposition in Dagestan.

In November 2019 a state television channel broadcast a speech by Kadyrov in which he advocated the killing, imprisonment and intimidation of those who 'assaulted the honour' of others online. Several incidents involving the murder or attempted murder of prominent opponents of Kadyrov abroad occurred during 2020. In February a Chechen dissident, Imran Aliyev, was found dead in a hotel in Lille, France. In July Mamikhan Umarov, a vehement critic of Kadyrov, was shot dead in Austria, after which two Chechen suspects were arrested in that country.

In July 2020 the USA imposed new sanctions against Kadyrov and close relatives. In the same month Putin awarded Kadyrov the military rank of Major-General. In October a Chechen refugee beheaded a schoolteacher in a town outside Paris, France, after he had shown students cartoons depicting Muhammed, the prophet of Islam, during a debate on freedom of speech in a class on moral and civil education. Kadyrov criticized French President Emmanuel Macron's subsequent vigorous defence of the teacher's actions during his memorial service. The US Administration on 10 December further extended sanctions against Kadyrov to five of his prominent associates, including a deputy premier, Vakhit Usmayev, and six companies owned or controlled by him. In January 2021 Kadyrov announced that six militants, including Aslan Byutukayev, who was considered to be the commander of the remaining Chechen wing of the Caucasus Emirate, had been killed in a special operation by security forces. The European Union (EU) in March 2021 imposed sanctions against a commander of the *Terek* special unit, and a former head of police, for human rights abuses. Also in March, Kadyrov nominated a relative, Khas-Magomed Kadyrov, as Mayor of Groznyi; he was confirmed in the post at the end of the month.

At elections to the republican Parliament on 19 September 2021, YeR secured 89.2% of the votes cast on a proportional basis. By the end of the year 37 of the 41 deputies had joined the YeR faction. Kadyrov was on the same day re-elected Head of the Republic by 99.7% of votes cast, according to official results, with a participation rate of 94.6%.

In late 2021 large-scale exercises were jointly staged by Chechnya's security forces and the federal National Guard in Groznyi. Chechen opposition activists and human rights defenders in exile in December reported the detention or disappearance of many relatives, and accused the Chechen authorities of abducting up to 50 people.

Kadyrov immediately welcomed the Russian invasion of Ukraine on 24 February 2022 and special forces from Chechnya were dispatched to Ukraine to support the war efforts. In March Kadyrov claimed that he had personally travelled to the besieged port city of Mariupol to meet the Chechen troops fighting there, and later that month it was announced that President Putin had awarded him the military rank of Lieutenant-General. Kadyrov in May called for the voluntary mobilization of Chechen citizens, while recruitment for the war in Ukraine was also conducted through the Republic's mixed martial arts club funded by him. In June Kadyrov announced the creation of four new *Akhmat* military battalions comprising ethnic Chechens, subordinate to the federal Ministry of Defence. Meanwhile, Chechen opposition leaders in exile travelled to Ukraine, in a demonstration of support for Ukraine.

In September 2022 the US Treasury applied additional sanctions against Kadyrov and some close relatives, who were designated as 'facilitators of Russia's aggression in Ukraine'. In response, Kadyrov accused the USA of attempting to foment terrorism in the North Caucasus, and announced the establishment of a further special task force, *Akhmat-1*, to be deployed in Ukraine. However, Kadyrov declared that an order issued by President Putin on 21 September for the partial mobilization of military reservists in each region would not apply in Chechnya, since it had already deployed around 20,000 troops to Ukraine; on that day a small anti-war rally by women was held in Groznyi (the first recorded protest to be staged during the incumbent Kadyrov administration). Kadyrov also openly criticized Russian territorial losses in Ukraine and federal decisions such as a recent Russian-Ukrainian prisoner exchange.

The Chechen-language form of Kadyrov's title was amended in February 2023 to a term used to mean 'father of the people'. In July Zarema Musayeva, the mother of three Chechen anti-torture activists who had fled abroad, was sentenced to over five years in prison for fraud and attacking a police officer. She had been abducted by Chechen security officers in Nizhnii Novgorod Oblast and forcibly returned to Chechnya. A Russian investigative journalist, who had planned to report on Musayeva's sentence, and a human rights lawyer were severely assaulted in Groznyi on the same day.

In July 2023 Yakub Zakriyev, hitherto republican Deputy Prime Minister and Minister of Agriculture, who was also a relative of Kadyrov, was appointed as the head of French multinational food corporation Danone's Russian subsidiary, after the federal Government ordered the state to assume temporary control of the company's assets in Russia. In early August Kadyrov announced that a total of 29,000 combatants, including 13,000 volunteers, had been dispatched to Ukraine from Chechnya since February 2022; it was reported that Chechen units had been deployed to patrol the occupied southern Ukrainian town of Enerhodar, where the Zaporizhzhya Nuclear Power Plant, the largest in Europe, was located. Meanwhile, it was announced that Groznyi (following St Petersburg) had established 'sister city' relations with the occupied southern Ukrainian city of Mariupol.

In September 2023 Kadyrov published a video showing his 15-year-old son, Adam, violently assaulting a prisoner in pre-trial detention accused of burning a copy of the Qur'an. He commended his son's actions, bestowing on him the state award 'Hero of the Chechen Republic'. In October the heads of the Republic of Tatarstan and the Karachai-Cherkess Republic also conferred regional awards on Adam Kadyrov. Ramzan Kadyrov, who had dismissed further media reports of his deteriorating health, appointed Adam as his head bodyguard in early November, also appointing an elder son, Akhmat, as a deputy minister for physical culture, sports and youth policy. Ramzan Kadyrov was part of a Russian delegation that accompanied President Putin in meetings with the leaders of the United Arab Emirates and Saudi Arabia during visits to those countries in early December.

ECONOMY

In 2021 Chechnya's gross regional product (GRP) amounted to 268,069m. roubles, or 177,860 roubles per head, the second lowest figure recorded in any federal subject, after that of Ingushetiya. There is an airport at Groznyi.

Chechnya's agriculture consists mainly of horticulture, the production of grain and sugar beet, and animal husbandry. Agriculture employed 21.7% of the workforce in 2021 and contributed 12.7% of GRP. Conflict in 1994–96 and 1999–2009 seriously damaged the economic infrastructure. (The Republic had previously been the principal producer of aviation fuel in Russia.) Attempts were made to restore industry in the Republic, and a major programme of reconstruction was implemented in the second half of the 2000s. In 2014 the state-controlled company Rosneft (the local operations of which were subsequently placed under the control of the republican authorities) announced that it was to construct a new oil refinery in Groznyi. Industry employed 22.8% of the workforce and contributed 15.4% of GRP in 2021, when manufacturing employed 6.9% of the workforce and contributed 2.6% of GRP.

The economically active population numbered 582,881 in 2022, when the rate of unemployment was 11.0%, while the average monthly wage was 33,700 roubles. There was a budgetary deficit of 2,072.6m. roubles in 2021. Export trade amounted to US $23m. in 2021 (6.5% of which was with CIS countries), while import trade amounted to $49m. (of which 23.8% was with CIS countries).

DIRECTORY

Head of the Republic: RAMZAN A. KADYROV.

Chairman of the Republican Government: MUSLIM M. KHUCHIYEV.

Office of the Head of the Republic and the Government: 364000 Chechen Rep., Groznyi, ul. Garazhnaya 10A; tel. (8712) 22-00-01; fax (8712) 22-20-14; e-mail info@chechnya.gov.ru; internet chechnya.gov.ru.

Republican Parliament: 364014 Chechen Rep., Groznyi, ul. Vostochnaya 48; tel. (8712) 22-42-26; fax (8712) 22-42-25; e-mail spiker@parlamentchr.ru; internet parlamentchr.ru; Chair. MAGOMED KH. DAUDOV.

State Duma Representative (1): ADAM S. DELIMKHANOV (YeR).

Federation Council Representatives: SULEIMAN S. GEREMEYEV, MOKHMAD I. AKHMADOV.

Republic of Dagestan

The Republic of Dagestan is situated in the eastern North Caucasus. Azerbaijan lies to the south, Georgia to the south-west, the Chechen Republic and Stavropol Krai to the west, and the Republic of Kalmykiya to the north and the Caspian Sea to the east. Dagestan occupies 50,270 sq km (19,409 sq miles). The principal rivers are the Terek and the Sulak. The north of the Republic is flat, while in the south are Greater Caucasus foothills and peaks. At January 2023 Dagestan had a population of 3,209,781 and a population density of 63.9 per sq km. Only 45.2% of the population was urban in 2023. The capital, Makhachkala, had an estimated 622,660 inhabitants at January 2023. Other major cities are Khasavyurt (157,466), Derbent (126,078) and Kaspiisk (125,747). Of residents who stated their ethnicity at the 2021 census, 30.5% were Avar, 16.6% were Dargin, 15.8% Kumyk, 13.3% Lezgin, 5.2% Lak, 4.0% Tabasaran, 3.7% Azeri, 3.3% Russian, 3.2% Chechen, 1.2% Nogai, 0.9% Aghul, and 0.9% were Rutul. Dagestan is in the time zone UTC+3.

HISTORY

Dagestan came under Russian rule in 1723, when the khanates on its territory were annexed from Persia. The Dagestani peoples mounted rebellions, including the Murid

Uprising of 1828–59, before Russian control could be established. The Dagestan Autonomous Soviet Socialist Republic was established on 20 January 1920.

Dagestan voted against the new Russian federal Constitution in 1993. It adopted a republican Constitution in 1994, providing for the creation of a supreme executive body, the State Council, to comprise representatives of the 14 largest ethnic groups in the Republic. This was headed by the erstwhile Chairman of the republican Supreme Soviet, Magomedali Magomedov, a Dargin. Constitutional changes, approved in March 1998, permitted Magomedov to serve a further term and removed the ethnicity requirements for senior positions. In June Magomedov was reappointed. A new parliament, the People's Assembly, was elected in March 1999.

Growth in support for Islamist groups was evident from the 1990s. In May 1998 over 200 fighters of the Soyuz Musulman Rossii (Union of Russian Muslims) occupied a government building in Makhachkala, while 2,000 demonstrators gathered to demand the resignation of the republican Government. In August militants seized three villages in Buinaksk district, establishing 'a separate Islamic territory', which remained under rebel control until intervention by federal forces in September 1999.

Chechen Islamist militants led by Shamil Basayev invaded Dagestan on 2 August 1999. The invading forces were repelled, but they returned on 5 September, after an explosion in Buinaksk had killed about 60 people. Following the recommencement of federal military operations in Chechnya in late 1999, several explosions in Dagestan were attributed to supporters of Chechen separatism, including a bombing in May 2002 in Kaspiisk, in which 45 people were killed.

In March 2003 Magomedov was elected to serve a third term as Chairman of the State Council. In July a new republican Constitution entered into effect. A directly elected presidency was to be established, with effect from 2006, despite fears that so doing would exacerbate ethnic tensions.

Instability further heightened in the 2000s, with opposition to Magomedov's administration being voiced by prominent politicians in the northern city of Khasavyurt, supported by elements close to the Chechen leader, Ramzan Kadyrov, and by the local Nogai community. In May 2005 the republican Minister of the Interior, Zagir Arukhov, was assassinated in a bombing organized by an Islamist group, Shari'a Jamaat, which in that month united with militants from across the North Caucasus to form a 'Caucasus Front'. In July republican security forces killed the leader of Shari'a Jamaat, Rasul Makshapirov. Relations with Chechnya were strained on several occasions in 2005, as a result of incursions by Chechen security forces.

In February 2006 the People's Assembly appointed Mukhu Aliyev, hitherto legislative speaker, to the new post of President of the Republic. He was succeeded as Chairman of the People's Assembly by Magomedsalam Magomedov, the son of the outgoing Chairman of the abolished State Council.

In July 2007 Shari'a Jamaat claimed responsibility for the killing of a senior Islamic cleric (the 11th such killing in nine years). Three successive leaders of the organization were assassinated during 2007–08. In April 2009 Umalat Magomedov (Al Bar) became leader of Shari'a Jamaat in Dagestan. During that year militants killed several senior political, security and religious officials in Dagestan, including the republican Minister of the Interior, Adilgerei Magomedtagirov. Ali Magomedov, a colonel in the Federal Security Service (FSB), was appointed as the Minister of the Interior in July.

In February 2010 the republican parliament voted to endorse the appointment of Magomedsalam Magomedov as President of Dagestan, precipitating protests by Kumyks who objected to the domination of senior republican posts by Avars and

Dargins. In March Magomed Abdulayev, an Avar, was named premier; Magomedsultan Magomedov, a Kumyk, was approved as parliamentary speaker. Federal President Dmitrii Medvedev dismissed Ali Magomedov as republican Minister of the Interior in August, appointing Col Abdurashid Magomedov in his place, and also announced that new volunteer detachments, comprising some 800 men, would be deployed in the mountainous areas of the Republic to combat Islamist militancy.

Magomedali Vagabov, the recently appointed leader of Shari'a Jamaat and the leading suspect behind an attack on the Moscow Metro, which had killed 40 people, was killed by security forces in August 2010. Two subsequent leaders of Shari'a Jamaat were assassinated in 2011–12. Meanwhile, in December 2011 the founder of an independent newspaper, Khadzhimurad Kamalov, was shot dead in Makhachkala.

In August 2012 Sunni Islamist militants injured eight people in a gun attack at a Shi'a mosque in Khasavyurt. In the same month a suicide bomber killed a Sufi leader, the second Sufi leader to have been killed in recent months in Dagestn. Meanwhile, the kidnapping and torture of Salafi Muslims, by either militants or security forces, were reported.

In January 2013 President Vladimir Putin dismissed Magomedsalam Magomedov, appointing Ramazan Abdulatipov as his acting successor as republican leader. The People's Assembly endorsed the nomination of Mukhtar Medzhidov as premier. In April Dagestan announced that it would not introduce popular elections to the regional leadership, as permitted by new federal legislation.

The mayor of Makhachkala, Said Amirov, was arrested in June 2013 on suspicion of arranging the killing of a local investigator; he was subsequently sentenced to life imprisonment for terrorism and murder. In July Abdulatipov dismissed the Government. Abdusamad Gamidov became the new Head of the Government. In September the People's Assembly elected Abdulatipov as republican President; his title was subsequently changed to Head of the Republic. Later in the month a judge of the republican Supreme Court was killed in Makhachkala.

After FSB operatives killed Umarov in March 2014, an Avar, Aliaskhab Kebekov (Ali Abu-Mukhammad), became leader of the Caucasus Emirate organization. The replacement in May of the Presidential Representative to the North Caucasus Federal Okrug, Aleksandr Khloponin, by Lt-Gen. Sergei Melikov, previously the commander of the joint forces of the federal Ministry of Internal Affairs in the North Caucasus, in part reflected dissatisfaction with the deteriorating security conditions in Dagestan. In September the People's Assembly adopted legislation that abolished direct elections for the heads of districts in Dagestan, in favour of a system under which they would be selected by municipal councils. In 2014, according to the news publication *Kavkazskii Uzel*, 208 people (163 suspected militants, 21 security officials and 24 civilians) were killed in the insurgency in Dagestan, substantially fewer than the total of 341 people killed in 2013, although it remained the most violent North Caucasus territory.

The arrests of imams and Salafi Islamist activists were reported from early 2015. Meanwhile, divisions increased within the Caucasus Emirate between those, allied with Kebekov, who remained affiliated with the al-Qa'ida organization, and those allied with the Islamic State organization. On 19 April special forces killed Kebekov. His successor as leader of the Caucasus Emirate, Magomed Suleimanov (Abu Usman Gimrinskii), was announced in July; however, he was assassinated in August.

In December 2015 Islamic State claimed responsibility for an attack on tourists outside the historic fortress in Derbent, as a result of which one person was killed and

12 others injured. According to *Kavkazskii Uzel*, 126 people (mostly suspected militants) were killed as a result of the insurgency in Dagestan during 2015.

Meanwhile, the Dagestan authorities continued the practice of the mass arrest of attendees of Salafi mosques and their inclusion in registers maintained by the Ministry of Internal Affairs. A Salafi imam in Khasavyurt was detained in April; in October he was sentenced by a military court in Rostov-on-Don (Rostov Oblast) to five years' imprisonment on charges of inciting terrorism.

YeR secured 75.5% of the votes cast on a proportional basis at elections to the People's Assembly held on 18 September 2016. The republican authorities were reported to have encouraged candidates of the nationalist Rodina (Motherland) party and of a local anti-corruption party to withdraw from the elections. Seventy-two of the 90 deputies had joined the YeR parliamentary faction by the end of the year.

In late 2016 Chechens in Dagestan appealed to President Putin and Abdulatipov to expedite their repossession of residences in Novolak district (following mass deportations of Chechens, principally to Central Asia, in 1944); this was dependent on the provision of federal funding to support the resettlement of several thousand ethnic Laks from the villages concerned. Meanwhile, Chechen representatives issued demands for the revision of the borders of Novolak district (which was to be renamed Aukh district) to incorporate two villages, Leninaul and Kalininaul, that had formed part of the district until 1944. Both issues exacerbated ethnic tensions in the region. Also in June, around 5,000 Nogais held a congress in Dagestan, which condemned the republican Government's proposals to deprive the Nogai community of access to agricultural land and appealed to Putin to overturn the decision.

On 27 September 2017 Abdulatipov retired as Head of the Republic. He was succeeded in an acting capacity by Vladimir Vasilyev, a former security official and a YeR State Duma deputy. A large-scale anti-corruption operation began in Dagestan in 2018. Among those arrested were the mayor of Makhachkala, Musa Musayev. On 5 February FSB forces detained and transferred to Moscow Gamidov, two deputy chairmen of the republican Government and a former minister. Vasilyev consequently dismissed the republican Government; Artyom Zdunov, hitherto Minister of the Economy of Tatarstan, became premier. In October a court sentenced Musayev to four years in prison for abuse of office; custodial sentences were also issued to Gamidov and to his former deputy.

Kavkazskii Uzel recorded that the annual total of people killed as a result of the insurgency in Dagestan had fallen significantly during 2017, to 47, and further to 35 in 2018; in both years the vast majority of fatalities comprised suspected militants. In February 2017 an Islamic State militant killed five people at a church in the northern town of Kizlyar, before being shot dead by security forces.

On 9 September 2018 the People's Assembly elected Vasilyev as Head of the Republic. From late 2018 unofficial border negotiations between Dagestani and Chechen officials prompted increasing discontent in Dagestan. The Chairman of the People's Assembly, Khizri Shikhsaidov, stated that demarcation of the joint border would be finalized by the end of 2019, and that no territorial claims had been made by either party (despite the Chechen authorities having published a map that appeared to lay claim to some territories within Dagestan). In March a Dagestani activist reported that the Chechen authorities had unilaterally registered about 18 ha of border land in Kizlyar district. Shikhsaidov and his Chechen counterpart, Magomed Daudov, announced the suspension of any further demarcation activities in April. Nevertheless, in November local residents criticized the opening by Chechen security forces of new border checkpoints. In December Kadyrov publicly maintained Chechnya's claim to disputed territory near Kizlyar, and it was reported that the Chechen authorities had referred the case to the federal Supreme Court. On 23 February 2020 around 10,000 people participated in a rally in Novolak district to mark the 76th anniversary of the Soviet deportation of Chechens and Ingush to Central Asia; Chechen activists attending renewed demands for the restoration of a former Chechen-majority district in Dagestan. In May six militants believed to be connected to Islamic State were killed by security forces in Khasavyurt.

President Putin accepted the resignation of Vasilyev on 5 October 2020. Sergei Melikov, hitherto a representative of Stavropol Krai in the Federation Council, the upper chamber of the federal legislature, was appointed Acting Head of the Republic. On 24 November Abdulpatakh Amirkhanov became Acting Chairman of the Government, replacing Zdunov (who had been appointed Acting Head of the Republic of Mordoviya). At elections to the People's Assembly on 19 September 2021, YeR secured 73.7% of votes cast on a proportional basis; SR took 12.7% and the KPRF 11.6%. By the end of the year 68 of the 90 deputies had joined the YeR faction, 11 that of SR, and 10 that of the KPRF. Meanwhile, on 14 October the People's Assembly voted to confirm Melikov as Head of the Republic, with the support of 82 deputies.

Following the resignation of Amirkhanov, on 22 February 2022 the People's Assembly unanimously approved the appointment of Abdulmuslim Abdulmuslimov (previously a Deputy Chairman of the Government) as premier.

In mid-September 2022 Melikov (together with other regional heads) expressed support for an initiative announced by Chechen President Kadyrov for the federal subjects to 'self-mobilize' by dispatching volunteer combatants in support of the ongoing Russian invasion of Ukraine. However, an order by federal President Putin shortly afterwards, on 21 September, for the partial mobilization of military reservists precipitated protests in major towns across Dagestan and elsewhere in the North Caucasus. On 25 September anti-mobilization rallies erupted in the village of Endirey, near Khasavyrut, and in Makhachkala, where violent confrontations between protesters and police resulted in some 100 arrests. Ukrainian President Volodymyr Zelensky issued an appeal, urging citizens from Dagestan to resist the mobilization. At least another 110 people were arrested Makhachkala on the following day.

In March 2023 a militant was killed by security forces in Kaitag district, after a police operation in which a civilian died, and in May a further two suspects were killed in an armed confrontation in Kuli district. On 28 June President Putin made a working visit to Dagestan, which was interpreted by some observers as an effort to improve his popularity; he met Melikov and received a strong welcome from the local population in Derbent, where he visited the Juma Mosque (the oldest in Russia) on the occasion of the Muslim holiday Eid al-Adha (Feast of the Sacrifice). Residents of Makhachkala blockaded the city centre on 9 August in protest at the perceived inaction of the regional authorities over lengthy power outages.

Following the intensification of the conflict between the Palestinian Islamist militant and political organization Hamas and Israel in October 2023, police in Makhachkala dispersed an unauthorized pro-Palestinian protest rally. On 29 October an estimated 1,200 protesters chanting anti-Semitic slogans stormed the airport in Makhachkala seeking passengers who had arrived on a flight from Israel, in apparent response to posts on the social media platform Instagram. The rioters surrounded the aircraft and attempted to identify Jewish passengers at the terminal. Around 20 people, including nine police officers, were injured in clashes, and some 60 participants in the rioting were arrested. Melikov denounced the actions of the protesters, while the federal Government attributed the violence to 'outside interference' by the West. In early November the region's deputy interior minister and deputy head of police were both arrested in early November on charges of bribery. By late November more than 500 people were reported to have been charged in connection with the rioting.

ECONOMY

In 2021 the gross regional product (GRP) of Dagestan amounted to 814,427m. roubles, or 259,076 roubles per head. The economic situation in the Republic was severely affected by unrest in the 2000s and 2010s. The Republic's major industrial centres are at Makhachkala, Derbent and Kaspiisk. In 2021 there were 509 km of railways in the Republic. There are fishing and trading ports in Makhachkala. The major railway line between Rostov-on-Don and Baku (Bakı), Azerbaijan, runs across the territory, as does the Caucasus highway. There is an airport at Makhachkala.

Dagestan's economy is largely based on animal husbandry, particularly sheep breeding. Its agriculture also consists of grain production, viniculture, horticulture and fishing. Agriculture employed 19.4% of the workforce (a higher proportion than in any other federal subject) in 2021 and contributed 19.6% of GRP. Dagestan's main industries are petroleum and natural gas production, electricity generation, mechanical engineering, metal working and food processing. Industry employed 21.2% of the workforce and contributed 21.0% of GRP in 2021, when manufacturing employed 7.4% of the workforce and contributed 3.3% of GRP.

Dagestan's economically active population comprised 1,259,001 inhabitants in 2022, when the rate of unemployment was 12.1%, while the average monthly wage was 35,082 roubles. There was a budgetary surplus of 4,840.0m. roubles in 2021, when export trade amounted to US $68m. (of which 55.9% was with countries of the CIS), and import trade to $147m. (of which 20.9% was with CIS countries).

DIRECTORY

Head of the Republic: SERGEI A. MELIKOV.

Chairman of the Government: ABDULMUSLIM M. ABDULMUSLIMOV.

Office of the Head of the Republic and of the Government: 367015 Dagestan, Makhachkala, pl. Lenina; tel. (8722) 67-30-59; fax (8722) 67-30-60; e-mail pressa@e-dag.ru; internet president.e-dag.ru; internet e-dag.ru.

People's Assembly: 367015 Dagestan, Makhachkala, pl. Lenina; tel. (8722) 67-30-55; fax (8722) 67-30-66; internet nsrd.ru; Chair. ZAUR A. ASKENDEROV.

State Duma Representatives (3): ABDULKHAKIM K. GADZHIYEV (YeR), MURAD S. GADZHIYEV (YeR), DZHAMALADIN N. GASANOV (YeR).

Federation Council Representatives: ILYAS M.-S. UMAKHANOV, SULEIMAN A. KERIMOV.

Republic of Ingushetiya

The Republic of Ingushetiya is situated on the northern slopes of the Greater Caucasus. The Chechen Republic lies to the east and north and North Osetiya—Alaniya to the west. There is an international border with Georgia to the south. The Assa is the main river. The Republic is mountainous, with some peaks over 3,000m high. The Republic occupies 3,628 sq km (1,401 sq miles). At January 2023 its population was 519,078 and the population density 143.1 per sq km. Only 54.8% of the population was urban in 2023. The administrative centre is at Magas, founded in 1998. At January 2023 it had an estimated 16,931 inhabitants. The largest city in the Republic is Nazran, with an estimated 124,086 inhabitants. Of residents who stated their ethnicity at the 2021 census, 96.4% were Ingush and 2.5% were Chechen. Only 0.7% were ethnically Russian—the lowest proportion of any federal subject. The Ingush are a Muslim people indigenous to the Caucasus Mountains and closely related to the Chechens (the two peoples are collectively known as Vainakhs). Their native tongue is a dialect of the Nakh group of the Caucasian family of languages. Ingushetiya is in the time zone UTC+3.

HISTORY

The Ingush are descended from the western Nakh people, whose reaction to Russian colonization of the Caucasus region in the 1860s distinguished them from their eastern counterparts (subsequently known as the Chechens); the latter resisted the invaders violently and were driven into the mountains, while the Ingush responded more passively and settled on the plains. In 1920 their territory was temporarily integrated into the Mountain People's Republic, but became the Ingush Autonomous Oblast on 7 July 1924. In 1934 the region was merged into a Checheno-Ingush Autonomous Oblast, which became an Autonomous Soviet Socialist Republic (ASSR) in 1936. In February 1944 the entire Ingush (and Chechen) population was deported to Soviet Central Asia, and the territory was subsequently handed over to the Osetiyans, although the Ingush were permitted to return from 1957.

With the ascendancy in the Checheno-Ingush ASSR of the secessionist All-National Congress of the Chechen People in 1991, a de facto separation between Chechen and Ingush territories was achieved. In June 1992 the federal Supreme Soviet recognized the existence of an Ingush Republic, with undetermined borders. The Republic claimed some eastern regions of North Osetiya and part of the North Osetiyan capital, Vladikavkaz. Prigorodnyi district, with a majority of Ingush inhabitants, was at the centre of the dispute. Armed hostilities between informal militias ensued for six days in October, with the Osetiyan militias receiving support from federal security forces, and tens of thousands of Ingush fled North Osetiya. Some 500 people were killed during the fighting, and a peace agreement was signed in 1994. The implementation of subsequent agreements signed between the leaders of Ingushetiya and North Osetiya—Alaniya, permitting Ingush to return to their former homes in Prigorodnyi, was obstructed by continuing tension.

In February 1994 some 97% of the electorate endorsed a new republican Constitution. In 1996 the territory was renamed the Republic of Ingushetiya. In March 1998 Ruslan Aushev (republican leader since 1992) was re-elected republican President. He subsequently sought to incorporate aspects of Islamic *Shari'a* law into republican law, in contravention of the federal Constitution.

In December 2001 Aushev resigned as President. Murat Zyazikov, a Federal Security Service (FSB) general, was elected his successor in April 2002. In September 70 people were killed near Galashki, when Chechen rebels clashed with federal forces.

According to human rights organizations, more than 40 instances of kidnapping in Ingushetiya occurred during the first half of 2004. In June a series of raids, led by the Chechen Islamist Shamil Basayev, took place against interior ministry targets in Ingushetiya, resulting in more than 90 deaths. As attacks on security officials became increasingly frequent, in December military aircraft and heavy artillery attacked southern regions in which rebel bases were believed to be located.

In June 2005 the republican legislature appointed Zyazikov to a further term of office. Numerous assassination attempts against several republican ministers occurred in 2006, while Islamists abducted and held hostage a People's Assembly deputy for two months. In September eight people were killed in a gun battle between Ingush traffic police and Chechen special forces. Federal officials subsequently permitted special forces from Chechnya and North Osetiya—Alaniya to operate in Ingushetiya.

In July 2007 militants killed an Islamic cleric, an ally of Zyazikov; on the same day an attack was attempted on the republican presidential motorcade. The federal Ministry of Internal Affairs subsequently dispatched reinforcements to Ingushetiya, but attacks against state officials military personnel persisted.

In August 2008 a rebel militia attacked a private residence belonging to Prime Minister Kharun Dzeitov. In that month the owner of an opposition news website, Magomed Yevloyev, was shot dead. In October a suicide bomber narrowly failed to kill the republican Minister of the Interior, Musa Medov. Amid much instability, on 30 October federal President Dmitrii Medvedev dismissed Zyazikov. One day later the

People's Assembly approved Medvedev's nomination of a military intelligence officer, Yunus-bek Yevkurov, as republican President. In November the People's Assembly approved the appointment of Rashid Gaisanov (a former republican Minister of the Economy) as Prime Minister. In that month Medov was dismissed.

In November 2008 Medvedev adopted federal legislation requiring the formal delineation of the administrative borders of Ingushetiya, the resolution of the status of the disputed Sunzha and Malgobek districts (claimed by both Chechnya and Ingushetiya), and the formal renunciation of any Ingushetiyan claim to Prigorodnyi.

Yevkurov issued an amnesty to members of illegal armed formations in March 2009, provided that they surrendered voluntarily and had not been involved in grave crimes; he announced his readiness to negotiate with the rebels, including the Ingush branch of Shari'a Jamaat, led by Akhmed Yevloyev (Emir Magas), the commander-in-chief of the Caucasus Emirate organization. However, in June the deputy chairman of Ingushetiya's Supreme Court and a former republican deputy premier were both assassinated in Nazran. In that month a suicide bomb attack against a car seriously injured Yevkurov and killed four of his companions.

The assassinations of senior republican officials, including two government ministers, continued in 2009. On 17 August some 21 police officers were killed in a bomb attack in Nazran. Medvedev responded by replacing the republican Minister of the Internal Affairs, Ruslan Meiriyev, with his deputy, Valerii Zhernov, and installing the federal Deputy Minister of Internal Affairs, Col-Gen. Arkadii Yedelev, as republican chief of police. In September Ingushetiya's Prosecutor-General, Yurii Turygin, announced that the perpetrators of the attack against Yevkurov had been identified, and that two had been killed. On 5 October Yevkurov dismissed the Government, citing its tolerance of corruption. On 20 October the People's Assembly approved the appointment of Aleksei Vorobyov, the Secretary of the republican Security Council, as Prime Minister.

A prominent Islamist militant, Said Buryatskii (Aleksandr Tikhomirov), was killed by security officials near Nazran in March 2010. In that month Medvedev dismissed Zhernov. In June federal forces captured Akhmed Yevloyev, who was deemed responsible for the attempt to assassinate Yevkurov; he was sentenced to life imprisonment in 2013.

Meanwhile, President Yevkurov dismissed the Government in March 2011, after Vorobyov was transferred to a post in Moscow City. The erstwhile republican Minister of Finance, Musa Chiliyev, became Prime Minister. Soon afterwards, Yevkurov's title was changed to Head of the Republic.

In July 2012 a public dispute erupted between Yevkurov and Chechen leader Ramzan Kadyrov, who claimed that Chechen security personnel had carried out a special operation in the Ingushetiyan village of Galashki in which three Chechen militants had been killed. Yevkurov, however, strongly denied that the operation had taken place. Kadyrov's rhetoric on the apparent inability of the Ingushetiyan authorities to suppress insurgent activity intensified following a suicide bombing that killed seven police officers. With preparations beginning for the formal demarcation of the Chechen–Ingush border, Kadyrov presented claims for the restoration of a pre-1934 border that would substantially reduce Ingushetiyan territory. In April 2013 a Chechen security operation, purportedly seeking Umarov, in the border village of Arshty, precipitated a clash with Ingushetiyan police.

In May 2013 Dzhamaleil Mutaliyev (Emir Adam), the head of the Ingushetiyan branch of the Caucasus Emirate organization, was killed in a counter-terrorism operation in Nazran. In August Akhmed Kotiyev, the head of the Security Council, and his driver were killed by Caucasus Emirate gunmen.

Yevkurov was re-elected as Head of the Republic by the People's Assembly on 8 September 2013. Later in the month Abubakar Malsagov, hitherto republican Minister of Construction, became Prime Minister.

As in other republics of the North Caucasus, a marked downturn in the level of violence was evident from 2014. Meanwhile, antagonism increased between Yevkurov and the republican mufti, Isa Khamkhoyev, an ally of Kadyrov. In March 2016 an assassination attempt was made against a prominent Salafi cleric, Sheikh Khamzat Chumakov, whose followers had clashed with those of Khamkhoyev. In April 2016 Yevkurov dissolved the muftiate.

YeR secured 75.9% of the votes cast on a proportional basis in elections to the People's Assembly held on 18 September 2016. Twenty-six of the 32 deputies had joined the YeR parliamentary faction by the end of the year.

Yevkurov was re-elected Head of the Republic by the People's Assembly on 9 September 2018. On the same day the People's Assembly voted to appoint its outgoing Chairman, Zyalimkhan Yevloyev, as Prime Minister.

On 26 September 2018 a border demarcation agreement was signed by Yevkurov and Kadyrov, providing for territorial exchanges between Chechnya and Ingushetiya. The agreement was highly advantageous to Chechnya, which acquired much of Sunzha district (renaming its newly acquired portion Sernovodskoye district). A campaign of protests in Ingushetiya against the accord intensified after the People's Assembly approved it on 4 October. On 30 October the republican Constitutional Court overturned the agreement, stating that a referendum was required to determine territorial questions. However, Yevkurov referred the matter to the federal Constitutional Court, which in December upheld the legitimacy of the agreement. In March 2019 a further large rally against the agreement was staged in Magas. One day later demonstrators blockading a major highway near Nazran to demand Yevkurov's resignation were forcibly dispersed by police and more than 50 people were detained. Amid continuing tensions, on 24 June Yevkurov resigned. President Vladimir Putin appointed Makhmud-Ali Kalimatov, a former public prosecutor of Ingushetiya and hitherto a senior official in Samara Oblast, as Acting Head of the Republic. The People's Assembly formally elected Kalimatov Head of the Republic on 8 September, approving his nomination of Konstantin Surikov, a banking official from Tomsk Oblast, as the new Chairman of the Government four days later.

On 2 November 2019 the head of the Ingushetiyan Department for Combating Extremism, Ibragim Eldzharkiyev, was shot dead in Moscow. Islamic State claimed responsibility for an attack in Magas in December, in which one police officer was killed and three others injured. In March 2020 a suspected militant was killed in a special operation in Sunzha district. A further two suspected militants were killed in a counter-terrorist operation in Malgobek district in August.

In November 2020 Ingushetiya was declared officially bankrupt by the federal Government. Kalimatov was obliged to sign an agreement under which the financial policy of Ingushetiya would be managed directly by the federal Ministry of Finance.

At elections to the People's Assembly on 19 September 2021, YeR secured 82.1% of the proportional vote. By the end of the year 27 of the 32 deputies had joined the YeR faction. In November excavation work initiated by the Chechen authorities by the Fortanga River, at the Ingushetiyan border, was denounced by the Ingushetiyan Minister of Natural Resources. Following heightened tensions, it was agreed that any

Chechen works would be undertaken in co-ordination with Ingushetiya's neighbouring Sunzha district. In December a court in Stavropol Krai sentenced seven Ingushetiyan activists who had led the protest rally in Magas in March 2019 to prison terms of up to nine years, on charges of creating an extremist group and assaulting law enforcement officers.

In June 2022 Ingushetiyan deputy premier Magomed Yevloyev denied a claim by the federal Minister of Natural Resources and Ecology, Aleksandr Kozlov, that the Ingushetiyan authorities had approved the transfer of part of a nature reserve located in the east of the region to Chechnya, under the 2018 territorial exchange agreement.

A militant attack against a police post on the border with North Osetiya—Alaniya was staged on 28 March 2023, injuring two officers. In response, the Ingushetiyan authorities undertook a counter-terrorism operation regime in Malgobek district. In early April three police officers were killed and eight injured, and at least one militant was killed in the district. A suspect wanted in connection to the series of attacks on law enforcement forces nearby was killed in an exchange of fire in September.

ECONOMY

In 2021 the gross regional product (GRP) of Ingushetiya amounted to 77,237m. roubles, or 148,587 roubles per head, the lowest figure recorded in any federal subject. In 2021 there were 39 km of railways in the Republic.

The primary agricultural activity in Ingushetiya is cattle-breeding. In 2021 the sector employed 17.1% of the workforce and contributed 11.0% of GRP. Ingushetiya's industry consists of electricity production, petroleum refining and food processing. Industry employed 25.4% of the workforce and contributed 13.8% of GRP in 2021, when manufacturing employed 14.2% of the workforce and contributed 2.0% of GRP.

The economically active population numbered 198,749 in 2022, when 28.5% of the labour force were unemployed (the higher proportion among the federal subjects), and the average monthly wage was 32,801 roubles. There was a budgetary surplus of 19.3m. roubles in 2021, when export trade amounted to US $6m. (24.2% of which was with CIS counties), and import trade to $5m. (of which 9.3% was with CIS countries).

DIRECTORY

Head of the Republic: MAKHMUD-ALI M. KALIMATOV.

Chairman of the Government (Prime Minister): VLADIMIR SLASTENIN.

Office of the Head of the Republic and Government: 386100 Ingushetiya, Magas, pr. I. Zyazikova 12–14; tel. (8734) 55-11-06; e-mail admin@ingushetia.ru; e-mail prav-vo@inbox.ru; internet ingushetia.ru; internet pravitelstvori.ru.

People's Assembly: 386000 Ingushetiya, Magas, pr. I. Zyazikova 16; tel. (8734) 55-17-35; e-mail parlament@ingushetia.ru; internet parlamentri.ru; Chair. MAGOMET U. TUMGOYEV.

State Duma Representative (1): MUSLIM B. TATRIYEV (YeR).

Federation Council Representatives: BELAN B. KHAMCHIYEV, MUKHARBEK O. BARAKOYEV.

Kabardino-Balkar Republic

The Kabardino-Balkar Republic is situated on the northern slopes of the Greater Caucasus and on adjoining flatlands. North Osetiya—Alaniya lies to the east, Georgia to the south-west, Stavropol Krai to the north, and the Karachai-Cherkess Republic to the west. The Republic's major rivers are the Terek and the Baksan. The Republic occupies 12,470 sq km (4,815 sq miles), and includes the highest peak in Europe, Elbrus, with a summit of 5,642 m (18,517 feet). At January 2023 the Republic's population was an estimated 903,266 and its population density 72.4 per sq km. Some 51.8% of the population was urban in 2023. The capital of the Republic is Nalchik, with an estimated 245,961 inhabitants at January 2023. Of residents who stated their ethnicity at the 2021 census, 57.1% were Kabardin, 19.8% were Russian, 15.2% were Cherkess, 13.7% were Balkar, 1.9% were Turks, and 0.8% were Osetiyan. Both the Kabardins and the Balkars are Sunni Muslims. The Kabardins' native language belongs to the Abkhazo-Adyge group of Caucasian languages. The Balkars speak a language closely related to Karachai, part of the Kipchak group of the Turkic branch of the Uralo-Altaic family. Both peoples almost exclusively speak their native tongue as a first language, but many are also fluent in Russian. The Kabardino-Balkar Republic is in the time zone UTC+3.

HISTORY

The Circassian Kabardins are believed to be descended from the Adyges and the Alans. They were converted to Islam in the 16th century, but in 1561 appealed to Tsar Ivan IV for protection against Tatar rule. In 1739 Kabardiya was established as a neutral state between the Ottoman and Russian Empires, but the region again became Russian territory in 1774. In the 1860s many Kabardins migrated to the Ottoman Empire. The Turkic Balkars, closely related to the Karachai people, were pastoral nomads until the mid-18th century, when they were forced to retreat further into the North Caucasus Mountains, their territory coming under Russian control in 1827, following which many ethnic Russians migrated to the region. In 1921 autonomous Balkar and

Kabardin Okrugs were created within the Mountain People's Republic. In January 1922 the two districts (which had been reconstituted as Autonomous Oblasts) were merged into a Kabardino-Balkar Autonomous Okrug, which became an Autonomous Soviet Socialist Republic (ASSR) on 5 December 1936. In 1944 the Balkars were deported to Kazakhstan and Central Asia, and the territory became the Kabardin ASSR. The Balkars were rehabilitated in 1956, and the Republic reverted to its previous name in 1957.

Valerii Kokov, a Kabardin, was elected as President in January 1992; he was re-elected in 1997. Meanwhile, in 1991 a Balkar association joined the Assembly of Turkic Peoples, and in November 1996 the first congress of the State Council of the Balkar People was held.

A new republican Constitution was adopted in July 2001. In January 2002 Kokov was re-elected republican President. Republican legislative elections to a unicameral legislature (replacing its bicameral predecessor) took place in December 2003.

From 2004 a rise in support for militant Islamist groups among Balkars was reported. Islamists associated with the Yarmuk Jamaat group, aligned with the Chechen rebel leader, Shamil Basayev, claimed responsibility for an attack on government offices in Nalchik in December, in which four people were killed. Two successive leaders of Yarmuk Jamaat were shot dead in early 2005. In August the authorities in Nalchik prohibited public rallies, following the killing of six police officers in the previous month.

In September 2005 Kokov submitted his resignation; the republican legislature endorsed a former State Duma deputy, Arsen Kanokov, as his successor as republican President. On 13 October some 100 militants linked with Basayev staged a series of co-ordinated attacks against government, police and commercial buildings across Nalchik. In ensuing clashes, some 130 people were killed, including 93 suspected militants and 12 civilians. Following the attacks, Kanokov pledged to reopen the unofficial mosques that had been closed by Kokov, and announced other measures to appease disaffected citizens.

In March 2006 federal President Vladimir Putin issued a decree dismissing the republican Minister of the Interior, Lt-Gen. Khachim Shogenov. Later in the month the republican Supreme Court ordered the dissolution of the State Council of the Balkar People. In June a new Prime Minister, Andrei Yarin, was appointed.

In July 2007 the recently established Sovet Stareishin Balkarskogo Naroda (SSBN—Council of Elders of the Balkar People) organized an unauthorized protest against policies of the republican authorities that it regarded as unfavourable to Balkars; the office of the republican prosecutor suspended the operations of the organization in November, deeming it extremist. However, in March 2008 the federal Supreme Court annulled an order issued by its republican counterpart demanding the dissolution of the SSBN.

The voter turnout in the Republic in elections to the State Duma on 2 December 2007 was reported at 96.7%, with the ruling YeR winning 96.1% of the votes cast. In April 2008 the trial began in Nalchik of 58 suspects charged with participating in the October 2005 attacks in the city. Attacks against Balkar activists were increasingly reported; in June 2008 the Balkariya organization convened a rally in Nalchik to protest against the failure of the republican leadership to protect the rights of the Balkar population. In October Kanokov met Balkar representatives for the first time. Shortly afterwards, the SSBN was refused permission to conduct its annual congress in a public building in Nalchik.

In June 2009 several hundred protesters in the Elbrus district blocked a highway in support of demands for the revision of a 2005 law that had deprived many Balkar inhabitants of their traditional grazing lands. President Kanokov persuaded the demonstrators to disperse. In July some 1,500 Balkars gathered in Nalchik, issuing a statement threatening to lobby federal President Dmitrii Medvedev for the removal of Kanokov from office should the implementation of Constitutional Court rulings to overturn the 2005 land legislation not be expedited. On 21 August Kanokov dismissed the Government and installed Aleksandr Merkulov, formerly a federal presidential official, as premier. The presentation to the republican Parliament in October of draft legislation intended to mollify Balkar concerns, providing for the transfer of some 200,000 ha of grazing land from republican control to that of Balkar-populated villages, led to protests among Kabardin groups. In May 2010 the republican Supreme Court again ruled that the SSBN was an extremist organization whose operations should cease, after attendees at a meeting had called for the establishment of a separate Balkar republic, to comprise around 40% of the Kabardino-Balkar Republic's territories. In September 2010 the republican Parliament voted to approve the reappointment of Kanokov as President (his title was subsequently changed to Head of the Republic).

In April 2011, following the dismissal of Merkulov, the republican Parliament approved the appointment of Ivan Gertler, a former deputy premier, as Prime Minister. In 2012 the federal authorities launched an extensive anti-corruption operation in the Republic. In July the head of the federal treasury's branch in the republic was dismissed and charged with the misappropriation of government funds.

On 1 November 2012 Kanokov dismissed Gertler's Government; on the same day the republican Parliament unanimously voted to support the appointment of Ruslan Khasanov as Prime Minister.

On 6 December 2013 Putin announced that he had accepted Kanakov's resignation. He appointed Yurii Kokov, the former head of the anti-extremism directorate of the federal Ministry of Internal Affairs, as Acting Head of the Republic. The recently elected republican Parliament voted to confirm Kokov's reappointment as Head of the Republic on 9 October 2014. Ali Musukov, hitherto republican Minister of Economic Development, became Prime Minister.

During 2014, according to figures compiled by the news publication *Kavkazskii Uzel*, a total of 49 people (all but five of whom were suspected militants) were killed in the insurgency in the Kabardino-Balkar Republic, compared with 92 people (including 52 suspected militants) in 2013, and 107 (including 80 suspected militants) in 2012.

The trial at the Republic's Supreme Court of those accused of involvement in the 2005 Nalchik attacks concluded on 23 December 2014; five defendants were sentenced to life imprisonment, while 49 were imprisoned for at least 10 years.

A significant upsurge in violence occurred in 2015, as regional members of the Caucasus Emirate network pledged allegiance to the Islamic State organization. In April Putin replaced the republican Minister of the Interior with a senior security officer, Igor Romashkin. The Federal Security Service (FSB) led a series of large-scale operations in Nalchik. According to *Kavkazskii Uzel*, 45 suspected militants and two security officials were killed as a result of the insurgency in the Republic during 2015. Violence abated substantially in subsequent years.

In August 2016 the federal National Anti-terrorist Committee announced it had killed four members of the Kabardino-Balkar Republic's militant network in a special operation in St Petersburg, including Zalim Shebzukhov, the commander of the Caucasus Emirate in the Kabardino-Balkar and Karachai-Cherkess Republics. Also in August the trial of 10 residents of Nalchik on charges of plotting to seize a government building and proclaim an Islamic caliphate, began at the North Caucasus Military Court in Rostov-on-Don (Rostov Oblast). In May 2017 the defendants received prison sentences of up to 16 years. In the same month the FSB reported that 183 residents of the Republic were involved in military operations in the Syrian Arab Republic and Iraq for Islamic State.

In June 2018 more than 200 prominent figures in the Republic adopted a resolution demanding the resignation of all four of the Republic's deputies in the State Duma, after they had voted to support educational reforms that required a significant reduction in the study of regional languages in schools; further protest demonstrations against the measure ensued.

On 19 September 2018 federal special police, together with National Guard forces from neighbouring republics, were dispatched to quell ethnic unrest around the village of Kendelen, which had erupted after local residents (mostly Balkars) had prevented Kabardin horsemen from riding through the village to mark the anniversary of the 1708 Kanzhal War, a Circassian victory. At least 45 people were injured, and around 120 arrests ensued. On 26 September Kokov resigned as Head of the Republic. On the same day he was appointed to the federal Security Council, while Kazbek Kokov, the son of former republican President Valerii Kokov and hitherto a presidential adviser, became Acting Head of the Republic. Further insecurity was reported in Nalchik in early 2019, with the arrest of several Ingushetiyan opposition leaders who had taken refuge there.

At the elections to the republican Parliament held on 8 September 2019, YeR obtained 65.0% of the proportional vote, ahead of the KPRF, with 12.2%, and SR, with 10.4%. On 3 October the republican Parliament confirmed Kazbek Kokov as Head of the Republic. Later in the month Musukov was reappointed as Prime Minister. By January 2020, 48 of the 70 deputies had joined the YeR parliamentary faction, nine that of the KPRF, and seven that of SR.

In March 2020 three suspected militants were killed in armed clashes in Baksan district. A further four militants were killed in Chegem district in July; the FSB subsequently announced that weapons and explosives had been seized at a residence in Nalchik, and claimed to have prevented an attack by members of Islamic State. In July 2021 a special security operation was carried out in Baksan, after which five suspected militants were declared to have been killed.

In May 2022 a total of 115 members of Russia's National Guard, and around 385 other servicemen from the Kabardino-Balkar Republic were officially dismissed for refusing assignments to participate in the Russian invasion of Ukraine which had begun on 24 February. A military court in Nalchik upheld the dismissal of the National Guard members after they attempted to appeal against the decision. An order issued by President Putin on 21 September for the partial mobilization of military reservists (in association with the ongoing Russian invasion of Ukraine) precipitated protests across the North Caucasus, including in Nalchik and Baksan.

Two militants were reported to have been killed during an operation near Prokhladnyi in early October 2022 a further two militants were killed in an exchange of fire with security officers on the outskirts of Nalchik on 26 December.

ECONOMY

Gross regional product (GRP) in the Kabardino-Balkar Republic amounted to 199,326m. roubles in 2021, or 229,153 roubles per head. The Republic's main industrial centres are at Nalchik, Tyrnauz and Prokhladnyi. In 2021 there were 133 km of railways in the Republic. Prokhladnyi is an important junction on the North Caucasus Railway. There is an international airport at Nalchik.

The Republic's main agricultural activities are the production of grain, fruit and vegetables, and animal husbandry. Agriculture employed 19.0% of the workforce in 2021 and contributed 16.3% of GRP. The Republic is rich in minerals, with reserves of petroleum, natural gas, gold, iron ore, garnet, talc and barytes. The industrial sector chiefly comprises mechanical engineering, metal working, non-ferrous metallurgy, food processing, the production of electricity, and the production and processing of tungsten-molybdenum ores. Industry employed 25.6% of the workforce and contributed 22.0% of GRP in 2021, when manufacturing employed 11.4% of the workforce and contributed 8.3% of GRP.

The economically active population numbered 404,503 in 2022, when 10.0% of the labour force were unemployed, while the average monthly wage was 35,251 roubles. There was a budgetary surplus of 1,572.1m. roubles in 2021, when export trade amounted to US $22m. (of which 82.8% was with countries of the CIS), and import trade to $79m. (of which 12.8% was with CIS countries).

DIRECTORY

Head of the Republic: KAZBEK V. KOKOV.

Prime Minister: ALII T. MUSUKOV.

Office of the Head of the Republic and the Government: 360028 Kabardino-Balkar Rep., Nalchik, pr. Lenina 27; tel. (8662) 40-20-66; fax (8662) 47-61-74; e-mail apkbr@kbrnet.ru; e-mail admin@kbr.ru; internet glava.kbr.ru; internet pravitelstvo.kbr.ru.

Republican Parliament: 360051 Kabardino-Balkar Rep., Nalchik, pr. Lenina 55; tel. (8662) 40-47-95; fax (8662) 47-27-13; e-mail parlam_kbr@mail.ru; internet parlament.kbr.ru; Chair. TATYANA B. YEGOROVA.

State Duma Representative (1): ADALBI L. SHKHAGOSHEV (YeR).

Federation Council Representatives: MUKHARBII M. ULBASHEV, ARSEN B. KANOKOV.

Karachai-Cherkess Republic

The Karachai-Cherkess Republic is situated on the northern slopes of the Greater Caucasus. It borders Krasnodar Krai to the north-west, Stavropol Krai to the north-east and the Kabardino-Balkar Republic to the east. There is an international boundary with Georgia (mainly the separatist region of Abkhazia) to the south. Its major river is the Kuban. The Republic occupies 14,277 sq km (5,512 sq miles). At January 2023 it had a population of 468,444 and a population density of 32.8 per sq km. Only 41.4% of the population was urban in 2023. The capital, Cherkessk, had an estimated 112,789 inhabitants at January 2023. Of residents who stated their ethnicity at the 2021 census, 44.4% were Karachai, 27.5% were Russian, 12.7% Cherkess, 8.1% Abazin, and 3.7% were Nogai. Both the Karachai and the Cherkess are Sunni Muslims of the Hanafi school. The Cherkess speak a language closely related to Kabardin, from the Abkhazo-Adyge group of Caucasian languages, while the Karachais' native tongue, from the Kipchak group, is the same as that of the Balkars. The Karachai-Cherkess Republic is in the time zone UTC+3.

HISTORY

Mongol tribes drove the Karachai, a group descended from Turkic Kipchak tribes, into the North Caucasus highlands in the 13th century. Their territory was annexed by the Russian Empire in 1828. In the 1860s–70s many Karachai emigrated to the Ottoman Empire to escape oppression, as did many Cherkess, a Circassian people. They had come under Russian control in the 1550s, having sought protection from the Crimean Tatars and some Turkic tribes, including the Karachai. Following the Treaty of Adrianople in 1829, by which the Ottomans abandoned their claim to the Caucasus region, a series of rebellions by the Circassians and reprisals by the Russian authorities occurred. In 1864 Russia completed its conquest of the region.

The Karachai and Cherkess Autonomous Oblasts were founded in 1926 and 1928, respectively, both subordinate to the territory governed from Stavropol. Following the deportation of the Karachai to Central Asia in 1943, the combined region became the

Cherkess Autonomous Oblast, until the Karachai were permitted to return in 1957. In 1992 federal President Boris Yeltsin presented draft legislation providing for the formation of a Karachai Republic. However, a referendum held in the Autonomous Oblast in March demonstrated widespread opposition to the subdivision of the territory, which was itself separated from Stavropol Krai and upgraded to republican status in the same month.

The Republic's first presidential election, in 1999, provoked unrest when a second round of voting reversed the positions achieved by the two leading candidates in the first round: Stanislav Derev, a Cherkess, and Gen. Vladimir Semyonov, a Karachai (whose share of the vote had increased from 18% to 85%). Semyonov's victory was confirmed in August; he was sworn in on 14 September. (The leader of the region in 1979–99, Vladimir Khubiyev, was also a Karachai.)

In an election in August 2003, in which all candidates were Karachai, Mustafa Batdyyev was elected President, defeating Semyonov. In October 2004 Ansar Tebuyev, a Deputy Chairman of the republican Government, was assassinated in Cherkessk. The killing, in November, of seven shareholders in a cement company controlled by Ali Kaitov, Batdyyev's former son-in-law, led to some 400 people demonstrating outside the offices of the republican presidency to demand Batdyyev's resignation, and then ransacking and occupying the building. In December 2006 Kaitov was one of 16 people to receive a substantial custodial sentence for charges relating to the murder.

In June 2005 some 200 members of the local Abazin population invaded the republican parliamentary building to protest at changes to local administrative structures. In July the changes were suspended, and in December a referendum approved the creation of a new Abazin district. Batdyyev supported similar Nogai demands for an autonomous district, the establishment of which was overwhelmingly approved by referendum in October 2006.

A local insurgent leader, Rustam Ionov (Abu Bakr), was killed in September 2007 as he attempted to escape into Georgia. In early 2008 the director of the Federal Security Service (FSB), Nikolai Patrushev, announced that the principal local Islamist militia, the Karachayevo Jamaat, had been dissolved. In July, nevertheless, militants killed three police patrol officers in Karachayevsk.

In August 2008 the People's Assembly voted to confirm the nomination of Boris Ebzeyev, hitherto a judge at the federal Constitutional Court and a Karachai, as republican President. He assumed office in September, appointing Vladimir Kaishev, an ethnic Greek, as Chairman of the Government. The Cherkess community objected strongly to Kaishev's appointment. An extraordinary congress of the local branch of the pan-Circassian Adyge Khase organization was convened in Cherkessk in November; delegates adopted a resolution demanding the establishment of a Circassian republic by the unification of those regions of Adygeya, the Kabardino-Balkar Republic and the Karachai-Cherkess Republic in which Circassians (Adyges, Kabardins and Cherkess) constituted a demographic majority.

In elections to the People's Assembly, held on 1 March 2009, YeR secured 69.2% of the votes cast. In April some 29 Islamists linked with the Chechen rebel commander, Doku Umarov, were brought to trial in Cherkessk, accused of plotting to overthrow the republican authorities and of membership of illegal armed groups; 22 defendants received custodial sentences in 2011. In April 2010 Muradin Kemov succeeded Kaishev as republican Prime Minister.

In February 2011 federal President Dmitrii Medvedev accepted Ebzeyev's resignation as republican President. Medvedev's nomination of Rashid Temrezov, a Karachai, as Ebzeyev's successor, was endorsed by the People's Assembly on 1 March. In March Temrezov appointed Indris Kyabishev, previously the Minister of Economic Development, as Prime Minister. The title of President was replaced by that of Head of the Republic in April.

Cherkess youth activists issued an appeal to federal President Vladimir Putin over alleged mistreatment by the Karachai-Cherkess police in September 2012, complaining that the Republic's police regularly attempted to repress displays of symbols of Circassian nationhood. In November Kyabishev resigned as premier, after he was elected to the People's Assembly. He was succeeded by Murat Kardanov.

In April 2013 Temrezov announced that he favoured the abolition of (recently reintroduced) direct elections for the Head of the Republic, owing to concerns that such elections could exacerbate ethnic tensions. In July Ruslan Rakhayev, the former deputy chief of the police in Cherkessk, was sentenced to 13 years' imprisonment by Cherkessk City Court for beating a detainee to death.

At elections to the People's Assembly, held on 14 September 2014, YeR obtained some 73.2% of the votes cast on a proportional basis. Overall, 37 of the 51 deputies elected joined the YeR parliamentary faction. On 27 August 2015 Temrezov dismissed the Government. On 14 September a new, substantially reorganized Government, headed by Ruslan Kazanokov (republican premier in 2003–05), assumed office. In October 2016 six people were arrested in the Republic on suspicion of involvement in the Islamic State organization.

Upon the expiry of Temrezov's mandate, on 27 February 2016 Putin appointed him Acting Head of the Republic. On 18 September Temrezov was overwhelmingly re-elected by the People's Assembly, receiving the votes of all 49 deputies attending.

In December 2017 five suspected militants, who were believed to be planning a terrorist attack on behalf of Islamic State against a civilian target, were killed by security officials in the central village of Zelenchukskaya.

Rauf Arashukov, a representative of the Republic in the Federation Council, the upper chamber of the federal legislature, was arrested in the legislative chamber in January 2019, after his colleagues had voted to remove his immunity from prosecution; charges of murder, in association with at least two contract killings, embezzlement and creating a criminal enterprise were brought against him. His senatorial status was revoked in May. In June 2021 a court ordered the seizure of property worth 1,300m. roubles from Arashukov and his father; a Moscow court in 2022 sentenced both to life imprisonment.

Meanwhile, in elections to the People's Assembly held on 8 September 2019 YeR won 65.0% of the votes cast on a proportional basis, ahead of the KPRF, with 12.2%. Of the 50 deputies elected, by January 2020 some 34 had joined the parliamentary faction of YeR and six that of the KPRF.

In August 2021 President Putin presented three candidates, including Temrezov, for the post of Head of the Republic. On 19 September all 48 deputies attending the session of the People's Assembly re-elected Temrezov to the office.

ECONOMY

In 2021 the gross regional product (GRP) of the Karachai-Cherkess Republic amounted to 109,390m. roubles, or 235,355 roubles per head. The Republic's major industrial centres are at Cherkessk and Karachayevsk. In 2021 it contained 51 km of railway track; the Stavropol–Sukhumi (Abkhazia, Georgia) highway passes through the Republic.

The principal crops cultivated by the Republic's agricultural sector include grain, sunflower seeds, sugar beet and vegetables, while animal husbandry is also significant. The sector employed 14.3% of the workforce in 2021 and contributed 19.5% of GRP. The Republic's main industries are petrochemicals, chemicals, mechanical engineering and metal working, while the manufacture of building materials, food processing and coal production are also important. Industry employed 25.1% of the workforce and contributed 25.4% of GRP in 2021, when manufacturing employed 11.7% of the workforce and contributed 9.4% of GRP.

The economically active population numbered 196,295 in 2022, when the rate of unemployment was 9.8%, while the average monthly wage was 35,463 roubles. There was a budgetary surplus of 995.3m. roubles in 2021, when export trade amounted to US $16m. (of which 73.3% was with countries of the CIS), while import trade amounted to $40m. (of which 23.8% was with CIS countries).

DIRECTORY

Head of the Republic: Rashid B. Temrezov.

Chairman of the Government: Murat O. Argunov.

Office of the Head of the Republic and Government: 369000 Karachai-Cherkess Rep., Cherkessk, pl. Lenina; tel. (8782) 25-40-08; fax (8782) 25-40-20; e-mail kchrdoc@mail.ru; internet kchr.ru.

People's Assembly (Parliament): 369000 Karachai-Cherkess Rep., Cherkessk, ul. Krasnoarmeiskaya 54; tel. (8782) 26-67-79; e-mail nskchr09@gmail.com; internet parlament09.ru; Chair. Aleksandr I. Ivanov.

State Duma Representative (1): Soltan Dzh. Uzdenov (YeR).

Federation Council Representatives: Akhmat A. Salpagarov, Krym O. Kazanokov.

Republic of North Osetiya—Alaniya

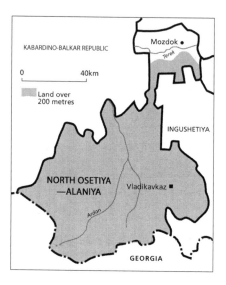

The Republic of North Osetiya—Alaniya is situated on the northern slopes of the Greater Caucasus. The Kabardino-Balkar Republic lies to the west, Stavropol Krai to the north, and the Chechen Republic and Ingushetiya to the east. There is an international boundary with Georgia (largely with the separatist territory of South Ossetia) in the south, along the Greater Caucasus Range. The major river is the Terek. In the north are the steppelands of the Mozdok and Osetiyan plains, while further south in the foothills are mixed pasture and beech forest. Narrow river valleys lie in the southern mountainous regions. North Osetiya covers 7,987 sq km (3,084 sq miles). At January 2023 it had a population of 680,748 and a population density of 85.2 per sq km. Some 63.2% of the population was urban in 2023. The capital, Vladikavkaz, in the east, had an estimated 292,886 inhabitants at January 2023. Of residents who stated their ethnicity at the 2021 census, 68.1% were Osetiyan, 18.9% Russian, 3.8% Ingush, 2.8% Kumyk, 1.8% Armenian, and 1.0% were Georgian. The Osetiyans speak an Indo-European language of the Persian group. The Republic is in the time zone UTC+3.

HISTORY

The Osetiyans (Ossetins, Oselty) are descended from the Alans, a tribe of the Samartian people, who were driven into the Caucasian foothills by the Huns in the fourth century, and whose descendants were forced further into the mountains by Tatar and Mongol invaders. The Georgians converted the Osetiyans to Orthodox Christianity in the 12th–13th centuries; a sub-group, the Digors, adopted Islam in the 17th–18th centuries. Perpetual conflict with the Kabardins forced the Osetiyans to seek Russian protection, and the Ottomans ceded their territory to Russia at the Treaty of Kuçuk Kainavci in 1774. The Russians fostered good relations with the Osetiyans. The strategic Darial pass is situated in the region, through which the construction of the Georgian Military Highway in 1799 facilitated the Russian conquest of Georgia.

North Osetiya was established as an Autonomous Oblast in July 1924, and as an Autonomous Soviet Socialist Republic in 1936. In 1944, when the Digors were deported to Central Asia, the territory was expanded to include former Ingush territories and part of Stavropol Krai.

The Republic declared sovereignty in mid-1990. From 1991 there was debate about unification with South Ossetia, where armed hostilities had broken out after the Georgian Supreme Soviet voted to abolish the South Ossetian territory, and from where thousands of refugees had fled to North Osetiya. Meanwhile, the Republic refused to recognize claims by the Ingush to the territory (Prigorodnyi district) that they had lost in 1944; violence between informal militia groups from Ingushetiya and North Osetiya (the latter obtaining some support from federal troops) ensued in October 1992. Around 500 people were killed in six days of fighting, and tens of thousands of Ingush fled North Osetiya. A peace settlement was agreed in 1994. In December the Republic's name was amended to North Osetiya—Alaniya.

In 1998 Aleksandr Dzasokhov, a former member of the Kommunisticheskaya Partiya Sovetskogo Soyuza (Communist Party of the Soviet Union) Politburo, was elected as republican President.

Regional instability increased from 1999. A bomb exploded in Vladikavkaz in March, killing 42 people. In January 2002 Dzasokhov was re-elected as President. Following republican legislative elections held in mid-2003, supporters of YeR held a working majority in the chamber. In June a suicide bomber detonated explosives close to a bus carrying federal airforce personnel near Mozdok (a principal base for federal troops fighting in Chechnya), killing 17 people. In August more than 50 people were killed, following a suicide bombing near a military hospital at Mozdok.

On 1 September 2004 some 32 Islamist militants seized control of a school in Beslan, taking at least 1,100 pupils, parents and teachers hostage. Federal special forces officers stormed the school on 3 September. Official figures claimed that over 330 hostages were killed, including 186 children, although independent estimates placed the number of fatalities at 600. The Republic's chief Federal Security Service (FSB) official and interior minister both resigned in response. After 3,500 demonstrators gathered in Vladikavkaz on 8 September to demand Dzasokhov's resignation, A new republican Government was appointed on 10 September.

Dzasokhov resigned as President on 31 May 2005. The nomination by federal President Vladimir Putin of Taimuraz Mamsurov, hitherto Chairman of the republican Parliament, to the renamed post of Head of the Republic, was approved by that body on 7 June. In May 2006 Nurpasha Kulayev, a Chechen who was reported to be the sole survivor of the instigators of the Beslan siege, was sentenced to life imprisonment.

The announcement, in February 2006, by the Presidential Representative to the Southern Federal Okrug (then including the territories of the North Caucasus), Dmitrii Kozak, of a revised plan for the resolution of the Prigorodnyi dispute precipitated considerable controversy and the opposition of the Ingushetiyan authorities; Kozak proposed that the displaced Ingush should be rehoused in new settlements elsewhere in North Osetiya.

The increase of tensions between Georgia and the Russian-backed 'Republic of South Ossetia' in mid-2008, which escalated into a military conflict between Russia and Georgia in August, prompted a mass evacuation of civilians to North Osetiya; refugees were estimated to number some 14,000 at the height of the conflict. After the Russian forces gained full control of South Ossetia, its internationally unrecognized

'President', Eduard Kokoyev (Kokoiti), repeated pledges to seek unification of the territory with North Osetiya.

In November 2008 the Head of Vladikavkaz city administration, Vitalii Karayev, was shot dead. In late April 2010 the republican Parliament voted to approve Mamsurov to a second term as Head of the Republic. A car bomb attack on the central market in Vladikavkaz in September, attributed to Ingush Islamist militants, resulted in at least 18 deaths.

At elections to the republican Parliament held in October 2012, YeR obtained 46.2% of the votes cast on a proportional basis. The small Russian nationalist party, PR, was placed second, with 26.6%.

In November 2013 the republican Parliament approved the first draft of legislation abolishing direct gubernatorial elections, and providing for the Head of the Republic to be elected by the republican parliament. In November 2014 a consular office of the separatist South Ossetian authorities opened in Vladikavkaz.

On 5 June 2015, as Mamsurov's term of office expired, President Putin appointed Tamerlan Aguzarov, a former Chairman of the republican Supreme Court, and a deputy of the federal State Duma, as Acting Head of the Republic. On 13 September the republican Parliament confirmed his appointment. A new republican Government, led by Vyacheslav Bitarov, assumed office later in the month. In February 2016 Aguzarov died of pneumonia. He was succeeded as Head of the Republic, in an acting capacity, by Bitarov, while Taimuraz Tuskayev became the interim Chairman of the Government. Bitarov was elected Head of the Republic in the Parliament on 18 September. Meanwhile, at a memorial service for the Beslan massacre on 1 September, police arrested several activists belonging to the Golos Beslana (Voice of Beslan) organization who had displayed placards criticizing Putin; penalties were subsequently imposed against six women on charges of violating public order. The European Court of Human Rights, ruling in April 2017 on a case filed by relatives of the people killed and injured in the seizure of the Beslan school, found that their rights had been violated, after the Russian authorities had failed to take the necessary measures to fully investigate the act, and awarded 409 complainants a total of around €3m.

In elections to the republican Parliament held on 10 September 2017, YeR secured 59.2% of the votes cast, ahead of PR, with 15.7%, SR, with 10.2%, and the KPRF, with 6.6%. The LDPR, which won only 2.1% of the votes cast, demanded a recount of the voting results; however, the region's Central Election Commission refused to acknowledge video recordings of apparent violations that were released online. By the end of the year 46 of the 70 deputies had joined the parliamentary faction of YeR, 12 that of PR, eight that of SR, and five that of the KPRF.

A large-scale fire occurred at a metallurgical plant (the largest contributor to the Republic's economy) in Vladikavkaz in October 2018, in which one person was killed. With widespread public support, in 2019 the closure of the plant was announced.

On 20 April 2020 some 2,000 demonstrators protested in Vladikavkaz against the restrictions introduced by the local authorities in order to contain the COVID-19 pandemic, and demanded Bitarov's resignation. The protest was violently dispersed by police. The protest had been instigated by a prominent North Osetiyan opera singer resident in St Petersburg, Vadim Cheldiyev, who had accused the North Osetiyan authorities of exaggerating the scale of the pandemic and using it as a pretext to expand state control. After being arrested in St Petersburg and placed in pre-trial detention in North Osetiya, in April Cheldiyev was fined 75,000 roubles by a Vladikavkaz court for disseminating false information. In July 2021 a total of 10 defendants received prison sentences of up to six-and-a-half years at a court in Rostov-on-Don (Rostov Oblast) for participating in the protest rally of April 2020; a further four protesters received custodial sentences in November 2021. In July 2022 Cheldiyev was sentenced to 10 years' imprisonment; two associates were also imprisoned.

On 9 April 2021 President Putin accepted the resignation of Bitarov as Head of the Republic; on the same day he appointed Sergei Menyaylo, the erstwhile Presidential Representative to the Siberian Federal Okrug (and former Governor of Sevastopol City) as Acting Head of the Republic. Menyaylo was confirmed in office by the Republican Parliament on 19 September. On 8 October Boris Dzhanayev, previously the Deputy Chairman, was appointed as Chairman of the Government, replacing Tuskayev.

In May 2022 the outgoing President of South Ossetia, Anatolii Bibilov, scheduled a referendum on his longstanding aim that South Ossetia unify with North Osetiya—Alaniya and become part of the Russian Federation for July. However, Bibilov failed to win re-election, and his successor, Alan Gagloyev, at the end of May cancelled the planned referendum, despite his own support for unification. Although Menyaylo and federal government representatives had prior to Bibilov's electoral defeat declared support for the referendum initiative, federal government officials welcomed Gagloyev's decision.

In legislative elections held on 11 September 2022 YeR obtained some 67.9% of the votes cast on a proportional basis, followed by SR (which had absorbed PR in 2021), with 14.3%, and the KPRF, with 12.4%. By the end of the year 51 deputies had joined the YeR parliamentary faction, 10 that of SR and nine that of the KPRF.

On 28 September 2022 Menyaylo imposed restrictions on vehicles arriving from other parts of Russia, after an order by President Putin for the partial mobilization of military reservists from all regions precipitated the increased flight of men out of the country, resulting in a traffic blockage at the main border crossing with Georgia.

ECONOMY

In 2021 the gross regional product (GRP) of North Osetiya—Alaniya amounted to 202,602m. roubles, or 293,366 roubles per head. Its major industrial centres are at Vladikavkaz, Mozdok and Beslan. In 2021 the Republic contained 144 km of railways and one of the two principal road routes from Russia to the South Caucasus, the Transcaucasian Highway. There is an international airport at Vladikavkaz.

Agriculture in North Osetiya consists mainly of vegetable and grain production, horticulture, viniculture and animal husbandry. Agriculture employed 9.0% of the workforce in 2021 and contributed 14.8% of GRP. The Republic's main industries are radio-electronics, non-ferrous metallurgy and food processing. There are five hydro-electric power stations. Industry employed 21.9% of the workforce and contributed 14.6% of GRP in 2021, when manufacturing employed 10.4% of the workforce and contributed 4.9% of GRP.

The economically active population in the Republic numbered 282,501 in 2022, when the rate of unemployment was 11.9%, while the average monthly wage was 36,360 roubles. There was a budgetary surplus of 1,238.3m. roubles in 2021, when export trade amounted to US $123m. (of which 61.3% was with countries of the CIS), and import trade to $34m. (of which 10.4% was with CIS countries).

DIRECTORY

Head of the Republic: Vice-Adm. SERGEI I. MENYAYLO.

Chairman of the Government: BORIS B. DZHANAYEV.

Office of the Head of the Republic and Chairman of the Government: 362038 North Osetiya—Alaniya, Vladikavkaz, pl. Svobody 1; tel. (8672) 53-53-38; fax (8672) 53-57-72; e-mail apinf@globalalania.ru; internet alania.gov.ru.

Republican Parliament: 362038 North Osetiya—Alaniya, Vladikavkaz, pl. Svobody 1; tel. (8672) 53-55-13; fax (8672) 53-96-32; e-mail parliamentosetia@mail.ru; internet parliament-osetia.ru; Chair. TAIMURAZ R. TUSKAYEV.

State Duma Representative (1): ARTUR B. TAIMAZOV (YeR).

Federation Council Representatives: TAIMURAZ D. MAMSUROV, VITALII V. NAZARENKO.

Stavropol Krai

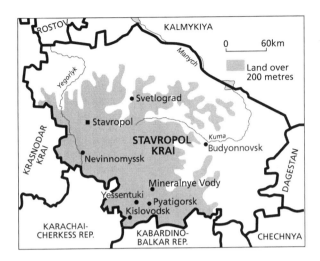

Stavropol Krai is situated in the central Caucasus and extends from the Caspian lowlands in the east to the foothills of the Greater Caucasus Mountains in the west. It borders Krasnodar Krai to the west, Rostov Oblast and the Republic of Kalmykiya to the north-west, and the Republic of Dagestan to the east. There are borders to the south with (from east to west) the Chechen Republic, North Osetiya—Alaniya, the Kabardino-Balkar Republic and the Karachai-Cherkess Republic. Much of the territory is steppe. Its total area is 66,160 sq km (25,545 sq miles). At January 2023 the population was an estimated 2,891,204 and the population density 43.7 per sq km. Some 60.7% of the population was urban in 2023. The administrative centre is Stavropol, with an estimated 550,147 inhabitants at January 2023. Other major cities are the administrative centre of the North Caucasus Federal Okrug, Pyatigorsk (144,955), Kislovodsk (126,674), Yessentuki (121,534) and Nevinnomyssk (115,826). Of residents who stated their ethnicity at the 2021 census, 82.9% were Russian, 4.9% Armenian, 2.1% Dargin, 1.4% Gypsy (Roma), 0.9% Greek, and 0.8% were Nogai. Stavropol Krai is in the time zone UTC+3.

HISTORY

Stavropol city was founded in 1777. The territory was created on 13 February 1924, and was originally known as the South-Eastern Oblast (also incorporating territories of Krasnodar Krai) and, subsequently, North Caucasus Krai. It was named Ordzhonikidze Krai in 1937–43, before adopting its current title. The Krai included a Karachai-Cherkess Autonomous Oblast (now Republic) until 1992.

In June 1995 the town of Budyonnovsk, in the east of the Krai, was the scene of a hostage-taking operation at a hospital carried out by Chechen forces led by Shamil Basayev: over 1,000 civilians were seized, and more than 100 people were killed. In the gubernatorial election of November 1996 the incumbent was defeated by the KPRF candidate, Aleksandr Chernogorov; he was re-elected in 2000. There were a series of bomb attacks in the Krai by Chechen separatists in 2000–03, as a result of which more than 75 people were killed.

In October 2005 the provincial legislature approved President Vladimir Putin's appointment of Chernogorov to a further gubernatorial term. In February 2006 some 300 special forces troops launched operations in the eastern village of Tukui-Mekteb against Nogai Islamist militants. According to official reports, eight militants and at least seven law enforcement officials were killed in the ensuing clashes.

At elections to the provincial State Duma in March 2007 SR, led locally by the Mayor of Stavropol Dmitrii Kuzmin, secured 37.6% of the votes cast; the ruling YeR was placed second, with 23.9%. After its failure to become the leading party in the regional legislature, the federal leadership of YeR revoked Chernogorov's membership of the party (which he had joined in late 2006, after leaving the KPRF).

In April 2008 Chernogorov resigned as Governor. The provincial State Duma approved the nomination by President Dmitrii Medvedev of Valerii Gayevskii (a federal official) as Governor on 23 May. In 2009 there were renewed indications of ethnic tension in the Krai. In June 12 Russian nationalists were detained in the city of Georgiyevsk and accused of creating public disorder, while later in the month clashes occurred between Dargins and Nogais, injuring at least eight. In August a Dargin was killed when fights broke out between several hundred ethnic Russians and Dargins in the village of Pelagiada.

Upon the foundation of the North Caucasus Federal Okrug in 2010 the town of Pyatigorsk, in the south of the Oblast, became its administrative centre, although the administration was initially temporarily based in another city in the Krai, Yessentuki. In May of that year a bomb placed outside a concert hall in Stavropol by Islamists killed six people and injured around 40 others.

Gayevskii resigned as Governor on 2 May 2012; Medvedev nominated Valerii Zerenkov, a YeR State Duma deputy, as his successor. The provincial State Duma voted to endorse his appointment on 5 May.

On 27 September 2013 Putin (who had again been elected President) dismissed Zerenkov as Governor. He was replaced in an acting capacity by Vladimir Vladimirov, a native of the Krai, but hitherto the First Deputy Governor of the Yamalo-Nenets Autonomous Okrug. In September 2014, Vladimirov was overwhelmingly elected Governor, receiving 84.2% of the votes cast.

During 2014, according to figures published by the news publication *Kavkazskii Uzel*, 10 people (seven civilians and three suspected militants) were killed in insurgency-related violence in Stavropol Krai, following 13 recorded deaths in the previous year; such violence largely abated in the Krai thereafter.

YeR secured some 53.1% of the proportional votes in elections to the Provincial State Duma held on 18 September 2016; by the end of the year 41 of the 50 deputies had joined the YeR parliamentary faction.

Vladimirov was elected to a further term as Governor on 8 September 2019, obtaining 79.6% of the votes cast and defeating four other candidates.

At elections to the Provincial State Duma held on 19 September 2021, YeR secured 60.3% of the votes cast on the basis of proportional representation; the KPRF obtained 15.7%. By the end of the year 44 of the 50 deputies had joined the YeR faction and four that of the KPRF.

ECONOMY

In 2021 Stavropol Krai's gross regional product (GRP) was 1,024,560m. roubles, or 367,687 roubles per head. Its main industrial centres are at Stavropol, Nevinnomyssk and Budyonnovsk. In 2021 there were 922 km of railway lines in the Krai.

The Krai contains extremely fertile soil. Agriculture consists mainly of grain, sunflower seeds, sugar beet and vegetables. Horticulture, viniculture, bee-keeping and animal husbandry are also important. Agriculture employed 14.0% of the workforce in 2021 and contributed 14.2% of GRP. The main industries are food processing, mechanical engineering, the production of building materials, chemicals and petrochemicals, natural gas, petroleum, non-ferrous metal ores and coal, mineral fertilizer, and electrical energy. Industry employed 22.4% of the labour force and contributed 28.3% of GRP in 2021, when manufacturing employed 10.4% of the workforce and contributed 13.4% of GRP.

The economically active population of Stavropol Krai numbered 1,320,286 in 2022, when 4.3% of the labour force were unemployed, while the average monthly wage was 41,402 roubles. There was a budgetary surplus of 13,585.5m. roubles in 2021, when export trade amounted to US $1,511m. (of which 28.3% was with countries of the CIS), while import trade amounted to $739m. (of which 17.6% was with CIS countries).

DIRECTORY

Governor: VLADIMIR V. VLADIMIROV.

Office of the Governor: 355025 Stavropol, pl. Lenina 1; tel. (8652) 35-11-72; fax (8652) 35-03-30; e-mail gsk@stavkray.ru; internet gubernator.stavkray.ru.

Provincial State Duma: 355025 Stavropol, pl. Lenina 1; tel. and fax (8652) 35-16-84; e-mail dumask@dumask.ru; internet dumask.ru; Chair. NIKOLAI T. VELIKAN.

State Duma Representatives (4): MIKHAIL V. KUZMIN (YeR), OLGA V. TIMOFEYEVA (YeR), OLGA M. KAZAKOVA (YeR), YELENA V. BONDARENKO (YeR).

Federation Council Representatives: MIKHAIL A. AFANASOV, GENNADII V. YAGUBOV.

VOLGA FEDERAL OKRUG

Presidential Representative to the Volga Federal Okrug: IGOR A. KOMAROV, 603082 Nizhnii Novgorod, Kreml, kor. 1; tel. (831) 431-47-65; e-mail press-pfo@yandex.ru; internet pfo.ru.

Republic of Bashkortostan

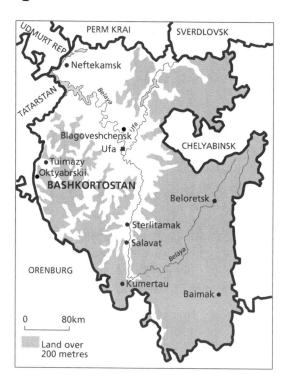

The Republic of Bashkortostan is situated in the Southern Urals. It borders Perm Krai in the north, the Udmurt Republic in the north-west, the Republic of Tatarstan in the west, and the Oblasts of Orenburg in the south, Chelyabinsk in the east and Sverdlovsk in the north. The Republic occupies 142,947 sq km (55,192 sq miles). At January 2023 it had a population of 4,077,600 and a population density of 28.5 per sq km. 62.3% of the population was urban in 2023. The capital is Ufa, with an estimated 1,157,994 inhabitants at January 2023. Other major cities include Sterlitamak (279,174), Salavat (147,296), Neftekamsk (133,300) and Oktyabrskii (116,282). Of residents who stated their ethnicity at the 2021 census, 37.5% were Russian, 31.5% Bashkir, 24.2% Tatar, 2.1% Mari, and 2.0% were Chuvash. Bashkir, spoken by the majority of ethnic Bashkirs, is a Kipchak language closely related to Tatar, and has two distinct dialects: Kuvakan, spoken in the north; and Yurmatin, spoken in the south. Most Bashkirs and

Tatars are Sunni Muslims of the Hanafi school, although some Bashkirs, the Nagaibak, are Orthodox Christians. Bashkortostan is in the time zone UTC+5.

HISTORY

The Bashkirs originated as a distinct ethnic group during the 16th century, out of the Tatar, Mongol, Volga Bulgar, Oguz, Pecheneg and Kipchak peoples. Russia annexed the territory in 1557. Rebellions against Russian control, most notably that led by Salavat Yulai in 1773, were unsuccessful. Immigration by ethnic Russians to the region in the late 19th century resulted in their outnumbering the Bashkir population. The Bashkir Autonomous Soviet Socialist Republic was formed on 23 March 1919.

The territory declared its sovereignty, as the Bashkir Autonomous Republic, on 11 October 1990. In December 1993, when Murtaza Rakhimov (hitherto President of the republican Supreme Soviet) was elected to the new post of President, a republican majority voted against acceptance of the new Russian federal Constitution. On 24 December the republican Supreme Soviet adopted a new Constitution, stating that its own laws had supremacy over federal laws. The name of Bashkortostan was adopted and a bicameral legislature, the Kurultai, established. Further autonomy was granted under treaties signed in 1994 and in 1995. Rakhimov was re-elected in 1998.

In November 2000, in response to demands of federal President Vladimir Putin, a new republican Constitution was introduced. A provision in the text that republican legislation should take precedence over federal law was rescinded in 2001. In June 2002 the federal Supreme Court ruled that 37 articles of the new Constitution breached of federal law, and in December a further Constitution was adopted, which increased presidential powers and referred to the 'statehood', rather than the 'sovereignty', of the Republic. The power-sharing treaties signed in the 1990s were annulled.

At elections to a new, unicameral Kurultai, held in 2003, YeO-YeR (later renamed YeR) obtained 91 of the 120 seats. Rakhimov was only re-elected President after two rounds of popular voting in December, and after his opponent ceased campaigning.

The seizure by police officers of up to 1,000 people over a period of five days in December 2004, following an attack against a police patrol in Blagoveshchensk, north-east of Ufa, became a matter of contention. In March 2005 around 20,000 people were reported to have participated in a demonstration in Ufa, to oppose human rights abuses, and to demand Rakhimov's resignation. In August the imposition of custodial sentences by the republican Supreme Court against nine members of the proscribed Hizb ut-Tahrir al-Islami (Hizb ut-Tahrir—Party of Islamic Liberation) represented the first use of federal anti-extremist legislation approved in 2003. In October 2006 the Kurultai approved the appointment of Rakhimov to a further term of office.

In April 2008 Rafael Baidavletov resigned as Prime Minister, after he was appointed to the upper chamber of the federal legislature, the Federation Council. Rail Sarbayev was appointed as his successor.

President Rakhimov resigned on 15 July 2010. He was succeeded, initially in an acting capacity, by Rustem Khamitov, a former head of the federal water resources agency. Khamitov additionally assumed the post of Prime Minister in an acting capacity, until May 2011 when Azamat Ilimbetov was appointed to the position.

In September 2014 Khamitov was directly elected to a new presidential term. His title was changed to Head of the Republic in January 2015. In November Ilimbetov was replaced as Prime Minister by the erstwhile first deputy premier (and former Chairman of the republican Bank), Rustem Mardanov.

A court in Ufa sentenced defendants convicted of membership of Hizb ut-Tahrir to prison terms of up to 24 years in July 2018. In elections to the Kurultai held on 9 September YeR won 58.3% of the votes cast on a proportional basis (representing a sharp decline in support compared with previous elections), while the KPRF received 18.8% and the LDPR 10.0%. Some 89 of the 120 deputies had joined the YeR parliamentary faction by the end of the year. On 11 October Khamitov resigned as Head of the Republic, after senior officials of the Republic's Office of the Prosecutor were arrested on corruption charges. Putin appointed Radii Khabirov, a state official, as his acting successor. Khabirov implemented substantial changes to the republican Government, and accepted the resignation of Mardanov as Prime Minister on 3 December.

In November 2018 an Ufa court fined Fail Alsynov, leader of the Bashqort cultural and linguistic organization, 150,000 roubles for organizing an unauthorized public gathering (which had degenerated into violent clashes). However, in December the republican Supreme Court overruled the sentence. In March 2019 a local opposition politician, Airat Dilmukhametov, was arrested and charged with inciting the violation of Russia's territorial integrity, after he had called for the ethnic republics and regions be accorded greater autonomy; he was subsequently additionally charged with promoting extremism and supporting terrorism. In May 2020 the republican Supreme Court banned Bashqort, which it had determined promoted extremism, and in August Dilmukhametov was sentenced by a military court to nine years' imprisonment.

Meanwhile, Khabirov was elected Head of the Republic on 8 September 2019, obtaining 82.0% of the votes cast, defeating seven other candidates. On 17 September 2020 the Kurultai endorsed the appointment of Andrei Nazarov, hitherto the first deputy premier, to the post of Prime Minister (vacant since December 2018).

In September 2021 the FSB announced that five residents of Ufa had been detained on suspicion of planning a series of terrorist acts. In November Liliya Chanysheva, who had headed the local branch of imprisoned opposition leader Aleksei Navalnyi's regional campaign groups, was arrested in Ufa and placed in pre-trial detention in Moscow on charges of belonging to an extremist organization. A Bashkir activist and former leader of Bashqort, Ruslan Gabbasov, in early December fled to Lithuania, where he appealed for asylum. Gabbasov subsequently formed the Committee of the Bashkir National Movement Abroad, which reported in September 2023 that Bashkir activists fighting in support of Ukraine had announced the creation of the Bashkir Liberation Army. Former Bashqort leader Alsynov was charged in October with inciting hatred, after making a speech at a rally in April in which he criticized government plans to start gold mining near a village in the region and to use migrant labourers; his trial began *in camera* in December.

Following elections to the Kurultai held on 10 September 2023, YeR held 87 of the 110 seats in the expanded chamber, increasing its representation there. In January 2024 a court in Baymak, in south-eastern Bashkortostan, sentenced Alsynov to four years' imprisonment for inciting hatred at an illegal protest. His trial and sentencing precipitated demonstrations, which were forcibly suppressed by police.

ECONOMY

In 2021 Bashkortostan's gross regional product (GRP) amounted to 2,000,038m. roubles, or 499,045 roubles per head. Bashkortostan's major industrial centres are at Ufa, Sterlitamak, Salavat and Ishimbai. In 2021 there were 1,451 km of railways in the Republic. There is an international airport at Ufa.

Bashkortostan is one of the principal agricultural regions of the Russian Federation. The main agricultural activities are animal husbandry, beekeeping, and grain and vegetable production. Agriculture employed 6.8% of the workforce and contributed 5.4% of GRP in 2021. Bashkortostan contains substantial petroleum reserves, as well as deposits of natural gas, brown coal (lignite), iron ore, copper, gold, zinc, aluminium, chromium, salt, manganese, gypsum and limestone. Bashkortostan is one of Russia's key petroleum producing areas and the centre of its petroleum refining industry. Other industries include mechanical engineering, metal working, electricity generation, and chemicals and petrochemicals. Industry employed 29.9% of the workforce and contributed 44.8% of GRP in 2021, when manufacturing employed 14.8% of the workforce and contributed 30.3% of GRP.

The economically active population numbered 1,852,746 in 2022, when the rate of unemployment was 3.4%, while the average monthly wage was 49,460 roubles. There was a budgetary deficit of 8,788.8m. roubles in 2021, when export trade amounted to US $3,717m. (of which 22.0% was with countries of the CIS), and import trade to $902m. (of which 23.4% was with CIS countries).

DIRECTORY

Head of the Republic: RADII F. KHABIROV.

Prime Minister: ANDREI G. NAZAROV.

Office of the Head of the Republic and of the Government: 450101 Bashkortostan, Ufa, ul. Tukayeva 46; tel. (347) 280-85-20; fax (347) 250-02-81; e-mail aprb@bashkortostan.ru; e-mail priemnaya507@bashkortostan.ru; internet glavarb.ru; internet pravitelstvorb.ru.

State Assembly (Kurultai): 450008 Bashkortostan, Ufa, ul. Zaki Validi 46; tel. (347) 218-30-01; e-mail kurultay@gsrb.ru; internet gsrb.ru; Chair. KONSTANTIN B. TOLKACHYOV.

State Duma Representatives (6): PAVEL R. KACHKAYEV (YeR), RAFAEL M. MARDANSHIN (YeR), ELVIRA R. AITKULOVA (YeR), RIFAT G. SHAIKHUTDINOV (LDPR), ZAFIR Z. BAIGUSKAROV (YeR), DINAR Z. GILMUTDINOV (YeR).

Federation Council Representatives: LILIYA S. GUMEROVA, OLEG YE. GOLOV.

Chuvash Republic

The Chuvash Republic is situated in the north-east of European Russia. The Republic lies on the Eastern European Plain, on the middle reaches of the Volga. Ulyanovsk Oblast neighbours it to the south, the Republic of Mordoviya to the south-west, Nizhnii Novgorod Oblast to the west and the Republics of Marii-El and Tatarstan to the north and the east, respectively. The Republic's major rivers are the Volga and the Sura, and one-third of its territory is covered by forest. It occupies 18,343 sq km (7,082 sq miles). At January 2023 the Republic had an estimated population of 1,178,543 and a population density of 64.3 per sq km. Some 64.3% of the population was urban in 2023. The capital is Cheboksary, with an estimated 496,238 inhabitants at January 2023. The other major town is Novocheboksarsk (120,147). Of residents who stated their ethnicity at the 2021 census, 63.7% were Chuvash, 30.7% Russian, 2.7% Tatar, and 0.7% were Mordoviyan. Most of the Chuvash population speak Chuvash, which has its origins in the Bulgar group of the Western Hunnic group of Turkic languages, as a first language. The dominant religions in the Republic are Islam and Orthodox Christianity. The Republic is in the time zone UTC+3.

HISTORY

The Chuvash, traditionally a semi-nomadic people, were conquered by the Mongol Tatars in the 13th century. Their territory subsequently became part of the dominion of the Golden Horde, and many subjects converted to Islam. From the late 1430s the Chuvash were ruled by the Kazan Khanate. In 1551, when Cheboksary was founded, the region joined the Russian Empire. The construction of other towns and forts, intended to encourage migration into the area, followed. After 1917 the Chuvash people made vociferous demands for autonomy to the new Soviet Government. A Chuvash Autonomous Oblast was established in June 1920, which became an Autonomous Soviet Socialist Republic (ASSR) on 21 April 1925.

Chuvash nationalism re-emerged in the early 1990s: the Chuvash ASSR declared its sovereignty on 27 October 1990 and adopted the name of the Chuvash (Chavash) Republic in March 1992. In December 1993 the Republic voted against acceptance of the federal Constitution. In that month Nikolai Fyodorov, a former Minister of Justice in the federal Government, was elected republican President. In May 1996 the republican Government signed a power-sharing treaty with federal President Boris Yeltsin. Fyodorov was elected to further terms of office in 1997 and 2001, although on the latter occasion he won only a 41% share of the popular vote. In August 2005 the republican legislature approved federal President Vladimir Putin's nomination of Fyodorov to a further term of office.

In July 2010 the State Council voted to approve federal President Dmitrii Medvedev's nomination of Mikhail Ignatyev (Minister of Agriculture in the republican Government since 2002) as republican President. He assumed office on 29 August 2010. Shortly afterwards the State Council appointed Fyodorov as a representative of the Republic in the upper chamber of the federal legislature, the Federation Council. In December 2011 Oleg Makarov resigned as Prime Minister (a post he had held since February), following the relatively poor performance of YeR (with 44.9% of the vote) in recent elections to the State Council). He was succeeded by Ivan Motorin, hitherto the republican Minister of Economic Development and Trade. Several days later Ignatyev's position was renamed Head of the Republic.

On 13 September 2015, in a popular vote, Ignatyev was elected Head of the Republic, receiving 65.5% of the votes cast. YeR secured some 50.7% of the votes cast on a proportional basis in elections to the State Council held on 18 September 2016; 36 of the 45 deputies joined the YeR parliamentary faction.

On 28 January 2020 Ignatyev was expelled from YeR, after he advocated that journalists who criticized the state authorities be 'wiped out'. On the following day Putin dismissed him, appointing Oleg Nikolayev of SR, hitherto a member of the State Duma, as Acting Head of the Republic (and as Head of the Government). In May Ignatyev filed a case against Putin for wrongful dismissal at the federal Supreme Court (an unprecedented action among former officials); however, in June, shortly before proceedings on the case were due to begin, he died in hospital.

On 13 September 2020 Nikolayev was elected as Head of the Republic with 75.6% of the votes cast; of the four other candidates, Aleksandr Andreyev of the KPRF obtained 10.3%. Nikolayev was inaugurated as Head of the Republic on 22 September.

At elections to the State Council held on 19 September 2021, YeR secured 35.0% of the votes cast on the basis of proportional representation; the KPRF obtained 21.4%. By the end of the year 30 of the 44 deputies had joined the YeR faction, and seven that of the KPRF.

ECONOMY

In 2021 the Chuvash Republic's gross regional product (GRP) amounted to 392,958m. roubles, equivalent to 326,607 roubles per head. The major industrial centres are at Cheboksary, Novocheboksarsk and Kanash. At the end of 2021 there were 421 km of railways in the Republic.

The Republic's agriculture comprises mainly animal husbandry and grain, potato and hop production. The sector employed 9.4% of the workforce and contributed 8.0% of GRP in 2021. The Republic contains deposits of peat, sand, limestone and dolomite. Its main industries are mechanical engineering, metal working, electricity generation, the production of chemicals and petrochemicals, light industry and food processing. Industry employed 32.7% of the workforce and contributed 33.7% of GRP in 2021, when manufacturing employed 20.0% of the workforce and contributed 24.2% of GRP.

The economically active population amounted to 575,219 in 2022, when the rate of unemployment was 3.2%, while the average monthly wage was 41,527 roubles. There was a budgetary surplus of 151.5m. roubles in 2021, when export trade amounted to US $302m. (of which 68.7% was with countries of the CIS), and import trade to $322m. (of which 16.4% was with CIS countries).

DIRECTORY

Head of the Republic and Head of the Government: OLEG A. NIKOLAYEV.

Office of the Head of the Republic and Government: 428004 Chuvash Rep., Cheboksary, Prezidentskii bulv. 10; tel. (8352) 62-01-71; e-mail glava@cap.ru; e-mail km2@cap.ru; internet cap.ru.

State Council: 428004 Chuvash Rep., Cheboksary, Prezidentskii bulv. 10; tel. (8352) 64-21-51; fax (8352) 64-21-50; e-mail gs@cap.ru; internet gs.cap.ru; Chair. LEONID I. CHERKESOV.

State Duma Representatives (2): ANATOLII G. AKSAKOV (SR), ALLA L. SALAYEVA (YeR).

Federation Council Representatives: NIKOLAI V. FYODOROV, NIKOLAI N. VLADIMIROV.

Republic of Marii-El

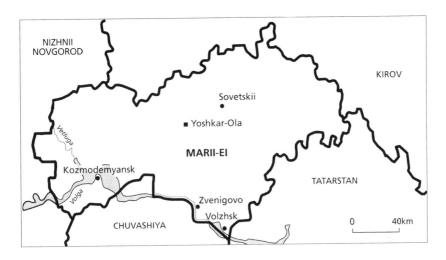

The Republic of Marii-El is situated in the Eastern European Plain in the middle Volga. The Republic of Tatarstan and the Chuvash Republic neighbour it to the south-east and to the south, respectively. The Oblasts of Nizhnii Novgorod and Kirov lie to the west and north, respectively. Marii-El occupies 23,375 sq km (9,025 sq miles). At January 2023 its population was an estimated 672,321 and the population density 28.8 per sq km. Some 68.8% of the population was urban in 2023. The capital is Yoshkar-Ola, with an estimated 283,469 inhabitants at January 2023. Of residents who stated their ethnicity at the 2021 census, 52.5% were Russian, 40.1% Mari (including 2.3% who were Hill Mari), and 4.8% were Tatar. Orthodox Christianity is the predominant religion, although many Mari adhere to aspects of their traditional animist religion. The Mari language belongs to the Finnic branch of the Uralo-Altaic family. Marii-El is in the time zone UTC+3.

HISTORY

The Mari emerged as a distinct ethnic group in the sixth century. In the eighth century they came under the influence of the Khazar Empire, but from the mid-ninth century to the mid-12th century they were ruled by the Volga Bulgars. In the 1230s Mari territory was conquered by the Mongol Tatars. It remained under the control of the Khanate of Kazan until its annexation by Russia in 1552. Mari nationalist feeling was not evident until the 1870s, when an animist religious movement, the Kugu Sorta (Great Candle), attacked the authority of the Russian Orthodox Church. A Mari Autonomous Oblast was established in 1920, becoming an Autonomous Soviet Socialist Republic in 1936.

The Republic declared its sovereignty on 22 October 1990. A presidential election was held in December 1991. In December 1993 elections were held to a new 300-seat State Assembly, which in June 1995 adopted a republican Constitution that designated the territory as the Republic of Marii-El.

At a presidential election in 2000, the incumbent, Vyacheslav Kislitsyn, was defeated by Leonid Markelov of the LDPR. He was re-elected in 2004 with support from YeR.

In the mid-2000s concern was expressed, both in Marii-El and by members of other Finno-Ugric peoples, at the marginalization of the cultural and political expression of Mari groups in the Republic, at the increasing restrictions placed upon the use of the Mari language in education and broadcasting, and at numerous instances in which Mari activists had been physically attacked.

In December 2009 the State Assembly approved Markelov's nomination to a third term of office; his position was renamed Head of the Republic in 2011.

In elections to the State Assembly held in September 2014, YeR obtained 65.4% of the votes cast on a proportional basis. A total of 46 of the 52 deputies subsequently joined the YeR parliamentary faction. In September 2015 Markelov was elected Head of the Republic, obtaining 50.8% of the popular vote. The second placed candidate was Sergei Mamayev of the KPRF, whose 32.3% share of support reflected continuing popular discontent with the federal authorities.

On 6 April 2017 Markelov submitted his resignation to President Putin, who on the same day appointed Aleksandr Yevstifeyev, a lawyer, and formerly the Deputy Presidential Representative to the Volga Federal Okrug, as Acting Head of the Republic. Shortly afterwards, Markelov was arrested and detained on suspicion of bribe-taking. He was indicted in January 2019 and property worth 2,200m. roubles was subsequently confiscated from him by court order. In September 2017 Yevstifeyev was elected Head of the Republic, winning 88.3% of the votes cast in an election contested by three other candidates.

Meanwhile, in July 2017, a speech made by Putin during a visit to Marii-El, in which he referred to the unacceptability of schools in Russia's ethnic republics forcing pupils to learn languages that were not their mother tongue, and in which he criticized a reduction in school hours devoted to learning Russian in some such republics, was a cause of local and national controversy.

In elections to the State Assembly, held on 8 September 2019, YeR obtained 37.5% of the votes cast on a proportional basis, ahead of the KPRF, with 26.9%, the LDPR, with 15.8%, and SR, with 7.8%. Of the 52 deputies elected, by January 2020 some 35 had joined the parliamentary faction of YeR, nine that of the KPRF, three that of the LDPR, and three that of SR.

Yevstifeyev tendered his resignation as Head of the Republic on 10 May 2022. Yurii Zaytsev, the Chairman of the Government, was immediately appointed by President Putin also as Acting Head of the Republic. On 11 September Zaytsev was elected as Head of the Republic with 82.4% of the votes cast, defeating Anton Mirbadalev of the LDPR (who received 7.9% of the votes) and two other candidates. Zaytsev subsequently formed a new Government, remaining its Chairman.

ECONOMY

In 2021 Marii-El's gross regional product (GRP) amounted to 221,991m. roubles, equivalent to 329,660 roubles per head. Its major industrial centres are at Yoshkar-Ola and Volzhsk. At the end of 2021 there were 152 km of railway lines in the Republic.

Marii-El's agriculture consists mainly of animal husbandry and the production of flax, vegetables, potatoes and grain. Agriculture employed 9.7% of the workforce and contributed 16.1% of GRP in 2021. The Republic's main industries are mechanical engineering, metal working, electricity production, and the processing of forestry and food products. Industry employed 33.1% of the workforce and contributed 34.4% of GRP in 2021, when manufacturing employed 21.1% of the workforce and contributed 24.9% of GRP.

The economically active population in the Republic numbered 311,591 in 2022, when the rate of unemployment was 3.6%, while the average monthly wage was 40,713 roubles. There was a budgetary surplus of 3,781.7 m. roubles in 2021, when export trade amounted to US $325m. (of which 27.5% was with countries of the CIS), and import trade to $134m. (of which 7.8% was with CIS countries).

DIRECTORY

Head of the Republic, Chairman of the Government: YURII V. ZAYTSEV.

Office of the Head of the Republic: 424001 Marii-El, Yoshkar-Ola, Leninskii pr. 29; tel. (8362) 64-15-25; fax (8362) 64-19-21; e-mail president@gov.mari.ru; internet mari-el.gov.ru.

State Assembly: 424001 Marii-El, Yoshkar-Ola, Leninskii pr. 29; tel. (8362) 64-14-17; fax (8362) 64-14-11; e-mail info@gsmari.ru; internet gsmari.ru; Chair. ANATOLII V. SMIRNOV.

State Duma Representative (1): SERGEI I. KAZANKOV (KPRF).

Federation Council Representatives: SERGEI A. MARTYNOV, KONSTANTIN I. KOSACHEV.

Republic of Mordoviya

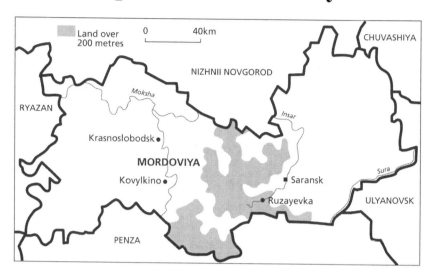

The Republic of Mordoviya is situated in the Eastern European Plain, in the Volga river basin. The north-west of the Republic occupies a section of the Oka-Don plain, and the south-east lies in the Volga Highlands. The Chuvash Republic lies to the north-east, the Oblasts of Ulyanovsk to the east, Penza to the south, Ryazan to the west and Nizhnii Novgorod to the north. The major rivers are the Moksha, the Sura and the Insar. Mordoviya occupies 26,128 sq km (10,088 sq miles). At January 2023 the Republic had an estimated population of 771,373 and a population density of 29.5 per sq km. Some 63.6% of the population was urban in 2023. The capital is Saransk, with an estimated 312,252 inhabitants at January 2023. Of residents who stated their ethnicity at the 2021 census, 54.1% were Russian, 38.7% were Mordoviyan (including 5.8% who were Erzya-Mordoviyan, and 1.3% who were Moksha-Mordoviyan) and 5.3% were Tatar. The majority of Mordoviyans inhabited the agricultural regions of the west and north-east. The dominant religion is Orthodox Christianity. The native tongue of the Mordoviyans belongs to the Finnic group of the Uralo-Altaic family. The Republic is in the time zone UTC+3.

HISTORY

The Mordoviyans first appear in historical records of the sixth century, when they inhabited the area between the Oka and the middle Volga rivers. In the late 12th and early 13th centuries a feudal society began to form in Mordoviya. One of its most famous fiefdoms was that headed by Prince Purgas. The Mordoviyans came under the control of the Mongols and Tatars between the 13th and the 15th centuries and, at the fall of the Khanate of Kazan in 1552, were voluntarily incorporated into the Russian state. Many thousands of Mordoviyans fled Russian rule in the late 16th and early 17th centuries to settle in the Ural Mountains and in southern Siberia, while those who remained were outnumbered by Russians. The region was predominantly agricultural until the completion of the Moscow–Kazan railway in the 1890s.

The Mordoviyan Autonomous Okrug was created in 1928, becoming an Autonomous Oblast in 1930 and an Autonomous Soviet Socialist Republic in 1934.

The Republic declared its sovereignty on 8 December 1990 and was renamed the Republic of Mordoviya in January 1994. A Constitution was adopted on 21 September 1995, establishing an executive presidency and a legislative State Assembly. Nikolai Merkushkin, Chairman of the republican legislature since January, became President. In February 1998 Merkushkin was elected Head of the Republic, with 96.6% of the votes cast. He was re-elected to a further term of office in 2003, receiving 87.3% of the votes cast. Merkushkin was subsequently appointed to the Supreme Council of YeR. In November 2005 the State Assembly confirmed Merkushkin's nomination to a further term of office.

In September 2007 the State Assembly adopted a resolution to dissolve itself and schedule early elections, for 2 December, to coincide with those to the State Duma. YeR secured 90.4% of votes cast in the elections to the State Assembly and 93.4% of votes cast locally to the State Duma. In October 2010 the State Assembly confirmed Merkushkin's appointment to a further term as Head of the Republic. At the elections to the State Assembly, held in December 2011 YeR was the only party to obtain seats elected by proportional voting.

Merkushkin resigned as Head of the Republic on 10 May 2012, after he had been appointed as Acting Governor of Samara Oblast, a transfer generally regarded as constituting a promotion. He was succeeded by Vladimir Volkov, the Chairman of the republican Government since 1995.

YeR secured 83.7% of the votes cast on a proportional basis in elections to the State Assembly held on 18 September 2016, ahead of the KPRF, with 6.2%, and the LDPR, with 5.9%. All but two of the 47 deputies had joined the YeR parliamentary faction by the end of the year. On 10 September 2017 Volkov was directly elected Head of the Republic, obtaining 89.2% of the votes cast.

On 18 November 2020 Volkov submitted his resignation to Putin, who on the same day appointed Artyom Zdunov, hitherto Chairman of the Government of the Republic of Dagestan, as Acting Head of Mordoviya. Zdunov was confirmed as Head of the Republic on 19 September 2021, when he received 78.3% of the votes cast in a direct election, defeating Dmitrii Kuzyakin of the KPRF (who obtained 11.5% of the vote) and two other candidates. He took office on 29 September. At elections to the State Assembly also held on 19 September, YeR secured 67.2% of the votes cast on a proportional basis (a fall of more than 16 percentage points compared with the 2016 elections), while the KPRF took 14.2% of the vote, the LDPR 9.9% and SR 6.8%. By the end of the year 42 of the 48 deputies had joined the YeR faction, three that of the KPRF, two that of the LDPR, and one that of SR.

On 6 October 2021 Vladimir Sidorov became Chairman of the Government. Following the retirement of Sidorov in December 2022, in January 2023 Zdunov, with the support of the State Assembly, appointed Dmitrii Pozdnyakov, hitherto the head of an agro-industrial enterprise, as his successor.

ECONOMY

In 2021 Mordoviya's gross regional product (GRP) was 298,023m. roubles, or 384,636 roubles per head. The territory's major industrial centres are at Saransk and Ruzayevka. At the end of 2021 there were 544 km of railway lines in the Republic.

The principal crops in Mordoviya are grain, sugar beet, potatoes and vegetables. Animal husbandry (especially of cattle) and beekeeping are also important. Agriculture employed 18.4% of the workforce and contributed 16.4% of GRP in 2021. The main industries are mechanical engineering and metal working. There is also some production of electricity, chemicals and petrochemicals, and food processing. Mordoviya is the centre of the Russian lighting equipment industry. Industry employed 27.7% of the workforce and contributed 35.3% of GRP in 2021, when manufacturing employed 16.3% of the workforce and contributed 28.6% of GRP. A new stadium, with a capacity of around 45,000 people, was constructed in Saransk in association with Russia's hosting of the 2018 football World Cup.

The economically active population numbered 419,136 in 2022, when the rate of unemployment was 3.6%, while the average monthly wage was 39,538 roubles. There was a budgetary surplus of 3,946.4m. roubles in 2021, when export trade amounted to US $376m. (of which 51.8% was with countries of the CIS), while import trade amounted to $147m. (of which 16.8% was with CIS countries).

DIRECTORY

Head of the Republic: ARTYOM A. ZDUNOV.

Chairman of the Government: DMITRII A. POZDNYAKOV.

Office of the Head of the Republic and Government: 430002 Mordoviya, Saransk, ul. Sovetskaya 35; tel. (8342) 32-77-11; fax (8342) 47-36-28; e-mail kanc@e-mordovia.ru; internet www.e-mordovia.ru.

State Assembly: 430002 Mordoviya, Saransk, ul. Sovetskaya 26; tel. (8342) 32-77-00; fax (8342) 32-74-27; e-mail gsrm@e-mordovia.ru; internet gsrm.ru; Chair. VLADIMIR V. CHIBIRKIN.

State Duma Representative (1): YULIYA V. OGLOBLINA (YeR).

Federation Council Representatives: SERGEI I. KISLYAK, PYOTR N. TULTAYEV.

Republic of Tatarstan

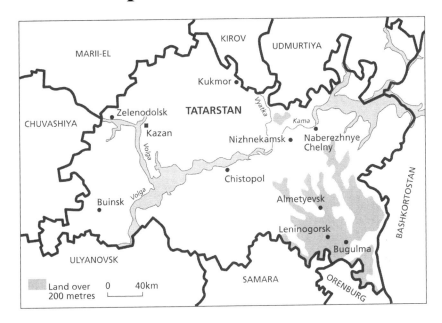

The Republic of Tatarstan is situated in the east of European Russia. Bashkortostan lies to the east, the Udmurt Republic to the north, Marii-El to the north-west, and the Chuvash Republic to the west. Ulyanovsk, Samara and Orenburg Oblasts lie to the south, and Kirov Oblast to the north. The major rivers are the Volga and the Kama. Tatarstan occupies 67,847 sq km (26,196 sq miles). At January 2023 it had an estimated population of 4,001,625 and a population density of 59.0 per sq km. Some 76.8% of the population was urban in 2023. The capital is Kazan, on the River Volga, with an estimated 1,314,685 inhabitants at January 2023. Other major cities include Naberezhnye Chelny (545,750), Nizhnekamsk (241,106) and Almetyevsk (164,145). Of residents who stated their ethnicity at the 2021 census, 53.6% were Tatar, 40.3% were Russian, and 2.3% were Chuvash. The Republic is in the time zone UTC+3.

HISTORY

The city of Kazan was founded in 1005. After the dissolution of the Mongol Empire in the 15th century, the region became the Kazan Khanate, which was conquered by Tsar Ivan IV 'the Terrible' in 1552.

A Tatar Autonomous Soviet Socialist Republic was established in May 1920. On 31 August 1990 the Chairman of the republican Supreme Soviet, Mintimer Shaimiyev, declared Tatarstan a sovereign republic; in 1991 he was elected republican President. Tatarstan rejected the Federation Treaty of 1992, and on 6 November adopted its own Constitution. In a procedure later emulated by numerous other federal subjects, in February 1994 the republican leadership signed a power-sharing treaty with the federal authorities, obtaining extensive economic and fiscal rights for the territory. Shaimiyev was re-elected to further terms of office in 1996 (unopposed) and in 2001.

Tatarstan became one of the principal territories to resist measures to harmonize regional and federal legislation after Vladimir Putin became federal President in 2000. In April 2002 a new republican Constitution entered into effect, after the federal Supreme Court demanded amendments to 42 articles of the previous text. In June the federal Prosecutor-General demanded the removal of references to Tatar citizenship and to the sovereignty of the Republic from the new text. Federal legislation of November requiring that all languages be printed in the Cyrillic script on official documents was also a source of controversy; the republican authorities had, in 1999, begun to introduce the Latin script for the Tatar language. In 2003 the power-sharing treaty signed in 1994 was annulled.

In March 2005 the republican legislature, the State Council, approved Shaimiyev's appointment to a further term of office. In October it approved a new draft power-sharing treaty with the federal authorities; although it gave less autonomy to the Republic than that of 1994, it permitted Tatarstan privileges not granted to other territories, including tax exemptions on natural resources and the right to grant the local language an official status. Both chambers of the federal legislature ratified a revised version of the treaty in July 2007.

In January 2010 Federal President Dmitrii Medvedev presented the nomination of Shaimiyev's preferred successor as President, Rustam Minnikhanov (republican Prime Minister since 1998), to the State Council, which unanimously endorsed it. Minnikhanov became republican President on 25 March, remaining Chairman of the Board of Directors of the state-owned Tatneft petroleum company. In March 2012 the death in custody of a citizen in Kazan, allegedly owing to torture by police officers, resulted in the removal from office of republican Minister of the Interior Asgat Safarov. Two months later, however, Minnikhanov appointed Safarov as a Deputy Prime Minister.

In July 2012 Tatarstan's mufti, Ildus Faizov, was injured in a bomb attack in Kazan, and his former deputy was shot dead. A follower of the Chechen Islamist Doku Umarov claimed responsibility for the attacks. In August, in an effort to counter the growth of Islamist fundamentalism, Minnikhanov approved new restrictions on religious organizations, including a prohibition on their being established by foreign nationals. In January 2013 an Islamic congregation, led by Rustem Safin, a member of the proscribed Hizb ut-Tahrir-al-Islami (Hizb ut-Tahrir—Party of Islamic Liberation), was ordered to cease worshipping in a mosque in Kazan. In May the republican Supreme Court ordered that the congregation be disbanded, and in September Safin was sentenced to two years' imprisonment for promoting extremism. In October two members of another proscribed group, Takfir wal-Hijra (Anathema and Exile), were given custodial sentences for planning a bomb attack. In late 2013 at least eight Orthodox churches in the Republic were set alight by arsonists, presumed to be militant Islamists.

In October 2014 four members of Hizb ut-Tahrir received custodial sentences at a Naberezhnye Chelny court for recruiting for the organization and distributing literature intended to incite hatred. In December a court in Kazan sentenced a local resident, Raif Mustafin, to over three years' imprisonment for fighting for an Islamist organization in the Syrian civil war. Also in December three residents of Kazan received custodial sentences for membership of Hizb ut-Tahrir. Meanwhile, a prominent Tatar nationalist activist, Rafis Kashapov, was detained, before being sentenced to three years' imprisonment for inciting separatism and ethnic hatred, in association with his opposition to the recent Russian annexation of Crimea from Ukraine.

Minnikhanov was elected President by popular ballot on 13 September 2015, obtaining 94.4% of the votes cast. He retained the title of 'President', the final regional leader in Russia to do so, even after the use of the title was outlawed in 2016.

In April 2017 republican Prime Minister Ildar Khalikov resigned, after the collapse of three banks based in Tatarstan (for all of which Khalikov was a board member), had precipitated public protests. Khalikov was succeeded as premier by his hitherto deputy, Aleksei Pesoshin.

In June 2017 the treaty granting extensive rights to Tatarstan, signed in its most recent form between the republican and federal authorities in 2007, and the final extant treaty of its type in the Federation, formally expired. A speech made by Putin in July 2017, in which he criticized what he termed the unacceptability of schools in Russia's ethnic republics forcing pupils to learn languages that were not their mother tongue, and the reported reduction in school hours accorded to learning Russian in some such republics, was a cause of particular controversy in Tatarstan. In September a group of Russian-language activists in Tatarstan launched a campaign in support of Putin's demands that the compulsory study of the Tatar language and literature should be ended. In November the State Council approved a revised school curriculum, in accordance with Putin's demands, and the republican Minister of Education resigned.

In elections to the State Council, held on 8 September 2019, YeR won 72.4% of the votes cast on a proportional basis. By January 2020 some 82 of the 100 deputies had joined the YeR parliamentary faction, eight had formed the Tatarstan—Novyi Vek (Tatarstan—New Century) faction (a YeR-allied pro-business group), and six joined that of the KPRF. Minnikhanov was re-elected as President on 13 September 2020, winning 83.3% of the votes cast and defeating four other candidates.

In November 2021 a prominent Islamic scholar was sentenced to six-and-a-half years in prison by a court in Kazan for leading a branch of the banned Nur (Light) movement. Meanwhile, on 25 October the State Council voted to reject draft legislation proposed in the newly elected State Duma, under which the title of 'President' held by Minnikhanov would be abolished. Legislation to that end was signed into force by Putin on 21 December. The Supreme Court of Tatarstan in June 2022 ordered the closure of the All-Tatar Public Centre, a prominent non-governmental organization involved in promoting and protecting Tatar history, culture and language, designating it as an extremist group. In July Putin issued an executive order that for the first time referred to Minnikhanov as 'Head' of the Republic. The Chairman of the State Council, Farid Mukhametshin, announced in response that the Republic would continue to refer to Minnikhanov as 'President' until the official title was formally amended in the regional Constitution. After Minnikhanov declared that he favoured the measure, however, in December the State Council voted overwhelmingly in favour of the amendments allowing the abolition of the title of 'President', although Minnikhanov was to retain the title until his term expired in September 2025; the provisions also included the removal of all references to Tatarstan's state sovereignty and special citizenship. However, on 26 January 2023 the State Council adopted further constitutional amendments without the previous stipulation for a transitional period, which were signed into law by Minnikhanov on the same day. These entered into effect on 6 February, when Minnikhanov's post was officially redesignated as 'Rais' (Leader).

A court in Tatarstan in September 2023 sentenced a blogger to three years in prison on charges of issuing calls online for Russian soldiers to desert the armed forces. In mid-October Tatar activists in Kazan met to commemorate the death of Tatars during the 1552 capture of the city, despite the refusal of the city administration from 2020 to permit a mass gathering to mark the anniversary.

ECONOMY

In 2021 Tatarstan's gross regional product (GRP) amounted to 3,454,700m. roubles, or an estimated 888,039 roubles per head. Its main industrial centres are Kazan, Naberezhnye Chelny, Zelenodolsk, Nizhnekamsk and Almetyevsk. Kazan is the most important port on the Volga and a junction in the national rail, road and air transport systems. An oil export pipeline to Europe starts in Almetyevsk. At the end of 2021 there were 877 km of railway lines in Tatarstan.

Tatarstan is one of the principal agricultural territories in Russia, with activities including grain production, animal husbandry, horticulture and beekeeping. The sector employed 7.1% of the workforce and contributed 4.2% of GRP in 2021. The Republic has significant reserves of hydrocarbons, and is a major producer of oil among the federal subjects. Kazan, Zelenodolsk and Vasilyevo are centres for light industry, the manufacture of petrochemicals and building materials, and mechanical engineering. The company Kazanorgsintez is the largest polyethylene producer in Russia. Industries connected with the extraction, processing and use of petroleum typically represent around 40% of the total industrial production. Industry employed 33.0% of the workforce and contributed 56.8% of GRP in 2021, when manufacturing employed 17.0% of the workforce and contributed 18.9% of GRP.

The economically active population numbered 1,981,753 in 2022, when the rate of unemployment was 2.3%, while the average monthly wage was 52,274 roubles. There was a budgetary surplus of 12,849.0m. roubles in 2021, when export trade amounted to US $12,073m. (of which 14.7% was with CIS countries), and import trade to $5,475m. (of which 6.3% was with CIS countries).

DIRECTORY

Rais (Leader): RUSTAM N. MINNIKHANOV.

Office of the Rais (Leader): 420014 Tatarstan, Kazan, Kreml; tel. (843) 567-89-01; fax (843) 292-70-88; e-mail ap.rt@tatar.ru; internet rais.tatarstan.ru.

Prime Minister: ALEKSEI V. PESOSHIN.

Office of the Prime Minister: 420060 Tatarstan, Kazan, pl. Svobody 1; tel. (843) 264-77-01; e-mail pr.pm@tatar.ru; internet prav.tatarstan.ru.

State Council: 420060 Tatarstan, Kazan, pl. Svobody 1; tel. (843) 267-63-00; fax (843) 267-64-89; e-mail gossov@gossov.tatarstan.ru; internet gossov.tatarstan.ru; Chair. FARID KH. MUKHAMETSHIN.

State Duma Representatives (6): ILYA S. VOLFSON (YeR), ILDAR I. GILMUTDINOV (YeR), OLEG V. MOROZOV (YeR), ALFIYA G. KOGOGINA (YeR), AZAT F. YAGAFAROV (YeR), MARAT A. NURIYEV (YeR).

Federation Council Representatives: GENNADII YE. YEMELYANOV, ALEKSANDR M. TERENTYEV.

Udmurt Republic

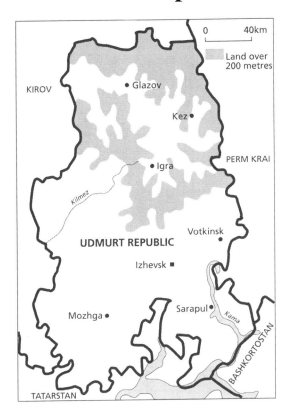

The Udmurt Republic occupies part of the Upper Kama Highlands. The Republic of Tatarstan lies to the south, the Republic of Bashkortostan to the south-east, Perm Krai to the east, and Kirov Oblast to the north and west. Its major river is the Kama. About one-half of its territory is forested. The Republic covers 42,061 sq km (16,240 sq miles). At January 2023 it had an estimated population of 1,442,251 and a population density of 34.3 per sq km. Some 65.8% of the population was urban in 2023. The capital is Izhevsk, with an estimated 620,591 inhabitants at January 2023. Of residents who stated their ethnicity at the 2021 census, 67.7% were Russian, 24.1% were Udmurt and 5.5% were Tatar. The dominant religion in the Republic is Orthodox Christianity. The Udmurt language is from the Permian group of the Finnic branch of the Uralo-Altaic family. The Republic is in the time zone UTC+4.

HISTORY

The first appearance of the Votyaks (as the Udmurts were formerly called) as a distinct ethnic group was recorded in the sixth century. Their territories were conquered by the Khazars in the eighth century, although Khazar influence gave way to that of the Volga Bulgars in the mid-ninth century. In the 13th century the Mongol Tatars occupied the region, but they were gradually displaced by the Russians from the mid-15th century.

By 1558 all Votyaks were under Russian rule. A Votyak Autonomous Oblast, established on 4 November 1920, was renamed the Udmurt Autonomous Oblast on 1 January 1932, and became an Autonomous Soviet Socialist Republic on 28 December 1934.

The Republic declared sovereignty on 21 September 1990, and adopted a Constitution in 1994. The Chairman of the legislature, the State Council, remained head of the Republic, and a premier chaired the Government. Following the approval by referendum of constitutional reforms in March 2000, the State Council adopted legislation introducing presidential rule. Aleksandr Volkov, hitherto the parliamentary speaker, was elected President in October; he was re-elected in March 2004.

From the 1990s the disposal of chemical weapons proved to be a serious social and ecological problem in the Republic, which was thought to contain around one-quarter of Russia's entire arsenal of such weapons. A new plant for the destruction of chemical weapons was inaugurated in 2006.

On 20 February 2009 the State Council voted to confirm Volkov's nomination to a further term as republican President (this title was subsequently amended to Head of the Republic).

In elections to the State Council held on 14 October 2012. YeR obtained 53.2% of the votes cast on a proportional basis, ahead of the KPRF, with 17.2%. Following the expiry of Volkov's mandate as Head of the Republic, on 20 February 2014 President Vladimir Putin appointed Aleksandr Solovyov, hitherto a representative of the Republic in the Federation Council, as Acting Head of the Republic. On 14 September Solovyov was directly elected Head of the Republic, obtaining 84.8% of the votes cast.

On 4 April 2017 President Putin dismissed Solovyov from his post, after he had been accused of taking bribes amounting to 140m. roubles, and on the same day appointed Aleksandr Brechalov, hitherto the head of the federal advisory Civic Chamber, as Acting Head of the Republic, pending an election in September. Solovyov was arrested on the charges immediately afterwards; he received a 10-year prison sentence in October 2020. Meanwhile, on 10 September 2017 Brechalov was elected Head of the Republic, receiving 78.2% of the votes cast. In concurrent elections to the State Council (which was reduced in size from 90 to 60 deputies), YeR obtained 63.2% of the votes cast to those seats elected on the basis of proportional representation, ahead of the KPRF, with 14.9%, and the LDPR, with 9.0%. By the end of the year 50 of the 60 deputies had joined the YeR parliamentary faction.

In republican legislative elections held on 11 September 2022, YeR obtained 51.1% of the proportional vote, followed by the KPRF, with 15.6%, the LDPR, with 13.6%, and SR, with 6.1%. By the end of the year 48 deputies had joined the YeR parliamentary faction, four that of the LDPR, three that of the KPRF and two that of SR. At a gubernatorial election held on the same day, Brechalov was re-elected as Head of the Republic, with 64.4% of the votes cast; his leading opponent among three other candidates, Aleksandr Syrov of the KPRF, received 19.8%.

ECONOMY

In 2021 the Udmurt Republic's gross regional product (GRP) amounted to an estimated 841,936m. roubles, equivalent to 565,472 roubles per head. The Republic possesses significant hydrocarbons reserves and is an important arms-producing region. Its major industrial centres are Izhevsk, Sarapul and Glazov and its main river-ports Sarapul and Kambarka. In 2021 there were 779 km of railways in the Republic.

Agriculture consists mainly of animal husbandry, and grain and potato production. Agriculture employed 5.6% of the workforce and contributed 5.7% of GRP in 2021. The main industries are the manufacture of weapons, mechanical engineering, metal working, car manufacturing, metallurgy, food processing, petroleum production and the production of peat. There are substantial reserves of coal and of petroleum. In early 2006 Sinopec, a company controlled by the state authorities of the People's Republic of China, purchased a 49% stake in the formerly republican-owned petroleum company Udmurtneft, representing the first instance of Chinese involvement in the Russian energy sector. (The remaining 51% of Udmurtneft was acquired by the Russian state-controlled firm Rosneft at the same time.) Industry employed 34.8% of the workforce and contributed 52.7% of GRP in 2021, when manufacturing employed 20.7% of the workforce and contributed 17.0% of GRP.

The economically active population numbered 717,552 in 2022, when the rate of unemployment was 2.9%, while the average monthly wage was 45,811 roubles. There was a budgetary deficit of 4,083.0m. roubles in 2021, when export trade amounted to US $600m. (of which 39.6% was with countries of the CIS), while import trade amounted to $565m. (of which 9.4% was with CIS countries).

DIRECTORY

Head of the Republic: ALEKSANDR V. BRECHALOV.

Chairman of the Government: YAROSLAV V. SEMYONOV.

Office of the Head of the Republic and Government: 426007 Udmurt Rep., Izhevsk, ul. Pushkinskaya 214; tel. and fax (3412) 49-72-00; e-mail president@udmurt.ru; e-mail premier@udmurt.ru; internet udmurt.ru.

State Council (Kun Keneshez): 426074 Udmurt Rep., Izhevsk, ul. 50 let Oktyabrya 15; tel. (3412) 91-31-05; e-mail gossovet@gossovet.udm.ru; internet udmgossovet.ru; Chair. VLADIMIR P. NEVOSTRUYEV.

State Duma Representatives (2): ANDREI K. ISAYEV (YeR), OLEG V. KARIN (YeR).

Federation Council Representatives: LYUBOV N. GLEBOVA, YURII V. FYODOROV.

Perm Krai

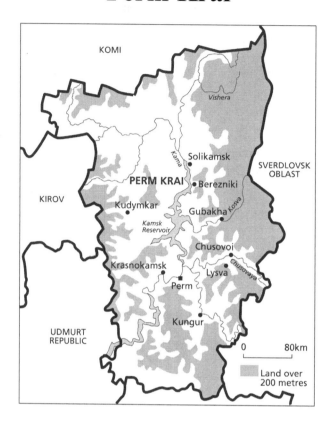

Perm Krai is situated on the western slopes of the Central and Northern Urals and the eastern edge of the Eastern European Plain. The Republic of Komi lies to the north, Kirov Oblast and the Udmurt Republic to the west, the Republic of Bashkortostan to the south, and Sverdlovsk Oblast to the east. The major rivers are the Kama, the Chusovaya and the Kosva. The Kamsk reservoir lies in the centre of the region. The Krai occupies 160,236 sq km (61,867 sq miles). At January 2023 its population was an estimated 2,508,352 and the population density 15.7 per sq km. Some 75.7% of the population was urban in 2023. The administrative centre, Perm, had an estimated 1,027,153 inhabitants at January 2023. The second largest city is Berezniki, with an estimated population of 135,533. Of residents who stated their ethnicity at the 2021 census, 89.4% were Russian, 4.1% Tatar, 2.2% Komi-Permyak, and 0.7% were Bashkir. Perm Krai is in the time zone UTC+5.

HISTORY

Perm city was founded in 1723. Perm Oblast was formed on 3 October 1938.

In December 1993 there were elections for a new regional parliament, the Legislative Assembly. In May 1996 the administrations of both Perm Oblast and the Komi-Permyak Autonomous Okrug (located in the north-west of the Oblast) signed power-sharing treaties with the federal President, Boris Yeltsin. In December the Governor of Perm Oblast appointed earlier that year, Gennadii Igumnov, retained his post following direct elections, and his reformist supporters secured a majority of seats in elections to the regional legislature in December 1997. Following the gubernatorial election held in December 2000, Igumnov was replaced by Yurii Trutnev, hitherto the Mayor of Perm. Elections to a new Legislative Assembly were held in December 2001.

In February 2003 the legislative bodies of Perm Oblast and the Komi-Permyak Autonomous Okrug voted in favour of the merger of their territories. More than 80% of participants in referendums held on 7 December in both territories supported the unification. On 26 March 2004, after the federal legislature endorsed the merger, President Vladimir Putin signed legislation on the formation of new territory, Perm Krai, with effect from 1 December 2005. He confirmed Oleg Chirkunov as Acting Governor of Perm Oblast, to serve until the new unified territory was constituted, after Trutnev became a federal minister.

The legislatures of both territories endorsed Chirkunov's appointment as Governor of Perm Krai on 10 October 2005. Chirkunov sought to develop Perm as a major international centre of culture and the arts. At elections held to the new provincial Legislative Assembly in December 2006, YeR was the most successful grouping, receiving 34.6% of the votes cast and 29 of the 60 elective seats. The pro-market SPS was second, with 16.4%, recording its most successful result in any regional election since the party's foundation.

In October 2010 the provincial Legislative Assembly approved the nomination of Chirkunov to a further term as Governor. In elections to the provincial Legislative Assembly held on 4 December 2011 the share of the vote attributed to YeR was 37.9%. The KPRF was second, with 20.1% of the votes cast, ahead of the LDPR, with 17.6%, and SR, with 15.2%. After the elections, YeR controlled 39 of the 60 seats in the provincial legislature, which elected the erstwhile provincial premier, Valerii Sukhikh, as its Chairman.

Chirkunov resigned as Governor on 28 April 2012. The provincial Legislative Assembly endorsed the appointment of the erstwhile federal Minister of Regional Development, Viktor Basargin, as his successor on 5 May.

YeR secured 43.8% of the votes cast on a proportional basis in elections to the Legislative Assembly on 18 September 2016; the KPRF took 17.8% of the votes, the LDPR 16.3% and SR 11.3%. By the end of the year 42 of the 60 deputies had joined the YeR parliamentary faction.

On 6 February 2017 Basargin submitted his resignation to President Putin, who appointed the erstwhile director of economic policy and development in Moscow City, Maksim Reshetnikov, as Acting Governor. On 10 September Reshetnikov was elected Governor, obtaining 82.1% of the votes cast, defeating three other candidates.

President Putin transferred Reshetnikov to the post of Minister of Economic Development in the federal Government on 21 January 2020. He appointed Dmitrii Makhonin, hitherto a prominent official of the Federal Antimonopoly Service, as Acting Governor on 6 February. On 13 September Makhonin was elected to the post of Governor; he was inaugurated on 7 October.

At elections to the regional Legislative Assembly held on 19 September 2021, YeR secured 33.1% of the votes cast on the basis of proportional representation; the KPRF obtained 22.7%, SR 11.3%, the LDPR 9.6%, and the recently established centre-right

NL 8.4%. By the end of the year 40 of the 60 deputies had joined the YeR faction, 11 that of the KPRF, three that of the LDPR, three that of SR, and two that of NL.

ECONOMY

In 2021 the gross regional product (GRP) of Perm Krai amounted to 1,740,525m. roubles, or 677,760 roubles per head. The major industrial centres are at Perm, Berezniki, Chusovoi and Krasnokamsk. At the end of 2021 there were 1,574 km of railways in the Krai.

Agriculture in the territory consists mainly of grain and vegetable production, beekeeping and animal husbandry. Agriculture employed 4.1% of the workforce and contributed 2.0% of GRP in 2021. The main industries are coal, petroleum, natural gas, potash and salt production, mechanical engineering, chemicals and petrochemicals, petroleum refining, and electricity generation. The territory is a major producer of mineral fertilizer and of paper. There is also a significant defence sector. Industry employed 34.3% of the workforce and contributed 60.0% of GRP in 2021, when manufacturing employed 19.9% of the workforce and contributed 26.8% of GRP.

The economically active population numbered 1,175,910 in 2022, when the rate of unemployment was 3.4%, while the average monthly wage was 53,234 roubles. There was a budgetary surplus of 27,628.1m. roubles in 2021, when export trade amounted to US $7,949m. (of which 10.3% was with countries of the CIS), and import trade to $847m. (of which 16.3% was with CIS countries).

DIRECTORY

Governor: DMITRII N. MAKHONIN.

Office of the Governor: 614006 Perm, ul. Kuibysheva 14; tel. (342) 217-71-58; internet permkrai.ru.

Legislative Assembly: 614006 Perm, ul. Lenina 51; tel. (342) 217-75-55; fax (342) 235-12-57; e-mail press@zsperm.ru; internet zsperm.ru; Chair. VALERII A. SUKHIKH.

State Duma Representatives (4): IGOR N. SHUBIN (YeR), ROMAN M. VODYANOV (YeR), DMITRII S. SKRIVANOV (YeR), IRINA V. IVENSKIKH (YeR).

Federation Council Representatives: ANDREI A. KLIMOV, ALEKSEI K. PUSHKOV.

Kirov Oblast

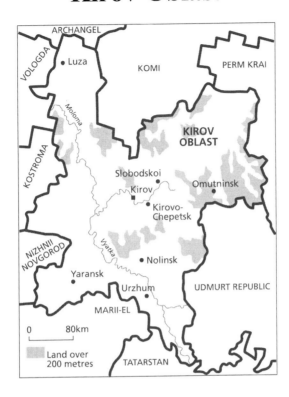

Kirov Oblast is situated in the east of the Eastern European Plain. It is bordered by Archangel Oblast and the Republic of Komi to the north, Perm Krai and the Udmurt Republic to the east, the Republics of Tatarstan and Marii-El to the south, and Nizhnii Novgorod, Kostroma and Vologda Oblasts to the west. Its main river is the Vyatka. The Oblast occupies 120,374 sq km (46,477 sq miles). At January 2023 its population was an estimated 1,138,112 and the population density 9.5 per sq km. Some 78.3% of the population was urban in 2023. The administrative centre is Kirov, a river-port with an estimated 471,754 inhabitants at January 2023. Of residents who stated their ethnicity at the 2021 census, 92.8% were Russian, 2.5% Tatar, 1.8% Mari, and 0.7% were Udmurt. The territory is in the time zone UTC+3.

HISTORY

The city of Khlynov was founded in 1181, and came under Muscovite rule in 1489. It was renamed Vyatka in 1781 and Kirov in 1934, when the Oblast was formed.

Vladimir Sergeyenkov, the KPRF candidate, was elected Governor in 1996, and re-elected in 2000. He was succeeded, following an election in December 2003, by Nikolai Shaklein. At elections to the regional Legislative Assembly, held on 12 March 2006, YeR secured 28.5% of the votes cast. The KPRF, the LDPR and the Rossiiskaya Partiya Pensionerov (Russian Party of Pensioners) all obtained over 10% of the vote. In December 2008 President Dmitrii Medvedev nominated Nikita Belykh (a former leader of the pro-market SPS) as Governor: after the Legislative Assembly approved his appointment, he assumed office on 15 January 2009. At elections to the Legislative Assembly on 13 March 2011, YeR obtained 36.7% of the votes cast on a proportional basis, ahead of the KPRF (22.4%), SR (21.1%) and the LDPR (17.1%). Of the 54 deputies, 29 subsequently joined the YeR parliamentary faction.

In 2013, after the anti-corruption campaigner Aleksei Navalnyi announced his intention of seeking election as Mayor of Moscow, a Kirov court brought charges of embezzlement against him, in relation to a state-owned timber company, Kirovles. It was reported that in January the offices of Belykh had been searched by federal security officials in connection with further corruption allegations against Navalnyi. In July Navalnyi was found guilty and sentenced to five years' imprisonment, although further arrests and periods of detention subsequently ensued on numerous grounds.

Belykh was elected as Governor in a direct popular election held in September 2014, receiving 70.0% of the vote. The second-placed candidate was Sergei Mamayev of the KPRF, with 16.0%. On 24 June 2016 Belykh was arrested in Moscow on charges of accepting a bribe. Belykh, who denied the charges against him, was dismissed as Governor on 28 July, when President Vladimir Putin appointed Igor Vasilyev, the former head of federal registration service Rosreyestr, as Acting Governor, pending an election to be held in September 2017. In February 2018, having been found guilty, Belykh was sentenced to eight years' imprisonment and fined 48.5m. roubles.

Meanwhile, YeR secured 35.9% of the votes cast on the basis of proportional representation at elections to the Legislative Assembly held on 18 September 2016 (one of the lowest levels of support for the party recorded in the regional elections on that day); the LDPR was second, with 25.9%. 37 of the 54 deputies had joined the YeR parliamentary faction by the end of the year. On 10 September 2017 Vasilyev was elected Governor, obtaining 64.0% of the votes cast, defeating three other candidates; the second-placed candidate was again Mamayev, with 19.0%.

At elections to the regional Legislative Assembly held on 19 September 2021, YeR secured only 27.3% of the votes cast on the basis of proportional representation; SR was second, with 19.7%, ahead of the KPRF, with 17.8%, the LDPR, with 13.8%, the recently established centre-right NL, with 8.8%, and the RPPS, with 6.2%. By the end of the year 24 of the 40 deputies had joined the YeR faction, nine that of SR, three that of the LDPR and two that of the KPRF. The factions of NL and the RPPS each comprised one deputy.

On 10 May 2022 Vasilyev tendered his resignation as Governor. Putin immediately appointed Aleksandr Sokolov, hitherto an official in the federal presidential administration, as Acting Governor. Sokolov was elected as Governor on 11 September, with 71.9% of the votes cast, defeating Sergei Mamayev of the KPRF (who obtained 13.4% of the votes) and three other candidates.

ECONOMY

In 2022 Kirov Oblast's gross regional product (GRP) was 395,924m. roubles, equivalent to 315,154 roubles per head. The main industrial centres are at Kirov and Slobodskoi. At the end of 2021 there were 1,095 km of railways in the Oblast.

The Oblast's agriculture consists mainly of animal husbandry and the production of grain, flax and vegetables. Agriculture employed 9.1% of the workforce and contributed 7.4% of GRP in 2021. There are significant deposits of peat and phosphorites. The main industries are mechanical engineering, the production of electrical energy, metal working, chemicals, and the processing of agricultural goods. Industry employed 29.8% of the workforce and contributed 40.7% of GRP in 2021, when manufacturing employed 20.4% of the workforce and contributed 33.6% of GRP.

The economically active population numbered 594,884 in 2022, when the rate of unemployment was 3.8%, while the average monthly wage was 40,833 roubles. There was a budgetary surplus of 6,995.3m. roubles in 2021, when export trade amounted to US $1,258m. (of which 11.4% was with CIS countries), and import trade to $454m. (of which 8.9% was with CIS countries).

DIRECTORY

Governor: ALEKSANDR V. SOKOLOV.

Office of the Governor and the Government: 610019 Kirov, ul. K. Libknekhta 69; tel. and fax (8332) 64-89-58; e-mail region@ako.kirov.ru; internet kirovreg.ru.

Legislative Assembly: 610019 Kirov, ul. K. Libknekhta 69; tel. (8332) 64-48-00; fax (8332) 38-17-50; e-mail zsko@zsko.ru; internet zsko.ru; Chair. ROMAN A. BERESNEV.

State Duma Representatives (2): RAKHIM A. AZIMOV (YeR), OLEG D. VALENCHUK (YeR).

Federation Council Representatives: VYACHESLAV S. TIMCHENKO, VIKTOR N. BONDAREV.

Nizhnii Novgorod Oblast

Nizhnii Novgorod Oblast is situated on the middle reaches of the Volga river. Mordoviya and Ryazan Oblast lie to the south, the Oblasts of Vladimir and Ivanovo to the west, Kostroma Oblast to the north-west, Kirov Oblast to the north-east, and Marii-El and the Chuvash Republic to the east. Its major rivers are the Volga, the Oka, the Sura and the Vetluga. The terrain in the north of the Oblast is mainly low-lying, with numerous forests and extensive swampland. The southern part is characterized by fertile black soil (*chernozyom*). The Oblast occupies 76,624 sq km (29,585 sq miles). At January 2023 it had an estimated population of 3,081,817 and a population density of 40.2 per sq km. Some 80.0% of the population was urban in 2023. The administrative centre is Nizhnii Novgorod, at the confluence of the Volga and Oka rivers, with an estimated 1,213,477 inhabitants at January 2023. Other major cities include Dzherinsk (216,598) and Arzamas (103,997). Of residents who stated their ethnicity at the 2021 census, 95.2% were Russian and 1.0% were Tatar. The territory is in the time zone UTC+3.

HISTORY

Nizhnii Novgorod city was founded in 1221 on the borders of the Russian principalities. With the decline of Tatar power, the city was absorbed by the Muscovite state. Industrialization took place in the late tsarist period. In 1905 mass unrest occurred in the region, and in late 1917 it was one of the first areas of Russia to be seized by the Bolsheviks. Nizhnii Novgorod Oblast was formed on 14 January 1929. In 1932–90 the city and region were named Gorkii, and for much of the time the city was 'closed', owing to its defence industry.

In 1991 Russian President Boris Yeltsin appointed Boris Nemtsov as regional Governor. Nemtsov instituted a wide-ranging programme of economic reform. In 1994 the Oblast was expanded to incorporate territories east of the River Volga hitherto within Ivanovo Oblast. Nemtsov secured popular election in 1995, and was a prominent advocate of democratization and decentralization. In 1996 he signed a power-sharing treaty with the federal Government. In 1997 Nemtsov was appointed to the federal Government; in the subsequent gubernatorial elections the pro-presidential candidate, Ivan Sklyarov (hitherto Mayor of Nizhnii Novgorod), defeated Gennadii Khodyrev, who was supported by the KPRF and the LDPR. In the 2010s Nemstov became a prominent liberal opposition activist, prior to his assassination in Moscow in 2015.

In July 2001 Khodyrev, by this time a KPRF deputy in the State Duma, the lower chamber of the federal legislature, was elected Governor. Following his election, Khodyrev suspended his membership of the KPRF (he was subsequently affiliated with YeR), and expanded the remit of the gubernatorial role to incorporate the duties hitherto held by a Chairman of the Government. In 2002 the power-sharing treaty of 1996 was annulled. Putin nominated the erstwhile Deputy Mayor of Moscow, Valerii Shantsev, as Khodyrev's successor in March 2005; the regional legislature voted to confirm this appointment in August.

In March 2007 security forces dispersed an unauthorized protest in Nizhnii Novgorod, organized by Drugaya Rossiya (Another Russia), an informal opposition coalition.

In June 2010 the regional Legislative Assembly approved the appointment of Shantsev to a second term of office. He was overwhelmingly elected Governor in a popular election in September 2014, obtaining 86.9% of the votes cast. YeR secured 54.9% of the proportional vote in elections to the Legislative Assembly held in September 2016. By the end of the year 41 of the 50 deputies had joined the YeR parliamentary faction.

On 26 September 2017 Shantsev resigned as Governor; he was succeeded in an acting capacity by Gleb Nikitin, the erstwhile federal First Deputy Minister of Industry and Trade. On 9 September 2018 Nikitin was elected Governor, obtaining 67.8% of the votes cast; the second-placed candidate, Vladislav Yegorov of the KPRF, obtained 16.6%.

At elections to the regional Legislative Assembly held on 19 September 2021, YeR secured 49.0% of the votes cast on the basis of proportional representation; the KPRF obtained 19.2%, SR 9.6%, the LDPR 7.0%, and the recently established centre-right NL 5.5%. By the end of the year 40 of the 50 deputies had joined the YeR faction, five that of the KPRF, two that of the LDPR, two that of SR, and one that of NL.

On 10 September 2023 Nikitin, the candidate of YeR, was overwhelmingly re-elected Governor with 82.8% of the votes cast, defeating four other candidates, including Yegorov of the KPRF, who was again placed second, with 9.7% of the votes.

ECONOMY

In 2021 Nizhnii Novgorod Oblast's gross regional product (GRP) amounted to 1,888,121m. roubles, or 597,431 roubles per head. Its principal industrial centres are at Nizhnii Novgorod, Dzerzhinsk and Arzamas. Nizhnii Novgorod contains a major river-port, from which it is possible to reach the Baltic, Black, White and Caspian Seas.

At the end of 2021 there were 1,208 km of railways in the Oblast. The city has an underground railway system and an international airport.

Agriculture consists mainly of animal husbandry, and the production of grain, sugar beet, flax, and onions and other vegetables. The sector employed 3.5% of the workforce and contributed 3.0% of GRP in 2021. The principal industries of the Oblast include mechanical engineering and metal working, ferrous metallurgy, chemicals, petrochemicals, and the processing of agricultural and forestry products. During the Soviet period the region was developed as a major military-industrial centre, with the defence sector accounting for around three-quarters of the regional economy. The Gorkii Automobile Plant (GAZ), which prior to 2022 assembled vehicles for numerous Western manufacturers as well as its own, is also a significant employer. In the 1990s the Oblast was among those territories of the Federation that dealt most successfully with the transition from military to civilian industry. Industry employed 31.8% of the workforce and contributed 34.7% of GRP in 2021, when manufacturing employed 19.5% of the workforce and contributed 26.5% of GRP. A new stadium, with a capacity of around 45,000 people, was constructed in Nizhnii Novgorod in association with Russia's hosting of the 2018 football World Cup.

The economically active population numbered 1,661,922 in 2022, when the rate of unemployment was 4.1%, while the average monthly wage was 48,368 roubles. There was a budgetary surplus of 4,493.4m. roubles in 2021, when export trade amounted to US $6,632m. (of which 25.6% was with countries of the CIS), and import trade to $3,212m. (of which 11.3% was with CIS countries).

DIRECTORY

Governor: GLEB S. NIKITIN.

Office of the Governor: 603082 Nizhnii Novgorod, Kreml, kor. 1; tel. (831) 419-90-12; fax (831) 439-00-48; e-mail official@kreml.nnov.ru; internet government-nnov.ru.

Legislative Assembly: 603082 Nizhnii Novgorod, Kreml, kor. 2; tel. (831) 439-05-38; fax (831) 439-17-17; e-mail zsno@sinn.ru; internet zsno.ru; Chair. YEVGENII B. LYULIN.

State Duma Representatives (5): ANATOLII F. LESUN (YeR), YEVGENII V. LEBEDEV (YeR), NATALYA V. NAZAROVA (YeR), VADIM YE. BULAVINOV (YeR), ARTYOM A. KAVINOV (YeR).

Federation Council Representatives: ALEKSANDR V. VAINBERG, OLGA V. SHCHETININA.

Orenburg Oblast

Orenburg Oblast is situated in the foothills of the Southern Urals. An international border with Kazakhstan lies to the south and east. Samara Oblast lies to the west, and Bashkortostan and Chelyabinsk Oblast to the north. There is a short border with Tatarstan in the north-west. The Oblast occupies 123,702 sq km (47,762 sq miles). At January 2023 the population of the Oblast was an estimated 1,841,377 and the population density 14.9 per sq km. Some 59.9% of the population was urban in 2023. The administrative centre, Orenburg, had an estimated 539,236 inhabitants at January 2023. The second largest city is Orsk (188,135). Of residents who stated their ethnicity at the 2021 census, 79.3% were Russian, 6.7% Tatar, 6.2% Kazakh, 2.1% Bashkir, 1.1% Mordoviyan, and 1.0% were Ukrainian. Orenburg Oblast is in the time zone UTC+5.

HISTORY

Orenburg was founded as a fortress in 1743. During the revolutionary period Orenburg was a headquarters of 'White' forces. The city, a centre of Kazakh nationalism, was the capital of the Kyrgyz Autonomous Soviet Socialist Republic (ASSR), within the Russian Socialist Federative Soviet Republic, in 1920–25. (The Kazakhs were known to the Russians as Kyrgyz at this time.) The region was then separated from the renamed Kazakh ASSR. Orenburg Oblast was formed on 7 December 1934.

A gubernatorial election in December 1995 was won by the incumbent, Vladimir Yelagin. He was defeated in the 1999 gubernatorial election by Aleksei Chernyshyov, who was re-elected in 2003. In June 2005 the Legislative Assembly voted to confirm Chernyshyov to a further term in office.

On 22 May 2010 the regional Legislative Assembly approved the nomination of Yurii Berg, hitherto the Mayor of Orsk, as Governor; he assumed office on 15 June. At elections to the regional Legislative Assembly, held in March 2011, YeR obtained 41.5% of the votes cast on a proportional basis.

In September 2014 Berg was overwhelmingly elected Governor in a popular election, obtaining 80.3% of the vote. YeR secured 41.1% of the proportional vote in elections to the Legislative Assembly held in September 2016; the LDPR took 23.0% and the KPRF 20.6%. By the end of the year 34 of the 47 deputies had joined the YeR parliamentary faction.

On 21 March 2019 President Putin accepted the resignation of Berg as Governor. On the same day he appointed Denis Pasler, the head of an electricity generation company and a former Chairman of the Government of Sverdlovsk Oblast, as Acting Governor. On 8 September Pasler was elected to the post, obtaining 65.9% of the votes cast. Maksim Amelin of the KPRF was second, with 23.7%.

At elections to the regional Legislative Assembly held on 19 September 2021, YeR secured 39.5% of the votes cast on the basis of proportional representation; the KPRF obtained 29.1%, the LDPR 10.6%, SR 10.1% and the RPPS 6.9%. By the end of the year 29 of the 47 deputies had joined the YeR faction and 12 that of the KPRF.

ECONOMY

Orenburg Oblast's gross regional product (GRP) was 1,394,280m. roubles in 2021, or 721,025 roubles per head. Its principal industrial centres are at Orenburg, Orsk and Novotroitsk. At the end of 2021 there were 1,454 km of railways in the Oblast.

Agriculture consists mainly of grain, vegetable and sunflower production, and animal husbandry. The intensive exploitation of petroleum and gas deposits has caused serious damage to arable land. Agriculture employed 11.9% of the workforce and contributed 6.9% of GRP in 2021. The Oblast's major industries are ferrous and non-ferrous metallurgy, mechanical engineering, metal working, natural gas production, electrical energy, and the production of petroleum, ores, asbestos and salt. The Oblast is among the principal producers of nickel and natural gas in Russia. Industry employed 28.4% of the workforce and contributed 63.5% of GRP in 2021, when manufacturing employed 12.3% of the workforce and contributed 11.3% of GRP.

The economically active population numbered 892,472 in 2022, when the rate of unemployment was 3.5%, while the average monthly wage was 43,540 roubles. There was a budgetary surplus of 17,656.6m. roubles in 2021, when export trade amounted to US $2,629m. (of which 53.2% was with countries of the CIS), while import trade amounted to $296m. (of which 49.7% was with CIS countries).

DIRECTORY

Governor: Denis V. Pasler.

Office of the Governor: 460015 Orenburg, pl. Lenina 1, Dom Sovetov; tel. (3532) 77-69-31; fax (3532) 77-38-02; e-mail office@gov.orb.ru; internet orenburg-gov.ru.

Legislative Assembly: 460015 Orenburg, pl. Lenina 1, Dom Sovetov; tel. (3532) 77-33-20; fax (3532) 77-42-12; e-mail speaker01@gov.orb.ru; internet zaksob.ru; Chair. Sergei I. Grachyov.

State Duma Representatives (3): Andrei A. Anikeyev (YeR), Oleg D. Dimov (YeR), Viktor M. Zavarzin (YeR).

Federation Council Representatives: Yelena V. Afanasyeva, Andrei A. Shevchenko.

Penza Oblast

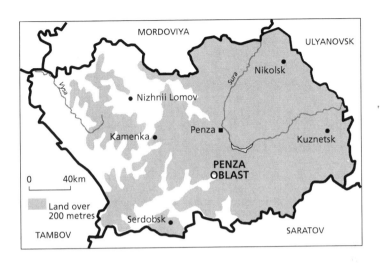

Penza Oblast is situated in the Volga Highlands. It borders the Republic of Mordoviya to the north, and the Oblasts of Ulyanovsk to the east, Saratov to the south, Tambov to the south-west and Ryazan to the north-west. The Oblast covers 43,352 sq km (16,738 sq miles). At January 2023 the population of the Oblast was an estimated 1,246,609 and the population density 28.8 per sq km. Some 68.8% of the population was urban in 2023. The administrative centre, Penza, had an estimated 492,376 inhabitants at January 2023. Of residents who stated their ethnicity at the 2021 census, 87.6% were Russian, 6.4% Tatar and 2.5% were Mordoviyan. The territory is in the time zone UTC+3.

HISTORY

The city of Penza was founded in 1663 as an outpost on the south-eastern border of the Russian Empire. Penza Oblast was formed on 4 February 1939.

In April 1993 the communist candidate, Anatolii Kovlyagin, defeated the incumbent in elections to head the regional administration. In 1998 Vasilii Bochkaryov, a technocrat, was elected as Governor. He was re-elected in 2002, with the support of YeO-YeR (now YeR). The Legislative Assembly approved Bochkaryov's appointment to further terms of office in 2005 and 2010.

At elections to the Regional Legislative Assembly in October 2012, YeR obtained 70.6% of the votes cast on a proportional basis. In May 2015, following the end of Bochkaryov's gubernatorial term, President Vladimir Putin appointed Ivan Belozertsev, hitherto the Chairman of the Regional Legislative Assembly, as Acting Governor. He was elected as Governor in September, obtaining 86.0% of the votes cast. At elections to the Regional Legislative Assembly in September 2017, YeR obtained 69.0% of the proportional vote, far more than the KPRF, with 13.1%, and the LDPR, with 7.0%. By the end of the year 32 of the 36 deputies had joined the YeR parliamentary association.

Belozertsev was one of five candidates to contest a gubernatorial election on 13 September 2020. He was re-elected with 78.7% of the votes cast. On 21 April 2021 Belozertsev was arrested on charges of having received a bribe of some 31m. roubles and of the illegal ownership of weapons; he was dismissed as Governor two days later. His trial was continuing in early 2024. Meanwhile, on 23 April 2021 Putin appointed Oleg Melnichenko, one of the Oblast's two representatives in the Federation Council, as Acting Governor. On 19 September Melnichenko was elected Governor with 72.4% of votes cast, defeating four other candidates. He assumed office on 29 September.

Elections to the regional legislature were held on 11 September 2022, when YeR obtained some 74.9% of the votes cast on the basis of proportional representation. The KPRF was second, with 8.5%. By the end of the year 33 of the 36 deputies had joined the YeR parliamentary association.

ECONOMY

In 2021 Penza Oblast's gross regional product (GRP) was 537,290m. roubles, or 418,946 roubles per head. The principal industrial centres are at Penza and Kuznetsk. At the end of 2021 there were 831 km of railways in the Oblast.

Around three-quarters of the agricultural land in the Oblast is of fertile black earth (*chernozyom*). Agriculture consists mainly of the production of grain and vegetables, and animal husbandry. Agriculture employed 9.5% of the workforce and contributed 20.2% of GRP in 2021. The main industries are mechanical engineering, the processing of timber and agricultural products, chemicals and petrochemicals, and light manufacturing. Industry employed 29.2% of the workforce and contributed 26.5% of GRP in 2021, when manufacturing employed 18.5% of the workforce and contributed 18.7% of GRP.

The economically active population in Penza Oblast numbered 607,161 in 2022, when the rate of unemployment was 3.7%, while the average monthly wage was 41,307 roubles. There was a budgetary surplus of 4,773.3m. roubles in 2021, when export trade amounted to US $358m. (of which 51.9% was with countries of the CIS), and import trade to $359m. (of which 18.1% was with CIS countries).

DIRECTORY

Governor: OLEG V. MELNICHENKO.

Chairman of the Regional Government: NIKOLAI P. SIMONOV.

Office of the Government: 440025 Penza, ul. Moskovskaya 75; tel. (8412) 56-23-33; fax (8412) 59-54-02; e-mail pravobl@obl.penza.net; internet pnzreg.ru.

Regional Legislative Assembly: 440025 Penza, ul. Kirova 13; tel. (8412) 59-05-02; fax (8412) 59-05-11; e-mail vkl@zspo.ru; internet zspo.ru; Chair. VADIM N. SUPIKOV.

State Duma Representatives (2): IGOR N. RUDENSKII (YeR), ALEKSANDR M. SAMOKUTYAYEV (YeR).

Federation Council Representatives: YULIYA V. LAZUTKINA, NIKOLAI F. KONDRATYUK.

Samara Oblast

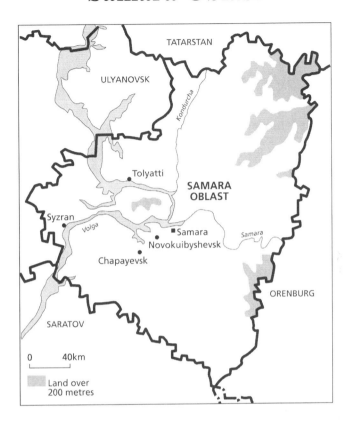

Samara Oblast is situated in the south-east of the Eastern European Plain on the middle reaches of the Volga river. Its southernmost tip lies on the border with Kazakhstan. It borders Tatarstan to the north and the Oblasts of Saratov (to the south-west), Ulyanovsk (west), and Orenburg (east). The Volga snakes through the west of the territory. The region occupies 53,565 sq km (20,682 sq miles). At January 2023 the region had an estimated population of 3,142,683 and a population density of 58.7 per sq km. Some 79.5% of the population was urban in 2023. The administrative centre, Samara, had an estimated 1,163,645 inhabitants at January 2023. Other major cities include Tolyatti (674,630) and Syzran (163,303). Of residents who stated their ethnicity at the 2021 census, 89.6% were Russian, 3.2% Tatar, 1.6% Chuvash, 1.0% Mordoviyan, and 0.7% were Armenian. The Oblast is in the time zone UTC+4.

HISTORY

Samara was founded in 1586 as a fortress. It became rich from the Volga grain trade and further increased in prosperity after the construction of the railways in the late 19th century. A Middle Volga Oblast was formed on 14 May 1928. It became a krai in 1929 and was renamed Kuibyshev Krai in 1935. (Samara city was similarly renamed.) On 5 December 1936 the Krai reverted to oblast status. Kuibyshev was the headquarters of the Soviet Government in 1941–43, when Moscow was threatened by German invasion. Both the city and Oblast assumed their current names in 1991.

The oblast legislature defied President Boris Yeltsin in the constitutional crisis of 1993 and was replaced by a Regional Duma. The head of the regional administration, Konstantin Titov, appointed to that position by Yeltsin in August 1991, was a proponent of liberal economic and political reform. In December 1996 Titov was elected Governor and was re-elected in July 2000. In April 2005 President Vladimir Putin nominated Titov to serve for a further term; this nomination was duly confirmed by the regional Duma. Later in the year Titov joined YeR.

Following Titov's resignation as Governor in August 2007, Putin nominated Vladimir Artyakov, hitherto head of the vehicle manufacturer AvtoVAZ (Volga Automobile Plant), based in Tolyatti, as his successor; the appointment was confirmed by the Regional Duma (which later renamed itself the Governorate Duma) on 29 August.

Artyakov resigned as Governor on 10 May 2012; he was succeeded, initially in an acting capacity, by Nikolai Merkushkin, Head of the Republic of Mordoviya since 1995. Merkushkin's appointment was confirmed by the Governorate Duma on 12 May.

On 14 September 2014, in a popular election, Merkushkin was overwhelmingly elected Governor, obtaining 91.4% of the votes cast. YeR secured 51.0% of the votes cast on a proportional basis at elections to the Governorate Duma held on 18 September 2016; the KPRF took 17.4% of the votes, the LDPR 14.5% and SR 5.8%. By the end of the year 41 of the 50 deputies had joined the YeR parliamentary faction.

Merkushkin was dismissed as Governor on 25 September 2017. He was succeeded in an acting capacity by Dmitrii Azarov, hitherto a representative of the Oblast in the Federation Council. On 9 September 2018 Azarov was elected Governor, obtaining 72.6% of the votes cast and defeating five other candidates.

At elections to the Governorate Duma held on 19 September 2021, YeR secured 44.3% of the votes cast on the basis of proportional representation; the KPRF obtained 20.4%, the LDPR 7.7%, SR 6.3% and the recently established centre-right NL 5.7%. By the end of the year 36 of the 50 deputies had joined the YeR faction, 10 that of the KPRF, and two that of SR. The factions of the LDPR and NL each comprised one deputy.

On 15 September 2023 Azarov was overwhelmingly re–elected Governor with 83.8% of the votes cast, defeating four other candidates. On 16 November the acting Vice-Governor, Chairman of the Government, Viktor Kudryashov, together with the Minister of Construction, was arrested on abuse of office charges related to the construction of a metro line in the Oblast. Natalya Katina, hitherto the Deputy Chairman of the Government, was appointed to succeed Kudryashov on 21 November, initially in an acting capacity.

ECONOMY

In 2021 Samara Oblast's gross regional product (GRP) amounted to 2,122,537m. roubles, or 675,335 roubles per head. The Oblast's major industrial centres are at Samara, Tolyatti and Syzran. At the end of 2021 there were 1,374 km of railways in the Oblast.

Agriculture in the Oblast consists mainly of the production of grain, sugar beet and sunflower seeds, and of animal husbandry and beekeeping. The sector employed 5.0%

of the workforce and contributed 4.9% of GRP in 2021. Samara Oblast is one of Russia's principal industrial regions, and there are some reserves of petroleum and natural gas in the Oblast. The territory has attracted substantial foreign investment. The main industries are mechanical engineering, metal working, the production and refining of petroleum, food processing, and chemicals and petrochemicals. The Oblast is home to AvtoVAZ (part of the Rostekh—Rostec State Corporation), manufacturer of the Lada automobile, and is the leading producer of automobiles in Russia. Industry employed 31.9% of the workforce and contributed 50.6% of GRP in 2021, when manufacturing employed 18.9% of the workforce and contributed 21.5% of GRP. A new stadium, with a capacity of around 45,000 people was constructed in the city in association with Russia's hosting of the 2018 football World Cup.

The economically active population of Samara Oblast numbered 1,619,700 in 2022, when the rate of unemployment was 2.7%, while the average monthly wage was 48,874 roubles. There was a regional budgetary surplus of 27,755.1m. roubles in 2021, when export trade amounted to US $5,182m. (of which 30.6% was with countries of the CIS), while import trade amounted to $2,879m. (of which 10.4% was with CIS countries).

DIRECTORY

Governor: DMITRII I. AZAROV.

Vice-Governor, Chairman of the Government: NATALYA I. KATINA (acting).

Office of the Governor and the Government: 443006 Samara, ul. Molodogvardeiskaya 210; tel. (846) 200-01-23; fax (846) 332-13-40; e-mail governor@samara.ru; internet samregion.ru.

Governorate Duma: 443100 Samara, ul. Molodogvardeiskaya 187; tel. (846) 242-42-02; fax (846) 248-38-08; e-mail info@samgd.ru; internet samgd.ru; Chair. GENNADII P. KOTELNIKOV.

State Duma Representatives (5): ALEKSANDR YE. KHINSHTEIN (YeR), LEONID I. KALASHNIKOV (KPRF), VIKTOR A. KAZAKOV (YeR), ANDREI F. TRIFONOV (YeR), MIKHAIL N. MATVEYEV (KPRF).

Federation Council Representatives: FARIT M. MUKHAMETSHIN, ANDREI I. KISLOV.

Saratov Oblast

Saratov Oblast is situated in the south-east of the Eastern European Plain. It has an international border with Kazakhstan to the south-east, and borders with the Oblasts of Volgograd (to the south), Voronezh and Tambov (to the west), and Penza, Ulyanovsk and Samara (to the north). Its main river is the Volga. Those regions of the Oblast to the west of the Volga are mountainous, those to the east are low-lying. The region occupies 101,240 sq km (39,089 sq miles). At January 2023 Saratov Oblast had an estimated 2,404,944 inhabitants and a population density of 23.8 per sq km. Some 76.8% of the population was urban in 2023. The administrative centre is Saratov, a major river-port, with an estimated 891,898 inhabitants at January 2023. Other major cities include Engels (223,333) and Balakovo (182,758). Of residents who stated their ethnicity at the 2021 census, 89.7% were Russian, 2.9% Kazakh, 1.7% Tatar, and 0.8% were Armenian. The region is in the time zone UTC+4.

HISTORY

Saratov was founded in 1590 as a fortress, to protect against nomad raids on the Volga trade route. In the mid-18th century the area was colonized by some 30,000 German settlers. Strategically placed on the Trans-Siberian Railway, Saratov city was seized by Bolshevik forces in late 1917. The Autonomous Commune of Volga German Workers was established in the region in 1918 and renamed the Volga German Autonomous Soviet Socialist Republic (ASSR) in 1924, with its capital at Pokrovsk (renamed Engels in 1931) on the opposite bank of the Volga from Saratov. Saratov Oblast was formed in 1936, having been part of a Saratov Krai from 1934. In 1941, during the Second World War, the Volga German ASSR was abolished and its inhabitants deported to Siberia, Central Asia and the North Caucasus. In 1972 they were permitted to return to the region, although from the 1980s German-Russians were allowed to emigrate to Germany, and many did so.

In September 1996 Dmitrii Ayatskov, head of the regional administration since April, was elected Governor. He carried out extensive reforms to the agro-industrial sector, including the adoption, in 1997, of the first law in Russia permitting the purchase and sale of agricultural land. He also signed a series of bilateral trade agreements with the Mayor of Moscow, Yurii Luzhkov. Ayatskov was re-elected in March 2000, amid accusations of electoral manipulation, which removed all other serious candidates from the contest, and of press censorship.

Ayatskov became the first incumbent Governor not to be reappointed under new arrangements, announced in 2004, whereby regional governors were subject to presidential appointment. In March 2005 the regional Duma approved the nomination of Pavel Ipatov, the former director of a nuclear power station, as Governor; he took office on 5 April. The Regional Duma voted to approve Ipatov's appointment to a second term as Governor in 2010.

In February 2012 a group of deputies from the Regional Duma issued an appeal to President Dmitrii Medvedev for Ipatov's dismissal, while Saratov City Duma endorsed a vote of no confidence in his governance. In March Ipatov resigned; he was succeeded by the erstwhile Chairman of the Regional Duma, Valerii Radayev.

Inter-ethnic riots in the eastern town of Pugachyov, in July 2013, were a focus of national attention. Unrest commenced after a Chechen youth murdered a local man (of Russian and Tatar parentage). Several hundred people gathered in the town's main square, demanding the expulsion from the region of all Chechens and other peoples from the Caucasus. Protests continued for several days, attended by Russian nationalists from outside the city. The local chief of police was dismissed, and the Presidential Representative to the Volga Federal Okrug visited the town, stating that any expulsion of Chechens would be unconstitutional. None the less, 13 Chechens resident in a nearby village were detained shortly afterwards and accused of lacking the requisite residence permit.

On 10 September 2017 Radayev was elected Governor, obtaining 74.6% of the popular vote, defeating three other candidates. In concurrent elections to the Regional Duma, YeR obtained 66.8% of the votes cast to those seats elected on a proportional basis (compared with the 77.9% it had won in 2012), ahead of the KPRF, with 14.7%, and the LDPR, with 8.1%. By the end of the year 37 of the 45 deputies had joined the YeR faction.

Radayev tendered his resignation as Governor on 10 May 2022. Putin immediately appointed Roman Busargin, hitherto Vice-Governor, Chairman of the Government, as Acting Governor. Later in May the Regional Duma adopted a proposal to change the structure of the Oblast's Government, combining the positions of Governor and Chairman of the Government.

Elections were held to the Regional Duma on 11 September 2022, when YeR obtained 60.5% of the votes cast on the basis of proportional representation, ahead of the KPRF, with 14.4%, the LDPR, with 9.2%, and SR, with 6.8%. By the end of the year 29 deputies had joined the YeR faction, five that of the KPRF, two that of the LDPR, and two that of SR. At a poll on the same day, Busargin was elected as Governor with 72.6% of the votes cast, defeating Olga Alimova of the KPRF, who obtained 14.2% of the votes, and three other candidates.

ECONOMY

In 2021 Saratov Oblast's gross regional product (GRP) amounted to 1,005,801m. roubles, or 422,955 roubles per head. The region's major industrial centres are at Saratov, Engels and Balakovo. At the end of 2021 there were 2,291 km of railways in the Oblast. The river port at Saratov is an important transshipment point on routes between Moscow and Central Asia, Siberia and southern Russia.

The Oblast's agriculture consists primarily of the production of grain (the Oblast is one of Russia's major producers of wheat) and sunflower seeds. Animal husbandry is also significant. Agriculture employed 7.8% of the workforce and contributed 15.2% of GRP in 2021. The Oblast's main industries are mechanical engineering and metal working, the production of electricity, petroleum refining, chemicals and petrochemicals, food processing, and the production of petroleum and natural gas. Significant quantities of cement and mineral fertilizer are also produced in the Oblast. Industry employed 25.3% of the workforce and contributed 34.1% of GRP in 2021, when manufacturing employed 13.7% of the workforce and contributed 20.7% of GRP.

The region's economically active population numbered 1,148,777 in 2022, when the rate of unemployment was 3.4%, while the average monthly wage was 42,917 roubles. There was a budgetary surplus of 3,387.7m. roubles in 2021, when export trade amounted to US $2,263m. (of which 24.5% was with countries of the CIS), and import trade to $955m. (of which 8.0% was with CIS countries).

DIRECTORY

Governor: ROMAN V. BUSARGIN.

Office of the Governor and the Government: 410042 Saratov, ul. Moskovskaya 72; tel. (8452) 27-20-86; fax (8452) 50-12-11; e-mail governor@saratov.gov.ru; internet saratov.gov.ru.

Regional Duma: 410031 Saratov, ul. Radishcheva 24A; tel. (8452) 26-00-68; fax (8452) 27-53-31; e-mail post@srd.ru; internet srd.ru; Chair. MIKHAIL A. ISAYEV.

State Duma Representatives (4): VYACHESLAV V. VOLODIN (YeR), NIKOLAI V. PANKOV (YeR), ANDREI V. VOROBYEV (YeR), ALEKSANDR M. STRELYUKHIN (YeR).

Federation Council Representatives: VALERII V. RADAYEV, ANDREI I. DENISOV.

Ulyanovsk Oblast

Ulyanovsk Oblast is situated in the Volga Highlands. The Republic of Mordoviya, the Chuvash Republic and the Republic of Tatarstan lie to the north. There are also borders with Samara, Saratov and Penza Oblasts in the south-east, south, and west, respectively. The region occupies 37,181 sq km (14,356 sq miles). At January 2023 its population was an estimated 1,186,333 and the population density 31.9 per sq km. Some 77.0% of the population was urban in 2023. The administrative centre, Ulyanovsk, had an estimated 613,334 inhabitants at January 2023. The other major city is Dimitrovgrad (109,547). Of residents who stated their ethnicity at the 2021 census, 77.5% were Russian, 11.1% Tatar, 5.8% Chuvash and 2.2% were Mordoviyan. The Oblast is in the time zone UTC+4.

HISTORY

Simbirsk was founded in 1648. The birthplace of the Soviet leader, Lenin (Vladimir Ulyanov), it was renamed Ulyanovsk in 1924. Ulyanovsk Oblast was formed in January 1943. In 1996 the incumbent Governor, Yurii Goryachev, backed by the KPRF, was elected to the post. He was defeated in a gubernatorial election by Lt-Gen. Vladimir Shamanov in 2000. In 2004 Sergei Morozov, the favoured candidate of YeR, was elected Governor after the second-placed candidate in the first round of voting was disqualified from participating in the run-off poll. Since 2005 the authorities have sought, unsuccessfully, to reduce the demographic downturn in the Oblast, providing prizes each year to mothers who give birth on Russia Day, 12 June. In 2006 and 2011 the regional legislature endorsed Morozov's appointment to further gubernatorial terms. On 18 September 2016 Morozov was directly elected Governor, receiving 54.3% of the vote. Aleksei Kurinnyi of the KPRF, with 25.5%, was second.

Elections to the Legislative Assembly were held on 9 September 2018. The KPRF was placed first in voting on a proportional basis, with 36.2%, narrowly ahead of YeR, with 34.0%. A total of 17 of the 36 deputies had joined the YeR parliamentary faction (which thereby lost its majority) by the end of the year, 12 that of the KPRF, four that of the LDPR, and one that of the KR.

On 8 April 2021 Morozov resigned as Governor, citing his wish to be a candidate in elections to the federal State Duma in September (when he gained election to the chamber on the YeR federal list). Meanwhile, Putin appointed Aleksei Russkikh, a representative of Moscow Oblast in the Federation Council, the upper chamber of the federal legislature, as Acting Governor. On 19 September 2021 Russkikh was overwhelmingly elected to the post of Governor with 83.2% of votes cast, defeating three other candidates.

Following elections to the Legislative Assembly held on 10 September 2023, YeR held 27 of the 36 seats in the expanded chamber, substantially increasing its representation there, although the rate of participation was only 34.7%. Among the three LDPR deputies elected was Viktor But, an arms dealer who had been imprisoned in 2012 in the USA on a 25-year sentence, before being released in 2022 as part of a prisoner exchange with Russia.

ECONOMY

In 2021 Ulyanovsk Oblast's gross regional product (GRP) amounted to 498,806m. roubles, or 411,847 roubles per head. Ulyanovsk and Melekess are major industrial centres. At the end of 2021 there were 697 km of railways in the Oblast.

Agriculture in the region consists primarily of animal husbandry, and the production of grain and sugar beet. The sector employed 6.8% of the workforce and contributed 7.5% of GRP in 2021. The main industries include mechanical engineering, food processing and electrical energy, while major companies include the UAZ automobile plant and the Aviastar-SP aeroplane manufacturer. Industry employed 32.2% of the workforce and contributed 34.5% of GRP in 2021, when manufacturing employed 20.9% of the workforce and contributed 23.6% of GRP.

The economically active population numbered 588,921 in 2022, when the rate of unemployment was 4.2%, while the average monthly wage was 41,523 roubles. There was a budgetary deficit of 7,192.7m. roubles in 2021, when export trade amounted to US $586m. (of which 26.3% was with countries of the CIS), and import trade to $729m. (of which 6.3% was with CIS countries).

DIRECTORY

Governor: ALEKSEI YU. RUSSKIKH.

Chairman of the Regional Government: ALEKSANDR A. SMEKALIN.

Office of the Governor and the Government: 432017 Ulyanovsk, pl. Lenina 1; tel. (8422) 41-20-78; fax (8422) 58-93-43; e-mail mail@ulgov.ru; internet ulgov.ru.

Legislative Assembly: 432063 Ulyanovsk, ul. Radishcheva 1; tel. (8422) 41-34-52; fax (8422) 41-20-74; e-mail zaksobr@mv.ru; internet zsuo.ru; Chair. VALERII V. MALYSHEV.

State Duma Representatives (2): VLADIMIR M. KONONOV (YeR), VLADISLAV A. TRETYAK (YeR).

Federation Council Representatives: SERGEI N. RYABUKHIN, AIRAT M. GIBATDINOV.

URALS FEDERAL OKRUG

Presidential Representative to the Urals Federal Okrug: Vladimir V. Yakushev, 620031 Sverdlovsk obl., Yekaterinburg, pl. Oktyabrskaya 3; tel. (343) 277-18-96; internet uralfo.gov.ru.

Chelyabinsk Oblast

Chelyabinsk Oblast is situated in the Southern Urals, with much of the region lying on the eastern slopes of the Southern Ural Mountains. Orenburg Oblast lies to the south, the Republic of Bashkortostan to the west, Sverdlovsk Oblast to the north and Kurgan Oblast to the east. There is an international border with Kazakhstan in the south-east. The major rivers in the Oblast are the Ural and the Miass and there are over 1,000 lakes. The Oblast covers an area of 88,529 sq km (34,181 sq miles). At January 2023 it had an estimated population of 3,407,145 and a population density of 38.5 per sq km. Some 82.6% of the population was urban in 2023. The administrative centre, Chelyabinsk, had an estimated 1,182,517 inhabitants at January 2023. Other major cities are Magnitogorsk (409,255), Zlatoust (159,662), Miass (147,449) and Kopeisk (146,125). Of residents who stated their ethnicity at the 2021 census, 86.3% were Russian, 4.4% Bashkir, 4.1% Tatar, and 1.0% were Kazakh. Chelyabinsk Oblast is in the time zone UTC+5.

HISTORY

Chelyabinsk city was established as a Russian frontier post in 1736. The Oblast was created on 17 January 1934.

Following the attempted coup by conservative communists in Moscow, the Russian and Soviet capital, in August 1991, President Boris Yeltsin dismissed the head of Chelyabinsk Oblast Administration, Pyotr Sumin, who had expressed sympathy for the putschists. He was replaced by Vadim Solovyov. Sumin subsequently became Chairman of the oblast legislature, which in January 1993 announced its intention of holding an election for a governor. Despite a ban on the election issued by the federal Supreme Court, voting proceeded in April, when Sumin was victorious. Yeltsin expressed support for Solovyov, and the federal Constitutional Court confirmed that the election was unlawful. The President re-established his authority locally in late 1993 and required the election of a Duma during 1994. In this body pro-Yeltsin forces obtained substantial support. In the gubernatorial election of 1996, however, Sumin was returned to power.

Sumin was re-elected Governor in 2000. In April 2005 the regional legislature voted to elect Sumin (as the nominee of President Vladimir Putin) to a further term of office.

In March 2010 Sumin announced that he would not seek a further term of gubernatorial office. On 22 March the regional Legislative Assembly voted to elect the hitherto Head of Chelyabinsk City Administration, Mikhail Yuryevich, as Governor; he assumed office in April.

On 15 January 2014 President Putin accepted Yuryevich's resignation as Governor, appointing Boris Dubrovskii, hitherto the Chairman and Director-General of the Magnitogorsk Iron and Steel Works (MMK), as Acting Governor. On 14 September Dubrovskii was elected Governor, obtaining 86.4% of the votes cast. YeR obtained 56.2% of votes cast on a proportional basis in elections to the regional Legislative Assembly held in September 2015, ahead of SR, with 15.9%, the KPRF, with 11.7%, and the LPDR, with 10.0%. In total, 48 of the 60 elected deputies joined the YeR parliamentary faction.

On 19 March 2019 Dubrovskii resigned as Governor. Putin appointed Aleksei Teksler, hitherto the federal First Deputy Minister of Energy, as Acting Governor. Dubrovskii had recently been placed under investigation by the Federal Antimonopoly Service, after it had emerged that in 2015–18 more than 90% of road contracts in the Oblast had been awarded to his Yuzhuralmost company. A court case against Dubrovskii was subsequently announced; on appeal in March 2021 he was acquitted, but in August Dubrovskii was again found guilty of anti-competitive practices.

Meanwhile, on 8 September 2019 Teksler was elected as Governor, receiving 69.3% of the votes cast, defeating four other candidates.

In elections to the Regional Legislative Assembly, held on 13 September 2020, support for YeR decreased to 42.6% of the proportional vote. SR was second, with 14.8%, ahead of the KPRF, with 11.9%, the LDPR (11.3%), the RPPS (5.7%), and the ecologist Zelyonaya Alternativa (Green Alternative), with 5.4%. A total of 41 deputies joined the YeR faction when the new chamber convened; seven joined the faction of SR, four that of the KPRF, three that of the LDPR, two that of the RPSS, and one that of the Zelyonaya Alternativa.

ECONOMY

In 2021 the gross regional product (GRP) of Chelyabinsk Oblast amounted to 2,042,593m. roubles, equivalent to 595,385 roubles per head. The region's major industrial centres are at Chelyabinsk, Magnitogorsk, Miass and Zlatoust. At the end of 2021 there were 1,795 km of railway track in the Oblast.

The Oblast's agriculture consists mainly of animal husbandry, horticulture and the production of grain. It is one of the principal meat producing federal territories. The sector employed 5.1% of the workforce and contributed 4.1% of GRP in 2021. Chelyabinsk Oblast became heavily industrialized during the Second World War, as industries relocated from Western regions of the USSR. The Oblast's main industries are ferrous and non-ferrous metallurgy, ore mining, mechanical engineering, metal working, and fuel and energy production. It is the principal steel producing region of Russia. In the north-west, Ozersk is a major plutonium processing and storage site, while centres for weapons manufacturing and space technology are located in the west. Industry employed 35.9% of the workforce and contributed 51.4% of GRP in 2021, when manufacturing employed 21.9% of the workforce and contributed 37.2% of GRP.

The economically active population numbered 1,729,809 in 2022, when 3.1% of the labour force were unemployed, while the average monthly wage was 50,104 roubles. There was a budgetary surplus of 48,580.1m. roubles in 2021, when export trade amounted to US $7,353m. (of which 38.3% was with countries of the CIS), while import trade amounted to $3,524m. (of which 53.6% was with CIS countries).

DIRECTORY

Governor: ALEKSEI L. TEKSLER.

Office of the Governor: 454089 Chelyabinsk, ul. Tsvillinga 27; tel. (351) 263-92-41; fax (351) 263-12-83; e-mail gubernator@chel.surnet.ru; internet gubernator74.ru; internet pravmin.gov74.ru.

Legislative Assembly: 454009 Chelyabinsk, ul. Kirova 114; tel. (351) 255-55-55; fax (351) 263-63-79; e-mail sovetnik@zs74.ru; internet zs74.ru; Chair. OLEG V. GERBER.

State Duma Representatives (5): VLADIMIR V. PAVLOV (YeR), VLADIMIR V. BURMATOV (YeR), VALERII K. GARTUNG (SR), VITALII V. BAKHMATYEV (YeR), OLEG A. KOLESNIKOV (YeR).

Federation Council Representatives: OLEG V. TSEPKIN, MARGARITA N. PAVLOVA.

Kurgan Oblast

Kurgan Oblast is situated in the south of the Western Siberian Plain. Chelyabinsk Oblast lies to the west, Sverdlovsk Oblast to the north and Tyumen Oblast to the north-east, and there is an international border with Kazakhstan to the south. The main rivers are the Tobol and the Iset, and there are more than 2,500 lakes in the south-east of the region. The Oblast occupies 71,488 sq km (27,602 sq miles). At January 2023 it had an estimated population of 761,586 and a population density of 10.7 per sq km. Some 64.2% of the population was urban in 2023. The administrative centre, Kurgan, had an estimated 305,505 inhabitants at January 2023. Of residents who stated their ethnicity at the 2021 census, 93.4% were Russian, 1.7% Tatar, 1.2% Kazakh, and 1.2% were Bashkir. Kurgan Oblast is in the time zone UTC+5.

HISTORY

The city of Kurgan was founded in 1553, on the edge of Russian territory. Kurgan Oblast was formed on 6 February 1943. The KPRF was the largest party in the regional Duma elected on 12 December 1993.

The KPRF candidate, Oleg Bogomolov, hitherto speaker of the regional Duma, was elected Governor in 1996, running unopposed in the second round of the election. He was re-elected in December 2000. In December 2004 Bogomolov, with the support of YeR, was again re-elected Governor. In December 2009, the Regional Duma approved Bogomolov's nomination by President Dmitrii Medvedev to a further term of office.

On 14 February 2014 Bogomolov resigned as Governor. He was succeeded in an acting capacity by Aleksei Kokorin, hitherto Mayor of Shadrinsk. Kokorin was overwhelmingly elected Governor on 14 September, obtaining 84.9% of the vote. YeR was the most successful party in elections to the Regional Duma held on 13 September 2015, obtaining 56.7% of the proportional vote, ahead of the LDPR, with 13.6%, the KPRF, with 13.2%, and SR, with 10.9%. A total of 28 of the 34 deputies joined the YeR parliamentary faction.

On 2 October 2018 Kokorin resigned as Governor. He was succeeded in an acting capacity by Vadim Shumkov, hitherto a Deputy Governor of Tyumen Oblast. On 8 September 2019 Shumkov was elected to the post, receiving 80.9% of the votes cast, defeating three other candidates.

In elections to the Regional Duma, held on 13 September 2020, the share of the vote for YeR to those seats elected on a proportional basis declined to 44.6%. The KPRF was second, with 19.1%, ahead of the LDPR (14.5%), SR (10.5%), and the RPPS (8.3%). When the new chamber convened, the YeR faction comprised 27 deputies, that of the KPRF three deputies, that of the LDPR two deputies, and that of SR one deputy.

ECONOMY

In 2021 the gross regional product (GRP) of Kurgan Oblast amounted to 268,495m. roubles, equivalent to 330,642 roubles per head. The Oblast's main industrial centres are at Kurgan, a river-port in the south-east of the region, and Shadrinsk, on the Iset. At the end of 2021 there were 746 km of railways in the Oblast.

Agriculture consists mainly of grain production and animal husbandry. The sector employed 9.0% of the workforce and contributed 9.7% of GRP in 2021. Kurgan Oblast's main industries are mechanical engineering, metal working, electricity production and food processing. The industrial sector employed 28.1% of the workforce and contributed 31.9% of GRP in 2021, when manufacturing employed 17.7% of the workforce and contributed 21.6% of GRP.

The economically active population numbered 340,545 in 2022, when the rate of unemployment was 6.5%, while the average monthly wage was 41,792 roubles. There was a budgetary surplus of 746.8m. roubles in 2021, when export trade amounted to US $142m. (of which 56.9% was with countries of the CIS), while import trade amounted to $113m. (of which 25.8% was with CIS countries).

DIRECTORY

Governor: VADIM M. SHUMKOV.

Office of the Governor: 640024 Kurgan, ul. Gogolya 56; tel. (3522) 42-92-36; e-mail kurgan@kurganobl.ru; internet kurganobl.ru.

Regional Duma: 640024 Kurgan, ul. Gogolya 56; tel. (3522) 42-72-17; fax (3522) 41-88-91; e-mail mail@oblduma.kurgan.ru; internet kurganoblduma.ru; Chair. DMITRII V. FROLOV.

State Duma Representative (1): ALEKSANDR V. ILTYAKOV (YeR).

Federation Council Representatives: YELENA A. PERMINOVA, SERGEI N. MURATOV.

Sverdlovsk Oblast

Sverdlovsk Oblast is situated on the eastern, and partly on the western, slopes of the Central and Northern Urals and in the Western Siberian Plain. Tyumen Oblast lies to the east (with its constituent Khanty-Mansii Autonomous Okrug to the north-east); there is a short border with the Republic of Komi in the north-west. Perm Krai lies to the west. To the south are Bashkortostan, Chelyabinsk and Kurgan. The region's major rivers are those of the Ob and Kama basins. The west of the region is mountainous, while much of the eastern part is taiga (forested marshland). The Oblast covers an area of 194,307 sq km (75,022 sq miles). At January 2023 the population was an estimated 4,239,161 and the population density 21.8 per sq km. Some 85.8% of the population was urban in 2023. The administrative centre, Yekaterinburg, had an estimated 1,539,371 inhabitants at January 2023. Other major cities are Nizhnii Tagil (334,209), Kamensk-Uralskii (162,177) and Pervouralsk (112,860). Of residents who stated their ethnicity at the 2021 census, 92.3% were Russian and 2.4% were Tatar. The territory is in the time zone UTC+5.

HISTORY

Yekaterinburg city was founded in 1821 as a military stronghold and trading centre. Like the Oblast (formed on 17 January 1934), it was renamed Sverdlovsk in 1924 but, unlike the Oblast, reverted to its pre-Soviet name in 1991. The city was where the last Tsar, Nicholas II, and his family were assassinated in 1918. The region became a major industrial centre after the Second World War.

Following the disintegration of the USSR, Sverdlovsk Oblast was among the most forthright territories in demanding the devolution of powers from the centre. In October 1993 the head of the regional administration, Eduard Rossel, proclaimed a 'Ural Republic'. He was dismissed in November and replaced by Aleksei Strakhov. In August 1995 Rossel was reinstated as Governor, having won a direct election to the post. In January 1996 he signed a power-sharing treaty with the federal authorities. He was re-elected in 1999.

Rossel subsequently adopted a less oppositional stance towards the federal authorities, while continuing to express support for radical reforms to the administrative structure of the Russian Federation, advocating the abolition of the ethnic republics. In November 2005 the regional legislature voted to confirm Rossel's nomination to a further term of office.

In the election to the federal presidency held in March 2008 the winning YeR-backed candidate, Dmitrii Medvedev, secured his lowest share of the votes cast in any federal subject (52.6%) in the Oblast. President Medvedev dismissed Rossel in November 2009; the regional legislature endorsed the appointment of his successor, Aleksandr Misharin, later in the month. Misharin appointed Rossel as the representative of the Oblast in the upper chamber of the federal legislature, the Federation Council; he remained in this position until his retirement in 2022.

Elections to a reconstituted unicameral regional Legislative Assembly were held in December 2011. YeR obtained 33.1% of the proportional vote, ahead of SR, with 27.3%, the KPRF, with 17.5%, and the LDPR, with 15.9%. Some 29 of the 49 deputies subsequently joined the YeR parliamentary faction. The share of the vote won by YeR in the Oblast in the concurrent State Duma elections (32.7%) was among the lowest in the Federation. Misharin resigned in May 2012. The returning federal President, Vladimir Putin, appointed Yevgenii Kuivashev, hitherto Presidential Representative to the Urals Federal Okrug, as Acting Governor; the regional Legislative Assembly confirmed his appointment on 29 May.

The election to the mayoralty of Yekaterinburg held in September 2013 was a focus of national attention, as the preferred candidate of the federal authorities and YeR failed to be elected. The victor was Yevgenii Roizman, a former State Duma deputy and activist who had established an anti-narcotics and rehabilitation centre, and who had previously been charged with inciting inter-ethnic hatred.

In August 2017, several weeks before a gubernatorial election in which Kuivashev was returned to office, Roizman criticized the requirement for candidates to collect the signatures of at least 5% of local parliamentary deputies, claiming that it prevented any strong opponents of the incumbent from contesting the election; the regional election commission had rejected his own candidacy. In May 2018 Roizman resigned as Mayor of Yekaterinburg, after the regional Legislative Assembly voted to abolish direct elections to the post.

In elections to the Legislative Assembly held on 9 September 2018 YeR obtained 31.6% of the proportional vote, ahead of the KPRF, with 23.0% and SR, with 20.7%. Some 35 of the 49 deputies joined the YeR parliamentary faction by the end of the year. By the next legislative elections, held on 19 September 2021, YeR's support had increased slightly, to 35.6% of the proportional vote; the KPRF obtained 23.0%. By the end of the year 33 of the 50 deputies had joined the YeR faction.

In August 2022 Roizman, who remained a prominent figure in Yekaterinburg, was detained on charges of 'discrediting the army' (a charge for which a custodial sentence may be awarded), after he described the Russian military actions in Ukraine as an 'invasion' and a 'war'. He was, in effect, placed under house arrest pending a trial, and in November was officially designated by the Ministry of Justice as a 'foreign agent'. His trial commenced in April 2023, and concluded in May, when he was found guilty and fined 260,000 roubles (around US $3,250), and prohibited from attending public events or using the internet.

On 11 September 2022 Kuivashev was re-elected as Governor with 65.8% of the votes cast, defeating four other candidates.

ECONOMY

In 2021 Sverdlovsk Oblast's gross regional product (GRP) amounted to 3,038,443m. roubles, equivalent to an estimated 710,381 roubles per head. The most important industrial centres are at Yekaterinburg, Nizhnii Tagil, Pervouralsk and Serov. At the end of 2021 there were 3,511 km of railways in the Oblast. There is an international airport, Koltsovo, near Yekaterinburg.

The Oblast's agriculture comprises mainly animal husbandry and grain production and employed 2.7% of the workforce and contributed 2.3% of GRP in 2021. The main industries are ferrous and non-ferrous metallurgy, the production of electrical energy, mechanical engineering, food processing, and the production of steel, copper and other ores, bauxite, asbestos, petroleum, peat and coal. There is a significant defence sector and some extraction of gold and platinum. In 2006 the titanium producer based in the Oblast, VSMPO-AVISMA (now part of the Rostekh—Rostec State Corporation), entered into a joint venture with the US aircraft manufacturer Boeing to produce aircraft parts. In 2019 a further joint venture between the two companies to manufacture titanium aeroplane fittings was announced; co-operation with Boeing was suspended in March 2022 in connection with the Russian invasion of Ukraine that had commenced in the previous month. Industry employed 31.6% of the workforce and contributed 42.6% of GRP in 2021, when manufacturing employed 20.2% of the workforce and contributed 31.7% of GRP.

The economically active population numbered 2,015,147 in 2022, when 3.5% of the labour force were unemployed, while the average monthly wage was 55,308 roubles. There was a budgetary surplus of 16,933.7m. roubles in 2021, when export trade amounted to US $9,287m. (of which 18.0% was with countries of the CIS), while import trade amounted to $8,011m. (of which 14.2% was with CIS countries).

DIRECTORY

Governor: YEVGENII V. KUIVASHEV.

Office of the Governor: 620031 Sverdlovsk obl., Yekaterinburg, pl. Oktyabrskaya 1; tel. (343) 354-00-84; fax (343) 354-02-23; e-mail so@midural.ru; internet gubernator96.ru; internet midural.ru.

Legislative Assembly: 620031 Sverdlovsk obl., Yekaterinburg, ul. B. Yeltsina 10; tel. (343) 354-75-60; e-mail zsso@zsso.ru; internet zsso.ru; Chair. LYUDMILA V. BABUSHKINA.

State Duma Representatives (7): ANDREI G. ALSHEVSKIKH (YeR), LEV I. KOVPAK (YeR), SERGEI V. CHEPIKOV (YeR), KONSTANTIN YU. ZAKHAROV (YeR), MAKSIM A. IVANOV (YeR), ZELIMKHAN A. MUTSOYEV (YeR), ANTON V. SHIPULIN (YeR).

Federation Council Representatives: ALEKSANDR G. VYSOKINSKII, VIKTOR A. SHEPTIN.

Tyumen Oblast

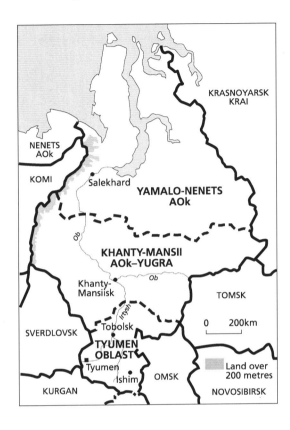

Tyumen Oblast is situated in the Western Siberian Plain, extending from the Kara Sea in the north to the border with Kazakhstan in the south. Much of its territory comprises the Khanty-Mansii Autonomous Okrug—Yugra and the Yamalo-Nenets Autonomous Okrug. To the west (going south to north) lie Kurgan and Sverdlovsk Oblasts, the Republic of Komi and the Nenets Autonomous Okrug—part of Archangel Oblast; to the east lie Omsk and Tomsk Oblasts and Krasnoyarsk Krai. The region has numerous rivers, its major ones being the Ob and the Irtysh. Much of its territory is taiga (forested marshland). The Oblast occupies 1,464,173 sq km (565,320 sq miles). At January 2023 its population was an estimated 3,851,234 and the population density 2.6 per sq km. Some 81.0% of the population was urban in 2023. The administrative centre, Tyumen, had an estimated 855,618 inhabitants at January 2023. Of residents who stated their ethnicity at the 2021 census, 76.4% were Russian, 6.4% Tatar, 2.3% Ukrainian, 1.3% Bashkir, 1.2% Nenets, 1.1% Azeri, 1.0% Khanty, 1.0% were Tajik, and 0.7% were Kazakh. The territory is in the time zone UTC+5.

HISTORY

Tyumen city was founded in 1585 on the site of a Tatar settlement, and subsequently became an important centre for trade with the Chinese Empire. Tyumen Oblast was formed on 14 August 1944.

On 21 October 1993 the Oblast Soviet repealed its earlier condemnation of government action against the federal parliament but refused to disband itself. Eventually, a new assembly, the Regional Duma, was elected.

From the mid-1990s the exact nature of the relationship between Tyumen Oblast and the two Autonomous Okrugs, which wished to retain a greater share of the income from their wealth of natural resources, became a source of intra-elite contention. In 1997 the two Autonomous Okrugs boycotted the oblast gubernatorial election. In 1998 Sergei Korepanov, the former Chairman of the Yamalo-Nenets legislature, was elected Chairman of the Regional Duma. At the gubernatorial election, held in January 2001, Sergei Sobyanin, a former speaker of the Khanty-Mansii legislature and the First Deputy Presidential Representative in the Urals Federal Okrug, defeated the incumbent Governor, Leonid Roketskii. In February 2005 the Regional Duma approved President Vladimir Putin's nomination of Sobyanin to a further term as Governor.

On 14 November 2005 Sobyanin was appointed head of the federal presidential administration (later becoming Mayor of Moscow); he was replaced as Governor by the hitherto Mayor of Tyumen, Vladimir Yakushev. In October 2010 President Dmitrii Medvedev nominated Yakushev to a second term as Governor; this was confirmed by a unanimous vote of the Regional Duma, and Yakushev was inaugurated to a new mandate on 24 November.

In September 2014 Yakushev was overwhelmingly elected Governor by popular vote. YeR secured some 56.6% of the votes cast on a proportional basis in elections to the Regional Duma held on 18 September 2016; the LDPR obtained 17.9%, the KPRF 11.8% and SR 8.8%. By the end of the year 39 of the 48 deputies had joined the YeR parliamentary faction.

Yakushev resigned as Governor on 18 May 2018, having been appointed to the federal Government as Minister of Construction, Housing and Utilities. On 29 May Putin appointed Aleksandr Moor, previously the Head of Tyumen City Municipal Establishment, as Acting Governor. On 9 September Moor was elected Governor, obtaining 65.9% of the votes cast. Artyom Zaitsev of the LDPR, who received 13.0%, was second.

At elections to the Regional Duma held on 19 September 2021, YeR secured 50.1% of the votes cast on the basis of proportional representation; the LDPR obtained 12.7%, the KPRF 11.9%, and SR 7.5%. By the end of the year 38 of the 48 deputies had joined the YeR faction, four that of the LDPR, four that of the KPRF, and two that of SR.

On 10 September 2023 Moor, the candidate of YeR, was re-elected Governor with 78.8% of the votes cast, defeating three other candidates.

ECONOMY

All figures in this survey include data for the two Autonomous Okrugs, which are also treated separately. Tyumen Oblast was considered to have great economic potential, owing to its vast hydrocarbons and timber reserves (mainly located in the Autonomous Okrugs). In 2021 Tyumen Oblast's gross regional product (GRP) amounted to 11,349,439m. roubles, equivalent to 2,992,775 roubles per head. Its main industrial centres are at Tyumen, Tobolsk, Surgut, Nizhnevartovsk (the last two in the Khanty-

Mansii Autonomous Okrug—Yugra) and Nadym (in the Yamalo-Nenets Autonomous Okrug). At the end of 2021 there were 2,442 km of railways in the Oblast.

Agriculture employed 2.6% of the workforce and contributed 0.6% of GRP in 2021. The region is the largest producer of oil and natural gas and of electrical energy in Russia. (Production of all three resources was concentrated in the two autonomous okrugs.) Industry employed 38.5% of the workforce and contributed 80.9% of GRP in 2021, when manufacturing employed 7.0% of the workforce and contributed 6.1% of GRP.

The economically active population amounted to 1,901,152 in 2022, when 2.7% of the workforce were unemployed, while the average monthly wage was 94,962 roubles. There was a budgetary surplus of 24,366.5m. roubles in 2021, when export trade amounted to US $24,828m. (of which 2.1% was with countries of the CIS), while import trade amounted to $3,579m. (of which 3.9% was with CIS countries).

DIRECTORY

Governor: ALEKSANDR V. MOOR.

Office of the Governor: 625004 Tyumen, ul. Volodarskogo 45; tel. (3452) 55-71-73; fax (3452) 46-55-42; e-mail kancelaria@72to.ru; internet gubernator.admtyumen.ru; internet admtyumen.ru.

Regional Duma: 625003 Tyumen, ul. Respubliki 52; tel. (3452) 45-50-81; fax (3452) 46-51-31; e-mail inbox@duma72.ru; internet duma72.ru; Chair. FUAT G. SAIFITDINOV.

State Duma Representatives (2): NIKOLAI G. BRYKIN (YeR), IVAN I. KVITKA (YeR).

Federation Council Representatives: PAVEL V. TARAKANOV, DMITRII YU. GORITSKII.

Khanty-Mansii Autonomous Okrug—Yugra

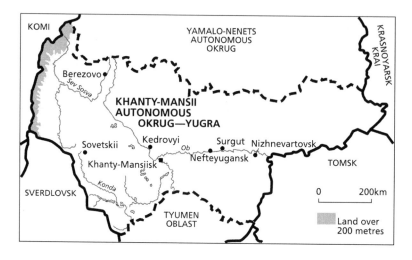

The Khanty-Mansii Autonomous Okrug—Yugra is situated in the Western Siberian Plain and the Ob-Irtysh river basin. The district forms part of Tyumen Oblast. The Yamalo-Nenets Autonomous Okrug (also part of Tyumen Oblast) lies to the north, while to the south lies the 'core' area of Tyumen Oblast. The Republic of Komi is to the west and Sverdlovsk to the south-west; to the south-east lies Tomsk and to the east Krasnoyarsk Krai. The district has numerous lakes, and much of its territory is Arctic tundra (frozen steppe) and taiga (forested marshland). The Autonomous Okrug occupies 534,801 sq km (206,488 sq miles). At January 2023 it had an estimated population of 1,730,353 and a population density of 3.2 per sq km. Some 92.2% of the population was urban in 2023. The administrative centre, Khanty-Mansiisk, had an estimated 109,745 inhabitants at January 2023. Larger cities in the Okrug include Surgut (406,938), Nizhnevartovsk (287,095) and Nefteyugansk (124,989). Of residents who stated their ethnicity at the 2021 census, 70.3% were Russian, 6.3% were Tatar, 3.3% Ukrainian, 2.4% Bashkir, 1.7% Tajik, 1.7% Azeri, 1.5% Khanty, 1.2% Lezgin, 1.1% Kumyk, 1.0% Uzbek, 0.9% Mansi, and 0.8% were Nogai. The Khanty and the Mansi languages are grouped together as an Ob-Ugrian subdivision of the Ugrian division of the Finno-Ugrian group. The Khanty-Mansii Autonomous Okrug—Yugra is in the time zone UTC+5.

HISTORY

The Khanty-Mansii region, known as Yugra in the 11th–15th centuries, came under Russian control from the late 16th century, as Russian fur traders established themselves in western Siberia. Attempts were made to assimilate the Khanty and Mansi into Russian culture, and many were forcibly converted to Orthodox Christianity. The modern territory was created in December 1930, as the East Vogul National

Autonomous Okrug. The territory became the Khanty-Mansii National Okrug in 1943, and an Autonomous Okrug in 1977, Yugra being appended to its designation in 2003.

After the Second World War the district became heavily industrialized, causing widespread damage to fish catches and reindeer pastures. In 1996 the okrug authorities appealed to the Constitutional Court against Tyumen Oblast's attempt to legislate for the control of district petroleum and natural gas reserves, and a protracted dispute ensued. As in the neighbouring Yamalo-Nenets Autonomous Okrug, the exact nature of the constitutional relationship between the Khanty-Mansii Autonomous Okrug and Tyumen Oblast remained ambiguous.

Aleksandr Filipenko, the head of the district administration appointed in December 1991, was returned to power in a elections in 1996 and 2000. Filipenko was more resistant than his counterpart in the Yamalo-Nenets Autonomous Okrug to the idea of a union with Tyumen Oblast: as the wealthiest of the three entities, Khanty-Mansii Autonomous Okrug would gain little from a merger. A power-sharing treaty, signed by representatives of the three entities in July 2004 and subsequently ratified by the three regional legislatures, delayed any possible unification until after the end of 2010. In February 2005 the District Duma unanimously endorsed President Vladimir Putin's nomination of Filipenko to a further term of office.

In February 2010 the District Duma unanimously endorsed President Dmitrii Medvedev's nomination of Nataliya Komarova, a YeR State Duma deputy, as Governor, to succeed Filipenko; she assumed office in March.

In December 2014, following the approval of legislation to that end by the State Duma (the proposals having first been approved by the District Duma and the Regional Duma of Tyumen Oblast), it was announced that future governors of the Autonomous Okrug would be elected indirectly, by members of the District Duma, from among three candidates proposed by the federal President. (Similar procedures were agreed in the Yamalo-Nenets Autonomous Okrug.) In September 2015, under these arrangements, the District Duma elected Komarova to a further term as Governor.

YeR secured some 46.9% of the votes cast on the basis of proportional representation at elections to the District Duma held on 18 September 2016; the LDPR obtained 25.3%, the KPRF 11.5%, and SR 8.1%. By the end of the year 25 of the 38 deputies had joined the YeR parliamentary faction.

Islamic State claimed responsibility for an attack in Surgut in August 2017, in which eight people were stabbed.

On 13 September 2020 the District Duma re-elected Komarova to a further gubernatorial term. At elections to the District Duma held on 19 September 2021, YeR secured 40.2% of the votes cast on the basis of proportional representation; the KPRF obtained 17.2%, the LDPR 14.6%, SR 7.7% and the RPPS 7.5%. By the end of the year 35 of the 49 deputies had joined the YeR faction and eight that of the KPRF.

ECONOMY

The district economy is based on industry, particularly on the extraction and refining of petroleum. In 2021 the district's gross regional product (GRP) amounted to 5,651,897m. roubles, equivalent to 3,334,557 roubles per head. The main industrial centre is at the petroleum-producing town of Surgut. The major river port is at Nizhnevartovsk. At the end of 2021 there were 1,084 km of railways in the Autonomous Okrug.

Agriculture in the district, which employed 1.3% of the workforce and contributed 0.2% of GRP in 2021, consists almost entirely of fishing. The extraction of petroleum and natural gas and the production of electricity are the principal areas of industrial activity. The district is a major producer of electrical energy, oil, and natural gas. The production of electrical energy amounted to 88,500m. kWh in 2013. Industry employed 42.2% of the workforce and contributed 83.4% of GRP in 2021, when manufacturing employed 5.9% of the workforce andcontributed 1.5% of GRP.

The economically active population of the district numbered 892,904 in 2022, when 2.0% of the labour force were unemployed, while the average monthly wage was 97,562 roubles. There was a budgetary deficit of 2,238.5m. roubles in 2021, when export trade amounted to US $17,484m. (of which 2.1% was with countries of the CIS), while import trade amounted to $459m. (of which 15.4% was with CIS countries).

DIRECTORY

Governor: Natalya V. Komarova.

Office of the Governor: 628011 Tyumen obl., Khanty-Mansii AO—Yugra, Khanty-Mansiisk, ul. Mira 5; tel. (3467) 33-20-95; fax (3467) 39-20-00; e-mail kominf@admhmao.ru; internet admhmao.ru.

District Duma: 628006 Tyumen obl., Khanty-Mansii AO—Yugra, Khanty-Mansiisk, ul. Mira 5; tel. (3467) 39-28-29; fax (3467) 33-16-84; e-mail dumahmao@dumahmao.ru; internet dumahmao.ru; Chair. Boris S. Khokhryakov.

State Duma Representatives (2): Pavel N. Zavalnyi (YeR), Vadim N. Shuvalov (YeR).

Federation Council Representatives: Eduard V. Isakov, Aleksandr V. Novyukhov.

Yamalo-Nenets Autonomous Okrug

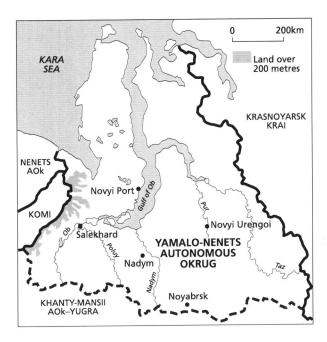

The Yamalo-Nenets Autonomous Okrug is situated on the Western Siberian Plain on the lower reaches of the Ob river. It forms part of Tyumen Oblast. The territory lies on the Asian side of the Ural Mountains and has a deeply indented northern coastline, the western section, the Yamal Peninsula, being separated from the eastern section by the Gulf of Ob. The rest of Tyumen Oblast, including the Khanty-Mansii Autonomous Okrug—Yugra, lies to the south. To the west lie the Nenets Autonomous Okrug (within Archangel Oblast) and the Republic of Komi, and to the east Krasnoyarsk Krai. The district occupies 769,250 sq km (297,009 sq miles). At January 2023 it had an estimated population of 512,387 inhabitants and a population density of 0.7 per sq km. Some 84.7% of the population was urban in 2023. The administrative centre, Salekhard, had an estimated 48,619 inhabitants at January 2023. The largest cities in the Autonomous Okrug were Novyi Urengoi (106,764) and Noyabrsk (101,235). Of residents who stated their ethnicity at the 2021 census, 62.9% were Russian, 8.9% Nenets, 4.7% Tatar, 4.5% Ukrainian, 2.5% Khanty, 1.7% Azeri, 1.5% Bashkir, 1.2% Kumyk, 0.9% Nogai, and 0.9% were Komi. The Yamalo-Nenets Autonomous Okrug is in the time zone UTC+5.

HISTORY

The Nenets were traditionally a nomadic people, who were totally dominated by Russia from the 17th century. The Yamalo-Nenets National Okrug was formed within Tyumen Oblast on 10 December 1930; it became an Autonomous Okrug in 1977. Environmental concerns provoked protests in the 1980s and 1990s, and prompted the district authorities (comprising an administration and, from 1994, an elected Duma) to seek greater control over the abundant natural resources, with the principal dispute being with the central Tyumen Oblast authorities.

At the gubernatorial election of 26 March 2000, the incumbent, Yurii Neyeyolov, who was regarded as sympathetic to the interests of the largest employer in the district, the domestic gas monopoly Gazprom, was overwhelmingly re-elected. In early 2004 Neyeyolov participated in several meetings with Sergei Sobyanin, Governor of Tyumen Oblast, to discuss proposals for the formal merger of the Oblast with its two constituent Autonomous Okrugs. However, a power-sharing treaty, signed by representatives of the three entities in July and subsequently ratified by the three regional legislatures, delayed any possible unification.

In March 2005 the District State Duma unanimously endorsed President Vladimir Putin's nomination of Neyeyolov to a further term as Governor. Dmitrii Kobylkin, hitherto a municipal leader, succeeded Neyeyolov as Governor in March 2010, after the district legislature approved his nomination.

In December 2014, following the approval of legislation by the federal State Duma (the proposals having first been approved by the district legislature and that of Tyumen Oblast), it was announced that future governors of the Autonomous Okrug would be elected indirectly by members of the Autonomous District Legislative Assembly (as the District State Duma had been renamed), from among three candidates proposed by the President. (Similar procedures were agreed in the Khanty-Mansii Autonomous Okrug—Yugra.) In March 2015, upon the expiry of Kobylkin's term of office, President Vladimir Putin requested that he remain in post in an acting capacity, until a new district legislature had been elected. In elections to the district legislature, held on 13 September, only two parties won deputies in proportional voting: YeR, with 70.1% of the votes, and the LDPR, with 13.3%. On 1 October the new legislature, in which 17 of the 22 deputies had joined the YeR parliamentary faction, confirmed Kobylkin to a new gubernatorial term.

In May 2018, after Kobylkin was appointed to the federal Government as Minister of Natural Resources and Ecology, Putin appointed Dmitrii Artyukhov, hitherto a Deputy Governor, as his acting successor. Artyukhov was elected Governor by the Autonomous District Legislative Assembly on 9 September.

In elections to the Autonomous District Legislative Assembly, held on 13 September 2020, the proportional vote for YeR declined slightly, to 64.6%. The second placed party was again the LDPR, with 15.3%, ahead of the KPRF, with 8.8%, and SR, with 6.1%. When the new chamber convened, 18 deputies joined the YeR faction, and two that of the LDPR; the factions of the KPRF and SR each comprised one deputy.

Artyukhov of YeR was re-elected Governor by 17 of the 21 votes cast in the Autonomous District Legislative Assembly, defeating two other candidates, on 10 September 2023.

ECONOMY

In 2021 the territory's gross regional product (GRP) amounted to 4,161,530m. roubles, equivalent to 7,572,420 roubles per head, the second highest in the Federation. At the end of 2021 there were 481 km of railways in the Autonomous Okrug. The major industrial centres include Noyabrsk, Novyi Urengoi and Urengoi.

Agriculture consists almost entirely of fishing. The sector employed 1.3% of the workforce and contributed 0.1% of GRP in 2021. The district's main industries are the extraction of natural gas and, to a lesser extent, petroleum, and the production of electricity. The territory is a major producer of both natural gas and oil. The Yamal–Europe natural gas pipeline, of which the state-controlled Gazprom is the major shareholder, connects the gas fields of the territory with Frankfurt-an-der-Oder on the German–Polish border. In 2017 a liquefied natural gas venture in the port of Sabetta, 50.1% owned by Russian independent gas producer Novatek and funded by Chinese banks, commenced commercial operation. Industry employed 46.1% of the workforce and contributed 89.0% of GRP in 2021, when manufacturing employed 2.8% of the workforce and contributed 5.2% of GRP.

The economically active population numbered 310,249 in 2022, when 1.7% of the labour force were unemployed, while the average monthly wage was 131,516 roubles, the second highest in the Federation. There was a budgetary surplus of 20,390.7m. roubles in 2021, when export trade amounted to US $5,722m. (of which less than 0.1% was with CIS countries), while import trade amounted to $1,977m. (of which 0.1% was with CIS countries).

DIRECTORY

Governor: DMITRII A. ARTYUKHOV.

Office of the Governor: 629008 Tyumen obl., Yamalo-Nenets AO, Salekhard, pr. Molodezhi 9; tel. (34922) 2-26-00; fax (34922) 4-52-89; e-mail apparat@apparat.gov.yanao.ru; internet yanao.ru.

Autonomous District Legislative Assembly: 629008 Tyumen obl., Yamalo-Nenets AO, Salekhard, ul. Respubliki 72; tel. (34922) 5-46-46; fax (34922) 5-46-80; e-mail sobranie@zs-yamal.ru; internet zs.yanao.ru; Chair. SERGEI M. YAMKIN.

State Duma Representative (1): DMITRII V. POGORELYI (YeR).

Federation Council Representatives: GRIGORII P. LEDKOV, VLADIMIR A. PUSHKAREV.

SIBERIAN FEDERAL OKRUG

Presidential Representative to the Siberian Federal Okrug: ANATOLII A. SERYSHEV, 630091 Novosibirsk, ul. Derzhavina 18; tel. (383) 220-17-80; internet sfo.gov.ru.

Republic of Altai

The Republic of Altai is situated in the Altai Mountains. It borders Kazakhstan to the south-west and Mongolia to the south-east. There is a short border with the People's Republic of China to the south. Kemerovo Oblast lies to the north, Khakasiya and Tyva to the north-east, and Altai Krai to the north-west. The Republic includes the highest peak in Siberia, Belukha, at 4,506 m (14,783 feet). The Republic occupies 92,903 sq km (35,870 sq miles). At January 2023 it had an estimated population of 210,769 and a population density of 2.3 per sq km. Only 30.8% of the population was urban in 2023—a lower proportion than in any other federal subject. The administrative centre, Gorno-Altaisk, had an estimated 64,957 inhabitants at January 2023. Of residents who stated their ethnicity at the 2021 census, 53.7% were Russian, 37.0% were Altai (including 1.7% who were Tubalar and 1.3% who were Telengit), and 6.4% were Kazakh. The Altai people can be divided into two distinct groups: the Northern Altai, or Tubalars, and the Southern Altai, including the Telengit. The languages spoken by both groups are from the Turkic branch of the Uralo-Altaic family. Although the traditional religions of the Altai were animist or Lamaism (Tibetan Buddhism), many converted to Christianity, and the dominant religion in the Republic is Russian Orthodoxy. The Republic is in the time zone UTC+7.

HISTORY

From the 11th century the Altai peoples inhabited Dzungaria (Sungaria—now mainly in the People's Republic of China). The region was under Mongol control until 1389, when it was conquered by the Tatar forces of Timur or Tamerlane 'the Great'; it subsequently became a Kalmyk confederation. In the first half of the 18th century many Altai moved westwards, almost as far as the Urals. In 1758 most of Dzungaria was incorporated into the Chinese province of Xinjiang (Sinkiang). China embarked on a war aimed at exterminating the Altai peoples. Only a few thousand survived, finding refuge in the Altai Mountains or in Russian territory. Russia annexed the region in 1866. In the early 1900s Burkhanism or Ak Jang (White Faith), a nationalist religious movement, pledging to liberate the Altai from Russian control, emerged. In February 1918 a Constituent Congress of the High Altai, which demanded the establishment of an Oirot Republic, to include the Altai, the Khakass and the Tyvans, was convened. In July 1922 the Soviet Government established an Oirot Autonomous Oblast as part of an Altai Krai (province). In 1948 the Oblast was renamed the Gorno-Altai (Mountainous Altai) Autonomous Oblast.

The region adopted a declaration of sovereignty in October 1990, and became the Republic of Altai, separate from Altai Krai, in March 1992. A resolution adopted on 14 October 1993 provided for the establishment of the El Kurultai (State Assembly) as the highest body of power in the Republic. The new post of Head of the Republic, Chairman of the Government was introduced in August 1997; this position was assumed initially by Vladilen Volkov, Chairman of the El Kurultai since February. In December Semyon Zubakin was directly elected as Chairman of the Government. In February 2001 the El Kurultai approved amendments to the republican Constitution, in order to conform with federal norms.

In January 2002, in an election to the post of Head of the Republic, Mikhail Lapshin, the leader of the Agrarnaya Partiya Rossii (APR—Agrarian Party of Russia), defeated Zubakin, having obtained support from YeO-YeR (later YeR) and the KPRF. In December 2005 the El Kurultai overwhelmingly voted in favour of the candidate for Head of the Republic proposed by President Vladimir Putin, Aleksandr Berdnikov, a former republican Minister of Internal Affairs, who had been an unsuccessful candidate in the most recent election to the post. At elections to the El Kurultai, held in March 2006, YeR obtained 27.2% of the votes cast on the basis of proportional representation, followed by Rodina (Motherland), with 10.5%, and the APR, with 10.4%.

In January 2010 the El Kurultai voted to endorse Berdnikov's appointment to a further term as Head of the Republic. At elections to the El Kurultai, held in March, YeR obtained 44.4% of the votes cast to those seats elected on the basis of proportional representation; the KPRF was second, with 24.8%.

Berdnikov was elected Head of the Republic in a popular election in September 2014, obtaining 51.8% of the votes cast; the second-placed candidate, with 37.3%, was Vladimir Petrov of GP. In the concurrent elections to the El Kurultai 44.7% of the votes cast on a proportional basis were awarded to YeR. A total of 29 of the 41 deputies subsequently joined the YeR parliamentary faction.

On 20 March 2019 Berdnikov tendered his resignation. Putin appointed Oleg Khorokhordin, previously a federal government official, as Acting Head of the Republic, pending an election on 8 September, to be held concurrently with voting to the El Kurultai. Khorokhordin was elected Head of the Republic on that date, obtaining 58.8% of the votes cast. The second placed candidate was Viktor Romashkin of the

KPRF, who obtained 31.6%, a notably high share of support for that party. In the elections to the El Kurultai, YeR obtained 34.2% of the votes cast on a proportional basis, narrowly ahead of the KPRF, with 29.5%, and the LDPR, with 12.0%. Of the 41 deputies elected, 24 joined the parliamentary faction of YeR and five that of the KPRF.

ECONOMY

The Republic of Altai's gross regional product (GRP) amounted to 71,336m. roubles in 2021, or an estimated 322,413 roubles per head. The main industrial centre in the Republic is Gorno-Altaisk. There are no railways or airports in the Republic.

Agriculture is largely based around livestock breeding (of horses, deer, sheep and goats). Agriculture employed 15.7% of the workforce and contributed 11.5% of GRP in 2021. The export of the antlers of Siberian maral and sika deer, primarily to South-East Asia, is an important source of convertible currency. The mountainous terrain often prevents the easy extraction or transport of minerals, but there are important reserves of manganese, iron, silver, lead and wolfram (tungsten). Stone, lime, salt, sandstone, gold, mercury and non-ferrous metals are also produced. There are food processing and construction materials industries. Industry employed 14.9% of the workforce (a lower proportion than in any other federal subject) and contributed 13.7% of GRP in 2021, when manufacturing employed 4.8% of the workforce and contributed 2.3% of GRP.

The economically active population of the Republic numbered 85,725 in 2022, when the rate of unemployment was 9.8%, while the average monthly wage was 43,974 roubles. There was a budgetary surplus of 302.6m. roubles in 2021, when export trade amounted to US $76m. (of which 68.9% was with countries of the CIS), and import trade to $16m. (of which 43.0% was with CIS countries).

DIRECTORY

Head of the Republic: OLEG L. KHOROKHORDIN.

Office of the Head of the Republic: 649000 Rep. of Altai, Gorno-Altaisk, ul. Chaptynova 24; tel. (38822) 2-31-32; fax (38822) 9-87-28; e-mail root@apra.gorny.ru; internet altai-republic.ru.

El Kurultai (State Assembly): 649000 Rep. of Altai, Gorno-Altaisk, ul. E. Palkina 1; tel. and fax (38822) 2-77-80; e-mail info@elkurultay.ru; internet elkurultay.ru; Chair. ARTUR P. KOKHOYEV.

State Duma Representative (1): ROMANI V. PTITSYN (YeR).

Federation Council Representatives: TATYANA A. GIGEL, VLADIMIR V. POLETAYEV.

Republic of Khakasiya

The Republic of Khakasiya is situated in the west of the Minusinsk hollow, on the left bank of the River Yenisei. It lies on the eastern slopes of the Kuznetsk Alatau and the northern slopes of the Western Sayan Mountains. Tyva lies to the south-east, the Republic of Altai to the south-west, Kemerovo Oblast to the west, and Krasnoyarsk Krai to the north and east. Khakasiya occupies 61,569 sq km (23,772 sq miles). At January 2023 it had an estimated population of 530,233 and a population density of 8.6 per sq km. Some 68.7% of the population was urban in 2023. The capital, Abakan, had an estimated 185,348 inhabitants at January 2023. Of residents who stated their ethnicity at the 2021 census, 82.1% were Russian, 12.7% were Khakass, and 0.7% were German. The Khakass language is primarily derived from the Uigur group of Eastern Hunnic languages of the Turkic family. Khakasiya is in the time zone UTC+7.

HISTORY

The Khakass or Khakasiyans (traditionally known as the Minusinsk, the Turki, or the Yenisei or Abakan Tatars) were semi-nomadic hunters, fishermen and livestock-breeders, and attained power through trade with Central Asia and the Chinese Empire. Russian settlers arrived in the 17th century. The annexation of Khakass territory by the Russians was completed during the reign of Peter (Pyotr) I 'the Great' (1682–1725). The Russians imposed Orthodox Christianity on the Khakass. After the construction of the Trans-Siberian Railway in the 1890s, the Khakass were heavily outnumbered. A Khakass national uezd (district) was established in 1923, becoming an okrug in 1925, and an autonomous oblast within Krasnoyarsk Krai in 1930. In 1992 it was upgraded to the status of a Republic, having declared its sovereignty in July 1991. The Republic adopted a Constitution in May 1995.

Aleksei Lebed, an independent candidate and the brother of Aleksandr Lebed (Governor of Krasnoyarsk Krai in 1998–2002), was elected Chairman of the Government (Head of the Republic) in 1996 and re-elected in 2000. Lebed was again re-elected on 26 December 2004. In concurrent elections to the republican legislature, YeR was the most successful grouping, closely followed by the Khakasiya bloc. The rate of participation in both elections was around 30%.

The Supreme Council confirmed President Dmitrii Medvedev's nomination of Viktor Zimin, hitherto a YeR State Duma deputy, as Head of the Republic in December 2008. He assumed office on 15 January 2009; Lebed was to serve as Khakasiya's representative in the State Duma. At the elections to the regional Duma held on 1 March, YeR secured 57.3% of votes cast on a proportional basis.

On 8 September 2013 Zimin was elected Head of the Republic, obtaining 63.4% of the votes cast. In concurrent elections to the Supreme Council, which was reduced in size from 83 to 53 deputies, YeR won 46.3% of the proportional vote. A total of 36 of the 53 deputies subsequently joined the YeR parliamentary faction.

Meanwhile, attempts to bring to justice those responsible for an explosion at the Sayano-Shushenskaya hydroelectric power station, situated on the border with Krasnoyarsk Krai, in 2009, as a result of which 75 people died, progressed only slowly; in December 2014 six managers and engineers received custodial sentences of up to six years, although three of them were granted amnesties shortly afterwards.

Elections to both the post of Head of the Republic and to the republican Supreme Council were held on 9 September 2018. In the elections to the Supreme Council, the KPRF was placed first, with 31.0% of the votes cast on a proportional basis, followed by YeR, with 25.5%, the LDPR, with 21.0%, the KR, with 8.0%, and SR, with 7.1%. The sharp decline in support for YeR in the Republic (one of three federal subjects in which it was surpassed by the KPRF in legislative elections on this occasion) was attributed, particularly, to discontent at plans to raise the national retirement age. Only 18 of the 50 deputies had joined the YeR parliamentary faction by the end of the year, meaning that the Assembly was one of the few regional legislatures in which the party did not enjoy a majority; 15 deputies joined the faction of the KPRF, eight that of the LDPR, two that of the KR, and two that of SR.

In the concurrent election for the post of Head of the Republic held on 9 September 2018, the KPRF candidate, Valentin Konovalov, was placed first, with 44.8% of the votes cast, ahead of Zimin, who received 32.4%. These two candidates were to proceed to a run-off. On 21 September 2018 Zimin announced his withdrawal from the election, owing to ill health. Another run-off election was subsequently scheduled for 7 October, to be contested by Konovalov and Andrei Filyagin of SR, the third-placed candidate in the first round of voting. Filyagin also withdrew from the contest on 2 October, and on 3 October President Putin appointed the federal Deputy Minister of North Caucasus Affairs, Mikhail Razvozhayev, as acting Head of the Republic. A further run-off poll scheduled for 21 October was again cancelled, as the final candidate of the first round, Aleksandr Myakhar of the Partiya Rosta (Party of Growth), declined to participate. Finally, on 11 November Konovalov proceeded to a second round unopposed, with a vote being held in which the options were to support or to oppose his candidacy. Some 57.6% of the votes were cast in support of Konovalov, the first occasion since 1997 in which a regional leader was elected unopposed.

On 10 September 2023 Konovalov of the KPRF was re-elected Head of the Republic with 63.1% of the votes cast, defeating Mikhail Molchanov of the LDPR, who received 14.3% of the votes, and Vladimir Grudinin of the KR, with 12.0%. A YeR candidate, State Duma deputy Sergei Sokol, had withdrawn his candidacy shortly before the poll on health grounds (although his defeat and a consequent further electoral crisis had been predicted). Following concurrent elections to the Regional Duma, YeR held 34 of the 50 seats in the expanded chamber, substantially increasing its representation there and ensuring it a majority; the rate of participation was 39.6%.

ECONOMY

Khakasiya's gross regional product (GRP) amounted to 307,517m. roubles in 2021, or an estimated 580,016 roubles per head. Khakasiya's major industrial centres are at Abakan, Sorsk, Sayanogorsk and Chernogorsk. At the end of 2021 there were 667 km of railways in the Republic.

The Republic's agriculture consists mainly of animal husbandry, and potato and vegetable production. Agriculture employed 6.0% of the workforce and contributed 2.7% of GRP in 2021. The Republic's main industries are ore mining and non-ferrous metallurgy. Electricity generation is also important; the Sayano-Shushenskaya plant is the fourth largest hydroelectric power station in the world. However, a large explosion at the plant in 2009 restricted operations, as three of the 10 power-generating units were destroyed; the repair of the plant was only completed in November 2014. There are significant reserves of coal and iron ore, while other mineral reserves include molybdenum, lead, zinc, barytes, aluminium and clay. There is also the potential for extraction of petroleum and natural gas. The territory is also renowned for its handicrafts (wood-carving and embroidery). Industry employed 25.9% of the workforce and contributed 54.9% of GRP in 2021, when manufacturing employed 11.2% of the workforce and contributed 20.6% of GRP.

The Republic's economically active population numbered 246,765 in 2022, when the rate of unemployment was 3.3%, while the average monthly wage was 54,522 roubles. There was a budgetary surplus of 2,131.8m. roubles in 2021, when export trade amounted to US $2,682m. (of which 2.4% was with countries of the CIS), and import trade to $419m. (of which only 2.1% was with CIS countries).

DIRECTORY

Head of the Republic, Chairman of the Government: Valentin O. Konovalov.

Office of the Head of the Republic: 655019 Khakasiya, Abakan, pr. Lenina 67; tel. (3902) 22-33-21; fax (3902) 22-50-91; e-mail gov@r-19.ru; internet r-19.ru.

Supreme Council: 655019 Khakasiya, Abakan, pr. Lenina 67; tel. (3902) 22-53-35; fax (3902) 24-30-71; e-mail info@vskhakasia.ru; internet vskhakasia.ru; Chair. Sergei M. Sokol.

State Duma Representative (1): (vacant).

Federation Council Representatives: Aleksandr A. Zhukov, Oleg A. Zemtsov.

Republic of Tyva

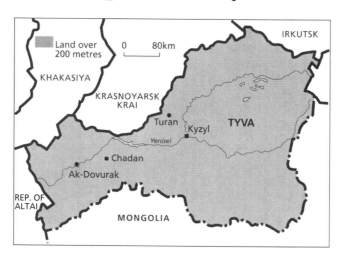

The Republic of Tyva is situated in the south of eastern Siberia in the Sayan Mountains. Tyva has an international border with Mongolia to the south and east. The Republic of Altai lies to the west, Khakasiya to the north-west and Krasnoyarsk Krai to the north. Irkutsk Oblast lies to the north-east and Buryatiya forms part of the eastern border. Tyva's major river is the Yenisei, which rises in the Eastern Sayan range. The territory of the Republic consists of a series of high mountain valleys. The Republic has more than 12,000 rivers and 8,400 freshwater lakes. Tyva occupies 168,604 sq km (65,098 sq miles). At January 2023 it had an estimated population of 337,271 and a population density of 2.0 per sq km. Some 55.3% of the population was urban in 2023. The capital, Kyzyl, had an estimated 128,149 inhabitants at January 2023. Of residents who stated their ethnicity at the 2021 census, 88.7% were Tyvan (Tuvinian), including 2.3% who were Tozhu Tyvan, and 10.1% were Russian. Lamaism (Tibetan Buddhism) is the predominant religion in the Republic. The Tyvan language belongs to the Old Uigur group of the Turkic branch of the Uralo-Altaic linguistic family. The Republic is in the time zone UTC+7.

HISTORY

The Tyvans (known at various times as Soyons, Soyots and Uriankhais) emerged as an identifiable ethnic group in the early 18th century. The territory of what is now Tyva was occupied in turn between the sixth and the ninth centuries by the Turkish Khanate, the Chinese, the Uigurs and the Yenisei Kyrgyz. The Mongols controlled the region from 1207 to 1368. In the second half of the 17th century the Dzungarians (Sungarians) seized the area from the Altyn Khans. In 1758 the Manzhous (Manchus) annexed Dzungaria, and the territory thus became part of the Chinese Empire. Russian influence dates from the Treaty of Beijing (Peking) of 1860, after which trade links were developed and a number of Russians settled there. One year after the Chinese Revolution of 1911 Tyva declared its independence. In 1914, however, Russia established a protectorate over the territory, which then became the Tannu-Tuva

People's Republic. This was a nominally independent state until October 1944, when it was incorporated into the USSR as the Tuvinian Autonomous Oblast, directly subordinate to the federal authorities. It became a nominally Autonomous Soviet Socialist Republic within the Russian Soviet Federative Socialist Republic on 10 October 1961.

Tyvan nationalism became an increasingly prominent force in the Republic from the late 1980s, and a growth in support for the Tyvan Democratic Movement, founded in 1990, was accompanied by an increase in inter-ethnic tensions. A series of attacks against ethnic Russians and against state institutions during that year resulted in some 90 deaths, and led to much of the ethnic Russian population leaving the territory. The Republic declared sovereignty on 11 December 1990 and renamed itself the Republic of Tuva in August 1991. On 21 October 1993 the republican Supreme Soviet resolved that the Republic's name was Tyva, in preference to the Russified 'Tuva', and adopted a new Constitution providing for a legislature, the Supreme Khural, and a supreme constitutional body, the Grand Khural. The new parliament was elected on 12 December, when the new republican Constitution was approved by 62.2% of votes cast. Only 32.7%, however, voted in favour of the Federal Constitution.

A new Constitution, which removed Tyva's rights of self-determination and of secession, was approved by referendum in May 2001. Various constitutional amendments brought the Republic further into compliance with federal norms. The Supreme Khural was renamed the Grand Khural and was reconstituted as a bicameral legislature, comprising an upper chamber, the 130-member Chamber of Representatives, and a lower chamber, the 32-member Legislative Chamber. In March 2002 the incumbent Chairman of the Government, Sherig-ool Oorzhak, was elected to serve a third term of office. Elections to the bicameral legislature were held in June.

Further elections to the Grand Khural took place in 2006. The ruling YeR secured 46.4% of the votes cast on a proportional basis, ahead of the Rossiiskaya Partiya Zhizhni (RPZh—Russian Party of Life), with 32.3%. Five members of the republican branch of the RPZh declared a hunger strike in protest at alleged electoral malpractice, and the party (which subsequently merged into SR) boycotted the Grand Khural. In 2007, shortly before the expiry of Oorzhak's mandate, the Grand Khural approved President Vladimir Putin's nomination of Sholban Kara-ool of YeR as Chairman of the Republic's Government.

A referendum held in April 2010 approved, by 95.4% of the votes cast, extensive constitutional reforms, including the restructuring of the Grand Khural on a unicameral basis, a reduction in the total number of parliamentarians, from 162 to 32, and an increase in the powers of the Chairman of the republican Government. At the elections to the new legislature, conducted on 10 October, YeR obtained 77.4% of the votes cast on a proportional basis.

The Grand Khural unanimously voted to reappoint Kara-ool as Chairman of the Government in March 2012; he additionally adopted the title of Head of the Republic in April. In elections to the Grand Khural, held in September 2014, YeR was the only party to secure seats on a proportional basis, having won 84.0% of the votes cast. Overall, YeR obtained 31 of the 32 legislative seats. In a popular election held on 18 September 2016, Kara-ool was elected Head of the Republic by 85.7% of the votes cast.

In elections to the Grand Khural held on 8 September 2019, YeR obtained some 80.1% of the votes cast on a proportional basis; the only other party to win seats on this basis was the LDPR, with 7.8%. Some 29 of the deputies elected joined the parliamentary faction of YeR, and two that of the LDPR.

On 7 April 2021 Putin accepted the resignation of Kara-ool as Head of the Republic; he appointed the hitherto General Director of the local energy concern Tyvaenergosbyt (and a former of Mayor of Kyzyl), Vladislav Khovalyg, as his acting successor. On 19 September Khovalyg was confirmed in post as Head of the Republic, defeating four other candidates in a direct election with 86.8% of the votes cast. He assumed office on 28 September.

ECONOMY

Tyva's gross regional product (GRP) was 88,771m. roubles, or an estimated 267,795 roubles per head, in 2021. The Republic's main industrial centres are at Kyzyl and Ak-Dovurak. There are no railways in Tyva.

Tyva's economy is relatively underdeveloped. Its agriculture consists mainly of animal husbandry, although forestry and hunting are also important. Agriculture employed 6.7% of the workforce and contributed 6.1% of GRP in 2021. Small-scale gold extraction was developed from the 1990s. Tyva's main industries are ore mining (asbestos, coal, cobalt and mercury), electricity production, food processing and non-ferrous metallurgy. In 2021 industry employed 14.2% of the workforce (the lowest level of any federal subject) and contributed 23.0% of GRP, when manufacturing employed 3.7% of the workforce and contributed 0.7% of GRP.

The economically active population of Tyva numbered 117,119 in 2022, when the rate of unemployment was 9.5% (the second highest rate in the Federation, after that of Ingushetiya), while the average monthly wage was 51,782 roubles. There was a budgetary deficit of 354.9m. roubles in 2021, when export trade amounted to US $140m. (of which 64.7% was with CIS countries), and import trade to $12m. (of which 12.3% was with CIS countries).

DIRECTORY

Head of the Republic: VLADISLAV T. KHOVALYG.

Office of the Head of the Republic: 667000 Tyva, Kyzyl, ul. Chuldum 18; tel. (39422) 2-27-07; fax (39422) 2-13-54; e-mail ods@tuva.ru; internet rtyva.ru.

Grand Khural (Parliament): 667000 Tyva, Kyzyl, ul. Lenina 32; tel. and fax (39422) 2-16-32; e-mail khural@inbox.ru; internet khural.rtyva.ru; Chair. KAN-OOL T. DAVAA.

State Duma Representative (1): ANDRIY N. SARYGLAR (YeR).

Federation Council Representatives: LYUDMILA B. NARUSOVA, DINA I. OYUN.

Altai Krai

Most of Altai Krai lies within the Western Siberian Plain. It has an international boundary to the south with Kazakhstan. Novosibirsk lies to the north, Kemerovo to the north-east and the Republic of Altai to the south-east. Its major river is the Ob. There are many thousands of lakes, about one-half of which are freshwater. About one-third of its total area is forested. In the east of the Krai are mountains, in the west steppe. The Krai occupies 167,996 sq km (64,864 sq miles). At January 2023 it had an estimated population of 2,130,950 and a population density of 12.7 per sq km. Some 58.3% of the population was urban in 2023. The administrative centre, Barnaul, had an estimated 623,057 inhabitants at January 2023. Other major cities are Biisk (181,678) and Rubtsovsk (124,687). Of residents who stated their ethnicity at the 2021 census, 95.5% were Russian, and 1.3% were German. (Only 0.1% were Altai.) Altai Krai is in the time zone UTC+7.

HISTORY

The territory of Altai Krai was annexed by Russia in 1738 (for more on the Altai people, see the Republic of Altai). The region was heavily industrialized during the Soviet period. Altai Krai was formed on 28 September 1937, at which time it included the territory of what is now the Republic of Altai. This territory, then known as the Gorno-Altai (Mountainous Altai) Autonomous Oblast, declared its sovereignty in 1990, and its secession from the Krai was formally recognized in 1992.

In March 1994 a new provincial legislature, the Legislative Assembly, comprising a lower chamber of 25 deputies and an upper chamber of 72 deputies, was elected to replace the provincial Soviet. The Chairman of the provincial Council of People's Deputies (the lower chamber), Aleksandr Surikov, a Communist, defeated the incumbent Governor, Lev Korshunov, in a gubernatorial election in 1996, and retained his post following an election in 2000. Later that year legislation was approved reforming the provincial legislature on a unicameral basis.

In the gubernatorial election of March–April 2004 Surikov was narrowly defeated by a comedian and actor, Mikhail Yevdokhimov. The victory of Yevdokhimov (which was opposed by the federal authorities) was regarded as indicating widespread dissatisfaction at the consequences of the extensive privatization programme implemented in the region in the early 1990s. However, the new Governor failed to bring about an improvement in the economic situation, and in March 2005 the leaders of the provincial branches of 21 political organizations, including YeR and the KPRF, urged President Vladimir Putin to dismiss Yevdokhimov. At the end of March the provincial legislature overwhelmingly approved a vote of no confidence in the Governor. A further vote of no confidence in Yevdokhimov was approved at the end of April, although the Governor stated that he would not resign. On 7 August Yevdokhimov was killed as a result of an automobile accident. Putin nominated Aleksandr Karlin, a former deputy Minister of Justice in the federal Government (a native of the Krai), as Governor; the provincial legislature confirmed this appointment in August.

YeR was the most successful party at elections to the Legislative Assembly held in March 2008, obtaining 53.4% of the votes cast. The KPRF was second, with 19.6%. In July 2009 the Legislative Assembly voted to confirm Karlin's appointment to a second term of office. At elections to the Legislative Assembly, held in December 2011, support for YeR declined to 39.8% of the vote, ahead of the KPRF, with 25.4%.

In a popular election held on 14 September 2014 Karlin was elected Governor, obtaining 73.0% of the votes cast. YeR secured 34.1% of the votes cast on a proportional basis in elections to the Legislative Assembly on 18 September 2016; the LDPR received 21.2%, the KPRF 21.0%, and SR 17.4%. A total of 42 of the 68 deputies had joined the YeR parliamentary faction by the end of the year.

Amid social discontent in the Krai, in March 2018 a regional ecological organization initiated a petition appealing to President Putin for the dismissal of Karlin, who was accused of economic mismanagement, and involvement in organized crime and corruption. After Karlin submitted his resignation on 30 May, Putin appointed Viktor Tomenko, hitherto the Chairman of the Government of Krasnoyarsk Krai, as Acting Governor. On 9 September Tomenko was elected Governor, obtaining 53.6% of the votes cast; the second-placed candidate, Vladmir Semyonov of the LDPR, received 16.2%.

At elections to the Legislative Assembly held on 19 September 2021, YeR secured 34.3% of the votes cast on the basis of proportional representation; the KPRF obtained 24.2%, SR 13.7%, the KR 12.1%, and the LDPR 10.7%. By the end of the year 31 of the 68 deputies had joined the YeR faction (therefore denying it a majority), 23 that of the KPRF, five that of SR, four that of the KR, and four that of the LDPR. On 10 September 2023 Tomenko, the candidate of YeR, was re-elected Governor with 76.2% of the votes cast, defeating three other candidates.

ECONOMY

Altai Krai's gross regional product (GRP) amounted to 845,430m. roubles in 2021, equivalent to an estimated 370,434 roubles per head. Its main industrial centres are Barnaul, Biisk, Rubtsovsk and Novoaltaisk. At the end of 2021 there were 1,567 km of railways in the Krai. There is an international airport at Barnaul and major river-ports at Barnaul and Biisk. A natural gas pipeline connects Tyumen to Barnaul.

The Krai's principal crops are grain, flax, sunflowers and sugar beet. Animal husbandry, including fur-farming and beekeeping, is also important. Agriculture employed 11.5% of the workforce and contributed 17.7% of GRP in 2021. There are substantial mineral resources, including salt, iron ore, soda and precious stones, most of which are not industrially exploited. Its main industries are mechanical engineering (including tractor-manufacturing), food processing, metal working, electricity production, and chemicals and petrochemicals. Barnaul contains one of the largest textiles enterprises in Russia, producing cotton fibre and yarn for cloth. Industry employed 24.4% of the workforce and contributed 30.6% of GRP in 2021, when manufacturing employed 13.9% of the workforce and contributed 22.9% of GRP.

The economically active population numbered 1,119,762 in 2022, when the rate of unemployment was 3.7%, while the average monthly wage was 39,270 roubles. There was a budgetary surplus of 8,832.9m. roubles in 2021, when export trade amounted to US $1,148m. (of which 58.4% was with CIS countries), and import trade to $681m. (of which 60.2% was with CIS countries).

DIRECTORY

Governor: Viktor P. Tomenko.

Office of the Governor: 656035 Altai Krai, Barnaul, pr. Lenina 59; tel. (3852) 35-38-05; fax (3852) 36-38-63; e-mail gubernator@alregn.ru; internet altairegion22.ru.

Legislative Assembly: 656035 Altai Krai, Barnaul, ul. Anatoliya 81; tel. (3852) 29-40-12; fax (3852) 63-02-69; e-mail info@akzs.ru; internet akzs.ru; Chair. Aleksandr A. Romanenko.

State Duma Representatives (4): Daniil V. Bessarabov (YeR), Mariya N. Prusakova (KPRF), Aleksandr S. Prokopyev (YeR), Ivan I. Loor (YeR).

Federation Council Representatives: Viktor V. Zobnev, Natalya S. Kuvshinova.

Krasnoyarsk Krai

Krasnoyarsk Krai occupies the central part of Siberia and extends from the Arctic Ocean coast in the north to the Western Sayan Mountains in the south. It is bordered by Sakha (Yakutiya) and Irkutsk Oblast to the east and by Tyva to the south. To the west lie Khakasiya, Kemerovo Oblast and Tomsk Oblast, as well as the Khanty-Mansii—Yugra and Yamalo-Nenets Autonomous Okrugs within Tyumen Oblast. Its major river is the Yenisei, one of the longest in Russia. Most of its area is covered by taiga (forested marshland). The Krai covers a total area of 2,366,797 sq km (913,825 sq miles), and is the second largest federal unit in Russia, measuring almost 3,000 km from south to north. The Krai lies within three climatic zones—arctic, sub-arctic and continental. At January 2023 it had an estimated population of 2,845,545 and a population density of 1.2 per sq km. Some 79.6% of the population was urban in 2023. The administrative centre, Krasnoyarsk, had an estimated 1,196,913 inhabitants at January 2023. The second-largest city is Norilsk (174,747). Of residents who stated their ethnicity at the 2021 census, 93.6% were Russian, and 0.8% were Tatar. The territory is in the time zone UTC+7.

HISTORY

The city of Krasnoyarsk was founded in 1628 as an ostrog (military transit camp) during Russian expansion across Siberia. The region gained importance after the discovery of gold deposits, and with the construction of the Trans-Siberian Railway. The Krai was formed on 7 December 1934.

In December 1992 Valerii Zubov, a supporter of President Boris Yeltsin, was elected Governor. Elections to a new parliament, the Legislative Assembly, were held in March 1994. In May 1998 Gen. (retd) Aleksandr Lebed, the former secretary of the National Security Council, defeated Zubov in a gubernatorial election.

Lebed died in a helicopter crash in April 2002. In September the former General Director of Norilsk Nickel and Governor of the Taimyr (Dolgano-Nenets) Autonomous Okrug, in the north of the Krai, Aleksandr Khlopanin, narrowly defeated the Chairman of the provincial legislature, Aleksandr Uss, who was supported by the aluminium company Rusal, to be elected Governor. The provincial electoral commission annulled the result, however, citing irregularities in Khlopanin's campaign. After a court overturned this ruling, President Vladimir Putin appointed Khlopanin Acting Governor, necessitating his resignation as Governor of the Taimyr Autonomous Okrug.

The unification of the Krai and its two Autonomous Okrugs (the Evenk Autonomous Okrug, in the centre of the Krai, being the second) was approved in referendums held in each of the territories on 17 April 2005; it took effect on 1 January 2007.

In June 2007 the Legislative Assembly approved the appointment of Khlopanin to a further term of office. He remained in office until January 2010, when he was appointed Presidential Representative to the North Caucasus Federal Okrug. In February the Legislative Assembly endorsed Lev Kuznetsov, the hitherto First Deputy Governor, as Governor.

In May 2014 Kuznetsov was appointed to the federal Government as Minister of North Caucasus Affairs; he was succeeded as Governor in an acting capacity by Viktor Tolokonskii, the erstwhile Presidential Representative to the Siberian Federal Okrug, and Governor of Novosibirsk Oblast in 2000–10. In September 2014 Tolokonskii was elected Governor, obtaining 63.3% of the popular vote.

YeR secured 38.6% of the proportional votes cast in elections to the Provincial Legislative Assembly held in September 2016, ahead of the LDPR, with 20.2%. By the end of the year 37 of the 52 deputies had joined the YeR parliamentary faction.

On 29 September 2017 Tolokonskii, who had become increasingly unpopular, resigned as Governor. (He later became senior advisor to the KPRF Mayor of Novosibirsk, Anatolii Lokot.) Putin appointed Uss as Acting Governor, pending an election. On 30 May 2018 Putin transferred the Krai's Chairman of the Government, Viktor Tomenko, to the post of Acting Governor of Altai Krai; he was succeeded, also in an acting capacity, by Yurii Lapshin. On 9 September Uss was elected Governor, obtaining 60.2% of the votes cast. In October Lapshin was confirmed in the post of Chairman of the Government.

At elections to the Provincial Legislative Assembly held on 19 September 2021, YeR secured 31.7% of the votes cast on the basis of proportional representation; the KPRF obtained 21.8%, the LDPR 14.7%, the recently established centre-right NL 8.0%, SR 7.1% and the Rossiiskaya Ekologicheskaya Partiya 'Zelyonyye' (REP-Z—Greens—Russian Ecological Party) 5.1%. By the end of the year 36 of the 52 deputies had joined the YeR faction, eight that of the KPRF, four that of the LDPR and two that of SR. The factions of NL and the REP-Z each comprised one deputy.

On 20 April 2023 President Putin appointed Mikhail Kotyukov, hitherto the federal Deputy Minister of Finance, as Acting Governor, after Uss resigned to become one of the representatives of the Krai to the Federation Council. Shortly afterwards, Sergei Vereshchagin, the Deputy Chairman of the Government, was appointed Acting First Deputy Governor, Chairman of the Government, following the resignation of Lapshin. On 10 September Kotyukov, the candidate of YeR, was elected Governor with 70.2% of the votes cast, defeating four other candidates. Vereshchagin was confirmed in his post on 29 September.

ECONOMY

Krasnoyarsk Krai contains vast timber reserves and deposits of minerals, gold and petroleum. In 2021 the Krai's gross regional product (GRP) amounted to 3,064,832m. roubles, or an estimated 1,074,424 roubles per head. The Krai's major industrial centres are at Krasnoyarsk, Norilsk, Achinsk, Kansk and Minusinsk. At the end of 2021 there were 2,078 km of railways in the Krai.

The principal crops are grain, potatoes and vegetables. Animal husbandry and beekeeping are also important. Agriculture employed 6.7% of the workforce and contributed 3.2% of GRP in 2021. The main industries are non-ferrous metallurgy, electricity production and ore mining (particularly of bauxite). The Krai contains the world's second largest aluminium smelter, Krasnoyarsk Aluminium, which forms part of the Krasnoyarsk Metallurgical Plant (KraMZ). The territory is, among the federal subjects, a major producer of nickel, coal and electrical energy. A new pipeline to carry oil from Kyumba, in the centre of the Krai, to Taishet, in Irkutsk Oblast, entered into operation in 2017. In 2021 the Segezha Group, based in Kareliya, announced the intention to construct a major pulp and paper mill at Lesosibirsk, 300 km north of Krasnoyarsk. Industry employed 28.0% of the workforce and contributed 64.0% of GRP in 2021, when manufacturing employed 13.5% of the workforce and contributed 33.4% of GRP.

The economically active population numbered 1,372,065 in 2022, when the unemployment rate was 2.7%, while the average monthly wage was 71,728 roubles. There was a budgetary surplus of 96,998.3m. roubles in 2021, when export trade amounted to US $7,165m. (of which 4.2% was with CIS countries), and import trade to $2,668m. (of which 11.3% was with CIS countries).

DIRECTORY

Governor: MIKHAIL M. KOTYUKOV.

First Deputy Governor, Chairman of the Government: SERGEI V. VERESHCHAGIN.

Office of the Governor and the Government: 660009 Krasnoyarsk, pr. Mira 110; tel. (391) 249-30-40; fax (391) 222-11-78; e-mail public@krskstate.ru; internet krskstate.ru.

Provincial Legislative Assembly: 660009 Krasnoyarsk, pr. Mira 110; tel. (391) 249-32-70; fax (391) 222-22-24; e-mail sobranie@sobranie.info; internet sobranie.info; Chair. ALEKSEI I. DODATKO.

State Duma Representatives (4): YURII N. SHVYTKIN (YeR), ALEKSANDR S. DROZDOV (YeR), SERGEI V. YEREMIN (YeR), ALEKSEI B. VELLER (YeR).

Federation Council Representatives: ANDREI A. KLISHAS, ALEKSANDR V. USS.

Irkutsk Oblast

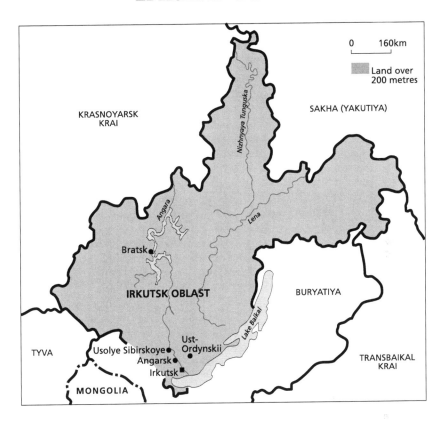

Irkutsk Oblast is situated in the south-east of the Central Siberian Plateau. The Republic of Sakha (Yakutiya) lies to the north-east, Krasnoyarsk Krai to the north-west and Tyva to the south-west. Most of the long south-eastern border is with the Republic of Buryatiya and, in the east, with Transbaikal Krai. Lake Baikal (which forms part of the border with Buryatiya) is the deepest lake in the world, and holds over 80% of Russia's, and 20% of the world's, surface freshwater resources. The Oblast's main rivers include the Angara, the Nizhnyaya Tunguska and the Lena. The Oblast covers 774,846 sq km (299,170 sq miles). At January 2023 its population was an estimated 2,344,360 and the population density 3.0 per sq km. Some 77.5% of the population was urban in 2023. The administrative centre, Irkutsk, had an estimated 611,215 inhabitants at January 2023. Other major cities include Bratsk (221,244) and Angarsk (218,386). Of residents who stated their ethnicity at the 2021 census, 92.2% were Russian, and 3.6% were Buryat. Irkutsk Oblast is in the time zone UTC+8.

HISTORY

The city of Irkutsk, founded as a military transit camp in 1661, became one of the largest economic centres of eastern Siberia. The region was part of the pro-Bolshevik Far Eastern Republic based in Chita (now in Transbaikal Krai) established in April

1920 and which merged with Soviet Russia in November 1922. The Buryat-Mongol Autonomous Soviet Socialist Republic (ASSR), created in 1923, was restructured in 1937. The Ust-Orda Buryat Autonomous Okrug, comprising the four westernmost raions (districts) of the ASSR, was established within Irkutsk Oblast.

In late 1993 the Regional Soviet was dissolved, and in 1994 a Legislative Assembly was elected in its place. An ally of the federal authorities, Boris Govorin, was elected Governor in 1997. He was re-elected in 2001. On 26 August 2005 the regional legislature voted to approve President Vladimir Putin's nomination of Aleksandr Tishanin as Govorin's successor.

Referendums held on 16 April 2006 in both the Ust-Orda Buryat Autonomous Okrug and Irkutsk Oblast overwhelmingly approved the merger of the territories. In February 2007 Tishanin was appointed additionally as Governor of the Autonomous Okrug.

The new unified territory officially came into existence on 1 January 2008. Tishanin served as Acting Governor until 15 April, when he was succeeded, also in an acting capacity, by Igor Yesipovskii. At elections to the new legislature, held on 12 October, YeR won 49.5% of the votes cast on a proportional basis, followed by the LDPR, with 15.1%. Yesipovskii was formally inaugurated as Governor on 13 December. On 10 May 2009, however, he was killed in a helicopter crash. In June the regional legislature endorsed President Dmitrii Medvedev's nomination of Dmitrii Mezentsev, hitherto a Deputy Chairman of the Federation Council, as Governor.

On 18 May 2012 Mezentsev, having failed to obtain sufficient signatories to permit his participation in the March presidential election, resigned as Governor. On 29 May the Legislative Assembly approved the appointment of Sergei Yeroshchenko, a business executive, as his successor. In elections to the Legislative Assembly held in September 2013, YeR obtained 42.4% of the votes cast on the basis of proportional representation. The KPRF was second, with 18.9%.

The first round of voting in a gubernatorial election, held on 13 September 2015, proved inconclusive. Yeroshchenko, representing YeR, with 49.6% of the votes cast, and the KPRF candidate, Sergei Levchenko, with 36.6%, proceeded to a second round of voting on 27 September, when Levchenko was elected Governor, winning 56.4% of the votes cast. He thus became one of the few regional governors to be nominally opposed to the federal authorities and to YeR.

Elections to the Legislative Assembly were held on 9 September 2018. The KPRF was placed first, obtaining 33.9% of the votes cast on a proportional basis, ahead of YeR, with 27.8%, the LDPR, with 15.8%, and SR, with 7.0%. The continuing relative strength of support for the KPRF in the Oblast was associated with discontent at plans by the federal authorities to raise the national retirement age. Some 18 of the 45 deputies had joined the KPRF parliamentary faction by the end of the year, compared with 17 that of YeR, four that of the LDPR, and three that of SR.

On 12 December 2019 Levchenko resigned as Governor; he had been subject to substantial criticism in relation to his administration's response to large-scale flooding in the region in June–July, as a result of which at least 23 people had died. He was succeeded as Acting Governor by Igor Kobzev, a former Deputy Minister in the federal Ministry of Civil Defence, Emergencies and Disaster Relief.

On 13 September 2020 Kobzev was elected as Governor, securing 60.8% of the votes cast; of the four other candidates, Mikhail Shapov of the KPRF was placed second, with 25.5%. Kobzev was inaugurated to office on 18 September.

Following elections to the Legislative Assembly held on 10 September 2023, YeR held 35 of the 45 seats in the expanded chamber, substantially increasing its representation there at the expense of the KPRF and giving it a large majority, although the rate of participation was only 24.2%.

ECONOMY

Irkutsk Oblast is one of the most economically developed regions in Russia, largely owing to its significant fuel, energy and water resources, minerals and timber, and its location on the Trans-Siberian Railway. In 2021 the Oblast's gross regional product (GRP) amounted to 1,924,361m. roubles, or an estimated 813,312 roubles per head. The region's main industrial centres are at Irkutsk, Bratsk, Ust-Ilimsk and Angarsk. At the end of 2021 there were 2,494 km of railways in the Oblast. The Oblast has two international airports, at Irkutsk and Bratsk. There are two major river-ports on the Lena river, at Kirensk and Osetrovo (Ust-Kut), which are used to transport freight to the northern seaport of Tiksi and other locations in the Republic of Sakha (Yakutiya).

Agriculture consists mainly of animal husbandry (fur animal, reindeer and livestock breeding), hunting and fishing, and grain and potato production. The sector employed 6.7% of the workforce and contributed 4.1% of GRP in 2021. The region contains substantial energy reserves, including the Kovytkinskoye gas field and the Angarsk oilfield. The main industries are non-ferrous metallurgy, the processing of forestry products, mining (coal, iron ore, gold, muscovite or mica, gypsum, talc and salt), mechanical engineering, metal working and electricity generation. Among the federal subjects, the Oblast is a major producer of electrical energy. Industry employed 27.4% of the workforce and contributed 53.1% of GRP in 2021, when manufacturing employed 11.6% of the workforce and contributed 10.9% of GRP.

The economically active population in Irkutsk Oblast numbered 1,096,569 in 2022, when the rate of unemployment was 5.0%, while the average monthly wage was 64,635 roubles. There was a budgetary surplus of 18,170.0m. roubles in 2021, when export trade amounted to US $8,386m. (of which 2.4% was with CIS countries), and import trade to $2,127m. (of which 24.5% was with CIS countries).

DIRECTORY

Governor: Igor I. Kobzev.

First Deputy Governor, Chairman of the Government: Konstantin B. Zaitsev.

Office of the Government: 664047 Irkutsk, ul. Lenina 1a; tel. (3952) 25-65-75; fax (3952) 24-17-73; internet irkobl.ru.

Legislative Assembly: 664027 Irkutsk, ul. Lenina 1a; tel. (3952) 25-60-38; fax (3952) 20-00-09; e-mail delo@izrs.ru; internet irzs.ru; Chair. Aleksandr V. Vedernikov.

State Duma Representatives (4): Mikhail V. Shchapov (YeR), Anton A. Krasnoshtanov (YeR), Sergei Yu. Ten (YeR), Aleksandr V. Yakubovskii (YeR).

Federation Council Representatives: Sergei F. Brilka, Andrei V. Chernyshev.

Kemerovo Oblast—Kuzbass

Kemerovo Oblast—Kuzbass is situated in southern central Russia. Krasnoyarsk Krai and Khakasiya lie to the east, Tomsk Oblast to the north, Novosibirsk Oblast to the west, and Altai Krai and the Republic of Altai to the south-west. The region lies in the Kuznetsk basin, the area surrounding the Tom River. The Oblast occupies 95,725 sq km (36,960 sq miles). At January 2023 its population was an estimated 2,568,238 and the population density 26.8 per sq km. Some 86.5% of the population was urban in 2023. The administrative centre, Kemerovo, had an estimated 549,362 inhabitants at January 2023. Other major cities are Novokuznetsk (533,565) and Prokopyevsk (174,859). Of residents who stated their ethnicity at the 2021 census, 95.3% were Russian, and 0.9% were Tatar. Kemerovo Oblast—Kuzbass is in the time zone UTC+7.

HISTORY

Kemerovo was founded in 1918 as Shcheglovsk. It became the administrative centre of the Oblast upon its formation on 26 January 1943. The city is at the centre of Russia's principal coal mining area. In 1997 the Governor appointed in August 1991, Mikhail Kislyuk, was dismissed by President Boris Yeltsin, following a dispute over pensions arrears.

In the December 1995 elections to the federal State Duma, the KPRF won 48% of the regional votes cast, its second highest share of the vote in any federal territory. Much of this support was attributed to the popularity of Aman-Geldy Tuleyev, speaker of the suspended Assembly. Tuleyev contested the federal presidency in 1991, 1996 and 2000, and served in the federal Government during 1996–97. Having been appointed Governor by Yeltsin in July 1997, Tuleyev's position was confirmed by a popular election to the post in October of that year, when he received 94.6% of the votes cast.

In 1998 Tuleyev signed a framework agreement with the federal Government on the delimitation of powers, which was accompanied by 10 accords aimed at strengthening the regional economy. Tuleyev was widely considered to be Russia's most popular regional leader. When he contested the federal presidency in 2000, Tuleyev received 51.6% of the votes cast in the Oblast, more than twice the number of votes cast there for the victor, Vladimir Putin. In January 2001 Tuleyev announced his resignation, but was overwhelmingly re-elected Governor in April, with 93.5% of the votes cast. In 2003 he was appointed to the Supreme Council of YeO-YeR (later YeR).

In 2005 the regional legislature unanimously supported Tuleyev's appointment to a further term of office. At elections to the Regional Council of People's Deputies held in 2008 YeR, with 84.8% of the proportional vote, was the only party to win representation on this basis. In 2010 the regional legislature approved President Dmitrii Medvedev's nomination of Tuleyev to a further gubernatorial term.

In elections to the Regional Council of People's Deputies held in September 2013, YeR was again the only party to obtain seats on a proportional basis, with 86.2% of the vote; 43 of the 46 deputies were affiliated with YeR. In September 2015, Tuleyev was overwhelmingly elected Governor, receiving 96.7% of the popular vote.

On 25 March 2018 a fire at a shopping centre in Kemerovo killed at least 64 people, including 41 children. A protest was staged in the city, attracting several thousand people, and demanding the resignation of the regional authorities; seven officials, including the head of the local building inspection agency, were subsequently arrested. President Putin, visiting the city, condemned 'criminal negligence' as the cause of the accident; in 2021 two senior officials of the company that owned the shopping centre, and six employees, were imprisoned on related charges. On 1 April 2018 Tuleyev (then the longest-serving regional leader in Russia) tendered his resignation (subsequently becoming Chairman of the Regional Council of People's Deputies, and remaining in that post for four months); on the same day Putin appointed the hitherto Deputy Governor, Sergei Tsivilyov, as Acting Governor.

On 9 September 2018 Tsivilyov was overwhelmingly elected Governor, with 81.3% of the votes cast. In concurrent elections to the Regional Council of People's Deputies, YeR won 64.4% of the votes cast on a proportional basis, ahead of the LDPR, with 10.1%, the KPRF, with 10.0%, and SR, with 7.8%. Some 38 of the 46 deputies subsequently joined the YeR parliamentary faction. Two deputies joined the KPRF faction, two that of the LDPR, two that of SR, and one that of PR.

On 27 March 2019 President Putin signed a decree amending the federal Constitution, appending the designation Kuzbass to the territory's official name. In December the Regional Council of People's Deputies was also renamed, becoming the Regional Legislative Assembly.

In February 2021 Vyacheslav Telegin was appointed (initially in an acting capacity) to the new post of First Deputy Governor, Chairman of the Government. He resigned, apparently on grounds of ill health in August 2022 and was succeeded in the following month by Ilya Seredyuk, hitherto Mayor of Kemerovo. In December Telegin was detained on charges of fraud in his earlier capacity as Mayor of Leninsk-Kuznetskii; he was subsequently placed under house arrest and his trial was due to commence in early 2024.

On 10 September 2023 Tsivilyov, the candidate of YeR, was overwhelmingly re-elected Governor with 85.2% of the votes cast, defeating three other candidates. Following concurrent elections to the Regional Legislative Assembly, YeR held 40 of the 46 seats in the chamber; the rate of participation, at 81.0%, was substantially higher than that in any of the other territorial elections held on that date.

ECONOMY

In 2021 Kemerovo Oblast's gross regional product (GRP) amounted to 1,807,387m. roubles, equivalent to an estimated 690,143 roubles per head. The Oblast's main industrial centres are at Kemerovo, Novokuznetsk, Prokopyevsk, Kiselyovsk and Leninsk-Kuznetskii. At the end of 2021 there were 1,678 km of railways in the Oblast.

Kemerovo Oblast's agriculture consists mainly of potato and grain production, animal husbandry and beekeeping. The sector employed 2.9% of the workforce and contributed 2.6% of GRP in 2021. The regional economy is based on industry. The region is rich in mineral resources and contains the Kuzbass basin, one of the major coal reserves of the world, while there are also significant deposits of iron ore. The Oblast is the largest producer of coal among the federal subjects, and a principal producer of steel. Production of complex ores, ferrous metallurgy and electricity generation are also important industries in the region. Industry employed 33.1% of the workforce and contributed 61.3% of GRP in 2021, when manufacturing employed 12.1% of the workforce and contributed 13.8% of GRP.

The economically active population numbered 1,195,422 in 2022, when the rate of unemployment was 4.1%, while the average monthly wage was 57,653 roubles. There was a budgetary surplus of 34,589.0m. roubles in 2021, when export trade amounted to US $15,327m. (of which 13.2% was with countries of the CIS), and import trade to $826m. (of which 26.7% was with CIS countries).

DIRECTORY

Governor: Sergei Ye. Tsivilyov.

First Deputy Governor, Chairman of the Government: Ilya V. Seredyuk.

Office of the Governor and the Government: 650064 Kemerovo, pr. Sovetskii 62; tel. (3842) 36-43-33; fax (3842) 36-34-09; e-mail postmaster@ako.ru; internet ako.ru.

Regional Legislative Assembly: 650099 Kemerovo, pr. Sovetskii 58; tel. (3842) 45-04-50; fax (3842) 58-54-51; e-mail office@zskuzbass.ru; internet zskuzbass.ru; Chair. Aleksei A. Zelenin.

State Duma Representatives (4): Anton V. Gorelkin (YeR), Dmitrii V. Islamov (YeR), Pavel M. Fedyayev (YeR), Aleksandr A. Maksimov (YeR).

Federation Council Representatives: Aleksei V. Sinitsyn, Nadezhda V. Ilina.

Novosibirsk Oblast

Novosibirsk Oblast is situated in the Western Siberian Plain. It borders Kazakhstan in the south-west, Altai Krai to the south, and the Oblasts of Omsk to the west, Tomsk to the north and Kemerovo to the east. The major rivers are the Ob and the Om. The Oblast occupies 177,756 sq km (68,632 sq miles). At January 2023 it had an estimated population of 2,794,266 and a population density of 15.7 per sq km. Some 79.7% of the population was urban in 2023. The administrative centre, Novosibirsk, had an estimated 1,635,338 inhabitants at January 2023. The second city is Berdsk (102,965). Of residents who stated their ethnicity at the 2021 census, 94.2% were Russian, 0.7% were Tatar, and 0.7% were German. The Oblast is in the time zone UTC+7.

HISTORY

Novosibirsk was founded as Novonikolayevsk in 1893, during the construction of the Trans-Siberian Railway. The Oblast was formed on 28 September 1937.

Viktor Tolokonskii, a former Mayor of Novosibirsk, was elected Governor in 2000. He was re-elected in 2003 and confirmed to a further term in 2007.

In September 2010 Tolokonskii became the Presidential Representative to the Siberian Federal Okrug. He was succeeded as Governor by his first deputy, Vasilii Yurchenko. At elections to the Regional Council of Deputies in October, YeR obtained 44.8% of the votes cast, ahead of the KPRF, with 25.3%.

In March 2014 President Vladimir Putin dismissed Yurchenko, after a criminal investigation into abuse of office was opened against him. (In 2017 Yurchenko received a three-year suspended sentence.) He was succeeded as Governor, in an acting capacity, by Vladimir Gorodetskii, a former Mayor of Novosibirsk. Anatolii Lokot of the KPRF was subsequently elected the new Mayor, reflecting the widespread discontent in the city with the ruling authorities. (Lokot was re-elected in 2019.)

In September 2014 Gorodetskii was directly elected Governor. Meanwhile, an attempt to stage a rally, in August, demanding the devolution of powers to Siberia was thwarted by the regional administration. Charges of 'vandalism motivated by political, ideological, racial, ethnic or religious hatred' were subsequently brought against activists, after Soviet imagery on a war memorial was daubed with the colours of the Ukrainian flag, as a protest against Russian support for forces in eastern Ukraine.

In elections to the regional legislature held on 13 September 2015, YeR received 44.6% of the votes cast on the basis of proportional representation. The KPRF was second, with 24.5%.

On 6 October 2017 Putin dismissed Gorodetskii, and appointed Andrei Travnikov, hitherto the Mayor of Vologda, as Acting Governor. On 9 September 2018 Travnikov was elected as Governor, receiving 64.5% of the votes cast. Travnikov subsequently appointed Gorodetskii as a representative of Novosibirsk Oblast in the Federation Council.

In elections to the Regional Legislative Assembly, held on 13 September 2020, support for YeR in the proportional vote decreased to 38.1%. The KPRF was second, with 16.6%, ahead of the LDPR, with 13.6%. When the new chamber convened, 46 of the 76 deputies joined the YeR faction, 13 joined that of the KPRF, and seven that of the LDPR.

Russia's invasion of Ukraine on 24 February 2022 was strenuously opposed in the Novosibirsk municipal council by an independent deputy, Khelga Pirogova, who had been elected in 2020 with the support of the Umnoye Golosovaniye (Intelligent Voting) initiative of later imprisoned opposition figure Aleksei Navalnyi. In May 2022 police in Novosibirsk searched the residences of two former associates of Navalnyi and also of two other regional independent legislators connected to his supporters. In July the founder of an independent news website based in Novosibirsk fled Russia, after action against the outlet by federal media regulatory agency Roskomnadzor was announced. Later that month Pirogova was briefly detained and a criminal investigation on charges of disseminating 'false information discrediting the armed forces' was subsequently opened against her. Pirogova fled to Georgia shortly afterwards and was placed on the federal 'wanted' list.

An order issued by President Putin on 21 September 2022 for the partial mobilization of military reservists in each region precipitated protests in Novosibirsk (and other major cities nationwide).

Saboteurs who claimed to be members of a Ukrainian-based Russian paramilitary group, the Legion 'Svoboda Rossii' (Freedom to Russia Legion) announced on social media that they had set fire to a mothballed Su-24 aircraft at the Sukhoi Superjet Company's aviation plant near Novosibirsk on 8 May 2023, one day before Russia's Victory Day annual celebrations; reports had suggested that the plane was to have been refurbished for use in combat.

On 10 September 2023 Travnikov, the candidate of YeR, was re-elected Governor with 75.7% of the votes cast, defeating three other candidates. In December the regional authorities detained a resident who was accused of being a member of a radical nationalist group and of planning to plant an explosive device at a military enlistment office in Novosibirsk.

ECONOMY

In 2021 Novosibirsk Oblast's gross regional product (GRP) was 1,617,011m. roubles, or an estimated 581,018 roubles per head. Novosibirsk is the principal industrial centre.

At the end of 2021 there were 1,505 km of railways in the Oblast. There is a port on the Ob river at Novosibirsk, and an international airport.

The Oblast's agriculture comprises the production of grain, vegetables, potatoes and flax, and animal husbandry. It employed 5.1% of the workforce and contributed 5.7% of GRP in 2021. Extractive industries involve the production of coal, petroleum, natural gas, limestone and clay. The Oblast's manufacturing industry includes non-ferrous metallurgy, mechanical engineering, and electricity generation. Industry employed 24.2% of the workforce and contributed 25.1% of GRP in 2021, when manufacturing employed 13.9% of the workforce and contributed 13.5% of GRP.

The economically active population amounted to 1,330,471 in 2022, when the rate of unemployment was 4.7%, while the average monthly wage was 53,757 roubles. There was a budgetary surplus of 17,071.7m. roubles in 2021, when export trade amounted to US $3,838m. (of which 25.9% was with countries of the CIS), and import trade to $3,750m. (of which 18.3% was with CIS countries).

DIRECTORY

Governor: ANDREI A. TRAVNIKOV.

Office of the Governor: 630011 Novosibirsk, Krasnyi pr. 18; tel. (383) 223-29-95; fax (383) 223-57-00; e-mail pochta@nso.ru; internet nso.ru.

Regional Legislative Assembly: 630011 Novosibirsk, ul. Kirova 3; tel. (383) 223-09-36; e-mail refl@zsnso.ru; internet zsnso.ru; Chair. ANDREI I. SHIMKIV.

State Duma Representatives (4): OLEG I. IVANINSKII (YeR), DMITRII I. SAVELYEV (YeR), ALEKSANDR S. AKSYONENKO (SR), VIKTOR A. IGNATOV (YeR).

Federation Council Representatives: VLADIMIR F. GORODETSKII, ALEKSANDR A. KARELIN.

Omsk Oblast

Omsk Oblast is situated in the south of the Western Siberian Plain on the middle reaches of the Irtysh river. Kazakhstan lies to the south. Tyumen Oblast lies to the north-west, and Tomsk Oblast and Novosibirsk Oblast lie to the east. The major rivers are the Irtysh, the Ishim, the Om and the Tara. The Oblast covers some 141,140 sq km (54,494 sq miles). At January 2023 it had an estimated population of 1,832,064 and a population density of 13.0 per sq km. Some 73.6% of the population was urban in 2023. The administrative centre is Omsk, which lies at the confluence of the Om and Irtysh rivers, with an estimated 1,110,836 inhabitants at January 2023. Of residents who stated their ethnicity at the 2021 census, 88.7% were Russian, 4.1% Kazakh, 1.7% German, 1.6% Tatar, and 1.1% were Ukrainian. The region is in the time zone UTC+6.

HISTORY

The city of Omsk was founded as a fortress in 1716. In 1918 it became the seat of Adm. Aleksandr Kolchak's 'white' 'All-Russian Government'. Omsk fell to the Bolsheviks in 1919, and Kolchak 'abdicated' in January 1920. Omsk Oblast was formed on 7 December 1934.

The regional Governor since 1991, Leonid Polezhayev, an ally of President Boris Yeltsin, was elected Governor in 1995. In 1996 the regional and federal administrations signed a power-sharing treaty. Polezhayev was re-elected in 1999.

The Oblast was one of only four regions in which the KPRF candidate, Gennadii Zyuganov, received a larger proportion of the votes cast than Vladimir Putin in the federal presidential election of March 2000. The power-sharing treaty was abolished in 2001. Polezhayev was re-elected Governor in September 2003.

On 24 May 2007 the Regional Legislative Assembly confirmed President Putin's nomination of Polezhayev to a new term as Governor. At elections to the Regional Legislative Assembly held in December 2011 YeR experienced a sharp decline in support, receiving 39.0% of the votes cast on a proportional basis, compared with the 55.6% it had obtained in 2007. The KPRF was second, with 26.1%. Some 26 of the 44 deputies joined the YeR parliamentary faction.

In early 2012 Polezhayev announced that he did not intend to seek re-appointment to a further term as Governor (criminal investigations into numerous members of his family having recently commenced). In April the Regional Legislative Assembly endorsed the nomination by the outgoing President, Dmitrii Medvedev, of Viktor Nazarov, a former regional executive of the state-owned gas Gazprom corporation, as Governor; this took effect from 30 May. Nazarov was directly elected Governor in September 2015.

YeR secured 36.3% of the votes cast on a proportional basis in elections to the Regional Legislative Assembly on 18 September 2016; the KPRF was second, with 29.5%. By the end of the year 31 of the 44 deputies had joined the YeR parliamentary faction.

On 9 October 2017 Putin dismissed Nazarov as Governor. He was succeeded in an acting capacity by Aleksandr Burkov, hitherto an SR State Duma deputy. On 9 September 2018 Burkov was elected Governor, obtaining 82.6% of the votes cast.

At elections to the Regional Legislative Assembly held on 19 September 2021, YeR secured 31.3% of the votes cast on the basis of proportional representation; the KPRF obtained 23.7%, the KR 11.0%, SR 9.8%, the recently established centre-right NL 8.3% and the LDPR 6.8%. By the end of the year 26 of the 44 deputies had joined the YeR faction, 10 that of the KPRF, three that of the KR, two that of SR, two that of NL, and one that of the LDPR.

On 29 March 2023 Burkov tendered his resignation as Governor. President Putin on the same day appointed Vitalii Khotsenko, hitherto Chairman of the Government of the 'Donetsk People's Republic' (DNR) in the eastern Donbas region of Ukraine (which Russia had formally annexed in September 2022), as Acting Governor. On 10 September 2023 Khotsenko was elected Governor with 76.3% of the votes cast, defeating three other candidates.

ECONOMY

In 2021 Omsk Oblast's gross regional product (GRP) amounted to 854,133m. roubles, equivalent to an estimated 451,537 roubles per head. The region lies on the Trans-Siberian Railway and is a major transport junction. At the end of 2021 there were 735 km of railways in the Oblast. There is an international airport at Omsk.

The Oblast's soil is the fertile black earth (*chernozyom*) characteristic of the region. Its agriculture consists mainly of animal husbandry (including fur-farming), hunting and the production of grain. Agriculture employed 11.4% of the workforce and contributed 9.5% of GRP in 2021. Omsk city is a major industrial centre, while the region's mineral reserves include clay, peat and lime. There are also deposits of petroleum and natural gas. The Oblast's main industries are electricity generation, fuel, chemical and petrochemical production, mechanical engineering, petroleum refining and food processing. There is a petroleum refinery at Omsk, operated by Sibneft. The region's exports primarily comprise chemical, petrochemical and petroleum products. The defence sector is also significant to the economy of the region. Industry employed 26.0% of the workforce and contributed 36.4% of GRP in 2021, when manufacturing employed 14.3% of the workforce and contributed 28.5% of GRP.

The economically active population numbered 931,746 in 2022, when the rate of unemployment was 5.3%, while the average monthly wage was 46,952 roubles. There was a budgetary deficit of 3,263.6m. roubles in 2021, when export trade amounted to US $997m. in 2021 (of which 46.5% was with countries of the CIS), and import trade to $414m. (of which 38.3% was with CIS countries).

DIRECTORY

Governor: VITALII P. KHOTSENKO.

Office of the Governor: 644002 Omsk, ul. Krasnyi Put 1; tel. (3812) 24-14-15; fax (3812) 24-40-11; e-mail omskadm@omskportal.ru; internet omskportal.ru.

Regional Legislative Assembly: 640002 Omsk, ul. Krasnyi Put 1; tel. (3812) 79-93-08; e-mail zakonodatel@omskparlament.ru; internet omsk-parlament.ru; Chair. ALEKSANDR V. ARTYOMOV.

State Duma Representatives (3): ANDREI A. ALEKHIN (KPRF), OLEG N. SMOLIN (KPRF), OKSANA N. FADINA (YeR).

Federation Council Representatives: DMITRII S. PERMINOV, IVAN A. YEVSTIFEYEV.

Tomsk Oblast

Tomsk Oblast is situated in the south-east of the Western Siberian Plain. The Oblasts of Kemerovo and Novosibirsk lie to the south, Omsk Oblast to the south-west, the Khanty-Mansii Autonomous Okrug—Yugra (in Tyumen Oblast) to the north-west, and Krasnoyarsk Krai to the east. Almost all the Oblast's territory is taiga (forested marshland). It occupies 314,391 sq km (121,387 sq miles). At January 2023 its estimated population was 1,052,106, and the population density 3.3 per sq km. Some 71.3% of the population was urban in 2023. The administrative centre, Tomsk, had an estimated 551,505 inhabitants at January 2023. The other major city is Seversk (105,797). Of residents who stated their ethnicity at the 2021 census, 93.4% were Russian, and 1.2% were Tatar. Tomsk Oblast is in the time zone UTC+7.

HISTORY

Tomsk city was founded as a fortress in 1604. It was a major trading centre until the 1890s, when the construction of the Trans-Siberian Railway promoted other centres. Tomsk Oblast was formed on 13 August 1944.

In a gubernatorial election held in 1995, the incumbent appointed in 1991, Viktor Kress, an ally of President Boris Yeltsin, won the popular mandate. He was re-elected in 1999 and 2003. On 10 March 2007 the regional State Duma endorsed President Vladimir Putin's nomination of Kress (now allied with YeR) for a fifth term.

In March 2012 Kress resigned as Governor, becoming a representative of the Oblast in the Federation Council. Sergei Zhvachkin, hitherto a gas sector official, was appointed as his successor.

YeR secured 41.2% of the votes cast on a proportional basis in elections to the Regional State Duma in September 2016; 30 of the 42 deputies had joined the YeR parliamentary faction by the end of the year. In September 2017 Zhvachkin was directly elected Governor, obtaining 60.6% of the votes cast.

At elections to the Regional State Duma held on 19 September 2021, YeR secured 33.2% of the votes cast on a proportional basis; the KPRF obtained 24.4%, the LDPR

12.6%, SR 11.0% and the recently established centre-right NL 10.2%. By the end of the year 27 of the 42 deputies had joined the YeR faction, seven that of the KPRF, three that of SR, three that of the LDPR, and two that of NL.

On 10 May 2022 Zhvachkin announced his retirement as Governor. On the same day President Putin appointed Vladimir Mazur, hitherto the deputy head of the presidential domestic policy directorate, as Acting Governor. Mazur was overwhelmingly elected as Governor, with 84.9% of the votes cast, on 11 September, defeating Galina Nemtseva of SR (who obtained 6.1% of the votes) and two other candidates.

ECONOMY

In 2021 Tomsk Oblast's gross regional product (GRP) was 706,392m. roubles, equivalent to an estimated 660,598 roubles per head. The major industrial centres are Tomsk, Kolpashevo and Asino. At the end of 2021 there were 344 km of railways in the Oblast.

The Oblast's agricultural sector consists mainly of animal husbandry, and the production of grain, vegetables and potatoes. The sector employed 5.0% of the workforce and contributed 4.1% of GRP in 2021. The Oblast has substantial reserves of coal, petroleum and natural gas. Its other main industries are mechanical engineering, metal working, chemicals and petrochemicals, non-ferrous metallurgy and electricity generation. In 2005 the federal authorities announced that one of six special economic zones to be established across the Federation, a technological research centre, was to be located in the Oblast. Industry employed 24.6% of the workforce and contributed 44.4% of GRP in 2021, when manufacturing employed 11.9% of the workforce and contributed 110.9% of GRP.

The economically active population numbered 506,366 in 2022, when the rate of unemployment was 5.2%, while the average monthly wage was 57,879 roubles. There was a budgetary deficit of 4,537.7m. roubles in 2021, when export trade amounted to US $426m. (of which 65.6% was with countries of the CIS), and import trade to $348m. (of which 21.3% was with CIS countries).

DIRECTORY

Governor: VLADIMIR V. MAZUR.

Office of the Governor: 634050 Tomsk, pl. Lenina 6; tel. (3822) 51-00-01; fax (3822) 51-07-30; e-mail ato@tomsk.gov.ru; internet tomsk.gov.ru.

Regional State Duma: 634050 Tomsk, pl. Lenina 6; tel. (3822) 51-04-24; fax (3822) 51-06-02; e-mail duma@tomsk.gov.ru; internet duma.tomsk.ru; Chair. OKSANA V. KOZLOVSKAYA.

State Duma Representatives (2): ALEKSEI N. DIDENKO (LDPR), TATYANA V. SOLOMATINA (YeR).

Federation Council Representatives: VIKTOR M. KRESS, VLADIMIR K. KRAVCHENKO.

FAR EASTERN FEDERAL OKRUG

Presidential Representative to the Far Eastern Federal Okrug: Yurii P. Trutnev, 690922 Maritime Krai, Vladivostok, o. Russkii, p. Ayaks, dom 10, lit n, korp. b; tel. (4232) 49-47-73; e-mail press@dfo.gov.ru; internet dfo.gov.ru.

Republic of Buryatiya

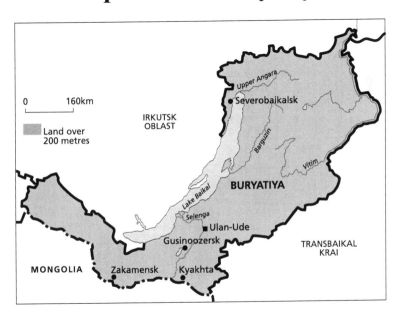

The Republic of Buryatiya is situated in the Eastern Sayan Mountains. It lies mainly to the east of Lake Baikal, although it extends westwards along the southern international boundary with Mongolia, with a short western border with Tyva. Irkutsk Oblast lies to the north and west, Transbaikal Krai to the east. Buryatiya's rivers mainly drain into Lake Baikal, including the Selenga, the Barguzin and the Upper Angara, but some, such as the Vitim, flow northwards into the Siberian plains. Lake Baikal, the oldest and deepest lake in the world, possesses over 80% of Russia's, and 20% of the world's, surface freshwater resources. Some 70% of Buryatiya's territory is open steppe. The Republic covers 351,334 sq km (135,651 sq miles). At January 2023 it had an estimated population of 974,628 and a population density of 2.8 per sq km. Some 59.1% of the population was urban in 2023. The capital is Ulan-Ude, with an estimated 436,138 inhabitants at January 2023. Of residents who stated their ethnicity at the 2021 census, 64.0% were Russian, and 32.5% were Buryat. The industrialized areas of the Republic are mainly inhabited by ethnic Russians. The Buryats are a native Siberian people of Mongol descent and their native tongue is a Mongol dialect. Some Buryats are Orthodox Christians, but others practise Lamaism (Tibetan Buddhism), which has been syncretized with the region's traditional animistic shamanism. Buryatiya is in the time zone UTC+8.

HISTORY

The territory east of Lake Baikal (Transbaikal) was formally incorporated into the Russian Empire by the Treaties of Nerchinsk (1689) and Kyakhta (1728), the latter of which ended a territorial dispute with the Chinese Manzhou (Manchu) Empire. Many Russians settled in the region, often inhabiting land confiscated from the Buryats, many of whom were 'russified'. A resurgence of Buryat nationalist feeling in the 19th century included an affinity with the Mongols, most of whom were ruled from China.

With the dissolution of the Far Eastern Republic, the Buryat-Mongol Autonomous Soviet Socialist Republic (ASSR) was established on 30 May 1923. In the early 1930s, amid a policy of collectivization, many Buryats fled the USSR or were found guilty of treason and executed. In 1937 the eastern section of the Republic was transferred to Chita Oblast (now Transbaikal Krai) and a westerly region to Irkutsk Oblast, in both of which territories small Buryat national (later autonomous) okrugs were established. Furthermore, the Buryat language's Mongolian script was replaced with a Cyrillic one. In 1958 the territory was renamed the Buryat ASSR.

The territory declared its sovereignty in 1990 and was renamed the Republic of Buryatiya in 1992. In 1994 the republican Supreme Soviet adopted a Constitution. The erstwhile Chairman of the Supreme Soviet, Leonid Potapov, became the Republic's first President, following elections, and a legislature, the People's Khural (Assembly), was established. A treaty on the division of powers was signed with the federal Government in 1995. Potapov was re-elected as President in 1998. In 2002 Potapov resigned from the KPRF, and oversaw the rescission of the 1990 declaration of sovereignty, before being re-elected as President with the support of YeO-YeR (now YeR). In 2007 the People's Khural voted to approve federal President Vladimir Putin's nomination of Vyacheslav Nagovitsyn, hitherto Deputy Governor of Tomsk Oblast, as Potapov's successor. He was re-appointed in 2012.

On 7 February 2017 Nagovitsyn resigned. Putin appointed the Republic's erstwhile Deputy Minister of Transport, Aleksei Tsydenov, as Acting Head of the Republic. On 10 September Tsydenov was overwhelmingly elected Head of the Republic.

Elections to the People's Khural were held on 9 September 2018. YeR won 41.1% of the votes cast on a proportional basis, ahead of the KPRF, with 25.6%. Some 41 of the 65 deputies had joined the YeR parliamentary faction by the end of the year, and 11 that of the KPRF. A presidential decree, issued in November 2018, transferred the Republic from the Siberian to the Far Eastern Federal Okrug.

In September 2019 around 200 people attended protest demonstrations (supported by local members of the KPRF) in Ulan-Ude calling for the release of detained supporters of a self-styled 'warrior shaman' (from the Republic of Sakha—Yakutiya), Aleksandr Gabyshev, a vocal critic of the Putin administration, and expressing discontent at the conduct of the recent mayoral election in the city. Demonstrations continued for several days, and were dispersed violently by riot police. Gabyshev himself was arrested in Buryatiya, as he travelled across Russia on a personal anti-Putin protest; he was later detained in a psychiatric hospital.

On 11 September 2022 Tsydenov was overwhelmingly re-elected Head of the Republic, with 86.2% of the votes cast, defeating three other candidates. Following elections to the People's Khural held on 10 September 2023, YeR held 51 of the 66 seats in the expanded chamber, substantially increasing its representation there, although the rate of participation was only 36.3%.

ECONOMY

In 2021 Buryatiya's gross regional product (GRP) amounted to 342,185m. roubles, or 347,738 roubles per head. Its major industrial centre is at Ulan-Ude, situated on the Trans-Siberian Railway. At the end of 2021 there were 1,227 km of railways in Buryatiya.

Agriculture, which consists mainly of animal husbandry (livestock and the breeding of animals for fur), and the production of grain, vegetables and potatoes, employed 7.0% of the workforce and contributed 4.3% of GRP in 2021. Buryatiya is rich in mineral resources, including gold, uranium, coal, wolfram (tungsten), molybdenum, brown coal, graphite and apatites. Apart from ore mining and the extraction of minerals, the main industries are mechanical engineering, metal working, food processing, timber production and wood working. The Republic is also a major producer of electrical energy. Industry employed 22.8% of the workforce and contributed 29.2% of GRP in 2021. Manufacturing employed 10.0% of the workforce and contributed 12.0% of GRP in 2021.

The economically active population numbered 394,691 in 2022, when the rate of unemployment was 7.4%, while the average monthly wage was 53,495 roubles. There was a budgetary deficit of 501.0m. roubles in 2021, when export trade amounted to US $1,330m. (of which 0.6% was with countries of the CIS), while import trade amounted to $88m. (of which 9.9% was with CIS countries).

DIRECTORY

Head of the Republic: ALEKSEI S. TSYDENOV.

Office of the Head of the Republic: 670001 Buryatiya, Ulan-Ude, ul. Lenina 54; tel. (3012) 21-51-86; e-mail pres_rb@icm.buryatia.ru; internet egov-buryatia.ru.

People's Khural: 670001 Buryatiya, Ulan-Ude, ul. Sukhe-Batora 9; tel. (3012) 21-49-61; e-mail hural@icm.buryatia.ru; internet hural-rb.ru; Chair. VLADIMIR A. PAVLOV.

State Duma Representative (1): VYACHESLAV A. DAMDINTSURNOV (YeR).

Federation Council Representatives: VYACHESLAV V. NAGOVITSYN, ALEKSANDR G. VARFOLOMEYEV.

Republic of Sakha (Yakutiya)

The Republic of Sakha (Yakutiya) is situated in eastern Siberia on the Laptev and Eastern Siberian Seas. Two-fifths of the Republic's territory lies within the Arctic Circle. To the west it borders Krasnoyarsk Krai. Irkutsk Oblast and Transbaikal Krai lie to the south-west, Amur Oblast to the south, Khabarovsk Krai and Magadan Oblast to the south-east, and the Chukot Autonomous Okrug to the north-east. The main river is the Lena, which drains into the Laptev Sea through a large swampy delta. Apart from the Central Yakut Plain, the region's territory is mountainous, and four-fifths is taiga (forested marshland). Sakha is the largest federal unit in Russia, occupying an area of 3,083,523 sq km (1,190,554 sq miles), making it larger than Kazakhstan, itself the second largest country, after Russia, in Europe or the former USSR. The north of the Republic lies within the Arctic zone, whereas the south has a more temperate climate. At January 2023 the Republic had an estimated population of 997,565 and a population density of 0.3 per sq km. Some 67.2% of the population was urban in 2023. The capital is Yakutsk, with an estimated 361,154 inhabitants at January 2023. Of residents who stated their ethnicity at the 2021 census, 55.3% were Yakut (Sakha), 32.6% Russian, 2.9% Evenk, 1.6% Even, 1.3% Kyrgyz, 0.8% Ukrainian, 0.8% Buryat, and 0.7% were Tajik. Orthodox Christianity is the dominant religion in the region. The Yakuts' native tongue is part of the north-eastern branch of the Turkic family, and is considerably influenced by Mongolian. The Republic spans three time zones: UTC+9 (Yakutsk), UTC+10 (Verkhoyansk) and UTC+11 (Kolyma).

HISTORY

The Yakuts (Iakuts), also known as the Sakha, traditionally a semi-nomadic people, were historically known as the Tungus, Jekos and the Urangkhai Sakha. They are believed to be descended from peoples from the Lake Baikal area, Turkish tribes from the steppe and the Altai Mountains, and indigenous Siberian peoples, including the Evenks. Their territory, briefly united by the toion (chief), Tygyn, came under Russian rule in the 1620s, and a fur tax was introduced. This led to violent, but ultimately unsuccessful, opposition between 1634 and 1642. Russians began to settle in the region, as the result of the completion of a mail route to the Far East, the construction of camps for political opponents to the tsars, and, in 1846, the discovery of goldfields. The territory became commercialized after the construction of the Trans-Siberian Railway in the 1880s and 1890s and the development of commercial shipping on the River Lena. The Yakut Autonomous Soviet Socialist Republic was founded in 1922. Collectivization and the purges of the 1930s greatly reduced the Yakut population. The region was rapidly industrialized, involving the extraction of gold, coal and timber.

Nationalist feeling re-emerged during the late 1980s. Cultural, ecological and economic concerns led to the proclamation of a 'Yakut-Sakha Soviet Socialist Republic' on 27 April 1990, although this effective declaration of independence from Russia (within the USSR) went unrecognized. On 22 December 1991 elections for an executive presidency were won by the erstwhile Chairman of the republican Supreme Soviet, Mikhail Nikolayev. The territory was renamed the Republic of Sakha (Yakutiya) in March 1992, and a new Constitution was promulgated in April. Elections were held to a new 60-seat bicameral legislature in December. In January 1994 the new parliament named itself the State Assembly (Il Tumen). In December 1996 Nikolayev was re-elected President. A power-sharing agreement with the federal authorities, signed in June 1995, was followed, in March 1998, by a framework agreement on federal-republican co-operation in mining and energy.

In December 2001 Nikolayev withdrew his candidacy from the forthcoming gubernatorial election, and urged voters to support Vyacheslav Shtyrov, the head of the local diamond producing company, Alrosa, the candidate of YeO-YeR (later YeR). Shtyrov was elected republican President in January 2002.

In March 2002 the republican legislature approved extensive amendments to Sakha's Constitution. Elections to a reformed, unicameral, 70-member State Assembly were held on 29 December. The republican legislature endorsed Federal President Vladimir Putin's nomination of Shtyrov to a second term of office in December 2006.

On 31 May 2010 Shtyrov announced his resignation as republican President. Federal President Dmitrii Medvedev's nomination of Yegor Borisov, the Chairman of the republican Government since 2003, as republican President was confirmed by a vote in the State Assembly in June 2010. He was succeeded as premier by Galina Danchikova.

In September 2014 Borisov was elected Head of the Republic (as the post of republican President had been redesignated), obtaining 58.8% of the votes cast; his nearest rival was Ernst Berezkin of GP, with 29.5%—a notably strong performance for a candidate of that party.

On 28 May 2018 Borisov resigned, following the federal Government's reported dissatisfaction at the level of support (64.4%) obtained in the Republic by Putin in the federal presidential election in March. Putin appointed Aisen Nikolayev, hitherto Head of Yakutsk City District, as the Acting Head of the Republic. On 9 September Nikolayev was elected Head of the Republic with 71.4% of the votes cast. In concurrent polls to the State Assembly, YeR won 50.8% of the votes cast on a proportional basis, ahead of the KPRF, with 19.4%, SR, with 16.3%, and the LDPR, with 9.6%. Some 43 of the 71 deputies had joined the YeR parliamentary faction by the end of the year, 10 that of the KPRF, nine that of SR, and four that of the LDPR. On 18 October the State Assembly confirmed Vladimir Solodov (acting premier since June) as Chairman of the Government.

On 3 April 2020 Solodov was transferred to the post of Acting Governor of Kamchatka Krai. Aleksei Kolodeznikov, the First Deputy Chairman of the Government, initially replaced him in an acting capacity, but in July the former Acting Governor of Maritime (Primorskii) Krai, Andrei Tarasenko, was appointed as Acting premier. Nikolayev confirmed Tarasenko's appointment on 10 November.

Wildfires concentrated in Sakha (Yakutiya) during July–August 2021 were particularly severe, destroying around 8.4m. ha of the Republic's forestland in that year overall. After wildfires in Far Eastern regions began in May 2022, on 19 July a federal state of emergency was declared in the Republic and in neighbouring Khabarovsk Krai in order to support regional efforts to combat their spread.

On 10 September 2023 Nikolayev, the candidate of YeR, was re-elected Head of the Republic with 75.8% of the votes cast, defeating three other candidates. Following concurrent elections to the State Assembly, YeR increased its representation to 55 of the 70 seats in the chamber. In early October Nikolayev appointed Kirill Bychkov, hitherto First Deputy Chairman of the Government, as Chairman, replacing Tarasenko.

ECONOMY

The gross regional product (GRP) of the Republic of Sakha (Yakutiya) in 2021 was 1,615,527m. roubles, or 1,636,734 roubles per head. The Republic's major industrial centres are at Yakutsk, Mirnyi, Neryungri and Lensk. Its main seaport is at Tiksi. A freight railway linking the Baikal–Amur main line with Nizhnii Bestyakh, on the opposite bank of the Lena from Yakutsk, commenced operations in 2014, but proposals to construct a bridge onwards to Yakutsk (otherwise connected to Nizhnii Bestyakh by ferry services, and, in winter, by an ice road) remained in abeyance. At the end of 2021 there were 964 km of railways in the Republic.

The Republic's agriculture consists mainly of animal husbandry (livestock and reindeer breeding), hunting and fishing. Grain and vegetable production tends to be on a small scale. The sector employed 5.9% of the workforce and contributed 1.1% of GRP in 2021. The main industries are non-ferrous metallurgy, mining (for gold, diamonds, tin, muscovite or mica, antimony and coal), and the production of electricity and natural gas. A new uranium field in the south of the Republic, at Elkonskii Gorst, was opened up for exploitation in the late 2000s; an adjacent gold mining facility was also to commence operations. In the early 2000s the local diamond-producing company Alrosa, the principal diamond-producer in Russia, acquired majority stakes in several petroleum and natural gas assets in the Republic. In early 2006 it was agreed by Alrosa's board of directors that the federal Government (which owned 37% of the company) would increase its holding to a majority stake (50% plus one share) in the company; by 2018 this share had been reduced, to 33%, although the Governments of Sakha and of several municipalities within the Republic owned a further 33%. The Eastern Siberia—Pacific Ocean Pipeline, that links Taishet (Irkutsk Oblast) with the port of Kozmino (Maritime Krai) passes through the Republic. Industry employed 32.1% of the workforce and contributed 70.2% of GRP in 2021, when manufacturing employed 3.9% of the workforce and contributed 0.9% of GRP.

The economically active population numbered 470,312 in 2022, when the rate of unemployment was 6.5%, while the average monthly wage was 96,728 roubles. There was a budgetary surplus of 39,051.4m. roubles in 2021, when export trade amounted to US $5,551m. (of which 0.2% was with countries of the CIS), while import trade amounted to $180m. (of which 0.9% was with CIS countries).

DIRECTORY

Head of the Republic: AISEN S. NIKOLAYEV.

Chairman of the Government: KIRILL YE. BYCHKOV.

Office of the Head of the Republic and Government: 677000 Sakha (Yakutiya), Yakutsk, ul. Kirova 11; tel. (4112) 43-53-88; fax (4112) 24-06-07; e-mail adm@adm.sakha.gov.ru; internet glava.sakha.gov.ru; internet prav.sakha.gov.ru.

State Assembly (Il Tumen): 677022 Sakha (Yakutiya), Yakutsk, ul. Yaroslavskogo 24/1; tel. (4112) 43-51-94; fax (4112) 43-53-33; e-mail gs@iltumen.ru; internet iltumen.ru; Chair. ALEKSEI I. YEREMEYEV.

State Duma Representative (1): PYOTR R. AMMOSOV (KPRF).

Federation Council Representatives: YEGOR A. BORISOV, SAKHAMIN M. AFANASYEV.

Kamchatka Krai

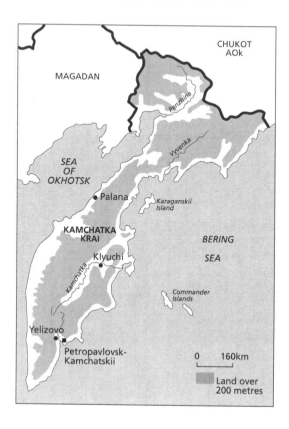

Kamchatka Krai occupies the Kamchatka Peninsula, some 1,600 km in length and 130 km in width, which separates the Sea of Okhotsk, in the west, from the Bering Sea, in the east. The Krai also includes Karaganskii Island, the Commander Islands and the southernmost part of the Chukotka Peninsula. There are land borders with the Chukot Autonomous Okrug to the north and Magadan Oblast to the west. The region is dominated by the Sredinnyi Khrebet mountain range, which is bounded to the west by a broad, poorly drained coastal plain, and to the east by the Kamchatka river valley. Two-thirds of the Krai's area is mountainous (including the highest point in the Russian Far East, Mt Klyuchevskaya, at 4,685 m), and it contains many hot springs. Kamchatka Krai covers 464,275 sq km (179,258 sq miles). There is a high annual rate of precipitation in the region, and temperatures vary considerably across the territory. At January 2023 the estimated population of the region was 288,730 and the population density 0.6 per sq km. Some 78.0% of the population was urban in 2023. The administrative centre is at Petropavlovsk-Kamchatskii, in the south-east, with an estimated 162,992 inhabitants at January 2023. Of residents who stated their ethnicity at the 2021 census, 88.3% were Russian, 2.4% Koryak, 1.5% Ukrainian, 0.7% Itelmen, and 0.7% were Even. Kamchatka Krai is in the time zone UTC+12.

HISTORY

Petropavlovsk came under Russian control in 1743. After 1917, Kamchatka was part of the short-lived Far Eastern Republic. Kamchatka Oblast was formed on 20 October 1923, forming part of Khabarovsk Krai until 23 January 1956.

At the gubernatorial election held in December 2000, the KPRF candidate, Mikhail Mashkovtsev, was elected Governor. He was re-elected in December 2004.

In April 2005 the legislatures of Kamchatka Oblast and the Koryak Autonomous Okrug (in the north of the Oblast) approved a request to President Vladimir Putin that the two territories be merged. In a referendum on unification, held in October, 84.9% of the votes cast in the Oblast (with 52.2% of the electorate participating) supported the proposal. Putin signed the merger, creating a territory called Kamchatka Krai, into constitutional law in July 2006.

Mashkovtsev resigned as Governor on 23 May 2007. Putin's nomination of Mashkovtsev's erstwhile deputy, Aleksei Kuzmitskii, as Governor of Kamchatka Krai was approved by the Kamchatka Oblast legislature on 30 May, and by the Koryak Autonomous Okrug legislature on 1 June. Kamchatka Krai was formally constituted on 1 July. At elections to the new provincial Legislative Assembly, conducted on 2 December, YeR won 62.9% of the votes cast.

In February 2011 President Dmitrii Medvedev (who had recently criticized the poor quality of infrastructure, social conditions and housing in Kamchatka Krai) accepted Kuzmitskii's resignation and nominated as his successor the erstwhile Federal Inspector to the Krai, Vladimir Ilyukhin. The provincial Legislative Assembly endorsed his appointment on 3 March. At elections to the provincial legislature, held on 4 December, YeR obtained 44.8% of the votes cast; the LDPR and the KPRF each obtained 17.6%, reflecting substantial dissatisfaction with the federal authorities locally. Ilyukhin was elected as Governor in a direct election on 13 September 2015, obtaining 75.5% of the votes cast.

YeR secured 48.3% of the votes cast on a proportional basis in elections to the Legislative Assembly on 18 September 2016. The LDPR was second, with 23.0%. Some 21 of the 28 deputies had joined the YeR parliamentary faction by the end of the year.

On 3 April 2020 President Putin (who had returned to that post in 2012) accepted the resignation of Ilyukhin (who had been criticized by federal officials for his poor management of the COVID-19 pandemic) and appointed Vladimir Solodov, hitherto the Chairman of the Government of the Republic of Sakha (Yakutiya), as Acting Governor. On 20 April Solodov appointed Aleksandr Kuznetsov, previously the Chief Federal Inspector for Sakhalin Oblast, as Acting Chairman of the Government, First Vice Governor.

Solodov was elected as Governor on 13 September 2020, with 80.5% of the votes cast. He was inaugurated to office on 21 September. Kuznetsov was subsequently confirmed in his post.

At elections to the provincial Legislative Assembly held on 19 September 2021, YeR secured 34.7% of the votes cast on the basis of proportional representation; the KPRF obtained 23.2%, the LDPR 11.7%, the recently established centre-right NL 10.3%, SR 8.4% and the RPSS 5.2%. By the end of the year 18 of the 28 deputies had joined the YeR faction, five that of the KPRF. The factions of the four other parties each comprised one deputy. In December Yevgenii Chekin succeeded Kuznetsov as Chairman of the Government (but without the designation of First Vice Governor), having previously held that role in the Republic of Sakha (Yakutiya) in 2016–18.

ECONOMY

The waters around Kamchatka (the Sea of Okhotsk, the Bering Sea and the Pacific Ocean) are extremely rich in marine life, and fishing, especially for crabs, is the dominant sector of the region's economy. The region's fish stocks comprise around one-half of Russia's total. In 2021 Kamchatka's Krai's gross regional product (GRP) was 337,505m. roubles, or 1,081,102 roubles per head. Petropavlovsk-Kamchatskii and Ust-Kamchatsk are the main industrial centres and ports in the territory. There is an international airport, Yelizovo, situated 30 km from Petropavlovsk-Kamchatskii. There are no railways in the Oblast.

Apart from fishing, which represents the overwhelming majority of agricultural output, agriculture in the territory consists of vegetable production, animal husbandry (livestock, reindeer, and fur animals) and hunting. Agriculture employed 11.5% of the workforce and contributed 30.1% of GRP in 2021. There are deposits of gold, silver, natural gas, sulphur and other minerals in the Krai, which were in the process of development in the 2000s. The industrial sector is based on the processing of agricultural products, non-ferrous metallurgy, and coal and electricity production. Three geothermal energy plants operate in the territory. Industry employed 22.7% of the workforce and contributed 18.6% of GRP in 2021, when manufacturing employed 7.8% of the workforce and contributed 5.0% of GRP.

The economically active population of the territory numbered 172,315 in 2022, when the rate of unemployment was 2.9%, while the average monthly wage was 103,540 roubles. There was a budgetary surplus of 705.7m. roubles in 2021, when export trade amounted to US $977m. (almost all of which was with non-CIS countries), while import trade amounted to $214m. (of which 1.2% was with CIS countries).

DIRECTORY

Governor: VLADIMIR V. SOLODOV.

Chairman of the Government: YEVGENII A. CHEKIN.

Office of the Governor and the Government: 683040 Kamchatka Krai, Petropavlovsk-Kamchatskii, pl. Lenina 1; tel. (4152) 41-20-68; fax (4152) 42-35-03; e-mail 41region@kamgov.ru; internet kamgov.ru.

Legislative Assembly: 683040 Kamchatka Krai, Petropavlovsk-Kamchatskii, pl. Lenina 1; tel. (4152) 42-56-06; internet zaksobr.kamchatka.ru; Chair. IRINA L. UNTILOVA.

State Duma Representative (1): IRINA A. YAROVAYA (YeR).

Federation Council Representatives: VALERII A. PONOMARYOV, BORIS A. NEVZOROV.

Khabarovsk Krai

Khabarovsk Krai is situated in the Far East, on the Sea of Okhotsk. Maritime Krai lies to the south, the Jewish Autonomous Oblast to the south-west, Amur Oblast to the west, the Republic of Sakha (Yakutiya) to the north-west and Magadan Oblast to the north-east. The island of Sakhalin (Sakhalin Oblast) lies off shore to the east, across the Tatar Strait. There is a short international border with the People's Republic of China in the south-west. Khabarovsk's main river is the Amur (Heilong Jiang). More than one-half of the Krai's total area of 787,633 sq km (304,107 sq miles) is forested, and almost three-quarters is made up of mountains or plateaux. The territory has a 2,500-km coastline. The climate is tropical in character, with hot, humid summers, with greater precipitation in the mountain regions. At January 2023 the population of Khabarovsk Krai was an estimated 1,284,090 and the population density 1.6 per sq km. Some 83.5% of the population was urban in 2023. The administrative centre, Khabarovsk, had an estimated 617,168 inhabitants at January 2023. The second city is Komsomolsk-on-Amur (Komsomolsk-na-Amure), with an estimated 236,158 inhabitants. Of residents who stated their ethnicity at the 2021 census, 92.9% were Russian, and 1.0% were Nanai. Khabarovsk Krai is in the time zone UTC+10.

HISTORY

Khabarovsk city was established as a military outpost in 1858. The region prospered significantly with the construction of the Trans-Siberian Railway, which reached Khabarovsk in 1905. The Krai was created on 20 September 1938, and until 1947 included Sakhalin Island. The province was industrialized from 1946. The Jewish Autonomous Oblast constituted part of the Krai until March 1991.

Elections to a new provincial legislature, the Legislative Duma, were held in 1994. In 1996 President Boris Yeltsin and the head of the provincial administration appointed in 1991, Viktor Ishayev, signed a power-sharing agreement. Ishayev was elected Governor later in 1996 and was re-elected in 2000 and 2004.

In June 2005 President Vladimir Putin ratified a treaty previously approved by the legislatures of Russia and the People's Republic of China, providing for the transfer of 340 sq km of territory from the Krai to China.

The provincial Legislative Duma appointed Ishayev to a further gubernatorial term in July 2007, but he was obliged to resign following his appointment, in April 2009, as Presidential Representative to the Far Eastern Federal Okrug. The provincial Legislative Duma approved the appointment of former State Duma deputy Vyacheslav Shport as Governor on 6 May. Shport was re-elected to the post by popular vote in September 2013, receiving 63.9% of the votes cast; his closest rival was Sergei Furgal of the LDPR, with 19.1%.

A gubernatorial election, contested by five candidates, was held on 9 September 2018. As no candidate obtained an absolute majority of the votes cast, the two leading candidates—Furgal and Shport, with 35.8% and 35.6% of the votes cast, respectively—proceeded to a run-off poll on 23 September. Furgal was elected Governor then, receiving 69.6% of the votes cast. The decisive defeat of the incumbent YeR candidate was attributed, in particular, to widespread discontent at federal plans to raise the national retirement age, as well as reflecting long-term dissatisfaction in the Krai with the federal authorities.

In March 2019 Ishayev (now an ally of Furgal) was arrested on suspicion of embezzlement; he was subsequently placed under house arrest. Having been found guilty, in 2021, of embezzling some 7.5m roubles from the state-owned oil company Rosneft, he received a five-year suspended sentence.

Meanwhile, on 13 December 2018 President Putin approved the transfer of the administrative centre of the Far Eastern Federal Okrug from Khabarovsk to Vladivostok, Maritime Krai; this entered fully into effect in 2020.

The low level of support for the federal authorities in the territory was again evident in elections to the Legislative Duma held on 8 September 2019. YeR was placed only third in proportional voting, obtaining 12.5% of the votes cast on that basis, behind the LDPR, with 56.1%, and the KPRF, with 17.2%. By January 2020 some 29 of the 36 elected deputies had joined the parliamentary faction of the LDPR, and two each those of YeR and the KPRF.

In July 2020 Furgal was arrested during a federal investigation into organized crime; one day later a Moscow court ordered that he be placed in pre-trial detention for two months, on charges of organizing the murder and attempted murder of several businessmen in 2004–05. Protests to demand the Governor's release ensued in cities across the Krai. The provincial authorities announced the extension of restrictions imposed in response to the COVID-19 pandemic, including a ban on mass gatherings. President Putin dismissed Furgal and appointed a hitherto deputy of the State Duma, Mikhail Degtyaryov, also of the LDPR, as Acting Governor on 20 July. Daily large rallies continued, with protesters rejecting Degtyaryov's appointment. Demonstrations in support of Furgal (and of detained opposition leader Aleksei Navalnyi) continued in central Khabarovsk, but with reduced numbers, into early 2021, resulting in the arrest of many activists by police. Furgal's trial, on charges of attempted murder and of ordering two killings, commenced in Lyubertsy, Moscow Oblast, in May 2022; Furgal subsequently undertook a hunger strike as the trial continued. In February 2023 Furgal was found guilty of two counts of murder and was sentenced to 22 years' imprisonment.

Meanwhile, Degtyaryov was confirmed in the post of Governor on 19 September 2021, when he secured 56.8% of the votes cast in a direct election. His closest rival was the SR candidate, television presenter Marina Kim (who obtained 25.4% of the vote). He assumed office on 24 September.

ECONOMY

In 2021 Khabarovsk Krai's gross regional product (GRP) was 987,187m. roubles, or 759,344 roubles per head. Its main industrial centres are at Khabarovsk, Komsomolsk-on-Amur, Sovetskaya Gavan and Nikolayevsk-on-Amur. The principal ports are Vanino, Okhotsk and Nikolayevsk-on-Amur. It is traversed by the Trans-Siberian and Baikal–Amur railways and by the Chita–Khabarovsk highway. At the end of 2021 there were 2,144 km of railways in the territory. A ferry service runs between the Krai and Sakhalin Oblast, and there is an international airport at Khabarovsk.

The principal land use is forestry. Agriculture consists mainly of the production of grain, soybeans, vegetables and fruit, animal husbandry (including reindeer breeding), and hunting. The sector employed 4.1% of the workforce and contributed 6.8% of GRP in 2021. The Krai's main industries are mechanical engineering, electricity production, metal working, non-ferrous and ferrous metallurgy, food processing, the processing of forestry products, the extraction of coal, ores and non-ferrous metals, shipbuilding (including oil rigs), and petroleum refining. Industry employed 26.4% of the workforce and contributed 28.1% of GRP in 2021, when manufacturing employed 10.0% of the workforce and contributed 11.1% of GRP.

The economically active population numbered 686,942 in 2022, when the rate of unemployment was 2.6%, while the average monthly wage was 65,897 roubles. There was a budgetary surplus of 6,155.0m. roubles in 2021, when export trade amounted to US $2,539m. (of which 15.1% was with countries of the CIS), while import trade amounted to $1,110m. (of which 31.9% was with CIS countries).

DIRECTORY

Governor: MIKHAIL V. DEGTYARYOV.

Office of the Governor: 680000 Khabarovsk, ul. K. Marksa 56; tel. (4212) 32-51-21; fax (4212) 32-87-56; e-mail main@adm.khv.ru; internet khabkrai.ru.

Legislative Duma: 680002 Khabarovsk, ul. Muravyeva-Amurskogo 19; tel. (4212) 32-50-27; fax (4212) 32-44-57; e-mail duma@duma.khv.ru; internet duma.khv.ru; Chair. IRINA V. ZIKUNOVA.

State Duma Representatives (2): BORIS M. GLADKIKH (YeR), PAVEL V. SIMIGIN (YeR).

Federation Council Representatives: SERGEI V. BEZDENEZHNYKH, ANDREI A. BAZILEVSKII.

Maritime (Primorskii) Krai

Maritime (Primorskii) Krai, or Primorye, is situated in the extreme south-east of Russia, on the Sea of Japan. Khabarovsk Krai lies to the north and the People's Republic of China to the west. There is a short border with the Democratic People's Republic of Korea (North Korea) in the south-west. The territory occupies 164,673 sq km (63,581 sq miles). At January 2023 the estimated population of the territory was 1,820,076 and the population density 11.1 per sq km. Some 78.4% of the population was urban in 2023. The administrative centre is at Vladivostok, which had an estimated 597,237 inhabitants at January 2023. Other major cities are Ussuriisk (179,862), Nakhodka (136,096) and Artyom (108,690). Of residents who stated their ethnicity at the 2021 census, 94.4% were Russian, and 0.8% were Ukrainian. Maritime Krai is in the time zone UTC+10.

HISTORY

The territories of Maritime Krai were recognized as Chinese possessions by Russia in 1687. They became part of the Russian Empire in 1860, following which the port of Vladivostok was founded. After the collapse of the Russian Empire, the territory was part of the pro-Bolshevik Far Eastern Republic until its integration into Soviet Russia in 1922. Maritime Krai was created on 20 October 1938.

The territory failed to obtain recognition as a republic in 1993. On 28 October the provincial Soviet (Council) was disbanded. Elections for a Governor, scheduled for October 1994, were cancelled by presidential decree. The incumbent, Yevgenii Nazdratenko, was elected, however, in December 1995, and re-elected in 1999, on both occasions by an overwhelming majority. An ongoing energy crisis forced his resignation in February 2001. Sergei Darkin, a local businessman, was elected Governor in June in a second round of voting, with 40.2% of the votes cast. After

Viktor Cherepkov, the former Mayor of Vladivostok, who was placed second in the first round, was barred from contesting the run-off poll, 33.7% of votes were cast 'against all candidates'.

In February 2005 the Legislative Assembly approved the nomination by President Vladimir Putin of Darkin to a further term as Governor. In January 2010 the Legislative Assembly approved President Dmitrii Medvedev's nomination of Darkin to a third gubernatorial term.

In elections to the Legislative Assembly held in December 2011 the proportion of the votes awarded to YeR declined sharply, to 33.7% (compared with 48.3% at the last elections, in 2006), while that of the KPRF increased to 23.8%. SR and the LDPR each obtained 19.8%. In concurrent elections to the State Duma, YeR's share of the votes cast in the province was lower still, at 33.0%. Later in December Putin (then Chairman of the federal Government) publicly criticized the high levels of corruption and crime in Maritime Krai. Darkin announced his resignation in February. In March the Legislative Assembly voted to endorse the appointment of Vladimir Miklushevskii, hitherto a university rector, as Governor. He was directly elected to the post on 14 September 2014.

YeR secured 39.5% of the votes cast on a proportional basis in elections to the Legislative Assembly held on 18 September 2016; the KPRF obtained 20.8%, the LDPR 20.4%, SR 7.2%, and the RPPS 5.4%. A total of 25 of the 40 deputies had joined the YeR parliamentary faction by the end of the year.

On 4 October 2017 Miklushevskii resigned as Governor. The erstwhile Director-General of the Rosmorport federal shipping and ports corporation, Andrei Tarasenko, succeeded him in an acting capacity. On 9 September 2018 Tarasenko was placed first in a direct gubernatorial election, obtaining 46.6% of the votes cast. Having failed to secure at least 50%, he proceeded, with the second-placed candidate, Andrei Ishchenko of the KPRF, who had obtained 24.6%, to a run-off poll on 16 September. On this occasion, amid allegations of electoral malpractice, Tarasenko was elected Governor. He was attributed 49.6% of the votes cast, and Ishchenko 48.1%. However, Ishchenko rejected the results. On 20 September the Provincial Electoral Commission declared the results invalid. On 26 September President Putin appointed Oleg Kozhemyako, a former Governor of Amur and Sakhalin Oblasts, as Acting Governor; and a further election was scheduled for 16 December. On 20 November the Provincial Electoral Commission debarred Ishchenko from participation. In the poll on 16 December, contested by four candidates, Kozhemyako was elected with 61.9% of the votes cast; Andrei Andreichenko of the LDPR was second, with 25.2%.

Meanwhile, in October 2018 Kozhemyako proposed that the administrative centre of the Far Eastern Federal Okrug be relocated from Khabarovsk to Vladivostok. Despite opposition from the Governor of Khabarovsk Krai, Sergei Furgal, on 13 December President Putin approved the transfer. On 27 November 2019 the Legislative Assembly adopted legislation amending the status of Vladivostok accordingly (with effect from 1 January 2020); the relocation of the Presidential Representative to the Far Eastern Federal Okrug was delayed until later in the year.

At elections to the provincial Legislative Assembly held on 19 September 2021, YeR secured 37.9% of the votes cast on the basis of proportional representation, ahead of the KPRF, with 31.0%. By the end of the year 18 of the 26 deputies had joined the YeR faction and five that of the KPRF.

On 10 September 2023 Kozhemyako, the candidate of YeR, was re-elected as Governor with 72.8% of votes cast, defeating four other candidates. Shortly afterwards, he appointed Aleksandr Rolik, hitherto the Chairman of the Legislative Assembly, as a representative of Maritime Krai in the Federation Council.

ECONOMY

Maritime Krai's gross regional product (GRP) was 1,308,884m. roubles, or 699,778 roubles per head, in 2021. Its major industrial centres are Vladivostok, Ussuriisk, Nakhodka and Dalnegorsk. The Krai's most important ports are at Vladivostok, Nakhodka and Vostochnyi (Vrangel). Maritime Krai has rail links with Khabarovsk Krai, as well as international transport links with the Democratic People's Republic of Korea (North Korea) and the People's Republic of China. In 2013 a railway linking Khasan, in the Krai, with the North Korean port of Rajin, closed for renovation since 2008, reopened. At the end of 2021 there were 1,559 km of railways in the Krai.

The Krai's agricultural sector consists mainly of grain, vegetable and soybean production, animal husbandry (including fur farming), beekeeping and fishing. The sector employed 8.3% of the workforce and contributed 10.2% of GRP in 2021. There are substantial reserves of coal and timber. The hydroelectric energy potential of the region's rivers is estimated at 25,000m. kWh. The main industries are food processing, fuel and electrical energy production, ore mining, the processing of forestry products, mechanical engineering and ship repairs. Industry employed 22.6% of the workforce and contributed 15.4% of GRP in 2021, when manufacturing employed 11.0% of the workforce and contributed 7.6% of GRP. The territory is geographically well placed for international trade, although perceptions of corruption and mismanagement have restrained its development. Significant development of infrastructure occurred prior to a summit meeting of the Asia-Pacific Economic Cooperation (APEC) forum in Vladivostok in 2012. In 2015 President Putin signed legislation granting the status of a free port to Vladivostok and other ports in Maritime Krai, and providing tax incentives and other benefits to companies operating in a large part of the Krai.

The economically active population numbered 949.854 in 2022, when the rate of unemployment was 3.4%, and the average monthly wage was 63,589 roubles. There was a budgetary surplus of 1,582.4m. roubles in 2021, when export trade amounted to US $3,428m. (of which 1.0% was with countries of the CIS), and import trade amounted to $7,219m. (of which 0.9% was with CIS countries).

DIRECTORY

Governor: OLEG N. KOZHEMYAKO.

Office of the Governor: 690110 Maritime Krai, Vladivostok, ul. Svetlanskaya 22; tel. (423) 222-38-00; fax (423) 222-17-69; e-mail administration@primorsky.ru; internet primorsky.ru.

Legislative Assembly: 690110 Maritime Krai, Vladivostok, ul. Svetlanskaya 22; tel. (423) 240-22-12; fax (423) 226-90-23; e-mail chairman@zspk.gov.ru; internet zspk.gov.ru; Chair. ANTON A. VOLOSHKO.

State Duma Representatives (3): ALEKSANDR V. SHCHERBAKOV (YeR), VLADIMIR M. NOVIKOV (YeR), VIKTORIYA V. NIKOLAYEVA (YeR).

Federation Council Representatives: ALEKSANDR I. ROLIK, LYUDMILA Z. TALABAYEVA.

Transbaikal Krai

Transbaikal Krai is situated in part of the region between Lake Baikal and the People's Republic of China. The Republic of Buryatiya lies to the west, Irkutsk Oblast to the north, and the Republic of Sakha (Yakutiya) and Amur Oblast to the east. To the south there are international borders with China and Mongolia. The western part of the region is situated in the Yablonovii Khrebet mountain range. The Krai covers 431,892 sq km (166,754 sq miles). At January 2023 its population was an estimated 992,429 and the population density 2.3 per sq km. Some 69.5% of the population was urban in 2023. The administrative centre, Chita, had an estimated 333,679 inhabitants at January 2023. Of residents who stated their ethnicity at the 2021 census, 89.2% were Russian, and 7.4% were Buryat. Transbaikal Krai is in the time zone UTC+9.

HISTORY

The city of Chita was established by Cossacks in 1653, at the confluence of the Chita and Ingoda rivers. Chita was pronounced the capital of the independent, pro-Bolshevik Far Eastern Republic upon its establishment in April 1920. It united the regions of Irkutsk, Transbaikal, Amur and the Pacific coast, and merged with Soviet Russia in November 1922. Chita Oblast was founded on 26 September 1937. The Buryat-Mongol Autonomous Soviet Socialist Republic (ASSR), created in 1923, was restructured in the same month, and the Aga-Buryat-Mongol Autonomous Okrug (renamed the Aga-Buryat Autonomous Okrug in 1958), hitherto the eastern-most section of the ASSR, was established within Chita Oblast.

A new regional Duma was elected in 1994. In a gubernatorial election held in October 2000 the incumbent, Ravil Geniatulin (who had been appointed as Governor by President Boris Yeltsin, before being elected in 1996), was re-elected. Geniatulin was elected to a further term in March 2004.

Referendums held in March 2007 overwhelmingly approved the merger of the Aga-Buryat Autonomous Okrug and Chita Oblast, by 90.3% of the votes cast in Chita Oblast and 94.0% of votes in the Aga-Buryat Autonomous Okrug; legislation to that end was signed into law by President Vladimir Putin on 23 July.

The new territory, Transbaikal Krai, was formed on 1 March 2008, when Geniatulin became its Governor. Elections to its Legislative Assembly were held on 12 October, at which YeR was the most successful party, winning 54.8% of the votes cast on a proportional basis.

Following the expiry of Geniatulin's mandate on 1 March 2013, Konstantin Ilkovskii, a former energy sector executive in the Republic of Sakha (Yakutiya) and an SR State Duma deputy, was appointed as Acting Governor. On 8 September he was elected as Governor, obtaining 71.6% of the popular vote. In the concurrent elections to the Legislative Assembly, YeR obtained 43.1% of the votes cast to seats elected on a proportional basis. The KPRF was second, with 14.2%.

On 17 February 2016 Putin accepted the early resignation of Ilkovskii as Governor; in addition to the reportedly inadequate implementation of a federal housing programme in the Krai, arrears in the payment of salaries to health and education sector employees had prompted strike action in late 2015. Ilkovskii was succeeded, in an acting capacity, by Natalya Zhdanova, hitherto Chairman of the provincial Legislative Assembly. She was elected Governor on 18 September, with 54.4% of the votes cast.

Elections to the Legislative Assembly were held on 9 September 2018. YeR won 28.3% of the votes cast to seats elected on a proportional basis, narrowly ahead of the LDPR and the KPRF, each of which received 24.6%, and SR, with 9.0%. Only 20 of the 50 deputies had joined the YeR parliamentary faction by the end of the year, meaning that the Assembly was one of the few regional legislatures in which the party did not enjoy a majority. Thirteen deputies joined the faction of the KPRF, 10 that of the LDPR, and three that of SR. Amid continuing economic difficulties, Zhdanova announced her resignation as Governor on 11 October. Two weeks later, Aleksandr Osipov, a former Deputy Minister of the Russian Far East in the federal Government, was appointed as Acting Governor. A presidential decree, issued in November 2018, transferred the Krai, along with the Republic of Buryatiya, from the Siberian to the Far Eastern Federal Okrug.

On 8 September 2019 Osipov was elected as Governor, obtaining 89.6% of the votes cast, defeating three other candidates. Following elections to the Legislative Assembly held on 10 September 2023, YeR held 42 of the 50 seats in the expanded chamber, substantially increasing its representation, although the rate of participation was only 26.6%.

ECONOMY

The gross regional product (GRP) of Transbaikal Krai amounted to 487,423m. roubles in 2021, equivalent to 464,887 roubles per head. The region's main industrial centres are at Chita, Nerchinsk and Darasun. At the end of 2021 there were 2,398 km of railways in the territory. The Chita–Khabarovsk highway, opened in 2003, forms part of a route between Moscow and Vladivostok.

Agriculture consists mainly of animal husbandry (livestock and reindeer breeding) and the hunting of animals for fur. The sector employed some 7.1% of the workforce and contributed 3.5% of GRP in 2021. The major industries are non-ferrous metallurgy, electrical energy, fuel extraction (including uranium), food processing and ore mining. Coal mining is centred around the Vostochnaya mine; gold and tin mining occurs at Sherlovaya Govra; lead and zinc ore mines are situated at Khapcheranga, while the principal uranium production facilities in the Federation are located at Krasnokamensk. Industry employed 22.6% of the workforce and contributed 41.6% of GRP in 2021, when manufacturing employed 7.3% of the workforce and contributed 2.0% of GRP.

The economically active population numbered 464,853 in 2022, when the rate of unemployment was 8.7%, while the average monthly wage was 59,413 roubles. There was a budgetary deficit of 1,107.7m. roubles in 2021, when export trade amounted to US $1,458m. (of which 3.7% was with CIS countries), and import trade to $633m. (0.3% of which was with CIS countries).

DIRECTORY

Governor: ALEKSANDR M. OSIPOV.

Office of the Governor: 672021 Transbaikal Krai, Chita, ul. Chaikovskogo 8; tel. (3022) 35-24-95; fax (3022) 35-74-89; e-mail ps@e-zab.ru; internet bit.ly/3a9fefq.

Legislative Assembly: 672021 Transbaikal Krai, Chita, ul. Chaikovskogo 8; tel. and fax (3022) 35-74-89; e-mail info@zaksobr.chita.ru; internet zaksobr-chita.ru; Chair. YURII M. KON.

State Duma Representatives (2): ALEKSANDR A. SKACHKOV (YeR), VASILINA V. KULIYEVA (LDPR).

Federation Council Representatives: BAIR B. ZHAMSUYEV, SERGEI P. MIKHAILOV.

Amur Oblast

Amur Oblast is situated in the south-east of Russia. Khabarovsk Krai lies to the east, the Jewish Autonomous Oblast to the south-east, Transbaikal Krai to the west and the Republic of Sakha (Yakutiya) to the north. To the south lies an international border with the People's Republic of China, along the Oblast's main river, the Amur (Heilong Jiang). A little under three-quarters of the Oblast's territory is forested. Its total area occupies 361,913 sq km (139,735 sq miles). At January 2023 the territory's population was an estimated 756,198 and the population density 2.1 per sq km. Some 68.4% of the population was urban in 2023. The administrative centre, Blagoveshchensk, had an estimated 240,572 inhabitants at January 2023. Of residents who stated their ethnicity at the 2021 census, 95.2% were Russian. Amur Oblast is in the time zone UTC+9.

HISTORY

The Amur region came under Russian control in the late 1850s. Amur Oblast was formed on 20 October 1932.

President Boris Yeltsin called for a gubernatorial election to be held in Amur Oblast in December 1992, when his appointed head of the administration, Albert Krivchenko, was defeated by Aleksandr Surat. In July 1993, after the Oblast unilaterally declared itself a republic, Surat was dismissed and the regional Soviet dissolved. In January 1996 the oblast administration brought action against the regional Assembly for adopting a Charter, described as a republican constitution, in contravention of federal legislation. In June Yeltsin dismissed the regional Governor, Vladimir Dyachenko, and appointed Yurii Lyashko in his place. In a gubernatorial election in September, Anatolii Belonogov of the KPRF narrowly defeated Lyashko, but the results were annulled on the grounds of irregularities. Belonogov became Governor following a new election in March 1997. In 2001 Leonid Korotkov defeated Belonogov to be elected Governor; the regional legislature approved Korotkov's appointment to a further term in 2005.

In May 2007 President Vladimir Putin signed a decree dismissing Korotkov (who had been charged with financial malpractice) as Governor. The oblast legislature approved the appointment as Governor of Putin's nominee, Nikolai Kolesov, hitherto a deputy in the legislature of Tatarstan, in June. This appointment proved controversial, not least as a result of Kolesov's appointment to senior positions of a number of his associates from Tatarstan. His position became increasingly untenable following the instigation of a court case on charges of embezzlement and abuse of office, in April 2008, against two of these ministerial appointees, and in October President Dmitrii Medvedev dismissed Kolesov. Later that month the oblast legislature voted to approve the appointment of Oleg Kozhemyako, a former Governor of the Koryak Autonomous Okrug (since absorbed into Kamchatka Krai) as Governor. On 14 October 2012, in a direct election, Kozhemyako was elected Governor, obtaining 77.3% of the votes cast.

On 25 March 2015 Putin (again President) transferred Kozhemyako to the post of Acting Governor of Sakhalin Oblast, appointing Aleksandr Kozlov (the Mayor of Blagoveshchensk) as the Acting Governor of Amur Oblast. Kozlov was elected Governor on 13 September, defeating three other candidates. Obtaining 50.6% of the vote, and thereby narrowly avoiding the necessity of contesting a run-off election, Kozlov, aged 34 years, became one of the youngest regional leaders in Russia. The second-placed candidate was the LDPR candidate, Ivan Abramov with 28.3% of the vote.

YeR secured 35.9% of the votes cast on a proportional basis in elections to the regional legislature held on 18 September 2016 (one of the lowest levels of support recorded for YeR at the regional elections held on that day); the LDPR was second, with 30.7%, while the KPRF obtained 17.4% and SR 5.1%. By the end of the year 24 of the 36 deputies had joined the YeR parliamentary faction, granting it a majority that it had hitherto lacked.

On 18 May 2018 Kozlov was appointed to the federal Government as Minister of Development of the Russian Far East. President Putin on 30 May appointed Vasilii Orlov, previously a regional Minister of Economic Development and hitherto a senior official of leading petrochemicals company Sibur, as Acting Governor, in his place. On 9 September Orlov was elected Governor, with 55.6% of the votes cast. Tatyana Rakutina of the KPRF was second, with 26.6%.

At elections to the regional Legislative Assembly held on 19 September 2021, YeR secured 33.2% of the votes cast on the basis of proportional representation; the KPRF obtained 21.5%, the LDPR 14.2%, the KR 8.3%, the recently established centre-right NL 7.2%, SR 6.3% and the RPPS 5.4%. By the end of the year 19 of the 27 deputies had joined the YeR faction, and three that of the KPRF. The factions of the five other parties represented comprised one deputy each.

On 10 September 2023 Orlov, the candidate of YeR, was re-elected Governor with 82.4% of the votes cast, defeating four other candidates.

ECONOMY

Amur Oblast's gross regional product (GRP) was 530,948m. roubles, or an estimated 683,168 roubles per head, in 2021. Its main industrial centres are Blagoveshchensk, Belogorsk, Zeya and Svobodnyi. At the end of 2021 there were 2,920 km of railways in the Oblast, including sections of the Trans-Siberian railway and the Baikal–Amur main line. The construction of a road bridge linking across the Amur linking Blagoveshchensk with Heihe, in the People's Republic of China, was completed in November

2019; it opened fully to traffic in May 2021. This constituted the first highway connection between Russia and China, and followed the opening of the first railway bridge between the two countries (the Russian side being located in the Jewish Autonomous Oblast) earlier in 2019. There is an international airport at Blagoveshchensk.

Agriculture in Amur Oblast consists mainly of grain and vegetable production, animal husbandry (including the breeding of reindeer and animals for fur), and beekeeping. The sector employed 5.7% of the workforce and contributed 5.9% of GRP in 2021. The region is rich in mineral resources, although they remain largely unexploited. Other raw material deposits include bituminous coal, lignite (brown coal) and kaolin. There are also substantial reserves of iron, titanium and silver ores. Coal mining is important, as are mechanical engineering, electricity generation, electrotechnical industry, and the processing of agricultural and forestry products. The region contains the Amur Shipbuilding Plant and produces nuclear-powered submarines. There is a hydroelectric power plant at Zeya, with a reservoir of 2,400 sq km. Two units of another power station, at Bureya, commenced operations in 2003; the entire complex, with a capacity of 2,010 MW, opened in 2009, and in the following year it produced more than 5,000m. kWh of electric energy. Industry employed 29.5% of the workforce and contributed 41.7% of GRP in 2021, when manufacturing employed 5.5% of the workforce and contributed 3.4% of GRP.

The economically active population numbered 385,590 in 2022, when the rate of unemployment was 4.2%, while the average monthly wage was 65,864 roubles. There was a budgetary deficit of 5,141.2m. roubles in 2021, when export trade amounted to US $627m. (of which 0.9% was with countries of the CIS), while import trade amounted to $532m. (of which 4.2% was with CIS countries).

DIRECTORY

Governor: Vasilii A. Orlov.

Office of the Governor: 675023 Amur obl., Blagoveshchensk, ul. Lenina 135; tel. (4162) 59-60-02; fax (4162) 44-62-01; e-mail governor@amurobl.ru; internet amurobl.ru.

Legislative Assembly: 675023 Amur obl., Blagoveshchensk, ul. Lenina 135; tel. (4162) 22-38-00; fax (4162) 42-38-54; e-mail zsamur@zsamur.ru; internet zsamur.ru; Chair. Konstantin V. Dyakonov.

State Duma Representative (1): Vyacheslav Yu. Loginov (YeR).

Federation Council Representatives: Ivan I. Abramov, Artyom G. Sheikin.

Magadan Oblast

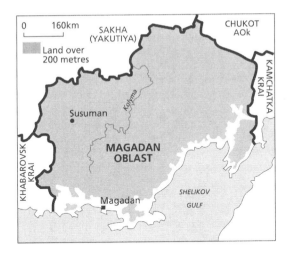

Magadan Oblast is situated in the north-east of Russia. To the north-east lies the Chukot Autonomous Okrug, and to the east, Kamchatka Krai. A coastline on the Sea of Okhotsk lies to the south-east, Khabarovsk Krai south-west and Sakha (Yakutiya) to the north-west. The main river is the Kolyma. Much of the territory is mountainous, whereas the south is dominated by forests and marshland. Much of the Oblast is tundra or forest-tundra. The Oblast occupies a total area of 462,464 sq km (178,558 sq miles). The climate in the region is severe, with winters lasting up to over seven months. At January 2023 the Oblast had an estimated population of 134,315 and a population density of 0.3 per sq km. Some 96.5% of the population was urban in 2023. The administrative centre, Magadan, had an estimated 89,834 inhabitants at January 2023. Of residents who stated their ethnicity at the 2021 census, 87.7% were Russian, 2.7% Ukrainian, 1.6% Even, and 0.7% were Uzbek. Magadan Oblast is in the time zone UTC+11.

HISTORY

Russians first reached the Magadan region in the mid-17th century. After the Bolshevik Revolution of 1917 Magadan was part of the Far Eastern Republic, which was integrated into Soviet Russia in 1922. The region held many penal establishments of the Gulag (State Corrective Camps) system established under Stalin (Iosif Dzhugashvili, 1924–53). Magadan Oblast was formed on 3 December 1953, incorporating the Chukot National District, which, as the Chukot Autonomous Okrug, was separated from the oblast in 1992.

A gubernatorial election in 1996 was won by a gold-mine proprietor allied with the KPRF, Valentin Tsvetkov. He was re-elected in 2000 but was killed in an apparent contract killing in Moscow in 2002. In February 2003 Nikolai Dudov, formerly First Deputy Governor, was narrowly elected Governor. In February 2008 the Regional Duma unanimously approved his nomination of Dudov to a further term.

Upon the expiry of Dudov's mandate as Governor, in February 2013 Vladimir Pechyonyi, hitherto Mayor of Magadan, was appointed his successor, in an acting capacity, before being elected by popular vote in September.

In elections to the Regional Duma held in September 2015 YeR won 57.7% of the proportional vote; 17 of the 21 deputies joined the YeR parliamentary faction.

Pechyonyi resigned as Governor on 28 May 2018. On the same day President Vladimir Putin appointed Sergei Nosov, a businessman and hitherto the Mayor of Nizhnii Tagil, in Sverdlovsk Oblast, as Acting Governor. On 9 September Nosov was overwhelmingly elected Governor, obtaining 81.6% of the vote.

In elections to the Regional Duma held on 13 September 2020 YeR obtained 58.3% of the proportional vote, ahead of the LDPR, with 11.6% and the KPRF, with 10.3%. When the new chamber convened, 16 of the 21 deputies joined the YeR faction.

On 10 September 2023 Nosov, the candidate of YeR, was re-elected Governor with 72.5% of the votes cast, defeating three other candidates.

ECONOMY

Magadan Oblast's gross regional product (GRP) was 314,708m. roubles, or 2,273,882 roubles per head, in 2021. The Oblast's main industrial centres are Magadan and Susuman. Magadan and Nagayevo are its most important ports. There are no railways in the Oblast. An international airport is located at Magadan.

Agricultural activities principally comprise fishing, animal husbandry and hunting. The sector employed 2.7% of the workforce and contributed 5.4% of GRP in 2021. Ore mining is important: in addition to being Russia's principal gold producing region, the Oblast contains considerable reserves of silver, tin and wolfram (tungsten). It is also rich in peat and timber, while prospecting for offshore petroleum deposits in the Sea of Okhotsk, in a zone thought to hold around 5,000m. metric tons of petroleum and natural gas, has also taken place. The Kolyma river is an important source of hydroelectric energy. The first units of a new hydroelectric plant at Ust-Srednekanskaya entered into operation on 2013; completion of the plant was expected by 2024. Other industry includes non-ferrous metallurgy, food processing, electricity generation, mechanical engineering and metal working. Industry employed 33.7% of the workforce and contributed 62.9% of GRP in 2021, when manufacturing employed 2.9% of the workforce and contributed 1.0% of GRP.

The economically active population numbered 80,278 in 2022, when the rate of unemployment was 4.1%, while the average monthly wage was 121,462 roubles. There was a budgetary surplus of 615.1m. roubles in 2021, when export trade amounted to US $552m. (of which 49.1% was with countries of the CIS), while import trade amounted to $95m. (of which 0.1% was with countries of the CIS).

DIRECTORY

Governor: Sergei K. Nosov.

Office of the Governor: 685000 Magadan, ul. Gorkogo 6; tel. (4132) 60-76-86; fax (4132) 60-78-07; e-mail government@49gov.ru; internet 49gov.ru.

Regional Duma: 685000 Magadan, ul. Gorkogo 8a; tel. (4132) 62-55-50; fax (4132) 60-70-42; internet magoblduma.ru; Chair. Sergei V. Abramov.

State Duma Representative (1): Anton A. Basanskii (YeR).

Federation Council Representatives: Sergei P. Ivanov, Anatolii I. Shirokov.

Sakhalin Oblast

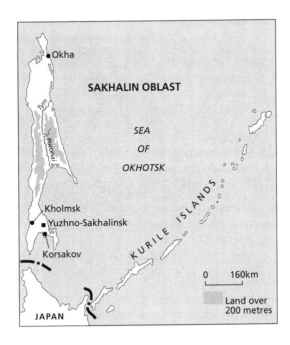

Sakhalin Oblast comprises the island of Sakhalin and the Kurile (Kuril) Islands in the Pacific Ocean. The island of Sakhalin lies off the coast of Khabarovsk Krai, separated from the mainland by the Tatar Strait. The Kurile Islands (annexed by the USSR in 1945, but claimed by Japan), an archipelago of 56 islands extending from the Kamchatka Peninsula in the north-east to Hokkaido Island (Japan) in the south-west, lie to the east. Sakhalin Island is 942 km (580 miles) in length and contains two parallel mountain ranges running north to south, separated by a central valley. The highest peaks on the island, both belonging to the eastern range of mountains, are Lopatin (1,609 m) and Nevelskogo (1,397 m). The north-west coast of the island is marshland, and much of its area is forested. The Kurile Islands are actively volcanic and contain many hot springs. There are some 60,000 rivers on Sakhalin Island, the major ones being the Poronai and the Tym (330 km), both of which are frozen during the winter months. The Kurile Islands contain around 4,000 rivers and streams and the largest waterfall in the Russian Federation, Ilya Muromets. Sakhalin Oblast covers a total area of 87,101 sq km (33,630 sq miles). At January 2023 the population was an estimated 460,535 and the population density 5.3 per sq km. Some 82.6% of the population was urban in 2023. The administrative centre, Yuzhno-Sakhalinsk, had an estimated 180,467 inhabitants at January 2023. Of residents who stated their ethnicity at the 2021 census, 91.2% were Russian, 3.7% were Korean, and 0.8% were Ukrainian. Sakhalin Oblast is in the time zone UTC+11.

HISTORY

Sakhalin Island was originally inhabited by the Nivkh (Gilyak) people. The Japanese conquered it in the late 18th century. After Russia established a military base at Korsakov in 1853, joint control of the island followed until 1875, when it was granted to Russia. Karafuto, the southern part of the island, was captured by Japan during the Russo–Japanese War (1904–05), but the entire island was ceded to the USSR in 1945. The Kurile Islands were divided between Japan and Russia in the 18th century and ruled jointly until 1875, when they were ceded to Japan. The USSR occupied the islands in 1945 and assumed full control in 1947. Four of the Southern Kuriles remained disputed thereafter. Sakhalin Oblast was formed on 20 October 1932 as part of Khabarovsk Krai. It became a separate administrative unit in 1947. Having been a place of exile for political opponents to the tsars, the region contained several penal institutions of the Gulag (State Corrective Camps) system established during the Soviet regime of Stalin—Iosif Dzhugashvili (1924–53).

In May 1996 the regional Government signed a power-sharing treaty with President Boris Yeltsin. The gubernatorial elections of October 1996 and October 2000 were won by the incumbent, Igor Farkhutdinov. In 1998 and 2000 the oblast signed co-operation accords with the Japanese province of Hokkaido, despite the continuing territorial dispute.

On 20 August 2003 Farkhutdinov and several senior oblast officials were killed in a helicopter crash. Ivan Malakhov, the new acting Governor, was formally elected to the post in December; he subsequently joined YeR.

In August 2006 the federal Government announced a strategy for improving economic conditions on the disputed islands, with a view to doubling their population over a 10-year period. In that month Russian security troops killed one Japanese fisherman and detained three others who had allegedly been fishing illegally in Russian waters; the captain of the Japanese vessel was subsequently fined. The revocation, in September, of an environmental permit associated with the Sakhalin-2 natural gas project, and the subsequent enforced reduction of the stake held in the project by Japanese companies, intensified tensions with Japan.

President Vladimir Putin accepted Malakhov's resignation in August 2007, having criticized him publicly for his conduct of relief measures following three recent earthquakes. Shortly afterwards the Regional Duma endorsed Putin's nominee as Governor, Aleksandr Khoroshavin, a former Mayor of the northern city of Okha.

In the elections to the Regional Duma held in October 2012. YeR obtained 50.2% of the votes cast on a proportional basis; a total of 21 of the 28 deputies subsequently joined the YeR parliamentary faction.

President Putin dismissed Khoroshavin as Governor on 25 March 2015, after investigations of corruption against him commenced. (In February 2018 Khoroshavin was sentenced to 13 years' imprisonment for bribery and money laundering.) Oleg Kozhemyako, hitherto Governor of Amur Oblast, was appointed as Acting Governor. On 13 September 2018 Kozhemyako was elected to the post, obtaining 67.8% of the vote. His nearest rival was Svetlana Ivanova of the KPRF, with 20.3%.

In elections to the Regional Duma, held on 10 September 2017, YeR obtained 44.6% of the votes cast on a proportional basis, ahead of the KPRF, with 16.5%, and the LDPR, with 13.0%. By the end of the year 20 of the 27 legislative deputies had joined the YeR parliamentary faction.

On 27 September 2018 Kozhemyako was transferred to serve as Acting Governor of Maritime Krai. Vera Shcherbina, the Chairman of the Oblast Government, became

Acting Governor until 7 December, when Valerii Limarenko, hitherto a senior official in the state atomic energy corporation, Rosatom, was appointed to the post, also in an acting capacity. A meeting between Putin and the Japanese Prime Minister, Shinzo Abe, in November 2018, at which the prospect was raised of renewing negotiations on a possible Russo-Japanese peace treaty in exchange for the return to Japanese rule of two of the Kurile islands, precipitated public protests, not only in Sakhalin Oblast, but also in Khabarovsk and in Moscow. On 8 September 2019 Limarenko was elected Governor, obtaining 56.1% of the votes cast.

After Russia invaded Ukraine in February 2022, Japan, now under the leadership of Fumio Kishida, reiterated its previous stance that the four disputed Southern Kurile Islands constituted an 'integral part' of Japan. In March Russia announced that it had frozen joint economic projects on the disputed islands, prior to staging a military drill nearby involving over 3,000 troops.

Elections to the Regional Duma were held on 11 September 2022, at which YeR won 47.2% of the votes cast on the basis of proportional representation. The second-placed party, with 14.3%, was the KPRF. When it convened, 21 of the 28 deputies in the new legislature were members of the YeR faction.

ECONOMY

Sakhalin Oblast's gross regional product (GRP) was 1,234,355m. roubles, equivalent to an estimated 2,545,593 roubles per head in 2021. The principal industrial centres are at Yuzhno-Sakhalinsk, Kholmsk and Okha. At the end of 2021 there were 835 km of railways in the Oblast. The Oblast's ports are at Kholmsk (from where a ferry links Sakhalin Island with Vanino, Khabarovsk Krai) and Korsakov. There is an international airport at Yuzhno-Sakhalinsk.

Fishing apart, agriculture in the region is minimal, owing to unfavourable climatic conditions, and consists mainly of potato and vegetable production and animal husbandry (reindeer breeding and fur farming). Annual catches of fish and other marine life amount to around 400,000–500,000 metric tons. The sector employed 5.7% of the workforce and contributed 2.2% of GRP in 2021. There is some extraction of coal and, increasingly, petroleum and natural gas in, and to the north of, Sakhalin Island. Some petroleum is piped for refining to a plant in Komsomolsk-on-Amur (Khabarovsk Krai), although the Oblast has its own refinery, with a capacity of some 200,000 metric tons per year. Industry employed 26.9% of the workforce and contributed 73.7% of GRP in 2021, when manufacturing employed 6.6% of the workforce and contributed 3.9% of GRP.

In the 1990s major consortiums were formed to exploit the region's natural resources. Sakhalin-1, a project to produce petroleum on the continental shelf of Sakhalin Island, initially comprised ExxonMobil of the USA (30%), Japan's Sodeco consortium (30%), the Russian state-owned Rosneft (20%) and India's Oil and Natural Gas Corporation (20%). Sakhalin-2, a project to exploit two fields containing an estimated 1,000m. barrels of petroleum and 408,000m. cu m of natural gas, was initiated by Sakhalin Energy Investment, comprising RoyalDutch/Shell (Netherlands/United Kingdom—UK, later Shell PLC of the UK), which held a 55% share, and Mitsui and Mitsubishi (both of Japan), with 45%. Sakhalin-2 was the single largest foreign direct investment project to be recorded in Russia, worth some US $10,000m., and was to include the world's largest liquefied natural gas (LNG) plant. Sakhalin-3, at first backed by a consortium of Mobil (now ExxonMobil), Texaco (now Chevron—of the USA) and Rosneft, was a project to seek to develop what was potentially the largest field on the Sakhalin shelf, containing an estimated 320m. metric tons of recoverable reserves. In 2004 the federal authorities annulled the tender to develop Sakhalin-3, and in 2005 it was announced that the project constituted one of the strategically important deposits of natural resources to be reserved for solely Russian exploitation. Production of gas from the project, now operated by a subsidiary of the state-controlled Gazprom corporation, commenced in 2013. Meanwhile, in 2006 Gazprom acquired a 50%-plus-one-share stake in Sakhalin-2, thereby reducing Shell's share to 27.5% and those of Mitsui and Mitsubishi to 12.5% and 10.0%, respectively. The hydrocarbon projects on Sakhalin were affected by the imposition of Western sanctions on Russia that followed Russia's invasion of Ukraine in February 2022. In August ExxonMobil announced it was to dispose of its stake in Sakhalin-1, where oil production had been reduced from 220,000 b/d to 10,000 b/d since May. In October a subsidiary of Rosneft, Sakhalinmorneftegaz-Shelf, started operating the project, and production was increased to 140,000 b/d on an interim basis, pending an eventual return to full operations. Meanwhile, Shell announced its withdrawal from Sakhalin-2; its shares were subsequently acquired by the Russian company Novatek.

Sakhalin Oblast's economically active population amounted to 262,711 in 2022, when 4.2% of the labour force were unemployed, while the average monthly wage was 102,684 roubles. There was a budgetary surplus of 1,703.6m. roubles in 2021, when export trade amounted to US $11,470m. (almost all of which was with non-CIS countries), while import trade amounted to $425m. (of which 0.1% was with CIS countries).

DIRECTORY

Governor: VALERII I. LIMARENKO.

Chairman of the Regional Government: ALEKSEI V. BELIK.

Office of the Government: 693009 Sakhalin obl., Yuzhno-Sakhalinsk, Kommunisticheskii pr. 32; tel. (4242) 67-01-14; e-mail pso@sakhalin.gov.ru; internet sakhalin.gov.ru.

Regional Duma: 693000 Sakhalin obl., Yuzhno-Sakhalinsk, ul. Chekhova 37; tel. (4242) 43-44-89; fax (4242) 72-15-46; e-mail duma@dumasakhalin.ru; internet dumasakhalin.ru; Chair. YELENA N. KASYANOVA.

State Duma Representative (1): GEORGII A. KARLOV (YeR).

Federation Council Representatives: ANDREI A. KHAPOCHKIN, GRIGORII B. KARASIN.

Jewish Autonomous Oblast

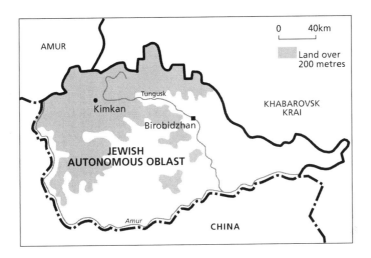

The Jewish Autonomous Oblast is part of the Amur river basin. Khabarovsk Krai, Amur Oblast, and the People's Republic of China lie to the north, north-west, and south. The Amur (Heilong Jiang) and the Tungusk are the major rivers. The region occupies 36,266 sq km (14,002 sq miles). At January 2023 it had an estimated population of 147,458 and a population density of 4.1 per sq km. Some 70.8% of the population was urban in 2023. The administrative centre, Birobidzhan, had an estimated 68,536 inhabitants at January 2023. Of residents who stated their ethnicity at the 2021 census, 95.7% were Russian, and 0.9% were Ukrainian. (Only 0.6% were Jewish.) The territory is in the time zone UTC+10.

HISTORY

The majority of Russian Jews came under Russian control following the Partitions of Poland in 1772–95. In 1835–1917 most Russian Jews were obligated to live within the 'Pale of Settlement' in the West of the Empire. Attempts by the Soviet authorities in the 1920s to create designated Jewish regions in Ukraine and Crimea largely failed, while the national Jewish district, established at Birobidzhan in 1928, never became the centre of Soviet Jewry. The district received the status of an Autonomous Oblast in May 1934 and formed part of Khabarovsk Krai until March 1991.

The incumbent governor, Nikolai Volkov, was re-elected by popular vote in 1996 and 2000 and by the regional Legislative Assembly in 2005. In 2010 the Legislative Assembly approved the appointment of Aleksandr Vinnikov, hitherto Mayor of Birobidzhan, as Governor.

Upon the expiry of Vinnikov's term of office in February 2015, President Vladimir Putin appointed Aleksandr Levintal, hitherto a deputy chairman of the Government of Khabarovsk Krai, as his acting successor. In September he was elected Governor, obtaining 75.4% of the votes cast.

On 12 December 2019 Putin dismissed Levintal and appointed Rostislav Goldshtein, hitherto a representative of the Oblast in the Federation Council, as Acting

Governor, pending an election. Goldshtein was confirmed to that post, securing 82.5% of the vote in an election held on 13 September 2020.

At elections to the regional Legislative Assembly held on 19 September 2021, YeR secured 51.9% of the votes cast on the basis of proportional representation; the KPRF obtained 19.0%, the LDPR 9.3%, the Partiya Partiya Pryamoi Demokratii (Party of Direct Democracy) 5.9% and SR 5.5%. By the end of the year 14 of the 19 deputies had joined the YeR faction and two that of the KPRF.

ECONOMY

The Jewish Autonomous Oblast's gross regional product (GRP) was 78,702m. roubles, or 507,212 roubles per head, in 2020. Birobidzhan is the region's main industrial centre. At the end of 2021 there were 512 km of railways in the Autonomous Oblast. In March 2019 the construction of a railway bridge providing a direct connection between Nizhneleninskoye, in the oblast, and the Chinese city of Tongjiang was completed, although transit over the bridge did not commence until November 2022.

Agriculture consists mainly of grain, soybean, vegetable and potato production, and animal husbandry. From the late 1990s the oblast authorities encouraged Chinese farmers to undertake agricultural activity in the region: an improvement in productivity ensued; in 2015 around one-quarter of the territory's land was being worked by Chinese farmers; extensive Chinese involvement in other areas of the regional economy was also recorded. Agriculture employed 7.4% of the workforce and contributed 3.7% of GRP in 2021. Major deposits of coal, peat, iron ore, manganese, tin, gold, graphite, magnesite and zeolite are largely unexploited. The main industries are mechanical engineering and metal working, the manufacture of building materials, the production of electricity, wood working, and light manufacturing. Industry employed 22.3% of the workforce and contributed 38.6% of GRP in 2021, when manufacturing employed 7.4% of the workforce and contributed 4.1% of GRP.

The economically active population numbered 73,031 in 2022, when the unemployment rate was 5.2%, while the average monthly wage was 56,957 roubles. There was a budgetary surplus of 2,483.3m. roubles in 2021, when export trade (almost all of which was with non-CIS countries) amounted to US $395 m. in 2021, while import trade amounted to $11m. (of which 0.9% was with CIS countries).

DIRECTORY

Governor: ROSTISLAV E. GOLDSHTEIN.

Office of the Governor: 679016 Jewish Autonomous Oblast, Birobidzhan, pr. 60-letiya SSSR 18; tel. (42622) 2-21-42; e-mail gov@eao.ru; internet eao.ru.

Legislative Assembly: 679016 Jewish Autonomous Oblast, Birobidzhan, pr. 60-letiya SSSR 18; tel. (42622) 2-04-02; e-mail zs@post.eao.ru; internet zseao.ru; Chair. ROMAN S. BOIKO.

State Duma Representative (1): ALEKSANDR P. PETROV (YeR).

Federation Council Representatives: VLADIMIR M. DZHABAROV, YURII K. VALYAYEV.

Chukot Autonomous Okrug

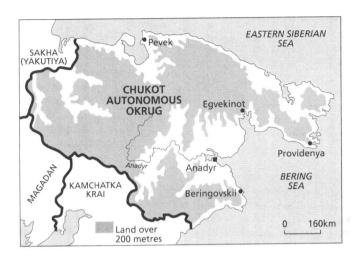

The Chukot Autonomous Okrug is situated mostly on the Chukotka Peninsula. It faces the Eastern Siberian Sea (Arctic Ocean) to the north and the Bering Sea to the south; the Anadyr Gulf, part of the Bering Sea, cuts into the territory from the south-east. The US state of Alaska lies eastwards across the Bering Straits. The western end of the district borders the Republic of Sakha (Yakutiya) to the west, and Magadan Oblast to the south. Also to the south lies Kamchatka Krai. The district's major river is the Anadyr. The Autonomous Okrug occupies 721,481 sq km (278,565 sq miles), of which approximately one-half lies within the Arctic Circle. Its climate is severe. At January 2023 it had an estimated population of 47,840 inhabitants and a population density of 0.1 per sq km. Some 69.1% of the population was urban in 2023. The administrative centre, Anadyr, had an estimated 12,998 inhabitants at January 2023. Of residents who stated their ethnicity at the 2021 census, 54.2% were Russian, 28.3% Chukchi, 3.2% Ukrainian, 3.1% Eskimo (Yupik), 2.7% Even, 1.6% Chuvan, 0.8% Kalmyk, and 0.7% were Tatar. The Chukchi (who call themselves the Lyg Oravetlyan, and are also known as the Luoravetlan, Chukcha and Chukot) speak the Chukotic language as their native tongue, which belongs to the Paleo-Asiatic linguistic family. Traditionally, they were divided into nomadic and semi-nomadic reindeer herders (the Chavchu or Chavchuven), and coastal dwellers (the An Kalyn). The Chukot Autonomous Okrug is in the time zone UTC+12.

HISTORY

Russian settlers first arrived in the territories inhabited by Chukchi (Chukot) tribes in the mid-17th century. Commercial traders, fur trappers and hunters subsequently established contact with the Chukchi, many of whom were forcibly converted to Orthodox Christianity and enserfed. A Chukot National Okrug was created within Magadan Oblast in December 1930. Collectivization was introduced, while industrialization resulted in an extensive migration of ethnic Russians to the area. Many

Chukchi abandoned their traditional way of life to work in industry. The okrug acquired nominally autonomous status in 1980.

In March 1990 Chukchi representatives participated in the creation of the Association of the Peoples of the North, and campaigned for the ratification of two international conventions that would affirm their right to the ownership and possession of the lands they traditionally inhabited. In February 1991 the autonomous okrug legislature declared the territory to be an autonomous republic. Although the federal authorities did not recognize this declaration, the district was acknowledged as a constituent member of the Russian Federation in March 1992 and, subsequently, as free from the jurisdiction of Magadan Oblast.

At the gubernatorial election held in December 2000, the incumbent Governor, Aleksandr Nazarov, withdrew his candidacy. Roman Abramovich, a prominent 'oligarch', was overwhelmingly elected in his place. Abramovich implemented numerous improvements to public services and utilities in the district.

In May 2004 an investigation conducted for the Audit Chamber of the State Duma declared the district to be insolvent. The Chamber also launched an investigation into possible fraud and misuse of public funds committed by Abramovich in connection with the sale of the Maiskoye gold mine. The Chairman of the Audit Chamber, Sergei Stepashin, demanded that Abramovich resign as Governor. However, although Abramovich divested much of his financial and business interests in Russia, taking up residence in the UK, the District Duma confirmed his appointment to a second term of office in 21 October.

In July 2008 Abramovich officially resigned as Governor. The District Duma approved the nomination of Abramovich's deputy, Roman Kopin, to succeed him. At a poll to fill one of three vacant seats in the District Duma on 12 October, Abramovich was elected to the legislature with 97.0% of the votes cast; he subsequently became the Chairman of the District Duma. YeR won an overwhelming victory in elections to the District Duma held in March 2011, obtaining 71.2% of the votes cast on a proportional basis. In July 2013 Abramovich resigned from the District Duma, in association with new federal legislation prohibiting holders of public office from owning property or bank accounts abroad. He was succeeded as Chairman of the District Duma by his ally, Aramais Dallakyan. On 8 September Kopin was directly elected as Governor, winning 79.9% of the vote.

YeR secured 61.7% of the votes cast on the basis of proportional representation at elections to the District Duma held on 18 September 2016, ahead of the LDPR, with 19.7%, the KPRF, with 8.8%, and SR, with 5.4%. By the end of the year 10 of the 15 deputies had joined the YeR parliamentary faction.

On 9 September 2018 Kopin was elected to a further term as Governor, obtaining 57.8% of the vote; Yuliya Butakova of the LDPR was second, with 18.5%.

At elections to the District Duma held on 19 September 2021, YeR secured 44.9% of the votes cast on the basis of proportional representation; the LDPR obtained 22.2%, the KPRF 15.9% and SR 12.3%. By the end of the year 10 of the 14 deputies had joined the YeR faction. The factions of the three other parties represented each comprised one deputy.

On 15 March 2023 Kopin tendered his resignation as Governor; on the same day President Vladimir Putin appointed Vladislav Kuznetsov, hitherto first deputy premier of the 'Lugansk People's Republic' (LNR) in the eastern Donbas region of Ukraine (which Russia had formally annexed in September 2022), as Acting Governor. On 10 September 2023 Kuznetsov, the candidate of YeR, was elected Governor with

72.3% of the votes cast, defeating three other candidates, including Butakova of the LDPR, who was again placed second, with 15.8%.

ECONOMY

The Chukot Autonomous Okrug's gross regional product (GRP) was 136,152m. roubles, or 2,734,863 roubles per head, in 2021. There are no railways in the district, and the infrastructure is relatively undeveloped. Anadyr is a major port, others being Pevek, Providenya, Egvekinot and Beringovskii.

The agricultural sector consists mainly of animal husbandry (especially reindeer breeding), hunting and fishing. The sector employed 5.1% of the workforce and contributed 2.0% of GRP in 2021. The district contains reserves of coal and brown coal (lignite), petroleum and natural gas, as well as gold, tin, wolfram (tungsten), copper and other minerals. It is self-sufficient in energy, containing two coal mines, six producers of electricity and one nuclear power station. Its main industries are electricity generation, ore mining, non-ferrous metallurgy and food processing. Industry employed 38.6% of the workforce and contributed 66.6% of GRP in 2021, when manufacturing employed 1.5% of the workforce and contributed 0.2% of GRP.

The economically active population numbered 29,390 in 2022, when the rate of unemployment was 1.9%, while the average monthly wage was 140,602 roubles, the highest in the Federation. There was a budgetary deficit of 2,082.3m. roubles in 2021, when export trade (of which 2.2% was with CIS countries) amounted to US $282m., while import trade amounted to $80m. (of which 3.1% was with CIS countries).

DIRECTORY

Governor: VLADISLAV G. KUZNETSOV.

Office of the Governor: 689000 Chukot AO, Anadyr, ul. Beringa 20; tel. (42722) 6-90-00; fax (42722) 2-29-19; internet bit.ly/389iCoz.

District Duma: 689000 Chukot AO, Anadyr, ul. Otke 29; tel. (42722) 2-93-50; fax (42722) 2-93-51; e-mail info@duma.chukotka.ru; internet dumachukotki.ru; Chair. VALENTINA V. RUDCHENKO.

State Duma Representative (1): YELENA A. YEVTYUKHOVA (YeR).

Federation Council Representatives: ANNA I. OTKE, ANASTASIYA G. ZHUKOVA.

PART THREE
Select Bibliography

Select Bibliography

Akaha, T., and Vassilieva, A. (Eds). *Russia and East Asia: Increasing and Informal Integration*. Abingdon, Routledge, 2014.

Askerov, A. *Historical Dictionary of the Chechen Conflict*. Lanham, MD, Rowman & Littlefield, 2015.

Barnes, I. *Restless Empire: A Historical Atlas of Russia*. Cambridge, MA, Harvard University Press, 2015.

Beer, D. *The House of the Dead: Siberian Exile under the Tsars*. London, Allen Lane, 2016.

Boeck, B. J. *Imperial Boundaries: Cossack Communities and Empire-building in the Age of Peter The Great*. Cambridge, Cambridge University Press, 2009.

Brown, J. D. J. *Japan, Russia and their Territorial Dispute: The Northern Delusion*. New York, Routledge, 2016.

Bruno, A. *The Nature of Soviet Power: An Arctic Environmental History*. Cambridge, Cambridge University Press, 2016.

Burgess, J. P. *Holy Rus': The Rebirth of Orthodoxy in the New Russia*. New Haven, CT, Yale University Press, 2017.

Chebankova, E. *Russia's Federal Reforms: Putin's Reforms and Management of the Regions*. Abingdon, Routledge, 2013.

Chenciner, R., and Magomedkhanov, M. *Dagestan – History, Culture, Identity*. Abingdon, Routledge, 2023.

Clover, C. *Black Wind, White Snow: Russia's New Nationalism*. New Haven, CT, Yale University Press, 2016.

Clowes, E. W., Erbslöh, G., and Kokobobo, A. (Eds). *Russia's Regional Identities: The Power of the Provinces*. Abingdon, Routledge, 2018.

Davidzon, I. *Regional Security Governance in Post-Soviet Eurasia: The History and Effectiveness of the Collective Security Treaty Organization*. Cham, Palgrave Macmillan, 2021.

De Waal, T. *The Caucasus: An Introduction*. Oxford, Oxford University Press, 2010.

Dinç, D. *Tatarstan's Autonomy within Putin's Russia: Minority Elites, Ethnic Mobilization, and Sovereignty*. Abingdon, Routledge, 2022.

Dollbaum, J. M., Lallouet, M., and Noble, B. *Navalny: Putin's Nemesis: Russia's Future?* London, Hurst & Co, 2021.

Dukes, P. *A History of the Urals: Russia's Crucible From Early Empire to the Post-Soviet Era*. London, Bloomsbury Academic, 2015.

Foxall, A. *Ethnic Relations in Post-Soviet Russia: Russians and Non-Russians in the North Caucasus*. Abingdon, Routledge, 2015.

Freeman, J. *From German Königsberg to Soviet Kaliningrad: Appropriating Place and Constructing Identity*. Abingdon, Routledge, 2022.

Galeeva, D. *Russia and the GCC: The Case of Tatarstan's Paradiplomacy*. London, I. B. Tauris, 2023.

Gammer, M. (Ed.). *Islam and Sufism in Daghestan*. Helsinki, Academia Scientiarum Fennica, 2010.

Garaev, D. *Jihadism in the Russian-Speaking World: The Genealogy of a Post-Soviet Phenomenon*. Abingdon, Routledge, 2023.

Gavrilova, S. *Russia's Regional Museums Representing and Misrepresenting Knowledge about Nature, History and Society*. Abingdon, Routledge, 2022.

Gelman, V. (Ed.). *Authoritarian Modernization in Russia: Ideas, Institutions and Policies*. Abingdon, Routledge, 2016.

Gessen, M. *Where the Jews Aren't: The Sad and Absurd Story of Birobidzhan, Russia's Jewish Autonomous Region*. New York, Schocken, 2016.

Giuliano, E. *Constructing Grievance: Ethnic Nationalism in Russia's Republics*. Ithaca, NY, Cornell University Press, 2011.

Gorbachev, M. *The New Russia*. Cambridge, Polity Press, 2016.

Greene, S. A., and Robertson, G. B. *Putin v. The People: The Perilous Politics of a Divided Russia*. New Haven, CT, Yale University Press, 2019.

Hauter, J. (Ed.). *Civil War? Interstate War? Hybrid War?: Dimensions and Interpretations of the Donbas Conflict in 2014–2020*. Stuttgart, Ibidem-Verlag, 2021.

Hill, F., and Gaddy, C. G. *The Siberian Curse: How Central Planners Left Russia Out in the Cold*. Washington, DC, Brookings Institution Press, 2003.

Hønneland, G. *Arctic Euphoria and International High North Politics*. Singapore, Palgrave Macmillan, 2017.

Huang, J., and Korolev, A. (Eds.) *The Political Economy of Pacific Russia: Regional Developments in East Asia*. Cham, Palgrave Macmillan, 2017.

Javeline, D. *After Violence: Russia's Beslan School Massacre and the Peace that Followed*. Oxford, Oxford University Press, 2023.

Khodarkovsky, M. *Bitter Choices: Loyalty and Betrayal in the Russian Conquest of the North Caucasus*. Ithaca, NY, Cornell University Press, 2011.

Kolstø, P., and Blakkisrud, H. (Eds). *Russia Before and After Crimea: Nationalism and Identity, 2010–17*. Edinburgh, Edinburgh University Press, 2018.

Konitzer, A. *Voting for Russia's Governors: Regional Elections and Accountability under Yeltsin and Putin*. Baltimore, MD, Johns Hopkins University Press, 2006.

Kuzio, T. *Russian Nationalism and the Russian-Ukrainian War: Autocracy-Orthodoxy-Nationality*. Abingdon, Routledge, 2022.

Lanskoy, M., and Akhmadov, I. *The Chechen Resistance: Independence Won and Lost*. New York, Palgrave Macmillan, 2010.

Lanzillotti, I. *Land, Community, and the State in the Caucasus: Kabardino-Balkaria from Tsarist Conquest to Post-Soviet Politics*. London, Bloomsbury Academic, 2021.

Laruelle, M. (Ed.). *New Mobilities and Social Change in Russia's Arctic Regions*. New York, Routledge, 2017.

Lee, R. W., and Lukin, A. *Russia's Far East: New Dynamics in Asia Pacific and Beyond*. Boulder, CO, Lynne Rienner Publishers, 2015.

Light, M. *Fragile Migration Rights: Freedom of Movement in Post-Soviet Russia*. Abingdon, Routledge, 2016.

Loftus, S. *Insecurity & the Rise of Nationalism in Putin's Russia: Keeper of Traditional Values*. Cham, Palgrave Macmillan, 2019.

Magocsi, P. R. *This Blessed Land: Crimea and the Crimean Tatars*. Toronto, ON, University of Toronto, 2014.

Maness, R. C., and Valeriano, B. (Eds). *Russia's Coercive Diplomacy: Energy, Cyber, and Maritime Policy as New Sources of Power*. Basingstoke, Palgrave Macmillan, 2015.

Matsuzato, K. (Ed.). *Russia and its Northeast Asian Neighbours: China, Japan and Korea*. Lanham, MD, Lexington Books, 2017.

Meyers, J. R. *The Criminal-Terror Nexus in Chechnya: A Historical, Social, and Religious Analysis*. Lanham, MD, Lexington Books, 2016.

Monaghan, A. *The New Politics of Russia: Interpreting Change*. Manchester, Manchester University Press, 2016.

Nathans, B. *Beyond the Pale: The Jewish Encounter with Late Imperial Russia*. Berkeley, CA, University of California Press, 2002.

Novikova, L. *An Anti-Bolshevik Alternative: The White Movement and the Civil War in the Russian North*. Madison, WI, University of Wisconsin Press, 2018.

Obydenkova, A. V., and Libman, A. *Causes and Consequences of Democratization: the Regions of Russia*. Abingdon, Routledge, 2015.

O'Neal, M. *Democracy, Civic Culture and Small Business in Russia's Regions: Social Processes in Comparative Historical Perspective*. Abingdon, Routledge, 2016.

Orttung, R. W. *Sustaining Russia's Arctic Cities: Resource Politics, Migration, and Climate Change*. New York, Berghahn Books, 2017.

Parts, L. *In Search of the True Russia: The Provinces in Contemporary Nationalist Discourse*. Madison, WI, University of Wisconsin Press, 2018.

Pleshkanov, K. *The Crimean Nexus: Putin's War and the Clash of Civilizations*. New Haven, CT, Yale University Press, 2017.

Pokalova, E. *Chechnya's Terrorist Network: The Evolution of Terrorism in Russia's North Caucasus*. Santa Barbara, CA, Praeger Publishing, 2015.

Prina, F. *National Minorities in Putin's Russia: Diversity and Assimilation*. New York, Routledge, 2015.

Przeworski, A. (Ed.) *Democracy in a Russian Mirror*. Cambridge, Cambridge University Press, 2015.

Reisinger, W. M., and Moraski, B. *The Regional Roots of Russia's Political Regime*. Ann Arbor, MI, University of Michigan Press, 2017.

Richardson, P. B. *At the Edge of the Nation: The Southern Kurils and the Search for Russia's National Identity*. Honolulu, HI, University of Hawai'i Press, 2018.

Robinson, P. *Russian Conservatism*. DeKalb, IL, Northern Illinois University Press, 2021.

Rogers, D. *The Depths of Russia: Oil, Power and Culture after Socialism*. Ithaca, NY, Cornell University Press, 2015.

Romaniello, M. P. *The Elusive Empire: Kazan and the Creation of Russia*. Madison, WI, University of Wisconsin Press, 2012.

Rubin, D. *Russia's Muslim Heartlands: Islam in the Putin Era.* London, Hurst & Co, 2017.

Sablin, I. *The Rise and Fall of Russia's Far Eastern Republic, 1905–1922: Nationalisms, Imperialisms, and Regionalisms in and after the Russian Empire.* Abingdon, Routledge, 2019.

Sahakyan, N. *Muslim Reformers and the Bolsheviks: The Case of Daghestan.* Abingdon, Routledge, 2022.

Saunders, E. *Kaliningrad and Cultural Memory: Cold War and Post-Soviet Representations of a Resettled City.* Oxford, Peter Lang, 2019.

Siikala, A.-L. *Hidden Rituals and Public Performances: Traditions and Belonging among the Post-Soviet Khanty, Komi and Udmurts.* Helsinki, Finnish Literature Society, 2011.

Simons, G. (Ed.). *The Image of Islam in Russia.* Abingdon, Routledge, 2021.

Simons, G., and Sumskaya, A (Eds). *Studies of Contemporary Journalism and Communication in Russia's Provinces.* Abingdon, Routledge, 2022.

Siroky, D. S., Dzutsati, V., and Bustikova, L. *Defection Denied: A Study of Civilian Support for Insurgency in Irregular War.* Cambridge, Cambridge University Press, 2022.

Smith-Peter, S. J. *Imagining Russian Regions: Subnational Identity and Civil Society in Nineteenth-Century Russia.* Leiden, Brill, 2018.

Socher, J. *Russia and the Right to Self-Determination in the Post-Soviet Space.* Oxford, Oxford University Press, 2021.

Sokirinskaia, E. *Bonds of Blood?: State-building and Clanship in Chechnya and Ingushetia.* London, Bloomsbury Academic, 2023.

Starodubtsev, A. *Federalism and Regional Policy in Contemporary Russia.* Abingdon, Routledge, 2017.

Steinwedel, C. *Threads of Empire: Loyalty and Tsarist Authority in Bashkiria, 1552–1917.* Bloomington, IN, Indiana University Press, 2016.

Tsyrempilov, N. *Under the Shadow of White Tara: Buriat Buddhists in Imperial Russia.* Leiden, Brill, 2022.

Tuna, M. *Imperial Russia's Muslims: Islam, Empire and European Modernity, 1788–1914.* Cambridge, Cambridge University Press, 2015.

Tynkkynen, V.-P., Tabata, S., Gritsenko, D., and Goto, M. (Eds). *Russia's Far North: The Contested Energy Frontier.* Abingdon, Routledge, 2021.

Van Herpen, M. *Putin's Wars: the Rise of Russia's New Imperialism.* 2nd edn. Lanham, MD, Rowman & Littlefield, 2015.

Ware, R. B. *The Fire Below: How the Caucasus Shaped Russia.* New York, Bloomsbury Academic, 2013.

Wegren, S. K. *Rural Inequality in Divided Russia.* Abingdon, Routledge, 2013.

Wilhelmsen, J. *Russia's Securitization of Chechnya: How War Became Acceptable.* Abingdon, Routledge, 2016.

PART FOUR
Indexes

Index of Principal Cities

This list includes all cities with a population of at least 200,000, according to official estimates at January 2023,6 and all smaller cities that are territorial capitals.

City	Territory	
Abakan	Republic of Khakasiya	261
Anadyr	Chukot Autonomous Okrug	317
Angarsk	Irkutsk Oblast	273
Archangel	Archangel Oblast	112
Astrakhan	Astrakhan Oblast	156
Balashikha	Moscow Oblast	80
Barnaul	Altai Krai	267
Belgorod	Belgorod Oblast	63
Birobidzhan	Jewish Autonomous Oblast	315
Blagoveshchensk	Amur Oblast	306
Bratsk	Irkutsk Oblast	273
Bryansk	Bryansk Oblast	66
Cheboksary	Chuvash Republic	204
Chelyabinsk	Chelyabinsk Oblast	241
Cherepovets	Vologda Oblast	128
Cherkessk	Karachai-Cherkess Republic	188
Chita	Transbaikal Krai	303
Dzherinsk	Nizhnii Novgorod Oblast	226
Elista	Republic of Kalmykiya	149
Engels	Saratov Oblast	236
Gorno-Altaisk	Republic of Altai	258
Groznyi	Chechen Republic	165
Irkutsk	Irkutsk Oblast	273
Ivanovo	Ivanovo Oblast	69
Izhevsk	Udmurt Republic	217
Kaliningrad	Kaliningrad Oblast	115
Kaluga	Kaluga Oblast	71
Kazan	Republic of Tatarstan	213
Kemerovo	Kemerovo Oblast—Kuzbass	276
Khabarovsk	Khabarovsk Krai	297
Khanty-Mansiisk	Khanty-Mansii Autonomous Okrug—Yugra	252
Khimki	Moscow Oblast	80
Kirov	Kirov Oblast	223
Komsomolsk-on-Amur	Khabarovsk Krai	297
Korolyov	Moscow Oblast	80
Kostroma	Kostroma Oblast	73
Krasnodar	Krasnodar Krai	152
Krasnoyarsk	Krasnoyarsk Krai	270
Kurgan	Kurgan Oblast	244
Kursk	Kursk Oblast	75
Kyzyl	Republic of Tyva	264
Lipetsk	Lipetsk Oblast	78
Lyubertsy	Moscow Oblast	80

INDEXES

Magadan	Magadan Oblast	309
Magas	Republic of Ingushetiya	178
Magnitogorsk	Chelyabinsk Oblast	241
Maikop	Republic of Adygeya	137
Makhachkala	Republic of Dagestan	172
Moscow	Moscow City	57
Murmansk	Murmansk Oblast	121
Mytishchi	Moscow Oblast	80
Naberezhnye Chelny	Republic of Tatarstan	213
Nalchik	Kabardino-Balkar Republic	183
Naryn-Mar	Nenets Autonomous Okrug	130
Nizhnekamsk	Republic of Tatarstan	213
Nizhnevartovsk	Khanty-Mansii Autonomous Okrug—Yugra	252
Nizhnii Novgorod	Nizhnii Novgorod Oblast	226
Nizhnii Tagil	Sverdlovsk Oblast	246
Novgorod/Velikii Novgorod	Novgorod Oblast	123
Novokuznetsk	Kemerovo Oblast—Kuzbass	276
Novorossiisk	Krasnodar Krai	152
Novosibirsk	Novosibirsk Oblast	279
Omsk	Omsk Oblast	282
Oryol	Oryol Oblast	83
Orenburg	Orenburg Oblast	229
Orsk	Orenburg Oblast	229
Penza	Penza Oblast	231
Perm	Perm Krai	220
Petropavlovsk-Kamchatskii	Kamchatka Krai	294
Petrozavodsk	Republic of Kareliya	106
Podolsk	Moscow Oblast	80
Pskov	Pskov Oblast	125
Pyatigorsk	Stavropol Krai	197
Rostov-on-Don	Rostov Oblast	159
Ryazan	Ryazan Oblast	85
St Petersburg	St Petersburg City	102
Salekhard	Yamalo-Nenets Autonomous Okrug	255
Samara	Samara Oblast	233
Saransk	Republic of Mordoviya	210
Saratov	Saratov Oblast	236
Sevastopol	Sevastopol City	133
Shakhty	Rostov Oblast	159
Simferopol	Republic of Crimea	141
Smolensk	Smolensk Oblast	87
Sochi	Krasnodar Krai	152
Staryi Oskol	Belgorod Oblast	63
Stavropol	Stavropol Krai	197
Sterlitamak	Republic of Bashkortostan	200
Surgut	Khanty-Mansii Autonomous Okrug—Yugra	252
Syktyvkar	Republic of Komi	109
Taganrog	Rostov Oblast	159
Tambov	Tambov Oblast	89
Tolyatti	Samara Oblast	233
Tomsk	Tomsk Oblast	285
Tula	Tula Oblast	91
Tver	Tver Oblast	93
Tyumen	Tyumen Oblast	249

Ufa	Republic of Bashkortostan	200
Ulan-Ude	Republic of Buryatiya	287
Ulyanovsk	Ulyanovsk Oblast	239
Velikii Novgorod/Novgorod	Novgorod Oblast	123
Vladikavkaz	Republic of North Osetiya—Alaniya	192
Vladimir	Vladimir Oblast	95
Vladivostok	Maritime (Primorskii) Krai	300
Volgograd	Volgograd Oblast	162
Vologda	Vologda Oblast	128
Volzhskii	Volgograd Oblast	162
Voronezh	Voronezh Oblast	97
Yakutsk	Republic of Sakha (Yakutiya)	290
Yaroslavl	Yaroslavl Oblast	100
Yekaterinburg	Sverdlovsk Oblast	246
Yoshkar-Ola	Republic of Marii-El	207
Yuzhno-Sakhalinsk	Sakhalin Oblast	311

Territories Renamed or Abolished after 1991

Adyge Autonomous Oblast	reconstituted as Republic of Adygeya
Aga-Buryat Autonomous Okrug	merged into Transbaikal Krai
Chechen Republic of Ichkeriya	created by split from Checheno-Ingush Autonomous Republic, later reconstituted as Chechen (Nokchi) Republic, subsequently the Chechen Republic
Checheno-Ingush Autonomous Republic . .	split into Chechen Republic of Ichkeriya and the Ingush Republic
Chita Oblast	merged into Transbaikal Krai
Evenk Autonomous Okrug	absorbed into Krasnoyarsk Krai
Gorno-Altai Autonomous Oblast . . .	reconstituted as Republic of Altai
Ingush Republic	created by split from Checheno-Ingush Autonomous Republic, later renamed Republic of Ingushetiya
Kalmykiya Khalmg-Tangch (Republic) . .	reconstituted as Republic of Kalmykiya
Kamchatka Oblast	merged into Kamchatka Krai
Karachai-Cherkess Autonomous Oblast . .	reconstituted as Karachai-Cherkess Republic
Komi-Permyak Autonomous Okrug . . .	merged into Perm Krai
Koryak Autonomous Okrug	merged into Kamchatka Krai
Kuibyshev Oblast	renamed Samara Oblast
Leningrad City	renamed St Petersburg City
Perm Oblast	merged into Perm Krai
Taimyr (Dolgano-Nenets) Autonomous Okrug	absorbed into Krasnoyarsk Krai
Tuva Autonomous Republic	reconstituted as the Republic of Tyva
Ust-Orda Buryat Autonomous Okrug . .	absorbed into Irkutsk Oblast
Yakut Autonomous Republic	reconstituted as Republic of Sakha (Yakutiya)

Alphabetical List of Territories

Adygeya, Republic of	137
Altai Krai	267
Altai, Republic of	258
Amur Oblast	306
Archangel Oblast	112
Astrakhan Oblast	156
Bashkortostan, Republic of	200
Belgorod Oblast	63
Bryansk Oblast	66
Buryatiya, Republic of	287
Chechen Republic	165
Chelyabinsk Oblast	241
Chukot Autonomous Okrug	317
Chuvash Republic	204
Crimea, Republic of	141
Dagestan, Republic of	172
Ingushetiya, Republic of	178
Irkutsk Oblast	273
Ivanovo Oblast	69
Jewish Autonomous Oblast	315
Kabardino-Balkar Republic	183
Kaliningrad Oblast	115
Kalmykiya, Republic of	149
Kaluga Oblast	71
Kamchatka Krai	294
Karachai-Cherkess Republic	188
Kareliya, Republic of	106
Kemerovo Oblast—Kuzbass	276
Khabarovsk Krai	297
Khakasiya, Republic of	261
Khanty-Mansii Autonomous Okrug—Yugra	252
Kirov Oblast	223
Komi, Republic of	109
Kostroma Oblast	73
Krasnodar Krai	152
Krasnoyarsk Krai	270
Kurgan Oblast	244
Kursk Oblast	75
Leningrad Oblast	119
Lipetsk Oblast	78
Magadan Oblast	309
Marii-El, Republic of	207
Maritime (Primorskii) Krai	300
Mordoviya, Republic of	210
Moscow City	57
Moscow Oblast	80
Murmansk Oblast	121
Nenets Autonomous Okrug	130
Nizhnii Novgorod Oblast	226
North Osetiya—Alaniya, Republic of	192
Novgorod Oblast	123
Novosibirsk Oblast	279
Omsk Oblast	282
Oryol Oblast	83
Orenburg Oblast	229
Penza Oblast	231
Perm Krai	220
Pskov Oblast	125
Rostov Oblast	159
Ryazan Oblast	85
St Petersburg City	102
Sakha (Yakutiya), Republic of	290
Sakhalin Oblast	311
Samara Oblast	233
Saratov Oblast	236
Sevastopol City	133
Smolensk Oblast	87
Stavropol Krai	197
Sverdlovsk Oblast	246
Tambov Oblast	89
Tatarstan, Republic of	213
Tomsk Oblast	285
Transbaikal Krai	303
Tula Oblast	91
Tver Oblast	93
Tyumen Oblast	249
Tyva, Republic of	264
Udmurt Republic	217
Ulyanovsk Oblast	239
Vladimir Oblast	95
Volgograd Oblast	162
Vologda Oblast	128
Voronezh Oblast	97
Yamalo-Nenets Autonomous Okrug	255
Yaroslavl Oblast	100

Federal Okrugs

Central

Belgorod Oblast	63
Bryansk Oblast	66
Ivanovo Oblast	69
Kaluga Oblast	71
Kostroma Oblast	73
Kursk Oblast	75
Lipetsk Oblast	78
Moscow City	57
Moscow Oblast	80
Oryol Oblast	83
Ryazan Oblast	85
Smolensk Oblast	87
Tambov Oblast	89
Tula Oblast	91
Tver Oblast	93
Vladimir Oblast	95
Voronezh Oblast	97
Yaroslavl Oblast	100

North-Western

Archangel Oblast	112
Nenets Autonomous Okrug	130
Kaliningrad Oblast	115
Republic of Kareliya	106
Republic of Komi	109
Leningrad Oblast	119
Murmansk Oblast	121
Novgorod Oblast	123
Pskov Oblast	125
St Petersburg City	102
Vologda Oblast	128

Southern

Republic of Adygeya	137
Astrakhan Oblast	156
Republic of Crimea	141
Republic of Kalmykiya	149
Krasnodar Krai	152
Rostov Oblast	159
Sevastopol City	133
Volgograd Oblast	162

North Caucasus

Chechen Republic	165
Republic of Dagestan	172
Republic of Ingushetiya	178
Kabardino-Balkar Republic	183
Karachai-Cherkess Republic	188
Republic of North Osetiya—Alaniya	192
Stavropol Krai	197

Volga

Republic of Bashkortostan	200
Chuvash Republic	204
Kirov Oblast	223
Republic of Marii-El	207
Republic of Mordoviya	210
Nizhnii Novgorod Oblast	226
Orenburg Oblast	229
Penza Oblast	231
Perm Krai	220
Samara Oblast	233
Saratov Oblast	236
Republic of Tatarstan	213
Udmurt Republic	217
Ulyanovsk Oblast	239

Urals

Chelyabinsk Oblast	241
Kurgan Oblast	244
Sverdlovsk Oblast	246
Tyumen Oblast	249
Khanty-Mansii Autonomous Okrug—Yugra	252
Yamalo-Nenets Autonomous Okrug	255

Siberian

Altai Krai	267
Republic of Altai	258
Irkutsk Oblast	273
Kemerovo Oblast—Kuzbass	276
Republic of Khakasiya	261
Krasnoyarsk Krai	270
Novosibirsk Oblast	279
Omsk Oblast	282
Tomsk Oblast	285
Republic of Tyva	264

Far Eastern

Amur Oblast	306
Republic of Buryatiya	287
Chukot Autonomous Okrug	317
Jewish Autonomous Oblast	315
Kamchatka Krai	294
Khabarovsk Krai	297
Magadan Oblast	309
Maritime (Primorskii) Krai	300
Republic of Sakha (Yakutiya)	290
Sakhalin Oblast	311
Transbaikal Krai	303